Samuel Rockwell Reed

The Vicksburg campaign,

And the battles about Chattanooga under the command of General U.S. Grant, in

1862-63; an historical review

Samuel Rockwell Reed

The Vicksburg campaign,
And the battles about Chattanooga under the command of General U.S. Grant, in 1862-63; an historical review

ISBN/EAN: 9783337814465

Printed in Europe, USA, Canada, Australia, Japan

Cover: Foto ©ninafisch / pixelio.de

More available books at **www.hansebooks.com**

THE
VICKSBURG CAMPAIGN,

AND THE

BATTLES ABOUT CHATTANOOGA

UNDER THE COMMAND OF

GENERAL U. S. GRANT,

IN 1862-63;

AN HISTORICAL REVIEW.

BY

SAM. ROCKWELL REED.

Dedicated to the Patriotic American Volunteers, the Best Soldiers in the World, whose Heroic Valor, Intelligence, and High Spirit, Without Reward and Without the Aid of Great Generalship, Fought the Great War Through to the Triumph of the Nation.

COPYRIGHT, 1882, BY SAMUEL ROCKWELL REED.

PREFACE.

Of heroic histories of generals of the great Civil War, written to show that the Nation was saved by a phenomenal military genius, there are enough. Enough of egoizing military biographies, brazenly self exalting, and derogating from officers of better service, who are kept silent by army subordination, or are silent in the grave. Enough of military lives written for political campaign lives, with the superlative rodomontade of such party literature. Enough of hero-worshiping myth which slights the heroic army. It is time to lift the history of the great war out of the degradation of selfish prescription; of menial body service; of timeserving party necessity; of the fungus of popular myth, up to the plane of independence and true criticism. It is time for real history to be written, to do justice to the patriotic volunteers, the best soldiers in the world, who, without the leading of a great military genius, and notwithstanding the leading of great military blunders, which multiplied their hardships and slaughter, and prolonged the war, fought it through with indomitable resolution, to the dearly earned triumph of the Nation. In this aim is this review written.

THE VICKSBURG CAMPAIGN.

CHAPTER I.

THE NATION'S REJOICING—THE PREPARATION OF THE PUBLIC MIND BY THE PRECEDING YEAR OF FAILURE.

The rejoicing of the country over the surrender of Vicksburg to Gen. GRANT's army, July 4, 1863, and its extravagant estimate of the importance of that event, may be better appreciated by a glance at the previous long course of the consuming of mighty energies, boundless patriotic sacrifices, and vast expenditure without adequate results, with very little to feed national glory, and without any positive progress toward ending the war. This seemed continually expanding, and the task of putting down the rebellion more discouraging. Yet the people never flinched. Still, volunteers continued to rise up in a continuous tide, rushing with eagerness to the slaughter under a combination of civil and military incompetency of leadership. Injustice would be done to the patriotism and pluck of a great people by pretending that all was then capable, successful, and glorious. It was an awful waste of brave and intelligent volunteers, and of colossal resources, and expenditure, by incapacity, and it was a long time of great discouragement. Yet the great people never weakened in their resolve to preserve the Union. It is time for the truth, and the truth is most glorious to the people.

After the slaughter at Pittsburg Landing, in which an army of as brave men as ever trod the soldier's brogans was sacrificed by sheer neglect in its Commanding General of all that belongs to the practice of a soldier, the national army rested. With BUELL's troops it was strong enough to have followed the enemy at once to Corinth, but it was in GRANT's department, and under HALLECK's general command, and it waited for HALLECK. After a battle our army always had a season of inactivity, rather the more after a victory than a defeat. The battle ended on the 7th of April, 1862. HALLECK ordered POPE's army of 25,000 from Missouri to Pittsburg. He kept BUELL's army. He laid open the entire West to gather troops to put into a state of suspended animation. The destroyed equipment of GRANT's army was replaced. HALLECK left St. Louis, April 19, to come and take command of an army raised to more than 100,000, to begin his famous siege approaches to Corinth, fifteen miles away, held by not half his number, and these recently repulsed with great slaughter.

HALLECK put GRANT into disgrace; on the other hand, he dispatched the War Department that it was the opinion of the army that Gen. SHERMAN saved the day, and he recommended his promotion to be Major General. This was done. It is an example of the way war reputations are made. GRANT was still nominally in command of the District of West Tennessee, but his army, which was now divided between right wing and reserve, was under the immediate command of THOMAS and McCLERNAND, to whom HALLECK sent orders direct, ignoring GRANT. HALLECK now moved on Corinth by siege approaches, intrenching in every part at each move, and moving at the average rate of half a mile a day. It was like McCLELLAN's approach toward Richmond. He was in constant apprehension of attack, and he made the evacuation of Corinth by the enemy his whole objective. There was no attempt to flank Corinth or cut off the enemy's retreat. HALLECK's only thought was of being attacked.

He was only too glad to have the enemy go away. His strategy was upon the advice of the Messina Magistrate to the watch:

Dogberry—You are to bid any man stand in the prince's name.
Watch—How if he will not stand?
Dog.—Why then take no note of him, but let him go; and presently call the watch together, and thank God you are rid of a knave.

When he had cautiously reached Corinth he found that the Confederate army had withdrawn at leisure. To cover up this impotent conclusion he dispatched Washington that he was making vigorous pursuit of the demoralized enemy, and that Gen. POPE reported the capture of 10,000 prisoners and 15,000 stand of arms. POPE had reported none and captured none, and there was no chance for this pursuit. But this achievement with the longbow got HALLECK present and lasting glory, and because of that he was presently, after MCCLELLAN'S retreat, called to Washington and made General in Chief to direct all things from Washington, and to be President LINCOLN'S military adviser. Thus was the nation organized for victory. This is another example of the way that the war made great military reputations and high ranks. And now that great army, which had been organized and disciplined by all this daily marching, bivouacking, intrenching, outpost duty, and constant vigilance in the face of the enemy, and which SHERMAN in the Memoirs says could have gone anywhere, was broken up and placed for the defensive.

In this as in all the war, in nearly all the commanders as in the administration, the paralyzing error was in the idea that the Union was to be restored by recovering territory and places, instead of destroying the Confederate armies. HALLECK had no need of BUELL for Corinth, even if with a capable commander he had at Pittsburg Landing. BUELL would have gone on from Nashville to Chattanooga or through Alabama. And now HALLECK ordered BUELL to move into East Tennessee. This was LINCOLN'S pet desire, and HALLECK supported it. LINCOLN fancied a great Union population there which, if protected, would restore Tennessee to the Union, and this political idea overruled military conditions. HALLECK insisted, against BUELL'S judgment, that he should make the Memphis & Charleston Railroad, running through Corinth, Northern Alabama, and Chattanooga, his line of communications and of movement.

For a distance of more than eighty miles this line was along the enemy's front. To protect this railroad was an impossibility. But all of HALLECK'S movements were as if afraid that the war would end too soon. BUELL proceeded to obey orders by repairing this road, and fortifying its stations and bridges. It was a great work, and at this time he asked the War Department for authority to feed and clothe the escaped slaves for this intrenching labor, but was informed that Congress had not appropriated for it. This, we think, was the first systematic proposal for the employment of the escaped slaves in a straightforward manner. BUELL, while obeying HALLECK'S order to repair the Memphis & Charleston road for his base line, proceeded also to provide one for practical use by giving orders for the repair of the roads from Nashville through Tennessee. While our army was thus scattering, and wasting its energies, part on the defensive and part on impossible undertakings, the Confederate armies in the great Interior, as in the East, were concentrating for a grand advance.

That of BRAGG, assisted by the co-operative columns of KIRBY SMITH on the east, and of VAN DORN on the west, was to carry forward the line of the Confederacy to the Ohio River, reinstate the rebel State government in Tennessee, set up a rebel State government in Kentucky, and make these States the great field for recruits and supplies, and the military base the Ohio. It was a brave undertaking, and the imbecility on our side made its opportunity. BUELL had brought from Corinth little over 24,000 men; about 16,000 more were distributed through Middle Tennessee and Northern Alabama, holding places which he had taken before he went to Pittsburg Landing. While he was repairing and fortifying railroads for his flank march in the enemy's front to East Tennessee, BRAGG'S grand advance began with 60,000 veteran troops, his movements veiled by a cloud of cavalry, and his lines of advance taking him into the friendly inhabitants of Kentucky.

This compelled BUELL to desist from his vain labors, and to gather up his troops from a wide region and take the field in the offensive defensive against BRAGG'S combined forces. Leaving a garrison to hold Nashville, he marched eastward to meet BRAGG, where he might be expected to debouch from the Cumberland ridge. Keeping his well disciplined troops completely in hand, protecting all his trains, his men never demoralized by this return march, nor by BRAGG's superior numbers, but, confident and high spirited, BUELL moved first to offer battle to BRAGG, but upon his own ground; then, BRAGG avoiding this, BUELL moved in a parallel line, always ready for battle, but with the condition that it must be upon his own ground, always threatening BRAGG while moving toward his own re-enforcements. The result of this skillful generalship was that when BRAGG got within about twenty-five miles of Louisville he found that he wanted to face about. BUELL, now re-enforced, as promptly faced about to march with him and attack him.

For this stroke of generalship, which against such heavy chances saved his army, saved Kentucky and Middle Tennessee, and saved the North, and whose skill and complete success has not been surpassed in any war, BUELL was summarily removed from command. This is another example of the way war makes reputations and dispenses rewards. The splendid success was marred by a reverse to a part of one wing of the army at Perrysville, where the disregard of instructions by the commander of that wing spoiled well laid plan for a general battle. But an army of 60,000 or 80,000 men spreads over a wide region, and the non-co-operation of its several commanders can defeat any Commanding General. Such disregard of instructions by the commander of a corps, in this instance, unknown to BUELL, defeated a plan of general battle, which would have made defeat destruction to BRAGG. It enabled him to have a nominal success in a dash at a few of our brigades, to carry back with his Kentucky State Government and great plan to plant the boundary of the Confederacy on the Ohio.

Meanwhile, in July, HALLECK had been ordered to Washington. On leaving he restored GRANT to command of his former troops, with headquarters at Corinth. The defensive policy and the holding of territory were pursued. A combined operation against PRICE, who had seized Iuka, failed by the neglect of that division which was with GRANT to attack, waiting while PRICE drew away from its front and marched on the double quick three miles and fell with his whole force on ROSECRANS. ROSECRANS, as was his wont, spoke his mind on this. Subsequently ROSECRANS, with about half the number of the enemy, gave VAN DORN a slaughtering repulse at Corinth. Although this was in the defensive line, yet it disabled VAN DORN for his part in the grand plan of invasion. After this ROSECRANS, much to GRANT's relief, BADEAU says, was ordered to the command of BUELL's army.

ROSECRANS' victory at Corinth was on the 4th of October. BADEAU says that on the 25th GRANT "assumed command of the Department of the Tennessee, which included Cairo, Forts Henry and Donelson, Northern Mississippi, and the portions of Kentucky and Tennessee west of the Tennessee River." Thus it appears that at this time GRANT was fully reinstated and his command enlarged in bounds, and that it followed ROSECRANS' victory at Corinth, for which the latter was promoted Major General. In the same month GRANT was largely re-enforced from the Northwestern States, and now he proposed to HALLECK, October 26, 1863, a concentration for an advance. He said: "I think I would be able to move down the Mississippi Central road, and cause the evacuation of Vicksburg."

BADEAU says, with due sense of the importance of this germ of the idea of the Vicksburg campaign: "This was the first mention, in the correspondence of the two commanders, of the place destined afterward to become so renowned." This was the initiative of the Vicksburg campaign, which was to occupy a great army and a great steamboat fleet and gunboat squadron for more than eight months, and which was now to begin after eight months, in which great forces and enormous expenditure were consumed in merely defensive operations, or in futile attempts, all of which had made no progress except to expand the war, and call continually for more men and money. In following articles we shall see how sped this great offensive campaign, which after long waiting, and immense consumption of men and means, at last brought rejoicing to a patriotic nation.

CHAPTER II.

THE CAMPAIGN ON THE INTERIOR LINE—ITS ENERGETIC START, ITS PAUSE, IRRESOLUTION, BACKING, AND FILLING, UNTIL RELIEVED BY VAN DORN'S DESTRUCTION OF ITS SUPPLIES.

Gen. GRANT, now in command of a department embracing the Mississippi River, and of a large army, wrote Gen. HALLECK, then in chief command at Washington, November 26, proposing an advance down the Mississippi Central Railroad, his objective being Vicksburg. Still the notion disabled all our military plans, that the recovery of places, not the destruction of armies, was the way to restore the Union. But GRANT'S line of operations was better than his main objective, for it was toward the enemy's main army. This was under PEMBERTON, who had been placed over VAN DORN, and was holding the line of the Tallahatchie which crosses the Central forty miles south of Grand Junction. This is on the same road, where crossed by the road from Memphis through Corinth, and is about midway between Corinth and Memphis, and was a central point for GRANT'S concentration of his divided forces. And yet, although GRANT'S forces were on three sides of Grand Junction, he had not occupied that place, and that road to Memphis was closed to him, and he had to communicate therewith by way of Columbus, Ky.

GRANT announced to HALLECK November 2: "I have commenced a movement on Grand Junction with three divisions from Corinth and two from Bolivar. Will leave here tomorrow and take command in person. If found practicable I will go to Holly Springs, and may be Grenada, completing railroad and telegraph as I go." Holly Springs is on the Central road, twenty-five miles south of Grand Junction, and about half way to the Tallahatchie. Grenada is about sixty miles further south, and is where the Yallabusha crosses the railroad. HALLECK replied: "I approve of your plan of advancing upon the enemy as soon as you are strong enough for that purpose." This was permission enough, properly leaving him discretion as to sufficiency of force and line of operation.

GRANT had force enough. His good fortune in all this operation was that he was supported by abundance of men, and supplies and appointments of every sort. November 4 he had moved to Grand Junction. He had ordered SHERMAN to co-operate by moving two divisions from Memphis, but on the 8th of November he informed SHERMAN that he estimated PEMBERTON'S force at 30,000, and that he felt "strong enough to handle that number without gloves." Therefore he countermanded the march from Memphis.

Unfortunately GRANT'S advance, which began so energetically, halted. A disturbing element had now come in. BADEAU relates it with charming simplicity. McCLERNAND was one of those whom SHERMAN and BADEAU call political Generals. He had proved himself a good soldier, but this only aggravated his fault. McCLERNAND had obtained from LINCOLN a special order to raise troops for an expedition to open the Mississippi River. HALLECK disapproved, but this was one of those peculiar military operations which LINCOLN took in hand. GRANT heard of McCLERNAND'S expedition through the newspapers, and it diverted his energies from PEMBERTON. He saw that such an expedition would gather up or at least subordinate SHERMAN, and would reap the glory of occupying Vicksburg if his operations caused its evacuation. For, not to destroy the enemy's army, but to occupy the evacuated Vicksburg, was GRANT'S objective with his great army.

He also suspected that this telegram from HALLECK, November 5, pointed to the diversion of troops from his command at Memphis to McCLERNAND: "Had not troops sent to re-enforce you better go to Memphis hereafter? I hope to give 20,000 additional men in a few days." GRANT, on the 9th, sent this feeler: "Re-enforcements are arriving very slowly. If they do not come in more rapidly I will attack as I am." In fact GRANT had only the day before countermarched SHERMAN'S two divisions back to Memphis, because, he said, he had force enough to handle PEMBERTON without them. BADEAU narrates that next day, growing more uneasy about McCLERNAND, GRANT telegraphed: "Am I to understand that I lie here still while an expedition is fitted out for Memphis, or do you want me to push as far south as possible? Am I to have SHERMAN subject to my orders, or is he and his force reserved for some special service?"

No one had caused GRANT to lie there still. He had HALLECK'S consent to his going, and he had turned back forces to Memphis, saying he had enough. HALLECK answered promptly:

"You have command of all troops sent to your department, and have permission to fight the enemy when you please." BADEAU relates that thereupon GRANT on the 14th informed SHERMAN: "I have now complete control of my department," and accordingly ordered him to "move with two divisions of twelve full regiments each, and if possible, with three divisions, to Oxford, or the Tallahatchie, as soon as possible. I am now ready to move from here (La Grange) any day, and only await your movements."

Thus were his plans backing and filling because of McCLERNAND. And now he had changed his mind again, and had ordered SHERMAN to join him with all his movable force for the march on PEMBERTON. This at last was a rational plan, but it was naught without execution, and the delay had already given the enemy time to recover. But so earnest was GRANT now in this plan that he telegraphed SHERMAN November 15 to meet him at Columbus, Ky., where he gave SHERMAN full instructions as to co-operation by moving three divisions so as to join GRANT at the Tallahatchie. SHERMAN marched promptly November 24.

HALLECK ordered the forces at Helena to co-operate by crossing the Mississippi and cutting the Central Railroad in PEMBERTON'S rear. And now all seemed resolved and promising. But again McCLERNAND'S shadow loomed across GRANT'S horizon. BADEAU says: "On the 23d HALLECK again broached the subject of the river expedition, doubtless urged on by the President. * * * He inquired how many men GRANT had in his department, and what force could be sent down the river to Vicksburg. GRANT replied that he had in all 72,000 men, of whom 18,000 were at Memphis, and 16,000 of these could be spared for the river expedition." He also announced next day that he had given orders for the advance of his entire force, including SHERMAN; had written to STEELE in Arkansas to threaten Grenada, and had asked Admiral PORTER to send boats to co-operate at the mouth of the Yazoo. He asked: "Shall I countermand the orders for this move?"

But HALLECK had not asked GRANT to tarry, nor to let any of his troops go in the river expedition unless he could spare them, and GRANT had said he could spare 16,000. HALLECK answered no. BADEAU says GRANT'S cavalry crossed the Tallahatchie on the 29th, and his headquarters were at Holly Springs, being an advance of twenty-five miles in twenty-three days, since the 4th; also, that "SHERMAN, too, was up, and would cross the Tallahatchie at Wyatt," which is six miles west of the railroad crossing, and that on the same day GRANT telegraphed HALLECK: "Our troops will be in Abbeville (just south of the Tallahatchie) to-morrow, or a battle will be fought." But the main body would not be at Abbeville for several days, and there was no enemy near for a battle. SHERMAN says in his Memoirs:

We reached Wyatt on the 2d day of December, and there learned that Pemberton's whole army had fallen back to the Yallabusha, near Grenada, caused, in great measure, by alarm at the demonstration on their rear from Helena. ° ° ° We had to build a bridge at Wyatt, which consumed a couple of days, and on the 5th of December my whole command was at College Hill, ten miles from Oxford, whence I reported to Gen. Grant at Oxford.

Oxford is ten miles south of the Tallahatchie, and twenty-five from Holly Springs. Halting as GRANT'S movement had been, the campaign was full of promise to a resolute General, and GRANT had double PEMBERTON'S force. But BADEAU shows that the shadow of McCLERNAND, with an independent command, coming down the Mississippi, weakened GRANT. At this point, where he had all in his hands for a campaign against PEMBERTON'S army, he wanted to turn back. He asked HALLECK from Abbeville: "How far South would you like me to go?" He had lost his object and his resolution.

He now wanted another change of plan. December 5 he suggested this to HALLECK: "If the Helena troops were at my command I think it would be practicable to send SHERMAN to take them and the Memphis forces south of the Yazoo River, and thus secure Vicksburg and the State of Mississippi." This was to turn his back on the Confederate Army to recover places by avoiding it. HALLECK'S answer gave GRANT the asked for addition to his command, and now GRANT countermarched SHERMAN again back to Memphis to command a river expedition to attack Vicksburg from the river, GRANT to await his operation and to "co-operate." But how to co-operate when, even with all his forces, he had decided it not safe to go further, is what GRANT could not tell. He ordered SHERMAN to "proceed to reduce Vicksburg, assisted by the gunboats," and he said, with a vagueness befitting such co-operation: "I will hold the forces here in readiness to co-operate with you in such manner as the movements of the enemy may make necessary."

BADEAU tells the objective of all this reversion of the plan of the campaign. He says:

Grant was still anxious lest McClernand should obtain the command of the river expedition, and therefore had hurried Sherman to Memphis on the very day that he secured the authority, so that if possible the latter might start before McClernand could arrive. Halleck, too, sent the permission without that deliberation which he sometimes displayed.

If BADEAU may be believed, GRANT's campaign had turned from PEMBERTON toward McCLERNAND, and HALLECK was co-operating. But they had not yet circumvented LINCOLN. Says BADEAU:

On the 18th came at last the unwelcome word from Washington: "It is the wish of the President that Gen. McClernand's corps shall constitute a part of the river expedition, and that he shall have the immediate command, under your direction."

This would put McCLERNAND in command of that which GRANT's altered plan had designed to be the winning side of the "co-operation;" then the subsequent proceedings would interest GRANT no more. His strategy was beaten.

But there was one turn left: If GRANT should return and take command of the river expedition, McCLERNAND would be subordinated. And now did GRANT's proverbial luck come to his relief in the shape of VAN DORN's cavalry, which, December 20, made a descent on Holly Springs, and destroyed the stores of GRANT's army. With the same trust in luck as at Pittsburg Landing, he had taken little care to fortify his supply depot. The rebels estimated the destruction at $4,000,000; but this, perhaps, was at Confederacy prices. Whatever the figure, it was enough for GRANT, who now decided that a river for a base, and gunboats to hold it, was the only practicable way of war in this country. So he decided to countermarch, and to join SHERMAN, and subordinate McCLERNAND, and, leaving PEMBERTON free to go to defend Vicksburg, to himself undertake to reduce that place from the river. Thus ended the first stage of the Vicksburg campaign. All this tended to make the final victory the more a cause for rejoicing. This, however, does not include SHERMAN's "co-operating" part; further along we shall see how that sped.

CHAPTER III.

THE CHANGE OF BASE—RETREAT FROM THE INTERIOR LINE—HOW SHERMAN WAS MARCHED UP AND DOWN—THE MANY REASONS WHY.

Gen. GRANT's movement down the line of the Mississippi Central Railroad, in the best time of year, when the roads were good, had advanced his headquarters from Grand Junction, November 4, to Oxford, December 5, forty-five miles in thirty-one days. Here he tarried till VAN DORN's visit at Holly Springs on the 20th, when he decided to go no further in a country of such impolite practices. This was not such a constant pressure as keeps an enemy busy in defense and retreat. And there is a being always at hand to find mischief still for the idle to do, as was exemplified by VAN DORN and FORREST behind GRANT's back.

Gen. SHERMAN, GRANT's energetic coadjutor, marched three divisions from Memphis, which is straight west of Grand Junction, November 24, by three roads, stopped two days at the Tallahatchie to make a bridge, and reached a point on GRANT's flank with his whole command December 5. All this was to find that he must march back again as fast, while GRANT waited for the new operation. Scraps which BADEAU prints from HALLECK's dispatches make appear that he was as irresolute as GRANT; but they show that he gave GRANT full discretion and support, and that when the enemy fell back from the Tallahatchie HALLECK became sanguine as to the interior line, and gave GRANT plenary authority, including the command of the Arkansas army. In conclusion he said: "Telegraph what are your present plans." BADEAU prints only this clause. GRANT's answer told the change of plan to a river expedition, he to co-operate on the interior line.

GRANT wrote SHERMAN December 8 inclosing HALLECK's dispatch, and asking SHERMAN to come to Oxford and confer on a plan, saying:

My notion is to send two divisions back to Memphis and fix upon a day when they should effect a landing, and press from here with this command at the proper time to co-operate. If I do not do this I will move our present force to Grenada, including Steele's. * * * When a good ready is had to move immediately on Jackson, Miss., cutting loose from the road. Of these two plans I look more favorably on the former.

In the former plan he was distinctly to meet SHERMAN at Vicksburg in a concerted attack. In the latter plan he would have only about as far to march from Grenada to Jackson, as he marched to the same place from Bruinsburg, after consuming a great army and navy and transport fleet for near six months. And the country was much better for the march.

Gen. SHERMAN had marched from Memphis with two divisions to join GRANT; had countermarched; had marched from Memphis again with three divisions, and by energetic movement had joined GRANT south of the Tallahatchie. And now he was to go back. BADEAU does not state what argument convinced SHERMAN of the propriety of this new back action; but SHERMAN started back immediately. As BADEAU lets out that this was to snatch the river expedition from McCLERNAND, we might suppose that GRANT took SHERMAN into his confidence, if it were not that SHERMAN, who is a very George Washington for inability to prevaricate, says that the idea of McCLERNAND'S coming did not enter into his dreams at that moment.

But after GRANT had sent back SHERMAN to head off McCLERNAND, came HALLECK'S announcement that McCLERNAND was to command the river expedition. This seemed an irreparable blow; but then VAN DORN came to GRANT'S relief by destroying his stores, and this supplied a reason for his going back to get command of the river expedition: Says BADEAU: "Since SHERMAN was not to command it, he was anxious to do so himself." But to show to HALLECK that it was not a retreat, but a "change of base," he telegraphed: "The enemy are falling back from Grenada." If so they were giving up the Yallabusha, the only obstacle to GRANT'S march directly to Jackson or Vicksburg. BADEAU says the destruction of supplies was but a "temporary inconvenience," but GRANT wanted to go back. Thus in the shifting of plans to circumvent McCLERNAND, SHERMAN was left to the sacrifice.

Although BADEAU finds so many reasons for GRANT'S turning back at the first impediment as to make VAN DORN'S visit a friendly service, yet he pauses to tell what might have been:

Grant has told me that had he known then what he soon afterward learned—the possibility of subsisting an army of 30,000 men without supplies other than drawn from an enemy's country—he could at that time have pushed on to the rear of Vicksburg, and probably have succeeded in capturing the place.

Very likely! but McCLERNAND might have been the first to get in.

BADEAU says: "GRANT was now convinced of the impossibility which he had foretold, of maintaining so long a line of supplies through hostile territory." He had undertaken a campaign to demonstrate his foretold impossibility. The Irish pilot was engaged by the skipper upon his solemn affirmation that he knew every rock in the channel; and when the ship struck, he exclaimed: "That's one of them!" When Generals set out on campaigns which they have foretold to be impossible, they generally succeed in proving their foretelling.

And when GRANT had found, during VAN DORN'S break of his communications, that he could draw sufficient supplies from the country, BADEAU fetches in the crowning reason for his turning back: "He discovered that PEMBERTON would not fight." GRANT'S great strategy, he says, was not to take places, but destroy armies. He had "indeed 'meant and hoped' to threaten Vicksburg, but his prime object was the defeat of PEMBERTON." But the facility with which, in BADEAU, GRANT'S afterthoughts reach back into his original plans, shows that at all times he "builded wiser than he knew." And now, as he came solely to fight PEMBERTON, and PEMBERTON would not stay and fight, what could he do as a military man, but turn back and leave him?

And thus, after we had spent an army of from 100,000 to 200,000 for a year to recover interior territory and "strategic" places which we fondly declared had broken the backbone of the rebellion, we then evacuated them to seek the backbone in another place, from which it vanished again like the pirates' buried treasure. The reader of the history of our wonderful war, who reads how well HALLECK employed an army greater than either that fought at Waterloo, in taking the great strategic point of Corinth, in 1862, will read also that in 1864, when Gen. GEORGE H. THOMAS was left by SHERMAN to defend Tennessee, Kentucky, and the North against Hood, Corinth was Hood's base. This is the way the war cost $7,000,000,000, and took four years.

GRANT's retreat began by the march of McPHERSON's division from the Tallahatchie January 4. But the retreat was slow; the roads were bad; they always are bad in times of indecision; "and as it had been determined to abandon Northern Mississippi, the accumulated Quartermasters' and ordnance stores had to be removed with the army." Happily VAN DORN's cavalry had lightened the labor of carrying stores back. "It was not till the 10th of January that the headquarters were established at Memphis." This completed the great interior campaign, with a striking parallel to the famous march of the King of France.

CHAPTER IV:

THE MOVEMENT IN CONCERT—THE DISCORDS.

Although Gen. GRANT, with an exalted patriotism which never stooped to count the cost of sacrifices in his country's affairs, had given up the interior campaign to take the command of the river expedition from Gen. McCLERNAND, yet the affair had now become so complicated by the orders from the War Department that McCLERNAND would be in command of the expedition, while GRANT, the commander of the department, would be left in the rear.

By judicious deliberation in forwarding the War Department's order to McCLERNAND at Springfield, Ill., happily spliced by the break of communications by VAN DORN and FORREST, it was hoped that SHERMAN would get started before McCLERNAND. Fortunately this was the event; but McCLERNAND received orders direct from the War Department, and followed about a week after, which left SHERMAN time for his assault on Vicksburg. Thus did GRANT do what he could to prevent the errors at Washington.

The last words which Gen. SHERMAN received from GRANT, December 14, defined GRANT's line of co-operation in the great concert of movements:

"The enemy are yet on the Yallabusha. I am pushing down on them slowly, but so as to keep up the impression of a continuous move. ° ° ° My headquarters will probably be in Coffeeville [ten miles above the Yallabusha] one week hence. ° ° ° It would be well if you could have two or three small boats suitable for navigating the Yazoo. It may be necessary for me to look to that base of supplies before we get through."

Gen. SHERMAN, in his Memoirs, writing of the failure of GRANT's column to attack in concert with ROSECRANS at Iuka, remarks: "In my experience these concerted movements generally fail, unless with the very best troops, and then in a country on whose roads some reliance can be placed, which is not the case in Northern Mississippi."

Perhaps there has not been in all the wars of ancient and modern Generals a plan of such farfetching and uncommunicable concerted movements as this, in which the concert of one army in the interior of Mississippi and another by a river expedition from Memphis, not hearing from one another for two weeks, was to be so exactly timed that their guns would unite on a given day in the fanfare finale at Vicksburg.

This is only one of the examples of the superiority of military genius in this fresh young country. Even through the tone of distinguished consideration which these eminent Generals preserve toward each other, GRANT in BADEAU, SHERMAN in his Memoirs, SHERMAN maintains that GRANT's orders required him to assault at Vicksburg, and gave him to expect to hear simultaneously the sound of GRANT's guns; while BADEAU plants GRANT impregnably on that clause of his first order which said: "I will hold the forces in readiness to co-operate with you in such manner as the movements of the enemy may make necessary;" and he maintains that GRANT did this literally in his retreat. And if the enemy's movements made that retreat necessary, who can deny the literal co-operation! Thus were both these distinguished commanders right, and each did alike distinguish his military genius.

Some notion of the immense resources called out by the government, may be formed from the narration that whereas SHERMAN, who had just bent all his energies to march three divisions from Memphis to Oxford to join GRANT for a campaign, left that place December 8th, to march back, his expedition from Memphis started on the 19th, the day before Van Dorn called on Grant at Holly Springs. The grand amphibious armada was composed of 12,000 men with all the equipment and supplies of an army, fifty-eight steamboats, and Commodore Porter's gunboat fleet of sixty vessels of all classes, carrying 280 guns and 800 men.

Gen. Sherman says:

The preparations were necessarily hasty in the extreme, but this was the essence of the whole plan—viz., to reach Vicksburg, as it were, by surprise, while Gen. Grant held in check Pemberton's army about Grenada, leaving me to contend with the smaller garrison at Vicksburg, and its well known strong batteries and defenses.

To gather such an expedition, and reach Vicksburg by surprise, was like those social surprise parties which send notice. And Van Dorn had done the surprising thing to Grant a week before Sherman reached the place of attack.

The sight of this armada, as "maneuvering by divisions" it descended the Mississippi, Gen. Sherman describes as grand and inspiring. It was also grandly dear to the country; for the necessities of our Generals, East and West, to have fleets to move their armies for inland operations, and to protect their bases, burned the candle at both ends. The armada reached Milliken's Bend, twenty miles above Vicksburg, on the Arkansas side, December 24. Leaving here a division which sent a brigade to break up the railroad leading from Vicksburg west toward Shreveport, La., the rest proceeded on the 26th to Johnson's plantation, just below the mouth of the Yazoo, and there debarked. The other division arrived and debarked the next night. And now Sherman's part in this great military symphony was to be played.

CHAPTER V.

Gen. Sherman's Assault on the Chickasaw Bluffs.

Gen. Sherman developed great talent for finding difficult places to assault, but even he could hardly have found one more difficult than this which he had turned back from a promising interior campaign to reach. He had landed his army on an island of five to six miles, between the Yazoo River and the line of bluffs running northeast from Vicksburg on the east side of the Yazoo. This island is formed by the Yazoo, the Mississippi, and bayous, and lies opposite that part of the Vicksburg Bluffs next to the town, which is called Chickasaw Bluffs or Walnut Hills. Further up the range is called Haines' Bluff, which the Yazoo runs near to in two places, twelve and twenty miles above Vicksburg, and thus Haines' Bluff effectually closed the Yazoo to our gunboats.

The island has on the north the crooked Yazoo, on the northeast a deep bayou, the Chickasaw, which runs from the Yazoo toward Chickasaw Bluffs to a broad, shallow, forked bayou called Old River, which comes down from above along the line of bluffs, and runs between the island and the bluffs to the Mississippi, just above Vicksburg. The big bayous have little bayous, cutting into the island, and it is dotted with lagoons and swamps. It is ten feet below high water, and, save on the Yazoo side, and some old cotton fields along Chickasaw Bayou, was heavily wooded. Sherman's reconnaissance found that the only part from which an assault seemed practicable was that which for about two miles below Chickasaw Bayou fronted Chickasaw Bluffs. To make the assault from there, Old River must first be crossed by two narrow causeways, each under a concentrated fire.

On the Walnut Hills side Old River had a levee to keep the flood from the strip of bottom between that and the hills. As Sherman states water marks ten feet high on the trees of the island, this levee must have been at least as high as that. This levee was the enemy's first line; it made a regular parapet, and was held by infantry. Between this levee and the line of hills was a road that ran along this bottom up to Yazoo City. The levee was a complete cover to this road, so that the enemy's forces could be moved along it, under cover, to meet Sherman's crossing at any point. At the foot of the bluffs, at places to command these two narrow causeways, were batteries to enfilade them. These were supported by infantry in rifle pits and on spurs of the hills. Along the foot of the hills were rifle pits, and the tops were crowned by elaborate works and batteries.

The official report of Gen. Sherman to Gen. Rawlins is a good description of the situation in which he had to storm the line of hills to carry out his part of the co-operative movement:

Immediately in our front was a bayou, passable at only two points, on a narrow levee or sandbar, which was perfectly commanded by the enemy's sharpshooters that lined the levee or parapet on its opposite bank. Behind this was an irregular strip of beach or table land, on which were constructed a series of rifle pits and batteries, and behind that a high abrupt range of hills, whose scarred sides were marked all the way up with rifle trenches, and the crowns of the principal hills presented heavy batteries.

The country road leading from Vicksburg to Yazoo City runs along the foot of these hills, and answered an admirable purpose to the enemy as a covered way, along which he moved his artillery and infantry promptly to meet us at any point at which we attempted to pass this difficult bayou. Nevertheless that bayou, with its levee parapets, backed by the line of rifle pits, batteries, and frowning hills, had to be passed before we could reach terra firma, and meet our enemy on anything like fair terms.

All these conditions made as nice a slaughter pen as the greatest strategist could find to send an army to. For this had he countermarched from a very promising interior campaign, and formed a grand armada. Gen. SHERMAN's report vindicates his failure by showing that success was impossible; but there is this indomitable quality in the soldiering of SHERMAN and GRANT, that the absolute impossibility of an assault, and the certainty of vain slaughter of men, was no reason for not sending them into it. Volunteers were food for powder, and there was an air of greatness in great slaughter. The very exuberance with which our young men volunteered made some of the regular officers extravagant in consuming them. And they had good fortune in this, for they who consumed most came to the top, and the few who achieved results with economy in men were thought little of.

A brigade of Gen. G. W. MORGAN's division was to carry the hills, supported by FRANK BLAIR's brigade of STEELE's division at the other crossing, a mile or more away. Gen. SHERMAN recites his plan, which was precise in its several stages, and complete; but in execution it stuck at the first stage. He tells the action in fewer words:

The assault was made and a lodgment effected on the hard table land near the county road, and the heads of the different assaulting columns reached different points of the enemy's works, but there met so withering a fire from the rifle pits and cross fire of grape and canister from the batteries that the columns faltered, and finally fell back to the point of starting, leaving many dead, wounded, and prisoners in the hands of the enemy.

Say 2,000 brave volunteers done for in that job.

Gen. SHERMAN's report pays a handsome tribute to the valor of the 6th Missouri Regiment, which was sent from A. J. SMITH's division to make a diversion from MORGAN. He says "the circumstances called for all the individual courage for which that regiment is justly celebrated." He continues:

The 6th Missouri crossed over rapidly by companies, and lay under the bank of the bayou, with the enemy's sharpshooters over their heads, within a few feet; so near that their sharpshooters held out their muskets, and fired down vertically upon our men. The orders were to undermine this bank and make a road up it, but it was found impossible; and after the repulse of Morgan's assault I ordered Gen. A. J. Smith to retire this regiment under cover of darkness.

In the Memoirs he says these men scooped out holes in the bank with their hands for shelter against the fire from above, and that they had to be recalled one at a time after dark. To cross a narrow sand spit, deploy against a steep parapet held by a line of the enemy, undermine a road through it, to carry an assault beyond up a steep hill thoroughly fortified, or to make a diversion while DE COURCEY's brigade did pretty much the same, seems like a forlorn hope. Gen. SHERMAN states the result:

When the night of the 29th closed in, we stood upon our original ground, and had suffered a repulse. The effort was necessary to a successful accomplishment of my orders, and the combination was the best possible under the circumstances.

SHERMAN meant to make another assault next day, and embarked STEELE's division to go up the Yazoo to Haines' Bluff "and make a dash at the hills;" but fortunately a heavy fog next day prevented the boats from moving. During the night the sound of trains was heard bringing in PEMBERTON's troops. A heavy rain set in, and, warned by the water marks on the trees, SHERMAN re-embarked his army. SHERMAN's official report was chivalrously just. He said:

I assume all the responsibility, and attach fault to no one, and am generally satisfied with the high spirit manifested by all. * * * I attribute our failure to the strength of the enemy's position, both natural and artificial, and not to his superior fighting.

Indeed the enemy had no opportunity to show great fighting qualities.

But when Gen. SHERMAN came to write his Memoirs, twelve years after, his view had changed. As with BADEAU'S Grant, after he had risen to greatness of superstructure, he seemed to think it necessary to strengthen his base by reconstructing history to show that he had been infallible from the beginning. He now wrote: "The attack failed, and I have always felt that its failure was due to the failure of Gen. GEORGE W. MORGAN to obey his orders, or to fulfill his promise made in person." That promise was to scale those hills. It can not be denied that MORGAN did not do it. SHERMAN says in these afterthoughts: "One brigade (DECOURCEY'S) of MORGAN'S troops crossed the bayou safely, but took cover behind the bank, and could not be moved forward." But this is the same cover which the 6th Missouri took, whose courage SHERMAN so commended in his report. Let us, like the two dutiful sons of NOAH, with averted faces, drop the mantle of charity over this exposure of military and moral weakness of a great General.

CHAPTER VI.

THE QUESTION BETWEEN GRANT AND SHERMAN OF GRANT'S FAILURE TO CO-OPERATE IN THE ATTACK ON VICKSBURG.

BADEAU makes an argument to refute the common supposition of the time "that SHERMAN'S reverse was the consequence of a failure on GRANT'S part to move south from Grenada and appear in the rear of Vicksburg at the time of the assault." He makes these strong points:

1. GRANT "meant, if he could, to hold PEMBERTON at Grenada, and thus allow SHERMAN to enter Vicksburg without any material opposition."

2. But if he had so held PEMBERTON it would have made no difference to SHERMAN; for "the strength of the works at Vicksburg was not fully appreciated when this arrangement was made; they were so strong that had GRANT been able to keep PEMBERTON'S entire force in his own front, there would have been no different result to SHERMAN'S endeavor."

3. SHERMAN "never could have anticipated a tactical co-operation from GRANT; for GRANT had neither promised nor suggested it;" therefore when at Oxford he laid out the plan of concerted movements, and his part in the interior, he said in his letter of instructions to SHERMAN—"I will hold the forces here in readiness to co-operate with you in such manner as the movements of the enemy make necessary"—he meant not tactical, but moral co-operation.

4. SHERMAN, in his report of the assault, shows that he was not looking for GRANT'S tactical co-operation in it, for he says: "Not one word could I hear from Gen. GRANT, who was supposed to be *pushing south*." "I proposed * * * to attack the enemy's right, which, if successful, would give us substantial possession of the Yazoo River, and *place us in communication with Gen. Grant*." The italics and gaps are BADEAU'S.

5. SHERMAN could not have expected "tactical co-operation" from GRANT, nor even moral co-operation in his assault; for this remark in SHERMAN'S report of the assault shows that he had before heard that GRANT was falling back: "The rumor of Gen. GRANT having fallen back behind the Tallahatchie became confirmed by my receiving no intelligence from him."

6. "SHERMAN himself declared that his failure was owing to 'the strength of the enemy's position, both natural and artificial.'" As one sufficient cause is in logic sufficient, ergo his failure was not owing to GRANT.

7. SHERMAN'S own report shows that the enemy's forces at Vicksburg were so large that, without regard to GRANT, success was impossible, for he says: "I supposed their (the rebel) organized forces to amount to about 15,000, which could be re-enforced at the rate of about 5,000 a day, *provided Gen. Grant did not occupy all the attention of Pemberton's forces at Grenada*." The italics in all these citations are BADEAU'S.

8. SHERMAN'S general letter of information of the campaign to the division commanders, which BADEAU cites as "*before the attack*"—in fact December 23, while coming down the river—told the plan of co-operation as "to act in concert with Gen. GRANT against PEMBERTON'S forces, supposed to have *Jackson, Miss., as a point of concentration*."

Also: "It may be necessary (looking to GRANT'S approach) before attacking Vicksburg, to reduce the battery at Haines' Bluff, so as to enable the gunboats and lighter transports to ascend the Yazoo and *communicate with Gen. Grant.*" Also: "*Grant's left and center were at the last accounts approaching the Yallabusha, near Grenada*, and the railroad to his rear, by which he drew his supplies, was reported to be seriously damaged. This may disconcert him somewhat, but only makes more important our line of operations." Again: "*At the Yallabusha Gen. Grant may encounter the army of Gen. Pemberton*, the same which refused him battle on the line of the Tallahatchie, which was strongly fortified, but as he (PEMBERTON) will hardly have time to fortify the Yallabusha, and in that event Gen. GRANT will immediately advance down the high ridge lying between the Big Black and the Yazoo, and will expect to meet us *on the Yazoo.*" The quotations in this number seem to show SHERMAN'S expectation of GRANT'S co-operation; but BADEAU quotes them as testimony to the contrary.

9. This same romantic letter of general intelligence, by Gen. SHERMAN to the several officers, issued while the grand armada was descending the Mississippi, showed that he contemplated, among other things, landing above Vicksburg and marching into the interior to attack Vicksburg from the east on the line of the railroad from that place to Jackson, thus: "I purpose to land our whole force on the Mississippi side, and then to reach the point where the Vicksburg and Jackson Railroad crosses the Big Black, after which to attack Vicksburg by land, whilst the gunboats assail it by water." This would offer to GRANT a fine opportunity to join him.

10. SHERMAN himself absolves GRANT from blame for lack of "tactical co-operation" in this assault, in his general absolution, in his report, when he says: "The effort was necessary to a successful accomplishment of my orders, and the combinations were the best possible under the circumstances. I assume all the responsibility, and attach the blame to no one."

BADEAU thus proves to his entire satisfaction, by these italicized citations from Gen. SHERMAN'S report, and from his previous letter of romantic anticipations, that he could not have expected any tactical co-operation from GRANT in the attack on Vicksburg, and did not expect it, and that GRANT'S inability to give the moral co-operation, which was all that he meant, by holding PEMBERTON on the Yallabusha, made no difference to SHERMAN, because the defenses of Vicksburg were so strong, by his own showing, and so strongly defended, without PEMBERTON, that SHERMAN would have been repulsed all the same. Therefore, what GRANT did was a matter of no consequence to SHERMAN, who thus, by the grand plan of movements in concert, was sent to slaughter his army in a solo.

Therefore does BADEAU conclude: "Of course those who think or have said that Gen. GRANT was to meet SHERMAN at Vicksburg, or to co-operate with him in the assault, never can have seen these papers." But he justifies SHERMAN by this left handed stroke: "SHERMAN deserves all praise for his determination to attempt the assault, when he knew not only that GRANT never intended to support him in its tactical execution, but that he was probably unable to render even the strategical support to the movement which had been originally planned." And he applies a poultice to SHERMAN to soothe his sole responsibility for his failure by this: "Indeed, when GRANT threw both his armies on the Mississippi, success still fled before him as coyly as in the interior."

On the other side, SHERMAN, in his Memoirs, prints GRANT'S letter, calling him to confer at Oxford on the new plan, GRANT saying: "My notion is to send two divisions back to Memphis, and fix upon a day when they should effect a landing, and press from here with this command at the proper time to co-operate." He also thought that the following in GRANT'S letter of instructions meant practical co-operation: "Inform me of the earliest practicable day when you will embark, and such plans as may then be matured. I will hold the forces here in readiness to co-operate with you in such manner as the movements of the enemy may make necessary."

Also a letter from GRANT, dated December 14, received by SHERMAN at Memphis, which he says "completes all instructions received by me governing the first movement against Vicksburg," had this as to co-operation: "The enemy are as yet on the Yallabusha. I am pushing them down slowly, but so as to keep up the impression of a continuous move. * * * My headquarters will probably be in Coffeeville one week hence. * * * It would be well if you could have two or three small boats suitable for navigating the Yazoo. It may become necessary for me to look to that base of supplies before we get through." Looking to the Yazoo for supplies, looked to a cutting loose from his interior base, and a march on the rear of Vicksburg.

Gen. SHERMAN also affirms that it was the plan and understanding of concert of action with GRANT that required him to make the assault immediately at Vicksburg, as "necessary to the successful accomplishment of my orders," without regard to the impossibility of successful assault. He says: "Up to that moment I had not heard a word from Gen. GRANT since leaving Memphis; and most assuredly I had listened for days for the sound of his guns in the direction of Yazoo City." In that belief he had intended another assault the next day, when the providential fog, preventing the boats from moving up to Haines' Bluff, saved the sacrifice of another 2,000 volunteers—perhaps twice as many.

Thus does each of these distinguished Generals make out his case, and prove that they suddenly turned back from a true military line, and divided the army, to enter upon a plan of remote concerted movements, in which there was to be no concert or co-operation, and in which the only definite idea was that SHERMAN was to go down and butt against the Vicksburg bluffs, which were as well known to be impregnable before as after he had sacrificed 2,000 brave volunteers in proving it. For Vicksburg was not a green spot, to be taken unprepared, but had been fortified a year before; and in the previous July had withstood a protracted bombardment by the united fleets of FARRAGUT and PORTER. To add to the completeness of the two arguments, SHERMAN gives his case away by an unqualified indorsement of BADEAU.

BADEAU makes very evident that GRANT and SHERMAN were thrown off the usual balance of their military judgment by LINCOLN's eccentricity in giving Gen. MCCLERNAND the command of an expedition to open the Mississippi. He had so far been a fortunate General. BADEAU says he had CÆSAR's fatal fault —he was ambitious. GRANT fancied that MCCLERNAND would have a great opportunity, and that irreparable irregularity might grow from the still higher elevation of a man who was not of the army class, and whom no regular officer could serve under. If GRANT and SHERMAN could have known then the military rudiments which they learned afterward, they could have gone on down Central Mississippi with an army of 70,000 men, and swept all before them, leaving to MCCLERNAND to go and sink his army in the bog. That they sacrificed the real campaign, and took their own army to the bog, to avert the apprehended mischief of MCCLERNAND's success, may prove that their military judgment was unhinged, but it nevertheless exalts their patriotism.

CHAPTER VII.

M'CLERNAND TAKES COMMAND—THE VICTORY OF FORT HINDMAN—TURNING THE MISSISSIPPI—GRANT'S EMBARRASSMENT WITH M'CLERNAND—GRANT COMES TO THE COMMAND.

Gen. SHERMAN's assault at Chickasaw Bluffs was on the 29th of December. The fog next day prevented his steamboat expedition up the Yazoo to Haines' Bluff "to make a dash at the hills." The rain set in; the water marks ten feet high on the trees warned him, and he ordered the re-embarkation of the stores, and preparations for the army to embark during the night of January 1, 1863. He says: "From our camps at Chickasaw (bayou) we could hear the whistle of trains arriving in Vicksburg, and could see battalions of men marching up toward Haines' Bluff and taking post at all points along our front."

Up to that moment, he says: "I had not heard a word from Gen. GRANT since leaving Memphis; and most assuredly I had listened for days for the sound of his guns in the direction of Yazoo City." On the morning of January 2 the command was all afloat, when SHERMAN heard that Gen. MCCLERNAND was at the mouth of the Yazoo. SHERMAN left his army there, and found Gen. MCCLERNAND "with orders from the War Department to command the expeditionary force on the Mississippi River." He reported to MCCLERNAND what had been done, and that troops were pouring into Vicksburg, which must be PEMBERTON's army, "and that Gen. GRANT must be near at hand." But MCCLERNAND surprised him by the information "that Gen. GRANT was not coming at all; that his depot at Holly Springs had been captured by VAN DORN, and that he had drawn back from Coffeeville and Oxford to Holly Springs and Lagrange; and, further, that QUIMBY'S division of GRANT'S army was actually at Memphis for stores when he passed down."

SHERMAN thought that this explained "how Vicksburg was being re-enforced;" also, that it made any attempt on the place from the Yazoo hopeless; therefore, "all came out of the Yazoo, and on the 3d of January rendezvoused at Milliken's Bend, about ten miles above." McCLERNAND'S order assuming command divided the "Army of the Mississippi" into two corps, of two divisions each, the first, his own, commanded by Gen. GEO. W. MORGAN, the second by Gen. SHERMAN. GRANT was still in the interior. A steamboat and her tow of barges, with SHERMAN'S ammunition, had been captured by a rebel boat, which came out of Arkansas River, and taken up that river forty miles, to Fort Hindman. Gen. SHERMAN says that he perceived that this liability in the rear would be unpleasant in operations at Vicksburg; therefore, he proposed to McCLERNAND to let him go up the Arkansas and take the fort, PORTER to send gunboats.

The conclusion was that PORTER and McCLERNAND went along, taking three ironclads and the whole army, which had not yet debarked, reaching the Arkansas on the 9th, the troops landing three miles below the fort next day. The enemy had a strong line of intrenchments below the fort, running from river to interior swamp. The front of this was a dead level much obstructed. The troops lay on their arms without fires or covering that January night, to be ready for assault in concert with the boats next day. This assault had to be made over a slaughterous place, but the volunteers went at it unflinchingly. Meanwhile the gunboats ran their bows into the bank in front of the fort, and, it being but little above the river, they poured their fire into the embrasures, putting the gunners to flight, they communicating their panic to the rest.

Outside the fort, at the strong line from river to swamp, the enemy made a more resolute defense, and our brave volunteers had to advance against a seeming impregnable line, under great exposure. In this operation they lost 977 killed and wounded. While this was going on, several officers in the fort hung out white flags; Commodore PORTER landed in the fort, and received the surrender. There was quarreling among Confederate officers over this alacrity with the white flag, but the surrender could not be recalled. Our forces dismantled the fort, carried off its small arms and stores, sent 4,791 prisoners North; re-embarked on the 13th; came down the Arkansas River in a snow storm, and stopped at Helena, at the mouth of that river.

Here McCLERNAND got a letter from GRANT, written before the result, sharply reprimanding him for making this side issue expedition. McCLERNAND replied, assuming the responsibility and defending the enterprise. BADEAU says that GRANT supposed that McCLERNAND planned the expedition, and he had no confidence in his military judgment, and therefore "he expressed his dissatisfaction both to McCLERNAND and HALLECK" But such a victory could not be repaired. and GRANT, finding that SHERMAN conceived the expedition, took a different view, and gave the credit to SHERMAN. SHERMAN says that McCLERNAND'S report did not give proper credit to the navy. This increased PORTER'S distrust of McCLERNAND'S military judgment, which he communicated to Washington.

It is evident that if the expedition had not gained a victory—an article long a stranger to that army—it would have disposed of Gen. McCLERNAND. As it was, it made Gen. GRANT still more unreconciled to him. GRANT visited the army afloat at Napoleon, and, as Gen. SHERMAN narrates: "On the 18th day of January ordered McCLERNAND with his own and my corps, to return to Vicksburg to disembark on the west bank, and to resume work on a canal across a peninsula, which had been begun by Gen. THOMAS WILLIAMS the summer before, the object being to turn the Mississippi River at that point."

Gen. GRANT at this time was greatly embarrassed by his anomalous relation to this expedition. He was in command of the department, but McCLERNAND had an order giving him command of the river expedition. He was GRANT'S subordinate by all regular military conditions, but yet he seemed in a degree independent. This is an instance of the way LINCOLN had of dispensing plums in the way of separate commands.

GRANT had abandoned his interior campaign, and left SHERMAN in the breach to go back and take the command of the river expedition away from McCLERNAND, but he found his plans blocked by that special order. His position was enough to perplex a Bonaparte. Indeed he could see no way to real military results but to dispose of McCLERNAND. One man must not be allowed to stop the way of such mighty forces as were now gathering at Vicksburg. Happily, GRANT'S patriotism was equal to the necessity.

GRANT had allowed no feeling of jealousy to cause him to withhold his counsel and orders from McCLERNAND. When he had first gotten back to Memphis January 10, he had written him vigorous words: "This expedition must not fail." His order at Helena to McCLERNAND to put his army at work to turn the Mississippi gave him opportunity for a great achievement. He repeated on the 22d: "I hope the work of changing the channel of the Mississippi is begun." But while thus generously planning, and giving McCLERNAND the chance for the glory, GRANT was not content. BADEAU says he had no confidence in McCLERNAND'S military ability; he must have known still less of his ability to turn the Mississippi River. Thus was McCLERNAND an obstacle to GRANT, and it was a military necessity that he should be disposed of.

After GRANT had visited the expedition at Napoleon, just from the fine but irregular victory of Fort Hindman, he wrote HALLECK, January 20: "I regard it as my duty to state that I found there was not sufficient confidence in Gen. McCLERNAND as a commander, either by the army or navy, to insure him a success." BADEAU states in addition that McCLERNAND was captious and insubordinate, insisting on "matters of military etiquette and law;" "raising objections to the orders of his commanding officer;" "making suggestions contrary to all the principles of military science," and so on. He cites an extreme case: McCLERNAND went so far as to object to GRANT'S receiving complaints from officers of his command, made not through him, and to GRANT'S practice of issuing orders to McCLERNAND'S subordinates, not through him, as creating confusion and insubordination. He added:

One thing is certain: two Generals can not command this army, issuing independent and direct orders to subordinate officers, and the public service be promoted.

In this McCLERNAND, a mere volunteer, was taking on rules, order and discipline as if he were a regular army officer, with all which that implies; whereas, there being regular officers under him, it was quite the regular thing for GRANT to send orders to them ignoring him. Besides, "suggestions contrary to the principles of military science" could not be tolerated.

All this undermining operation was promoting the discipline of the army in a sort that tended toward the great end, and it resulted in GRANT'S receiving permission from HALLECK to take command, which he assumed in person January 29, McCLERNAND thereby being set back to the command of his corps. And now at last was GRANT ready to begin his great campaign against the Mississippi River, three months after he had started on the interior line.

CHAPTER VIII.

THE WONDERFUL RIVER—THE MORE WONDERFUL MILITARY GENIUS—THE TRUE SOLDIER'S LIFE—THE SEESAW MILITARY POLICY.

The Mississippi River is creation's wonder. At no part are its elements more wonderfully combined than in the Vicksburg region; nor could there be found in its whole length more difficulties for a military operation from the river than that to which the force of circumstances had now brought Gen. GRANT. An idea of the region is requisite to an appreciation of the military achievement, and is interesting in itself. BADEAU draws from the memoir of Gen. J. H. WILSON, of the engineers, and this paper borrows from BADEAU:

All the way from Cairo to New Orleans the Mississippi meanders through a vast alluvial region, the whole of which is annually overflowed, except where levees have afforded a partial barrier. This great basin is nearly fifty miles in width, and extends on the east to the upland plains of Tennessee and Mississippi, while on the west it is bounded by the lesser elevations of drift alone. The bluffs that form the escarpment of the eastern plains are usually quite steep, and thickly overgrown with timber, underbrush, and vines. At various points in its course the river touches one extremity or the other of the bottom land, washing the base of the bluffs, and often cutting deep into the soft strata. Columbus, Fort Pillow, Memphis, Helena, Vicksburg, Grand Gulf, and Port Hudson are points of this kind, and rise from eighty to 200 feet above the freshets.

The alluvial region, throughout its entire extent, is higher near the banks of the river, and falls off gradually, till it reaches the line of the bluffs; the drainage is therefore toward the hills, and is the source of the intricate network of bayous for which the basin is remarkable. The Coldwater, the Tallahatchie, the Yazoo, the Washita, the Red, and Atchafalaya rivers, besides numerous other and smaller streams, are accordingly nothing more than huge side drains. During freshets, the water that breaks over the Mississippi banks or through the crevasses, flows through cypress swamps and a labyrinth of bayous, till it reaches the bluffs, and is again forced back into the parent stream.

Besides the bayous, crescent shaped lakes, the sole remains of the ancient meanderings of the river, abound on both sides, often at considerable distance from the present channel. The forests of the alluvial region are extremely luxuriant and dense; cottonwood, tulip, sweet gum, magnolia, sycamore, and ash are found, with an almost impenetrable jungle of cane and vine. The cypress swamps that occupy the lower portions of the bottom are nearly always under water; and this, with the slimy character of the soil, and the treacherous beds, and slippery steep banks of the bayous, renders the country almost impassable in summer, and entirely so, except by boats, in winter.

Into this domain of half creation had Gen. GRANT brought his fine army. Here in this very Slough of Despond was it to wrestle with the dense forests, the jungle of cane and vine, the deep bayous and lagoons, obstructed by sunken and overhanging trees, the cypress swamps, the slimy soil, and the treacherous bottom, for the next three months, in the most malarious conditions, with immense labors, all of which BADEAU says were destined to prove abortive, save to prove Gen. GRANT's fertility in resource; and all of which, in the consuming of men by disease, made the destruction of a campaign of battles in an open country a light matter.

The eastern line of bluffs coming down in a southwest course on the east side of the Yazoo, and called Haines' Bluff and Walnut Hills, meets the Mississippi at Vicksburg. Below* that place the river runs near the bluff for several miles; then diverges a little and a swamp intervenes; then comes to the bluff again at Warrenton, eight miles below Vicksburg, and so continues for three miles; then diverges widely in great crooks, and, with a turn to the northeast, strikes the bluff again at Grand Gulf, just below the mouth of Big Black River. Here it turns sharply to the southwest again, in the general course of the bluffs, but diverging, till at Bruinsburg, ten miles below Grand Gulf, and just below the mouth of Bayou Pierre, it is two miles from the bluffs.

At Vicksburg the bluffs were regarded as unassailable. They were of the same character below that place, and had heavy guns at different points. Warrenton was fortified. Grand Gulf was a little Vicksburg in its situation as to bluffs and rivers, and its easy defensibility. Where the river left the bluffs the swamps were a defense. At Bruinsburg, thirty-five miles below Vicksburg by land and twice as far by the river, was the first place where there was a landing not crowned by bluff. From here there was a road into the interior, and the line of bluff is two miles inland. Bruinsburg was easily defensible, but there was a limit to the enemy's extension of forces or to his vigilance. All along the west side of the river was a labyrinth of bayous, lakes, lagoons, and swamps, and of great crooks in the river. GRANT had for his camps and field of operations the great bottomless region west of the river, drawing all his supplies from the North. The Confederates had for their field the high land on the east side, drawing their supplies from the rich interior region of Northern Mississippi, now given up to them.

BADEAU, who is always exempt from the error of overstating Gen. GRANT's forces, states that the whole number now in his command was 130,000, all engaged in the Vicksburg operation, either immediately or in support. Fifty thousand were placed in camps at Young's Point, eight miles above Vicksburg, and at Millikin's Bend, twelve miles further up. McPHERSON's corps was at Lake Providence, forty miles above, to work at a bayou and swamp route of 400 to 600 miles to Red River. The base of supplies and reenforcements was at Memphis. Says BADEAU: "They were put in camps along the west bank of the river, on the low swamp land, overflowed this year to an unusual extent." He continues: "The camps were frequently submerged, and the diseases consequent to this exposure prevailed among the troops; dysentery and fevers made sad havoc, and even the smallpox was introduced." "The levees furnished the only dry land deep enough for graves, and for miles along the river bank this narrow strip was all that appeared above the water, furrowed its whole length with graves. The troops were thus hemmed in by the burial places of their comrades."

The old army song, "The soldier's life is always gay," is calculated to foster a levity which ill befits its danger. Our volunteers were taught the better lesson that a soldier's life is sad. How much better the moral effect of the generalship which constantly reminds a soldier of his mortality! The troops were also kept alert by a rising river above their heads, barred only by a treacherous levee. The great fleet of steamboats had to be kept for arks, in emergencies, as well as for the officers to live in, and to carry the troops on their various alligator expeditions. Meanwhile, this great army, sunk in the swamps west of the Mississippi, was as isolated from any co-operation or influence on any of the land operations, East or West, as if it had been sunk in the sea.

BADEAU says that GRANT bent all his energies to the river expedition. "He determined now to abandon the railroad from Jackson to Columbus (Ky.), and to move all his troops south, except those absolutely necessary to hold the line from Memphis to Corinth." He dismantled the river batteries between Memphis and Columbus, and removed the floating batteries. Interior territory, strategic places, and all other objects were set aside for this great enterprise to open the Mississippi. He wrote HALLECK that he should "require a large force for the final struggle," and advised that re-enforcements be held in readiness. "He also inquired if it would not be good policy to combine the four departments at the West—ROSECRANS', STEELE'S, BANKS'. and his own—under one commander," of which he, by his rank, would have the command.

This gives an idea of the way he was bending his own and would have bent all other energies in the west to the Vicksburg operation. This suggestion was not accepted at the time, save to place STEELE'S (the Arkansas) department under his control.

Our system of separate departments, without concert or co-operation, and HALLECK'S ingenious management from Washington, were so successful in alternating our several operations in the West that we gave up what we had gained in one department when we were to make an effort in another. Gen. GRANT'S withdrawal from North Mississippi and West Tennessee, and from the whole interior, to plant his army in the Vicksburg swamps, carried this see-sawing practice to perfection.

ROSECRANS had had a bloody battle at Murfreesboro December 31, 1862, and was organizing for his great Chattanooga campaign. And now VAN DORN'S and FORREST'S cavalry, set free by GRANT'S withdrawal, made BRAGG'S cavalry so superior to that of the Army of the Cumberland that it was hemmed in, and confined to the supplies which it transported from the North, while the rebel armies drew supplies from the greater part of Tennessee, and from all Northern Mississippi and Alabama, which might have fed our armies instead of the Confederate. And now, Gen. GRANT'S army being deeply planted in the bottomless region west of the Mississippi for an indefinite period, the Confederate forces, on their secure interior line, could move from one of our departments to the other wherever required.

This is the way the Confederate Generals, with not half so many men in arms, happened to match our numbers so well at the point of action. This is one of the parts of management which made the war last four years, cost $7,000,000,000, and call to arms at one time 1,200,000 men.

What STANTON and HALLECK could do in supporting a Commanding General in a campaign, when they tried, may be measured by their furnishing for this river expedition, to take a single place, 130,000 men, a transport fleet, a gunboat fleet, supplies of every sort in profusion, and a constant reserve and stream of re-enforcements to feed the dreadful waste from disease in the Mississippi swamps.

What STANTON and HALLECK could withhold from the support of an army in a true campaign, when they tried, may be measured by their treatment of ROSECRANS during the same period. They higgled over the cost of his requisition for saddles to mount 5,000 of his infantry; they called his request for repeating arms for the flank companies a fanciful innovation; they treated his plan to have a mounted force superior to the enemy, so that he might draw supplies from the country instead of they, as an excuse for delay;

they gave no heed to the conditions and possibilities of supplies; they assumed to know more of his situation than he could know on the ground.

They managed so as to withhold from him the co-operation of BURNSIDE in East Tennessee. STANTON, with an oath, refused him another man. They peremptorily ordered him to go forward with less than 65,000 men, on a campaign with a longer line of communication than that for which GRANT had abandoned an interior campaign because he declared it impossible. This down the interior where the Confederate forces from east and west could concentrate upon him. Thus did folly at Washington co-operate with divided commands and lack of concert in the field, to expand the war.

CHAPTER IX.

CHANGING THE BED OF THE MISSISSIPPI RIVER.

Gen. GRANT descended upon Vicksburg with several diverse plans. It was an application to military operations of the universal law of chances, which was discovered by the scientific philosopher, BUCKLE, by which, out of many, some one is likely to have a different fortune. They may be classified under three heads: First, plans to turn the course of the Mississippi River away from Vicksburg; second, plans on the east side to get to the Yazoo with gunboats for an operation from the interior toward the rear of Vicksburg; third, plans on the west side to find an interior route to get away from Vicksburg.

The first plan to which he applied his energies was to turn the Mississippi by a cut across the tongue of land opposite Vicksburg. As the object of the expedition was to open the Mississippi, and as Vicksburg was the obstruction, then, if the river could be induced to take a short cut away from Vicksburg, it would be opened, and, to use LINCOLN's poetic phrase, "the father of waters would flow unvexed to the sea." Thus, by a singular turn of events, had GRANT's great military campaign become converted to the work of changing the bed of the Mississippi.

It has been mentioned that the river makes a short bend to northeast, and runs five miles to the Vicksburg bluff, and then turns still shorter and runs back southwest, leaving a tongue of land which for five miles is little more than two miles wide. This seems an eccentric course in so great a river, in a dead level country, in which it can go where it pleases. Reasoning that the Mississippi is amenable to economical considerations, and would prefer the shorter way, it was thought that if it were led by a starter in the way of a canal, it would take this course, and wash out the rest for itself. And it appears that in all these great projects GRANT was his own engineer, and the engineer corps had only to do the details.

Accordingly the soldiers were set at work grubbing and digging this canal, the several brigades furnishing details for each day. Great trees had to be grubbed out, and the canal protected by levees, as the river was higher than the land. BADEAU relates that this "plan of turning a mighty river from its course" attracted the attention of the civilized world; "that the rebels loudly predicted failure, and the gibes of those who opposed the war at the North were incessant. Still GRANT toiled on. Four thousand soldiers were constantly employed on the work, besides negroes, who were comparatively of little use."

The scientific mind has not settled the question why rivers run crookedly. The Mississippi, running through the most level region in the world, all of which seems its own delta, is the crookedest river. There is nothing to hinder its running straight but its own self-contained forces. Indeed its banks, made by itself, are higher than the bottom beyond them, and as it annually flows over its banks, it has all the surface temptations to run away; but it retires each season within the same banks.

The Mississippi is not only like a snake in its sinuous course, but in shape, being biggest in the middle. Further south its side drains reach the gulf, and the river grows less. Along Vicksburg it rolls 120 to 130 feet in depth. In a depth of 120 feet below the bottom of GRANT's canal it was rushing along at the speed of five or six miles an hour. To dam the Nile with bulrushes was a feeble figure for this project. "Still GRANT toiled on," or the 4,000 soldiers did, and the rebels mocked.

But BADEAU vindicates GRANT's sagacity by this: "On the 4th of February he reported to HALLECK that he had lost all faith in the practicability of the scheme. The canal, he said, is at right angles with the thread of the current at both ends, and both ends are in an eddy—the lower coming out under bluffs completely commanding it. Warrenton, a few miles below, is capable of as strong defense as Vicksburg, and the enemy seeing us at work here, have turned their attention to that point." In so short a time, and after the work of only 4,000 soldiers, had GRANT'S far reaching mind perceived that the inlet to the canal was at an eddy, where the river ran up stream; likewise the outlet, and that the outlet ran against the same bluff whose cannon vexed the father of waters at Vicksburg.

"Still GRANT toiled on," still the details of 4,000 soldiers were sent every day to this exhilarating labor. The country had formed great expectations from the canal. To abandon it would give an impression of failure. Thus were our generals burdened with the necessity to satisfy public opinion in their rear. A wing was cut to a point higher up the river, to reach the current. The batteries opposite the outlet were ignored as a thing which it would be time enough to think about when the river had taken its destined bed. Dredges were procured, and deeper work was laid out, besides the long wing. And so the work went on after GRANT had vindicated his sagacity by pronouncing it useless as an attempt to divert the river, and that if diverted it would still be obstructed by the bluff batteries. Says BADEAU:

The troops who were engaged for two months on the canal were encamped immediately on its west bank, and protected from possible inundation by a levee; but the continued rise in the river made a large expenditure of labor necessary to keep the water out of the camps and canal.

Thus while they were digging to divert the river from its bed, they had to dam, to keep their heads above water:

The work was tedious and difficult, and seemed interminable; and toward the last it became also dangerous; for the enemy threw shells all over the peninsula, and as Grant had predicted, erected batteries which commanded the lower end of the canal.

BADEAU invariably makes the failure of GRANT'S plans praise his military sagacity by its fulfilling his prediction. Yet the canal was on the ragged edge of success, and soon the Mississippi would have had a chance to cut across and strike the new batteries on the bluff, when an untoward event spoiled all:

But at last there seemed some prospect of success; the dredgeboats worked to a charm; the laborers reached a sufficient depth in the soil; the wing was ready to connect with the main artery, and the undertaking was apparently all but completed; when, on the 8th of March, an additional and rapid rise in the river, and the consequent increase of pressure, caused the dam near the upper end of the canal to give way, and every attempt to keep the rush of water out proved abortive.

The torrent thus admitted struggled for a while with the obstacles that sought to stay its course, but finally, instead of coming out below, broke the levee of the canal itself, and spread rapidly across the peninsula, overwhelming every barrier, and separating the northern and southern shores as effectually as if the Mississippi itself flowed between them. It swept far and wide into the interior, submerging the camps, and spreading into the bayous, even to the Tensas and Lower Red. The troops were obliged to flee for their lives, horses were drowned, implements were broken and borne away by the current, and all the labor of many weeks was lost.

Thus the river, which was to be tempted by a chance to shorten its course, rushed out as if it had no regard for space. "Attempts were made to repair the damages, but on the 27th of March GRANT reported that all work except repairing the crevasses in the canal levee had been suspended for several days, the enemy having driven the dredges entirely out." "As he had foretold, the batteries erected on the hills below Vicksburg completely enfiladed the canal." Thus was his military prescience proved by the failure of his plan.

Although the plan of changing the river to this canal was not given up, yet while other projects were going forward work on it was resumed, upon the moderated plan of making it navigable for shallow craft to carry stores, for some yet inchoate purpose. Much labor was expended on it in establishing its levees, to recover the peninsula and the whole region from the river's overflow, and in removing the river's deposit.

But the river kept obstinately on its course, its mighty, rushing volume, 120 feet below, seemingly unconscious of this surface temptation. When the river was high it drowned the canal; when it fell the canal fell too; so it was never used. But BADEAU says it did good in furnishing occupation for the volunteers. And now Gen. GRANT's fertility in military resources was spread out in other plans.

CHAPTER X.

THE LAKE PROVIDENCE ROUTE FOR DIVERTING THE MISSISSIPPI AND THE ARMY—THE YAZOO PASS ROUTE—ESCAPE OF THE ARMY FROM A TRAP.

Although Gen. GRANT prosecuted the undertaking to change the bed of the Mississippi River with great energy and labor of the soldiers, and was at first sanguine of making "the father of waters flow unvexed to the sea," leaving Vicksburg, like Babylon, a monument of retribution, yet he did not trust all to this. At the same time, with McPHERSON's corps, he was prosecuting the Lake Providence plan. This plan comes under the third head—viz.: plans to get away from Vicksburg, and go somewhere.

Lake Providence is a crescent shaped lake, perhaps part of the former bed of the river, six miles long, a mile west of the river, forty miles above Vicksburg by an air line, and twice or thrice as far by the river. The plan was to cut a canal from the river to this lake. From the lake there was a partly defined channel called Bayou Baxter, running through a cypress swamp to Bayou Macon, one of a labyrinth of bayous. In its southerly course Bayou Macon, opposite Vicksburg, is forty miles from the river; about forty miles further south—or three or four times as far as by the course of the bayou—it joins the Tensas Bayou or river. All these bayous are rivers, and all the rivers bayous, differing only in size. The Tensas reaches the Washita about west of Natchez, and the Washita the Red River, and thus the Lake Providence route in a wonderfully tortuous course of 400 to 600 miles would reach the Mississippi about 200 miles below Vicksburg.

The object of this circumnavigation is stated by BADEAU: "Through these various channels it was thought possible to open a route by which transports of light draught might reach the Mississippi again below, and thus enable GRANT to re-enforce BANKS (then either on the Red River or the Atchafalaya) and to co-operate with him against Port Hudson." This was to give up Vicksburg till a more convenient season. This idea came alone from GRANT's active mind. There was no desire at Washington that he should abandon Vicksburg to go and re-enforce BANKS, "then on either the Red River or the Atchafalaya" or somewhere. And if BANKS was to be re-enforced it would be more natural to do it by way of the gulf than by this tortuous route and by abandoning the Vicksburg enterprise.

This route would be, by the course of the bayous, from 400 to 600 miles through the enemy's country, and through the greater part these bayous could be quickly shut in by felling across them the gigantic trees that grew along their banks. To this route for a line of supplies had GRANT come to avoid the difficulty of guarding a line on the Mississippi Central Railroad; and the objective was to go in search of Gen. BANKS, who was somewhere. But here again GRANT's proverbial luck interposed and saved from involving troops or supplies in this net. The nature of the undertaking, and the result, its great object in keeping the volunteers employed and working off their excessive spirit, and its demonstrating GRANT's fertility in military resource, are so well narrated by BADEAU that to comment on it would be to paint the lily:

The levee was cut, and a canal opened between the river and the lake, through which the water passed rapidly; but peculiar difficulties were encountered in clearing Bayou Baxter of the overhanging forests and fallen timber with which it was obstructed. The land from Lake Providence and also from Bayou Macon recedes until the lowest interval between the two widens out into a cypress swamp, where Bayou Baxter is lost. This flat was filled with water to the depth of several feet; and the work of removing the timber that choked the bayou for a distance of twelve or fifteen miles was in consequence exceedingly difficult and slow; but, if this could have been accomplished, the channel, in high water, would have been continuous, although intricate and circuitous to a remarkable degree.

So McPherson's corps was engaged in the undertaking for many weeks. The impossibility of obtaining the requisite number of light draught steamers, however, would have rendered this route useless, even had it been thoroughly opened. But no steamer ever passed through the tortuous channel, which served only to employ the superfluous troops, and to demonstrate the fertility and variety of devices developed during this anomalous campaign.

Thus the impossibility of using the route if it could have been opened reconciled GRANT to the impossibility of opening it, and each alike distinguished that fertility in resources which made this campaign "anomalous."

Besides, "the project excited attention and speculation," and many thought that it would divert the Mississippi to this route, and then by way of the Atchafalaya into the gulf, leaving Vicksburg and all the lower river towns. But BADEAU says that GRANT did not enter into this expectation. "He believed that Vicksburg was only to be won by hard fighting," and meanwhile he was "simply affording occupation for his men."

So this route was given up, after all the practicable occupation for the men had been got out of it, "at about the same time that all hope of effecting anything by the canal was abandoned." But during this time GRANT's remarkable fertility in resource had been directing another undertaking, by way of Yazoo Pass.

This plan comes under the second head, viz.: plans to get into the interior east of Vicksburg. Yazoo Pass is six miles below Helena, Ark., on the east side of the Mississippi, 160 miles above Vicksburg in a direct line, and twice or thrice as far by the river. It was a narrow and tortuous bayou that once ran from the river to Moon Lake—a crescent shaped lake, perhaps once the river bed—thence eastward to Coldwater River or bayou, thence southward to the Tallahatchie, which in a crooked course of about 100 miles unites with the Yallabusha at Greenwood to form the Yazoo—an exceedingly tortuous river or bayou. Greenwood is near 100 miles above Vicksburg in a line, and more than 200 by the course of the Yazoo. Yazoo Pass had long been closed at the Mississippi by a levee.

In all the Yazoo operations the enemy had an immense advantage in the free navigation of the Yazoo River above Haines' Bluff, and in a large fleet of steamboats which had taken refuge there. With these they could carry troops up the Yazoo, Tallahatchie, and Coldwater to place obstructions against GRANT's expedition. The levee was cut on the 2d of February, and the rush of water made an opening for steamboats into Moon Lake. But the impenitent "rebels had begun to make obstructions lower down by felling huge trees into the pass." "A single one of these barricades was a mile and a quarter in length, and composed of no fewer than eighty trees reaching completely across the stream."

Worse than this, of the various trees, nearly all were of wood that would not float. Consequently "the removal was a tedious task. Many of the trees, weighing at the least twenty tons, had to be hauled out upon the shore by strong cables." This served the great object of "occupation for the superfluous men." Besides, the crevasse "submerged the entire country, except a very narrow strip of land near the shore. The men, in parties of 500, were thus obliged to work in the water, as well as during almost incessant rains." But by this kind of labor the barriers were at last removed, "and a heavy growth of overhanging timber cut away, and the distance from Moon Lake to the Coldwater was finally cleared." But while thus occupied above, "the enemy had gained time to securely fortify below."

On the 15th of February the way to the Tallahatchie was declared practicable, and Gen. Ross, with 4,500 men, was ordered to move in. "He embarked in twenty-two light transports, preceded by two ironclad gunboats, and a mosquito fleet, as the light armored craft suitable for this navigation were called." There was some delay in getting light transports, but the expedition entered the pass February 24, and reached the Coldwater, twenty-five miles from the Mississippi, March 2. The Coldwater is of the same bayou character, and runs through a dense wilderness; the Tallahatchie is a similar stream, but larger. The expedition proceeding cautiously, through an almost unbroken forest, reached the Lower Tallahatchie March 10.

And now, says BADEAU: "GRANT determined to prosecute his entire campaign, if possible, in this direction. The idea was to reach the Yazoo, above Haines' Bluff, with his whole army. The distance from Milliken's Bend would have been nearly 900 miles." And half of this would be by narrow, tortuous bayous, and rivers, through an enemy's country, susceptible to all sorts of obstructions and defenses. QUINBY's division was ordered in to support Ross; then McPHERSON's whole corps, and a division from Memphis, as fast as transportation could be procured.

And now again did GRANT's proverbial luck interpose to save him from sending his whole army into this trap. Great difficulty was found in getting light draught and short steamboats for these narrow and crooked streams, and the great bulk of the troops was detained at Helena. Meanwhile Ross' flotilla had reached the junction of the Tallahatchie with the Yallabusha, which forms the Yazoo at Greenwood. Here the Confederates had made a battery called Fort Pemberton, which the gunboats engaged on the 11th of March, and again on the 13th, aided by a battery on shore, without success. The country was all under water, save narrow strips along the rivers; the troops had no way to flank the battery; therefore all depended on the ability of the gunboats to silence the battery, and thus the expedition came to a standstill.

As the site of the fort was little above the water, an effort was made to drown it by cutting the levee of the Mississippi, 300 miles away, at Austin, eighteen miles above Helena; but this did not work right. The enemy were now sending troops up to Greenwood by their free navigation of the Yazoo. Batteries would be as obstructive in the rear of our expedition as in front. Says BADEAU: "In order to relieve Ross, who was now in imminent danger of being surrounded, isolated as he was, away off in this tangled network of forest and bayou, GRANT devised still another scheme."

Thus, like a chapter of a serial novel, this chapter ends, leaving the Yazoo Pass expedition in a crisis on the Tallahatchie, and keeping the reader in suspense until the next chapter. GRANT, in order to relieve this expedition, shall devise another, which in its turn shall need rescue.

CHAPTER XI.

THE STEELE'S BAYOU PLAN—THE RELIEVING EXPEDITION RELIEVED.

Gen. GRANT'S next plan comes also under the second head—viz., plans to get by way of the Yazoo into the interior to operate on the rear of Vicksburg. It had also the present object of making a diversion to relieve the Yazoo Pass expedition, now in danger of being surrounded on the Tallahatchie. The plan was to go to the Yazoo "Along another of those labyrinthine routes that leaves the Yazoo River below Haines' Bluff, and after innumerable windings re-enters the same stream sixty miles above that point."

PORTER, with five ironclads and four mortar boats, and SHERMAN with his division, composed the expedition. This preparation indicates the high expectation. Steele's Bayou, running south, enters the Yazoo five miles from its mouth. The route was up the Yazoo to Steele's Bayou, up that to Black Bayou, east by that across to Deer Creek Bayou, up that to Rolling Fork Bayou, which diverges to a southeast direction and runs across to Big Sunflower Bayou, down the Big Sunflower to its confluence with the Yazoo, the route being about 150 miles.

As McPHERSON had failed to get transports for his corps for the Yazoo Pass expedition, GRANT now ordered him down to be ready to follow SHERMAN.

"The drift timber soon began to obstruct the channel, and the gunboats got entangled, but nevertheless forced their way through. The turns were so short that the Admiral was obliged to heave his vessels around the bends, not having a foot to spare. It took him twenty-four hours to advance four miles."

SHERMAN'S division was to land at necessary points to clear out the obstructions, and the gunboats got far ahead. PORTER had passed through Black Bayou with much difficulty, and had requested SHERMAN to clear it out, he working his way on in Deer Creek. During the 19th of March SHERMAN, at HILL'S plantation, on Black Bayou, heard frequent guns of the navy, and that night a negro brought him a message from PORTER, written on tissue paper, which the man had hid in a piece of tobacco, saying that PORTER had met infantry and artillery, which shot his men when they exposed themselves outside the armor to shove off the bows of the boats, on which he could not get steerage way. He besought SHERMAN to come to the rescue.

This is from SHERMAN'S graphic narrative. He had with him at HILL'S plantation GILES A. SMITH and 800 men. He ordered these to start up Deer Creek next morning. At the same time he went down Black Bayou in a canoe till he came luckily to the steamboat Silver Wave, just come up full of men. Taking some of the working parties into a coal barge, towed by a navy tug, he proceeded, followed by the Silver Wave. The night was dark, and they went "crushing through trees, carrying away pilot house, smokestacks, and everything above deck," but could only make two and a half of the four miles. We then disembarked and marched through the canebrake, carrying lighted candles in our hands, till we got into the open fields at Hill's plantation, where we lay down for a few hours' rest."

Sherman's narrative so well illustrates this "anomalous campaign" that it is continued verbatim:

On Sunday morning, March 21, as soon as daylight appeared, we started, following the same route which Giles A. Smith had taken the day before, the battalion of the 13th United States Regulars in the lead. We could hear Porter's guns, and knew that moments were precious. Being on foot myself, no man could complain, and we generally went at the double quick, with occasional rests. The road lay along Deer Creek, passing several plantations, and occasionally, at the bends, it crossed the swamps, where the water came above my hips. The smaller drummer boys had to carry their drums on their heads, and most of the men slung their cartridge boxes around their necks.

The soldiers generally were glad to have their general and field officers afoot, but we gave them a fair specimen of marching, accomplishing about twenty miles by noon. Of course our speed was accelerated by the sounds of the navy guns, which became more and more distinct, though we could see nothing. At a plantation near some Indian mounds we met a detachment of the 8th Missouri, that had been up to the fleet, and had been sent down as a picket to prevent any obstructions below. This picket reported that Admiral Porter had found Deer Creek badly obstructed, and turned back; that there was a rebel force beyond the fleet, with some six pounders, and nothing between us and the fleet.

So I sat down on the doorsill of a cabin to rest, but had not been seated ten minutes when in the woods just ahead, not 300 yards off, I heard quick and rapid firing of musketry. Jumping up I ran up the road, and found Lieut. Col. Rice, who said that the head of his column had struck a small force of rebels with a working gang of negroes, who on the first fire had broken and run back into the swamp. I ordered Rice to deploy his brigade, his left on the road, and extending as far into the swamp as the ground would permit, and then to sweep forward until he uncovered the gunboats. The movement was rapid and well executed, and we soon came to some large cotton fields, and could see our gunboats in Deer Creek, occasionally firing a heavy eight inch gun across the cotton field into the swamp beyond.

About that time a Major Reiley, of the 8th Missouri, galloped down the road on a horse he had picked up the night before, and met me. He explained the situation of affairs, and offered me his horse. I got on, bareback, and rode up the levee, the sailors coming out of their ironclads and cheering most vociferously as I rode by, and as our men swept forward across the cotton field in full view. I soon found Admiral Porter, who was on the deck of one of his ironclads, with a shield made of a section of smokestack, and I doubt if he was ever more glad to meet a friend than he was to see me. He explained that he had almost reached the Rolling Fork when the woods became full of sharpshooters, who, taking advantage of trees, stumps, and the levee, would shoot down every man that poked his nose outside the protection of their armor; so that he could not handle his clumsy boats in the narrow channel.

The rebels had evidently dispatched a force from Haines' Bluff up the Sunflower to the Rolling Fork; had anticipated the movement of Admiral Porter's fleet, and had completely obstructed the channel of the upper part of Deer Creek by felling trees into it, so that further progress in that direction was simply impossible. It also happened that at the instant of my arrival a party of about 400 rebels, armed and supplied with axes, had passed around the fleet and got below it, intending in like manner to block up the channel by the felling of trees, so as to cut off retreat. * * * I inquired of Admiral Porter what he proposed to do, and he said he wanted to get out of that scrape as quickly as possible. * * *

He informed me that at one time things looked so critical that he had made up his mind to blow up the gunboats and escape with his men through the swamp to the Mississippi River. * * * It took three days to back out of Deer Creek in Black Bayou, at Hill's plantation. * * * I reported the facts to Gen. Grant, who was sadly disappointed at the failure of the fleet to get through to the Yazoo above Haines' Bluff, and ordered us all to resume our camps at Young's Point.

The Confederates made poor use of their opportunity. The felling of half a dozen trees ahead was enough to detain Porter's squadron for their further operations. If instead of amusing themselves for twenty-four hours in popping with sharp-shooters behind trees and the levee at the heads of Porter's men whenever one was thrust out, they had first taken a score of negroes to the rear, and felled a dozen trees, they would have had that squadron trapped. And here the few families on the plantations were a shield to Gen. Sherman's troops; for, but for them, the reprehensible Confederates would have cut the levee, which would have let from six to eight feet of water upon them. But there was a blind goddess, called Fortune, watching over Grant in all these perilous undertakings.

Thus did the liberating expedition narrowly liberate itself. Meanwhile Ross and Quimby had gotten out of Yazoo Pass, and the army was restored to its former amphibious camps.

Yet there was a large slice of satisfaction

in this failure, for it illustrated what might have been had GRANT involved his whole army in the labyrinth of the Yazoo Pass route, or in the Lake Providence route, in which was as much as 200 miles of this narrow, tortuous, and easily trapped navigation. Thus did the narrow escapes of GRANT's army from his own various plans exemplify his proverbial luck.

CHAPTER XII.

THE PROCESS OF HARDENING THE SOLDIERS—THE SURVIVAL OF THE FITTEST—THE SWAMP ANGELS—THE PLAN TO GET AWAY FROM VICKSBURG.

This historical review follows chiefly BADEAU's Military Life of Gen. GRANT. This is not so much for the reason that it is accurate, truthful, or complete; nor that it does not withhold facts that enlighten, and suggest things that darken; but because it is sufficient for a view of the campaign; because it gives Gen. GRANT's inward thoughts and back-reaching afterthoughts; because BADEAU sees so fervently GRANT's great military genius, that he discerns in present failures the working of ultimate success; because even the line of argument which runs through his book involuntarily gives away information; finally, because the book is authentic, in that it was revised by Gen. GRANT, and is the same as his own. In our much quoting from BADEAU it may be received that when signs of quotation are used, the text is from BADEAU unless otherwise signified.

BADEAU says, with admirable candor, that all of GRANT's plans and expeditions had thus far been abortive in direct results, but he points out how these failures proved GRANT's variety of resources, and prepared for ultimate success; and he says:

These various attempts and expeditions on both sides of the Mississippi, although unsuccessful in their main objects, were yet productive of beneficial results. The national forces, so constantly employed, became hardened by exposure, and of course improved in spirits and health; they obtained also a thorough knowledge of the peculiar difficulties of the country in which they were operating, and were thus better able to encounter those difficulties.

The volunteers were from all sorts of occupations—mechanics, skilled artisans, professional men, students, clerks, railroad men, journalists, farmers' sons, and so on. Most of them, although accustomed to active lives, and standing pluckily the soldier's marching, bivouacking, fighting, and other work of the soldier, had not been trained in the heaviest labor. Comparatively few of the class which does the heavy unskilled labor enlisted. Consequently the most of the volunteers needed to be "hardened by the exposure" of working in the water in the swamps and bayous to pull out sunken trees by main strength, and of digging canals in the swampy ground, and other like serious labors, besides living in camp in swampy and sometimes submerged ground. Through this they became "of course improved in spirits," in the same manner as Mark Tapley was in jollity by the circumstances of the American Eden. And the "thorough knowledge which they obtained of the peculiar difficulties of the country in which they were operating," led their minds from its bottomless depths upward to revere the great military genius which had brought them to that region, and rejoiced them to get away.

Nature's great law of elevation by the survival of the fittest was working the preparation of that army for its future triumphs. The individual who goes down among the unfit is unable to see the benignity of this law, which all know to be wise in general. The volunteers who passed through that beneficial ordeal had gratifying testimony in the multitude of graves of their former comrades rising around them—now a great host of swamp angels—that they who still lived were of nature's elect. Said Gen. WM. E. STRONG, himself of that army—the Army of the Tennessee—in paying a tribute to its elect qualities, in his address at the dedication of the statue to Gen. McPHERSON at Clyde, July 22, 1881:

It was composed of men whose bodies were so inured to hardships that disease could make no impression upon them. Each man represented five others who had started with him; the five had succumbed to disease, or to the bullets of the enemy; four out of the five were under the sod that was to be made free soil by their exertions and the exertions of their comrades; the fifth was at home, discharged from the service by reason of disability, broken in health for life, or with a leg or an arm gone. The sixth man, to whom no swamp could give a fever, to whom wet clothes for a week could not give the rheumatism, to whom no march, however long, was a hardship—this culled and selected sixth man was there, robust, healthful, the ruddy glow of health coursing through every thousandth part of a square inch of his body, and visible through every pore of the skin, the patent seal and superscription of the Almighty that he was the genuine coin of the realm.

This was nature's supreme law of the survival of the fittest, in its most summary working.

But BADEAU is an historian of varied resources. When he comes to sum up the results of the campaign, and to compare it with BONAPARTE's about Ulm, much to BONAPARTE's inferiority, he states among other advantages which BONAPARTE had over GRANT: "Instead of moving fresh from a camp like that of Boulogne, the Army of the Tennessee had spent months amid the swamps and fevers of the Mississippi."

But the multitude is always devoid of reason. The populace is incapable of understanding any military operations save by results. The popular mind must be fed by battles; it can not appreciate the swamp method of sifting and hardening an army. Consequently there was great discontent in the people, which found so much expression as to awaken the administration. BADEAU says:

The country, meanwhile, and the government had become very impatient. Clamors were raised everywhere against Grant's slowness; the old rumors about his personal character were revived [for character read habits]; his soldiers were said to be dying of swamp fevers and dysentery in the morasses around Vicksburg; he was pronounced utterly destitute of genius or energy; his repeatedly baffled schemes declared to emanate from a brain unfitted for such trials; his persistency was dogged obstinacy, his patience sluggish dullness.

The people's feeling was the most stirred by the accounts of the consuming of the volunteers by the diseases incident to their swamp camps and labors. Although volunteers have higher spirit than regulars, and go to their death with more alacrity, yet they have faults, the chief of which is that they are intelligent, and can not be reduced to the quality of the unthinking machine, which, in our regular army, is the first requisite for a soldier. And each one has a lot of kinsfolk at home, who look upon his life as precious. Possessed of the invention of reading and writing, which has brought so much evil into the world, he writes home his experiences, and these circulate from tongue to tongue. In this way the sickness, death, and hardships of GRANT's troops, and his abortive plans, were spread among the people.

The newspaper war correspondents, although frowned upon in that campaign, could not be wholly extinguished, and they helped the evil news to spread. Thus does a republican government seem incompatible with regular army operations; because that which is called the spread of intelligence exposes a General to a fire in the rear. While his preparatory operation is putting the ordeal which sifts out the sixth man, the five who go down make a noise in the rear. BADEAU says that "some of GRANT's best friends failed him at the critical moment." He gives in a foot note this sad fall of a prominent Illinois politician whose political influence had been GRANT's main lift and stay:

A Congressman, who had been one of Grant's warmest friends, was found wanting at this juncture. He went to the President without being sent for, and declared that the emergencies of the country seemed to demand another commander before Vicksburg. To him Mr. Lincoln replied: "I rather like the man; I think we'll try him a little longer."

BADEAU shows that but for this happy-go-lucky temper of LINCOLN, McCLERNAND would have been put in command. But in spite of LINCOLN's *laissez faire* manner, the feeling of the people did disturb him. HALLECK also—than whom no regular army man in high rank could be content with less military progress—became sensible that some move must be made to quiet the public by seeming to do.

HALLECK wrote GRANT April 2d, remarking unfavorably on his "division of his forces into several eccentric operations," as frittering away his strength, besides being dangerous in the presence of an enemy. He continued:

What is most desired (and your attention is again called to this object) is that your forces and those of Gen. Banks shall be brought into co-operation as early as possible. If he can not get up to co-operate with you in Vicksburg, can not you get troops down to help him at Port Hudson? * * * As the President, who seems to be rather impatient about matters on the Mississippi, has several times asked me these questions, I repeat them to you.

HALLECK had written BANKS February 2: "Gen. GRANT's forces have for some time been operating in the vicinity of Vicksburg, and the President expects that you will permit no obstacle to prevent you from co-operating with him by some movement up the Mississippi River." The intention was that BANKS should take Port Hudson. But BANKS had been obliged to take the offensive, both east and west of the river, to prevent his being shut in by the active Gen. DICK TAYLOR, who had a wide range for recruiting west of the river and in Texas, to say nothing of Georgia, and although succeeding in his operations, he had not been able to spare a force for Port Hudson.

But such was now the stress of GRANT'S situation and of the administration; under the pressure of public opinion, that HALLECK and LINCOLN were anxious to have GRANT make a movement that should appear to be going forward, even to abandon Vicksburg to the hereafter, and go where no man could tell what was the object, or how the army was to be supplied, or how it was going to meet the danger of such a wide division in the face of the enemy. But to this plan to quiet the nation did HALLECK now consent, and GRANT addressed himself to it by inventing a new canal and bayou route to get away from Vicksburg. The rules of war justify stratagem to deceive the enemy, and they apply all the same when the military necessity is to satisfy your own people. That this route for boats was an impossibility from the beginning, was not a material point, so long as it served the present need of a diversion to the President and the nation.

During this time Mr. CHARLES A. DANA, then holding the "anomalous" position of Assistant Secretary of War, was sent by Secretary STANTON to view the situation, and report confidentially. A view taken at Gen. GRANT'S luxurious headquarters on one of the largest river steamers, brightened by the generous hospitalities of the staff, and of GRANT'S brilliant circle of Generals, who received him as a long lost brother, proved to his military eye that GRANT was the right man and in the right place. And as McCLERNAND was not of the circle, the Confidential Secretary of War became imbued with the belief that to have a "political General" in so important a command, ranking even next to GRANT, was "anomalous." The result of this conviction will appear further along.

CHAPTER XIII.

THE PORT HUDSON PLAN—A NEW CANAL—GRANT'S GENERALS ALL PROTEST—PRODDED BY THE FIRE IN THE REAR, HE PERSISTS—GRANT RESCUED BY HIS PROVERBIAL LUCK.

Gen. GRANT'S Port Hudson or Duckport Canal plan comes under the third general class—viz., plans to get away from Vicksburg. It was to cut a canal from the river at Duckport, just above Young's Point, three or four miles to a small bayou that came down from Milliken's Bend, called Walnut bayou; this bayou, eight or ten miles further down to the southeast, looped back in the most eccentric course to the northwest to Roundabout Bayou —very roundabout—on which is Richmond, about thirty miles west of Vicksburg. Bending to the southeast, this bayou runs into Bayou Vidal, which makes a turn to the west. By a turn to the northwest the Mississippi is right south of this part of Bayou Vidal, and on it is New Carthage, to which runs directly south a branch of Bayou Vidal, about four miles. Bayou Vidal fetches a circuit to the west and east and comes to the river at Mrs. PERKINS', which, in an air line from Duckport, is twenty miles, but by these bayous is sixty or more; to New Carthage from Duckport is about fifty miles. GRANT wrote HALLECK that these bayous were "navigable for large and small steamers, passing around by Richmond to New Carthage. There is also a good wagon road passing around by Richmond to New Carthage" (from Young's Point). "There is also a good wagon road from Milliken's Bend to New Carthage."

These roads followed these bayous, for the reason that along their banks the ground was the highest, and was a little above water during the Mississippi floods, if the river levees held. The term "good" applied to them was a bright anticipation. GRANT thus told HALLECK his plan:

The dredges are now engaged in cutting a canal from here into these bayous. I am having all the empty coal boats and other barges prepared for carrying troops and artillery, and have written to Col. Allen for some more, and also for six tugs to tow them. With them it would be easy to carry supplies to New Carthage and any points south of that.

BADEAU says the object and reason of this route were that GRANT now "proposed to send an army corps to co-operate with BANKS,

With this increased force Port Hudson could certainly be taken, and then BANKS' entire army might be combined with GRANT's, and moving up from below, a co-operative attack be made on Vicksburg."

GRANT's plan was to reach the Mississippi by this bayou route, at New Carthage; from there to take Grand Gulf, twenty-two miles below (by the river) by assault; to send from there an army corps of 20,000 to BANKS to operate against Port Hudson, four hundred miles below, holding the rest of the army at Grand Gulf, drawing its supplies by this bayou route from Milliken's Bend until Port Hudson had been taken, after which the army was to be supplied from New Orleans. And then "BANKS' entire army might be combined with GRANT's, and moving up from below, a co-operative attack be made on Vicksburg."

This was not that GRANT had not more men than he could use; and not that BANKS had any to spare, or could come up and join him on Vicksburg; for BANKS could not do this without losing Louisiana. The great objective was to get out of the Vicksburg predicament without revealing to the country the failure. The bayou route for this operation could be as easily obstructed as the Yazoo Pass and Steele's Bayou routes had been. And the road, such as it was, crooked around fifty or sixty miles in a hostile country, where the difficulty of guarding it would make mere play of the guarding a line of supplies by the Mississippi Central Railroad, which GRANT had given up as impossible. The whole plan depended on getting transports through his canal, and as it happened, none ever got through.

BADEAU says:

In order to accomplish this movement it was necessary for Grant to throw his whole force simultaneously south of Vicksburg, as a single corps would be exposed to the risk of attack from the garrison, as well as from the rebel army in the interior.

Therefore the forces were concentrated at Milliken's Bend. "HURLBUT (at Memphis) was stripped of every man that could be spared from the rear. Yawls and flatboats were collected from St. Louis and Chicago."

Had this plan been carried forward the military situation would have been complete, as follows: 20,000 of GRANT's army sent 400 miles below to Port Hudson, on the chances of a siege of that place; the rest of the movable army isolated at Grand Gulf, awaiting the result and return from Port Hudson, and hemmed in by the enemy from Vicksburg and the interior, its supplies depending on this circuitous route of fifty to eighty miles in a country affording every facility for hostile incursions and obstructions; Milliken's Bend held by a small force exposed to attacks from Vicksburg and the West; the river above Vicksburg exposed to the lodgments of Confederate forces from the interior, now wholly given up to them. And even before this, GRANT's transports had to be convoyed from Memphis.

When GRANT disclosed this remarkable plan to his general officers, it caused, as BADEAU represents, a sort of emeute:

When the idea became known to those in his intimacy, to his staff, and to his corps commanders, it seemed to them full of danger. To move his army below Vicksburg was to separate it from the North, and from all its supplies; to throw what seemed an insurmountable obstacle between himself and his own base; to cut his communications, and place his army exactly where it is the whole object and aim of war to get the enemy.

Says BADEAU: "SHERMAN, McPHERSON, LOGAN, WILSON, all opposed—all, of course, within the limits of soldierly subordination—but with all energy," and "strove to divert their chief from what they considered this fatal error:"

Even after the orders for the movement had been issued, Sherman rode up to Grant's headquarters, and proposed his plan. He asserted, emphatically, that the only way to take Vicksburg was from the north, selecting some high ground on the Mississippi for a base. Grant replied that such a plan would require him to go back to Memphis. "Exactly so," said Sherman; "that is what I mean.".

The earnest SHERMAN went back to his headquarters, and April 8 wrote a letter to RAWLINS, GRANT's Chief of Staff, setting forth his plan. In short, it was to take the main army back to Memphis, or other practicable high ground, and to the line down the Mississippi Central, which he and GRANT had abandoned on the 8th of December. Gen. SHERMAN was not a man who learned nothing and forgot nothing; he had learned more in that swamp in three months than had not been taught him in four years at West Point.

BADEAU says that GRANT read SHERMAN's letter in silence, and made no comment; and he adds as an example of GRANT's magnanimity to SHERMAN, "The letter has never since been mentioned between the two commanders." But GRANT persisted in the Port Hudson plan because "he believed that a retrograde movement, even if temporary, would be disastrous to the country, which was in no temper to endure another reverse; he was determined to take no step backward, and so declared." He means that the country "was in no temper to endure" another retrograde by GRANT, and that it would be disastrous to him. The continuance of Gen. GRANT's career of usefulness to his country depended on his seeming to go forward, whatever the fate of his army. Thus did the fire in the rear keep him from going back to the line which SHERMAN advised, and thus did it force him into a plan so strange that it alarmed all his Generals.

There was some excuse for these Generals for their lack of confidence in a plan which, BADEAU says, went counter to all "established principles of military science." GRANT had not till that time developed his great military genius. His affair at Belmont was called a blundering slaughter without any military object. His urgency for the Fort Henry march, suggested by Gen. C. F. SMITH, who had reconnoitered the place, was very creditable to his enterprise, but the navy took the fort, while GRANT's delay to invest it with his 18,000 men allowed the enemy's 2,000 infantry to retreat to Fort Donelson. GRANT waited at Fort Henry a week before moving to Fort Donelson, twelve miles. At Fort Donelson he waited for the navy to batter down the fort, and, that failing, he reported to HALLECK his purpose to intrench, anticipating "a protracted siege," for he said, "I fear the result of an attempt to carry the place by storm with new troops." He was next day unaccountably absent for six hours while a furious battle raged. And then the fort was taken by Gen. C. F. SMITH, leading in person a storming column of those "new troops," for which not SMITH but GRANT was promoted. At the surrender of Fort Donelson, GRANT had over 30,000 men, and the Confederate power was broken before him. He left his command without notice to HALLECK, and went off on a convivial time up the Cumberland for a week, on a government chartered steamer, during which HALLECK could get nothing from him. HALLECK reported him to Washington, and was authorized to arrest him. His explanation was that GRANT had returned to his "old habits." He induced HALLECK to plead for him, but HALLECK suspended him from command. While thus in disgrace GRANT was promoted to be Major General. HALLECK restored him to command just as SMITH had ordered SHERMAN to take position at Pittsburg Landing. GRANT lost his army at Pittsburg Landing. HALLECK had kept him suspended during the Corinth campaign. He had failed in his part of the concerted movements with ROSECRANS on Iuka. The only victory during his command in that department, as BADEAU says, was this of Iuka, and that of Corinth, which was won by ROSECRANS. He had failed in the Holly Springs campaign, and had now occupied a great army and navy for three months in abortive schemes in the swamps and bayous. He had been kept up thus far by the support of some very influential politicians. This was the property which distinguished GRANT and SHERMAN from those they called "political Generals," as well as from the regular officers of the army. Therefore, it could not be expected that these subordinate Generals would receive a plan which set at naught all military science—as BADEAU proudly claims—with that complete submission of military judgment which his commands carried after his military genius had developed.

There would be little encouragement to military heroes to write their own histories if they may not take some privileges therein. BADEAU ingeniously laps the energetic remonstrances of GRANT's Generals against his Port Hudson scheme, over to the operations in the rear of Vicksburg, into which he drifted after he had landed at Bruinsburg. In this way he carries forward their protests against a plan which GRANT abandoned, and lodges them upon his subsequent successful operation, which was quite the reverse of the other. Thus does he put all of GRANT's lieutenants in the category of remonstrants against his success.

This, however, is only a moderate use of the privilege of the historian of his own exploits. No one knew better than BONAPARTE the advantage of writing his own war bulletins. He taught his Marshals that his part was to take all the glory of victories; theirs to be content to shine by reflecting his beams. For all these Generals to be silent, while placed in their comander's history as protesting against his successful plan, when they had only protested against one so eccentric that he abandoned it, was only due subordination. Gen. SHERMAN, whose temper has been greatly misunderstood as impulsive and fiery, whereas he is a very MOSES for meekness, quietly assents to this representation of his letter. He even corroborates it by a plea that all he wrote it for was to get GRANT to call for the opinions of the rest of his corps commanders, and thereby expose McCLERNAND, of whom SHERMAN says he does not believe that he had any plan at all. He further corroborates by an unqualified indorsement of BADEAU's history of the Vicksburg campaign, in all of which, as in the rest of BADEAU's work, SHERMAN is patronized as a good subordinate to GRANT, but as needing GRANT's directing mind.

CHAPTER XIV.

A PRIZE OFFERED FOR A VICTORY—EXCUSES FOR THE NATION'S IMPATIENCE—GLANCE AT OTHER COMMANDERS—THE FEARFUL EXPENSES—HISTORY REPEATS ITSELF.

During the period of Gen. GRANT's Greco-Roman wrestling with the Mississippi swamps and bayous, Gen. HALLECK devised the original scheme of breaking the spell of ill fortune, which seemed to have settled upon our military operations everywhere, by proclaiming an offer of the vacant Major Generalship in the regular army to the General in the field who first won a victory.

There could hardly be a more delicate recognition of the motives which govern the regular army man, and of the distinction which Gen. SHERMAN, in his Memoirs, has beautifully defined between the professional General as one who "looked to personal fame and glory" alone, while the volunteers — the political Generals — look to these as "auxiliary and secondary to their political ambition." Of the commanders in the field, only Gen. ROSECRANS made response to this holding up of a Major Generalship as a bone to a lot of dogs to jump for. But ROSECRANS' long civil life had spoiled his regular army manners, and he was prone to speak out in a way that —speaking idiomatically—cooked his goose. He sent the following:

MURFREESBORO, March 6, 1863.
GENERAL: Yours of the 1st instant, announcing the offer of a vacant Major Generalship in the regular army to the General in the field who first wins an important and decisive victory, is received. As an officer and a citizen, I feel degraded at such auctioneering of honors. Have we a General who would fight for his own personal benefit when he would not for honor and his country? He would come by his commission basely in that case, and deserve to be despised by men of honor. But are all the brave and honorable Generals on an equality as to chances? If not, it is unjust to those who probably deserve most.
W. S. ROSECRANS, Major General.
Major General H. W. Halleck, Commander in Chief, Washington, D. C.

Of course the vacant Major Generalcy was not for ROSECRANS, and his getting out of command was only a question of time and opportunity.

Although Gen. GRANT's historian describes the impatience of the people and the government as so imminent that GRANT was compelled to set forth the Port Hudson plan, to get away from Vicksburg, in order to prevent his removal from command, and relates that "Senators and Governors went to Vicksburg and then to Washington to ask for his removal," and that "McCLERNAND and HUNTER and FREMONT and McCLELLAN were spoken of as his successors," and that "McCLERNAND's machinations at this time came very near succeeding," yet he generously makes excuse for this impatience. He says:

Indeed, it is not surprising that the government should have urged him on. No substantial victory had cheered the flagging spirits of the North since Grant's own successes at Corinth and Iuka, of the preceding autumn. Banks had achieved no military results with his mammoth expedition; Burnside, in December, had suffered the repulse of Fredericksburg; Rosecrans had not got further than Murfreesboro, and the great force of 60,000 or 70,000 men at Grant's disposal had accomplished absolutely nothing during six long, weary months of effort and delay.

Thus, in apologizing for the popular impatience, does he ingeniously set forth that no other commander had done any better.

To say that it had accomplished absolutely nothing during six months, does not give it justice. The peculiar property of this line of operation was that it placed that great army, and all its attachments, where it was as completely sequestered from all influence on other military operations; from co-operation with any; from holding or defending any part of the Confederacy or the North, as if it had been sunk to the bottom of that morass. The operations of the Army of the Potomac, those of ROSECRANS in Middle Tennessee: the expedition to East Tennessee; the campaign of BANKS against an enterprising commander in West Louisiana, and all other operations from the Potomac to the Indian Territory, and round the coast, had not the smallest material moral or strategical aid from this great army which was digging its graves in the swamps west of the Mississippi.

BANKS' "mammoth expedition" of about 30,000 men had to hold a large region against an active enemy, and the details of garrisons reduced his movable force to less than 14,000, and with this he had to take the field in an active campaign to defend Louisiana. ROSECRANS, with 43,400 men, had fought a very bloody pitched battle with BRAGG's army of about equal numbers, and was the victor. "The great force of 60,000 or 70,000 men at GRANT's disposal" was stated by BADEAU as 130,000 a short time previous. This, with the gunboat fleet, and the steamboat fleet of transports, kept constantly in attendance, made this by far the most "mammoth expedition" of the time.

And the place to which GRANT had brought this great expedition, in order to meet, as BADEAU says, and destroy PEMBERTON's army, was so strong that when GRANT wrote HALLECK, March 27, that he had learned that there were "not to exceed 10,000 in the city (Vicksburg) to-day," he added: "The batteries are the same, however, and would cause the same difficulty in landing that would be experienced by a heavy force." Thus he granted that 10,000 men, with the defenses of the place, could keep at bay his great land and naval forces. Some hints may be found, even in BADEAU's history, of the degree to which other armies were crippled to feed this swamp maelstrom.

For example, ROSECRANS had to enter on a winter campaign in the great interior, with nothing on the west to prevent concentration against him, with but 43,400 fighting men. Several of HALLECK's letters to GRANT give urgent orders not to detain the steamboats, "on account of the great entanglement it causes the Quartermaster's Department in supplying our Western armies." In particular the need to have them to transport supplies to ROSECRANS was urged. One of GRANT's answers to this urgency, dated March 29, explains that before he came he ordered McCLERNAND to send back the steamboats, but "on my arrival here I found the river rising so rapidly that there was no telling at what moment all hands might be driven to the boats." Thus was the great fleet of chartered steamboats kept for arks to rescue the army if the levees should break.

As an instance of McCLERNAND's insubordination, BADEAU gives two extracts from letters of McCLERNAND, at Vicksburg, to GRANT, at Memphis, adding: "These letters, it will be remembered, are addressed by a subordinate to his commanding officer." The first is the following, and the other is of the same urgent tenor:

Great prudence needs to be exercised in detaching transports from this fleet to return to Memphis, as the Mississippi is rising rapidly, and may deluge our troops at any time. You will at once perceive the great importance of this caution, as it involves the very existence of the army here.

The isolation of GRANT's great forces from any influence on the war is in part illustrated by his letter to HALLECK April 4, which has this:

From information from the South, by way of Corinth, I learn that the enemy in front of Rosecrans have been re-enforced from Richmond, Charleston, Savannah, Mobile, and a few from Vicksburg. They have also collected a large cavalry force of 20,000 men. All the bridges eastward from Savanna (Tenn.) and north from Florence are being rapidly repaired. Chalmers is put in command of North Mississippi, and is collecting all the partisan rangers and loose independent companies of cavalry that have been operating in this department. He is now occupying the line of the Tallahatchie. This portends preparations to attack Rosecrans, and to be able to follow up any success with rapidity. Also, to make a simultaneous raid into West Tennessee, both from North Mississippi and by crossing the Tennessee River.

The naming of Savanna and Florence as Confederate lines of operations recalls the beginning of the Halleck-Grant campaign up the Tennessee a year previous. These, together with the withdrawal from Northern Mississippi and Alabama, in order to open the Mississippi River, give some measure of our progress in recovering territory, which we had made our objective. Meanwhile the rapid rise of the premium on gold, which reached 72 while GRANT was exploring the Mississippi bayous, marked the fall of the faith of the money market in the progress of restoring the nation, and showed at what a discount the government was selling its bonds to pay these double expenses of a great army and navy aimlessly tied up in a morass.

The observation is profoundly made that history repeats itself. BADEAU makes it in likening GRANT's Vicksburg campaign to the first Italian campaign of BONAPARTE; the crossing of the Mississippi River under the protection of the navy in this being an historical repetition of BONAPARTE's crossing the Apennines, and the movements and victories which followed being an equally striking parallel. HALLECK thought it bore a striking parallel to BONAPARTE's campaign about Ulm. BADEAU accepts this, so far as it goes, but thinks the addition of the other requisite to fulness.

They who enjoy the projecting of these repeating histories may find in GRANT's Vicksburg campaign in 1862-3 a remarkable repeating of the history of Gen. McCLELLAN's Peninsular campaign in 1861-2. Each commander found that a navigable line for supplies, the navy to guard it, and a fleet of transports to carry the troops, were essential to his operations. Each withdrew his army from an interior line, leading into the heart of the Confederacy, and took it by water to an exterior line, which opened the interior and the North to the enemy, and wholly neutralized the army as to any influence on other operations. Each took his army into a morass, and set it at enormous labors which came to nothing.

Each retreated from practicable lines of operations in a healthy up-country and took it to the most unhealthy region and impracticable line attainable, which consumed more by sickness than by battles. Each chose a line which would give to the Confederates their best fortified place, and the secure possession of their territorial resources and lines of supply. Each claimed that his was the vital operation, and that interior armies should be drawn from to strengthen him. After consuming immense resources for months, each retreated from a hopeless operation, by a "change of base," to a new plan, whose success was as improbable. In each the volunteers, after all these discouragements, fought like veterans and heroes, as soon as they got a chance, enduring extraordinary hardship and privation, and marching by night and fighting by day, without murmuring, and eager to be led like soldiers to fight the enemy.

But here the historic parallel diverges, and one part turns toward success.

CHAPTER XV.

THE PORT HUDSON PLAN—THE PROGRESS IN "THROWING THE WHOLE ARMY AT ONCE" INTO GRAND GULF—THE NAVIGABLE ROUTE DROPS OUT—THE ARMY STUCK IN THE MUD—A NEW PLAN.

Orders were issued "in the last week in March" for concentrating all the forces at Milliken's Bend, for the Port Hudson plan. "HURLBUT" (at Memphis) "was stripped of every man that could be spared from the rear; yawls and flatboats were collected from St. Louis and Chicago, and on the 29th of March, McCLERNAND was sent by the circuitous roads that lead from Milliken's Bend, by way of Richmond and west of Roundaway Bayou, to New Carthage, twenty-seven miles below. McPHERSON and SHERMAN were to follow as rapidly as ammunition and rations could be forwarded."

The way, by crossing directly from Milliken's Bend to Bayou Vidal, was not more than half so long as the water route, which was to go by way of the Duckport Canal through the looping Walnut Bayou to Bayou Vidal. The canal had not yet been opened. The supplies for the army were to follow by the canal and bayou navigable route as soon as the canal was opened, and for this GRANT was collecting tugs and all sorts of shallow craft from all the North. The troops moved without tents or baggage, and with only wagons enough to carry, with what they carried on their backs, ten days' rations. The rest of the transportation teams of each corps was left behind to follow in mass after the whole army had passed. The artillery of each division accompanied it, but the usual supply of ammunition was cut down one-half.

The road was soft before, from overflow, and the passage of the troops made it a slough. In the greater part the soldiers had to build it up with logs. "New Carthage, however, was occupied on the 6th of April." "Occupied" is a strategic term; the advance had reached there with McClernand, but the corps was still struggling with the slough and the road building along Bayou Vidal. This bayou, after a southeast course, turns shortly to the west, corresponding to a bend in the river which here is south of the bayou. Just west of this turn in the bayou, and on its north side, is Smith's plantation, and at this point a branch running directly south connects Bayou Vidal with the river at New Carthage, the main bayou continuing in a circuit to the west.

The levee of this branch, between Smith's and New Carthage, was broken in several places, and the torrents pouring in made cross currents difficult for boats or floating bridges. "Boats were accordingly collected from all the bayous in the vicinity, and others were constructed of such material as was at hand. One division with its artillery was thus conveyed across Bayou Vidal and through the overflowed forest to the levee at New Carthage; but the ferriage of an entire army in this way would have been exceedingly tedious, and a new route was found from Smith's plantation * * * to Perkins', twelve miles below." This route kept along the north and west side of the main Bayou Vidal, which fetches a half circle and comes to the river at Mrs. Perkins' plantation, about eight miles below New Carthage, by the river, and sixteen by this road.

But Bayou Vidal, in the west part of its bend, was broken by cross bayous, all overflowed. "Four bridges, two of them 600 feet long, had to be laid across the swollen bayous which interrupted this route." McClernand says 2,000 feet of bridges had to be made. Says Badeau: "These were built of the barges and flats previously used at Smith's plantation, and of forest timber." Of course this protracted labor exhausted the ten days' rations, and the few teams which accompanied the divisions were kept going back and forth, and others were added, to try to keep McClernand supplied.

While McClernand's corps was struggling along all this way from Milliken's Bend to Smith's, building up a log way and bridges for his own wagons and artillery, and for the army which was to follow when he had made a road, he received valuable co-operation from Gen. Grant. Says Badeau: "Grant's orders had been explicit and urgent to McClernand to seize and occupy Grand Gulf. In order to appease the insatiable ambition and conceit of that subordinate, he had given him command of the advance, and charged him with an operation which, if successful, would have rendered McClernand famous at once. On the 12th of April he wrote to that officer: 'It is my desire that you should get possession of Grand Gulf at the earliest opportunity.'"

But "the insatiable ambition and conceit of his subordinate" had been appeased by sending his corps in the advance to build a road for itself and the rest of the army over the strangest and most impassable route ever chosen for the march or supply of an army. At that time not one of his divisions had reached the river, and it appears, by a scrap of the same dispatch of the 12th, that Grant was then concerned to know how McClernand was to get his troops from Smith's plantation to New Carthage. And as McClernand had then no means of crossing the river, if he had been there, the expectation must have been that his troops would swim for it, carrying their guns in their teeth.

Grand Gulf was a little Vicksburg in situation and defenses, and as little likely to be taken by direct attack. It had been fortified a year before, and was now armed and prepared. The opportunity which Grant gave to McClernand to make himself famous at once was of the same character as that which King David instructed Gen. Joab to give to Col. Uriah. But for many days after the 12th McClernand's troops were to be occupied in building roads and bridges for themselves and the rest of the army—a very useful, not to say vital, work to the expedition, but one not calculated to achieve fame.

On the 13th Grant sent to McClernand this necessary caution against going on from Grand Gulf:

> It is not desirable that you should move in any direction from Grand Gulf, but remain under the protection of the gunboats. The present plan, if not changed by the movement of the enemy, will be to hold Grand Gulf.

Meanwhile the difficulty of supplying the army by that single route, which it was base flattery to call a road, had become serious, even while the greater part of the army had not started. The operation did not realize the bright anticipation "to throw his whole force simultaneously south of Vicksburg."

At this time GRANT, at Milliken's Bend, was in labor with a grave dilemma, which he set forth to HALLECK in a letter dated April 12, fourteen days after McCLERNAND had started. The Duckport Canal, which was to let the transports into the bayous for the supply of this great movement, was not opened when McCLERNAND started. Flatboats and tugs were gathering for using it. But now a question presented itself. The road by which the army was plodding was only twenty inches above the water in the swamps. The river was near five feet higher than the land. To cut the levee and let the river into the canal might drown McCLERNAND's corps, and cut off all communication by the road. On the other hand, not to open the canal was to take away the main means which the plan had depended upon for supplying the army. Says GRANT to HALLECK:

There is nothing now in the way of my throwing troops into Grand Gulf, and then sending them on to Port Hudson to co-operate with Gen. Banks in the reduction of that place, but the danger of overflowing the road from here to New Carthage, when the water is let into the new canal, connecting the river there with the bayou coming out at New Carthage. One division of troops is now at New Carthage, and another on the way. * * * The wagon road (this road must now be nearly completed), by filling the lowest ground, will be about twenty inches above the water in the swamps. The river, where it is to be let into the canal, is four and eight-tenths feet above the land.

This gives the situation of the road building at that time, and of the progress of the movement, which BADEAU strategically makes dim. But the canal question was peculiar. "Nothing now in the way of throwing troops into Grand Gulf," excepting that if the river were let into the canal it might sweep away McCLERNAND's corps, and "throw" it into the bayous and cypress swamps. That of itself might not be objectionable, for McCLERNAND is the *bete noire* in the history of all the Vicksburg operations, but it might also make the road impassable without opening any water route. Well might GRANT say in this letter: "The embarrassment I have had to contend against on account of extreme high water can not be appreciated by any one not present to witness it."

But here again did GRANT's proverbial luck turn up to rescue him from the fatality of his plan. The embarrassing question was settled by the river's subsiding and leaving the Duckport Canal above water. BADEAU says one steamer got through, but says not what became of her; but "afterward the depth of water was insufficient to allow transports (this means barges and flatboats) of even the smallest draught to make their way, and all supplies of ordnance stores and provisions had to be hauled over the miserable muddy roads."

BADEAU leaves judiciously dim the time when the opening of the levee was made to let the river into the canal, but it appears by the result that it was when the river was falling fast, so that one steamer only caught it on the run. But Gen. GRANT, in a dispatch from Milliken's Bend to HALLECK, April 19, twenty-one days after McCLERNAND had started, states that the promise of the canal and bayou route was then all that his fancy had painted, thus:

By clearing out the bayous from timber there will be good navigation from here to New Carthage for tugs and barges, also small sternwheel steamers. The navigation can be kept good, I think, by using our dredges constantly, until there is twenty feet fall. On this subject, however, I have not taken the opinion of an engineer officer, nor have I formed it upon sufficient investigation to warrant me in speaking positively.

GRANT was his own engineer in all the bayou, canal, and road undertakings. BADEAU says he attended to all details, even to the duties of wagonmaster of the several corps. But at this time the need to encourage the administration and the country with news of the success of this remarkable undertaking caused an optimism in the dispatches, which was laudable for that purpose, but which somewhat impairs historical accuracy.

Thus had the water route, which was the main dependence for the supply of the army in the Port Hudson operation, vanished. The bottom had dropped out of the plan. McCLERNAND had one division at New Carthage, twenty-five miles above Grand Gulf by the river; another division bridging and building its way to Mrs. PERKINS' plantation on the river, sixteen miles below New Carthage by the Bayou Vidal route, and the others still floundering in the slough and rebuilding the road between SMITH's plantation and Milliken's Bend, from which the rest of the army had not yet started. To move the army and its supplies by that road was impracticable. To supply even McClernand's corps by it would be difficult; to do this while the rest of the army was moving on it, still more difficult. The Port Hudson expedition was at a deadlock, and some new means of supplying the army must be found, or it must withdraw its advance. The means invented to relieve the expedition from this dilemma, "demonstrate"—as Badeau remarked of the Lake Providence plan—"the fertility and variety of devices developed during this anomalous campaign."

CHAPTER XVI.

GEN. GRANT'S SPLENDID GENERALS—THEIR ZEALOUS WORKS WITHOUT FAITH—THE HEROIC SPIRIT OF THE VOLUNTEERS—RUNNING THE VICKSBURG GUNS—THE RESULTS.

Much praise is given by Gen. Grant's historian to his Generals for their zealous co-operation in his Port Hudson plan, when they found that "Grant was firmly determined to make the movement, and the disapproval of his ablest Generals had no effect to deter him." He continues:

Sherman, thinking the plan almost certain of defeat, for that reason felt the greater need of making the greater effort to insure its success. He did not fail, nor did any of those officers whose faith in the enterprise was least, to do their utmost to falsify their own opinions.

Indeed, had Grant's subordinates been less thoroughly subordinate, had they done less than their best to attain a result which they believed almost, if not quite, unattainable, no determination, nor daring, nor energy in their commander could have availed. But not a word of dissatisfaction or criticism escaped from these true soldiers after it once became evident that Grant was immovable.

This is a beautiful tribute. But, although Badeau takes the remonstrances which Sherman and others made against the plan of dividing the army, and sending part to Port Hudson on a campaign of indefinite length, holding the rest at Grand Gulf, trusting all to the supplies by this precarious route, and by a stroke of the pen extends them to Grant's operations in the rear of Vicksburg, which Grant took up after he had abandoned the Port Hudson plan, yet he is conscious of a chasm between these two, which he bridges in this admirable manner:

At this time, however, he had not himself determined to do all that he afterward attempted. His plans, indeed, were always ripened into their full fruition by the emergencies and opportunities of a battle or campaign; his judgment was always sharpened by events; his faculties were always brighter at a crisis; his decisions were most unerring when compelled to be most sudden and irrevocable.

Thus the march out to Jackson, to take Vicksburg, was the full fruition of the plan to abandon Vicksburg and go to Port Hudson. But although his brightened faculties abandoned his plan, and took another which was contrary, the objections of his Generals to the Port Hudson plan are extended by his veracious mouthpiece to the Jackson and Vicksburg plan, to show that he did it against all of them.

After thus bridging the chasm for Grant, and destroying the bridge for his Generals, Badeau thus repeats his present plan: "His design now was to move his army to some point below Vicksburg, where he might be able to supply himself by the roads and bayous in Louisiana, and thence send a corps to co-operate with Banks in the reduction of Port Hudson." (Banks was then in West Louisiana in an active campaign). "After that place should have fallen, Banks, with his whole army, and the corps from Grant, was to march up and unite in the campaign against Vicksburg." (Banks could not march up with his whole army, nor half of it, without losing Louisiana). * * * "In order to accomplish this movement it was necessary for Grant to throw his whole force simultaneously south, as a single corps would be exposed to the risk of attack from the garrison, as well as from the rebel army in the interior."

In this throwing of his whole army simultaneously he had got one corps strung out along this tortuous and miry defile of a road between Milliken's Bend and Perkins', forty miles, and the base of his plan—the navigable line of supplies—had dropped out, and the rest of the army was at Milliken's Bend, unable to move, because the question of supplying even the advanced corps had yet to be solved. And now it had become imperatively necessary to invent some new means to supply the expedition, or it would have to back out, and another cry of failure would go up in the rear. Under this pressure the desperate resort of sending the frail river steamboats laden with supplies past the Vicksburg batteries was resolved upon.

The result of previous experiments had not been encouraging. Some of the mailed vessels had gone by, but no ordinary river steamer. And the Vicksburg batteries had improved their gunnery. At the request of Admiral FARRAGUT, who wanted some vessels of light draught to operate against the enemy's ironclads in Red River, two of Col. ELLETT's rams ran past Vicksburg April 25; one was knocked to pieces, the other much damaged. This appears to be the last experiment made before the one now to be tried, on which depended the fate of the expedition. For now it was not only a question of supplies, but boats must be sent down to ferry McCLERNAND's corps over the Mississippi to attack Grand Gulf.

Three steamboats and ten barges laden with supplies, escorted by one wooden and six ironclad gunboats, composed the experimental expedition, which had to pass by "twenty eight heavy guns that commanded the river for fifteen miles." The steamboats were partly protected by bales of cotton and wet hay. They took the barges in tow. The gunboats engaged the batteries. The description of this passage is highly dramatic. The gunboats were considerably battered, but not disabled. One of the steamboats, the Henry Clay, was disabled by a shot, and while adrift was set on fire by a shell, and burned. Another, the Forest Queen, was hulled by a shot, and then disabled by another through the steam drum, but she drifted down below, and was taken up by a gunboat and landed. The third steamboat was unhurt. They cast off the barges when they got under fire.

As an example of the kind of men that composed our volunteer armies, the following is cited from BADEAU:

Only two of the steamboat masters were willing to encounter the danger; the crew of one transport [barge] also remained aboard, but all others shrank. When, however, it became known in the army that volunteers were wanted for the dangerous task, men enough to man a hundred steamers pressed themselves upon the commanders; pilots, masters, engineers, and men, all were found in the ranks and among the officers on shore, and from these crews were speedily improvised for the transport fleet.

The fate of the barges is left obscure. BADEAU says they were "materially damaged,"
and that "some of them went sweeping down the current even below New Carthage," which means that they went into the enemy's hands. In narrating an anecdote of the exultation of "an old rebel" at New Carthage, at whose house McCLERNAND had made his headquarters, at what he fancied was the destruction of the whole flotilla, BADEAU mentions this: "By daylight, however, the wrecks had all passed by, and after awhile a gunboat appeared below the bend, and then a transport; then, one after another, the whole fleet of ironclads and army steamers hove in sight from their perilous passage." BADEAU calls the barges transports, and he here mentions one, and the steamers and gunboats after "the wrecks had all passed by." Through this mist it appears that the passage went hard with the transports and steamers.

Gen. GRANT went to Smith's Plantation the day after this passage. After his return he wrote HALLECK, April 19, of the barges: "Whilst under the guns of the enemy's batteries they were cut loose, and I fear that some of them have been permitted to run past New Carthage undiscovered. They were relied upon to aid in the transportation of troops to take Grand Gulf."

Of course Gen. GRANT then knew whether the barges had gone by, but he wished to spare the country's feelings by breaking the news gently. The three steamboats that were towing the ten barges cast them loose as soon as under fire; one of the three was burned, another disabled, and herself had to be taken in tow. This left but one steamboat to pick up and land the ten barges after they had passed the fifteen miles of the Vicksburg guns, and then the Warrenton batteries, which left only about sixteen miles to New Carthage, and this in a river running five or six miles an hour, and on which, in high water, landings are very difficult, except at places prepared.

One steamboat could not do much in picking up and landing ten loaded barges in such conditions. As for the gunboats they were engaging the batteries and holding back against the current. Gen. GRANT says in the same letter: "Our vessels went down even slower than the current, using their wheels principally for backing." But the barges were speeding on with the current. It appears, therefore, that the most of the barges were lost. But the dramatic scene of this heroic running of the batteries electrified the country, and Gen. GRANT, in pursuance of the military necessity to send encouraging accounts, wrote HALLECK: "Our experiment of running the batteries at Vicksburg, I think, has demonstrated the entire practicability of doing so with but little risk."

CHAPTER XVII.

GRANT'S IMPASSIVENESS UNDER FAILURES—M'CLERNAND DELAYS ATTACKING GRAND GULF TILL HE CAN GET THERE—THE TIME WHEN THE NAVIGABLE BASE FAILED—SPARING HALLECK'S FEELINGS—MORE BOATS RUN PAST VICKSBURG—HALF ARE SUNK—CHANGE OF BASE TO HARD TIMES.

During all these operations Gen. GRANT had experienced many failures, which would seem to be severe disappointments, but he bore them all with stoicism, and indeed with seeming unconsciousness. In several of them BADEAU regards the failure in the end as approving GRANT's forecast in the beginning. The Duckport Canal and bayou route was the base of his Port Hudson plan. The dropping out of this navigable base must have been a severe disappointment; but it is not easy to find when this happened. BADEAU grows judiciously miscellaneous at times. The order of events in which he places it would make it much earlier than is shown by GRANT's dispatches to HALLECK, and these did not inform HALLECK that it had ever failed.

GRANT's letter of April 12 to HALLECK shows that he had then full faith in the navigable route, and that there were only two reasons why he did not then cut the levee and open the canal. First, that he had then but three tugs and fifteen barges "suitable for this navigation;" second, that the cutting of the levee might drown the road and McCLERNAND's corps. Therefore, he said it was necesssary to build the road to use until he got water craft enough, and until the river conditions got right for opening the canal. When he returned from Smith's Plantation he wrote HALLECK April 19 this favorable view of the navigable route: "By clearing out the bayous from timber there will be good navigation from here to New Carthage for tugs and barges, also small sternwheel steamers. The navigation can be kept good, I think, by using our dredges constantly until there is twenty feet fall"

Twenty feet fall is a pretty good margin for a dug way. He adds the condition, "by clearing out the bayous from timber," which, in Walnut Bayou, would have occupied McCLERNAND's corps all summer. He also guards his statement with the following, which illustrates the trust in luck with which GRANT embarked in expeditions involving the fate of a campaign and an army: "On this subject, however, I have not taken the opinion of an engineer officer, nor have I formed it upon sufficient investigation to warrant me in speaking positively." Not having consulted an engineer as to the practicability of a navigation on which his plan depended, and not having looked into it himself, he was in a situation to rest in a confiding trust in luck.

When GRANT went forward to Smith's Plantation the second time he wrote Gen. SHERMAN, April 24, before any attempt had been made to use the water route: "The water in the bayous is falling very rapidly; out of all proportion to the fall in the river, so that it is exceedingly doubtful whether they can be made use of for the purposes of navigation." This was only five days after he had written HALLECK that the navigable route was even more than his fancy had painted, and that with the dredges going it would be good, though the river fell twenty feet. Yet three days later than this he wrote HALLECK of the difficulty and "tedious operation" of moving troops from Smith's Plantation to the Mississippi, because of the flood and cross currents through the breaks in the levees of Bayou Vidal. Thus did GRANT's navigable route, which was the base of his Port Hudson plan, fade away while yet the river was so high as seriously to obstruct his operation. But he gave no sign of this to HALLECK. He spared HALLECK's feelings. And now the failure of this main dependence of the plan was eclipsed by the dramatic spectacle of running the Vicksburg guns. In following out the fate of the navigable base this paper has gone both back and ahead of events.

BADEAU states, with emphatic reflection on Gen. McCLERNAND, that GRANT wrote him on the 12th: "It is my desire that you should get possession of Grand Gulf at the earliest practicable moment." At that time McCLERNAND's corps was strung along the route from

Milliken's Bend to Smith's Plantation, building the road; and the means of getting over the flood and swift currents between Smith's and New Carthage had yet to be found. Again, on the 13th, GRANT cautioned him: "It is not desirable that you should move in any direction from Grand Gulf, but remain under protection of the gunboats." Again, on the 18th: "I would still repeat former instructions, that possession be got of Grand Gulf at the earliest practicable moment. * * * I will be over here again in a few days, and hope it will be my good fortune to find you in safe possession of Grand Gulf."

The last was written from Smith's Plantation, to which GRANT had come because of a message sent him from PORTER through SHERMAN, that he could not harmonize with McCLERNAND. Says BADEAU: "GRANT was suffering from boils at the time, but the day after receiving this request he rode forty miles, from Milliken's Bend to Perkins' Landing, and there gave McCLERNAND further instructions." But GRANT'S letter to HALLECK, April 19, shows that his ride was only to Smith's Plantation. BADEAU'S quotations show also that GRANT wrote from Smith's to McCLERNAND, who was then at New Carthage. But although this ride was only half so long as BADEAU thought, yet this and the boils together seem to have quickened Gen. GRANT'S military faculties to such a degree that he perceived that something more than desire was required to take Grand Gulf.

His letter to HALLECK states that "the whole of his (McCLERNAND'S) corps is between Richmond and New Carthage." Richmond is back on Bayou Vidal only nine miles from Milliken's Bend. What McCLERNAND'S troops were doing is told by GRANT'S letter to HALLECK, April 12: "The wagon road (this work must now be nearly completed), by filling up the lowest ground, will be about twenty inches above the water in the swamps." McCLERNAND'S corps was building a road for the army. GRANT also found at Smith's Plantation that there was great difficulty in getting troops from there to New Carthage. He also found that most of the barges he had sent down had gone to parts unknown, and, hence, that three things were requisite to an attack on Grand Gulf: First, to get the army to a place on the river where it could embark; second, boats to ferry it over; third, supplies.

So much was developed by the quickening of military sense by a horseback ride of twenty miles with boils. Thus did those boils do good service to their country. BADEAU says that by this ride "GRANT became convinced that nothing would be accomplished until he took command in person and remained with the advance," and that "he returned, therefore, to Milliken's Bend to hasten the transportation of McPHERSON'S corps." The word transportation here means the wagons that belonged to McPHERSON'S corps. And BADEAU explains this remarkable turn of GRANT to the rear from a conviction that his presence was vital at the front, by an admiring ascription that GRANT attended to all the details of every part of the transportation, movement, and supply of the army, directing the Quartermasters, commissaries, teamsters, and issuing orders not only to division, but to regimental commanders.

This representation that GRANT turned back to these minute details, from the capture of Grand Gulf, which he then held vital to his plan, and which he was convinced would not be done until he took command in person, is a remarkable tribute to the minuteness of Gen. GRANT'S mind; but it appears by what GRANT did that he discovered the three essentials above noted, and went back to provide means to supply his advanced corps by sending on more wagons, and to provide both means of supply and means to ferry his army over the river by sending more boats to run the batteries.

Going back a little this fine anticipation of present performance, and a valuable promise of present aid to Gen. BANKS are found in a dispatch from GRANT to BANKS, dated Milliken's Bend, April 14: "I am concentrating my forces at Grand Gulf. Will send an army corps to Bayou Sara by the 25th, to co-operate with you on Port Hudson." Fortunately the active enemy kept BANKS so busy that he did did not wait for this co-operating corps, which, at the time when it was promised at Bayou Sara, was still floundering in the slough of Bayou Vidal. But the information and the promise to Gen. BANKS illustrate the high intelligence and accurate plan which governed all the Vicksburg operations.

Gen. GRANT dispatched to HALLECK, April 23:

Six boats and a number of barges ran the Vicksburg batteries last night. All the boats got by more or less damaged. The Tigress sank at 3 a. m., and is a total loss—crew all saved. The Moderator was much damaged. I think all the barges went through safely. * * * Casualties, so far as reported, two men mortally wounded, and several (number not known) more or less severely wounded. About 500 shots were fired. I look upon this as a great success.

BADEAU narrates the affair more succinctly, save that in this place he calls the steamboats transports:

On the 26th of April six other transports [steamboats] attempted to run by the Vicksburg batteries; five of them succeeded, although in a damaged condition; one was sunk by being struck in the hull by a solid shot. The crews of all the transports [steamboats], like those of their predecessors, were composed of volunteers for the purpose from the army. Twelve barges, laden with forage and rations, were sent in tow of the last six steamers, and half of them got safely by.

Six of the twelve barges, laden with supplies, went down to form the Mississippi delta. Likewise one steamboat, which carried the hospital stores, preparatory to the Grand Gulf action. This was a dear way of supplying a great army, and this was to be the way until the Port Hudson expedition was over. But Uncle Sam was rich, and GRANT said it was a great success. And none of these steamers or barges could return for another load.

A shipyard was set up for repairs. In this again we have a hint at the quality of these volunteers:

Mechanics were found in the army to do the work; for it was a striking feature of the volunteer service throughout the war, that no mechanical or professional need arose when accomplished adepts could not be found in almost any regiment to perform the duty required.

The following shows that there is no mistake as to the amount of destruction, and also the next move:

The army craft was soon in a condition to be of use in moving troops; but the destruction of two transports and six barges reduced the number so that it was found necessary to march the men from Perkins' Plantation to Hard Times, twenty-two miles further, and a distance of seventy miles from Milliken's Bend.

The last extract anticipates events by a few days in this very important stage of the Port Hudson movement.

CHAPTER XVIII.

GEN. GRANT MOVES TO THE FRONT—GRAND GULF TO BE CARRIED BY STORM—THE 13TH CORPS DESTINED FOR THE SACRIFICE—CHANGE OF BASE TO HARD TIMES—VAST WORK IN ROAD BUILDING BY THAT CORPS.

Gen. GRANT's historian relates that on the 18th of April, at Smith's Plantation, he concluded that Grand Gulf would not be taken until he took command in person, "therefore" he returned to Milliken's Bend to attend to McPHERSON's wagon train. On the 21st he dispatched HALLECK, still from Milliken's Bend: "I move my headquarters to New Carthage to-morrow. Every effort will be made to get speedy possession of Grand Gulf, and from that point to open the Mississippi." A dispatch to HALLECK, 23d, was still dated at Milliken's Bend, but a letter of the 24th to SHERMAN showed that he had reached Smith's Plantation. Till now his orders to McCLERNAND had been to embark at New Carthage on barges and steamers, drop down to Grand Gulf, twenty-two miles, and carry it by assault. It was about the same as a similar attempt from Milliken's Bend on the Vicksburg bluff.

But when GRANT had reached Smith's Plantation now the second time, and had to direct operations, he found, as he wrote SHERMAN April 24: "The difficulties of getting from here to the river are great." Yet so far back as the 18th he had written Gen. McCLERNAND from there that he would be over there again in a few days, and expected to find him in possession of Grand Gulf. But now he wrote SHERMAN: "I foresee great difficulties in our present position;" and he suggested that possibly SHERMAN might find a chance to pitch in at Vicksburg or Haines' Bluff and relieve the situation. But GRANT had now found that to take the army to New Carthage was impracticable; also that, after so much destruction of boats by running past Vicksburg, he had not means of river transportation for so long a distance as to Grand Gulf.

McCLERNAND had found it impracticable to take his corps to New Carthage because of the flood and strong currents from the breaks in the levees of Bayou Vidal, and had built a road from Smith's Plantation by a circuit on the west side of Bayou Vidal to where it again fetches to the river at Perkins' Plantation, twelve miles below, where were either two or three of his four divisions. And now GRANT, in the progress of his knowledge of the situation, found that because of the destruction of boats in running Vicksburg, his means of transporting his army to the assault were too small, and that the passage was long. Therefore McCLERNAND marched by another interior half circle, following the course of Bayou St. Joseph, which fetches to the river again at Hard Times, by which GRANT's route of supply was attenuated to seventy miles from Milliken's Bend. Says BADEAU:

"The new road lay along the west bank of Lake St. Joseph, and across three large bayous, over which bridges were built by the troops, the materials being taken from plantation houses near by. The whole route was in a miserable condition, and after the march once began the roads became intolerable. But on the 29th of April the entire 13th Corps had arrived at Hard Times, 10,000 men having moved from Perkins' Plantation on transports."

Hard Times is four miles above Grand Gulf. GRANT's reconnaissances, BADEAU says, had found that between Warrenton and Grand Gulf, a distance of forty miles by the river, "there was but one point where a good road existed from the river to the bluffs, the whole still being overflowed on the left bank of the river. This dry point was at a place called Congo Island, and was so strongly protected by natural defenses that it was not judged advisable to attempt a landing there."

These natural defenses are thus alleged: "The road led to Cox's farm on the Big Black River, and to use the landing would have necessitated crossing Big Black in the face of the enemy." To avoid the necessity, after the landing, of crossing a narrow river against probable opposition, GRANT decided to storm the intrenchments of Grand Gulf, by landing in front of them from crowded barges towed by frail steamers. Grand Gulf is a little Vicksburg in situation and defensibility. The river runs a little north of east for five miles till it strikes the bluff, then turns a short corner and runs southwest, in the general line of the bluff. Its impact against the clay of the bluff has made a shape at this turn which gives the name of gulf. And thus the line of bluff is nigh the river bank.

Big Black River, connecting with the Mississippi at the upper end of Grand Gulf and the flooded bottom above, protected the place from approach in that quarter. On the south side of Big Black is a bold spur in the bluff, jutting out, and rising higher than the general range of the bluff. In a description made by Admiral PORTER, after Grand Gulf fell into our hands, he calls this elevation Point of Rocks. His description is as follows [Boynton's History of the Navy]:

"Grand Gulf is the strongest place on the Mississippi. * * * One fort on Point of Rocks, seventy-five feet high, calculated for six or seven guns, mounting two seven inch rifles and one eight inch and one Parrott gun, on wheels (carried off). On the left of this work is a triangular work, calculated to mount one heavy gun. These works are connected with another fort by a covered way and double rifle pits, extending three-quarters of a mile, constructed with much labor, and showing great skill on the part of the constructor. The third fort commands the river in all directions; it mounted one splendid Blakely 100 pounder, and one eight inch; two thirty-two pounders were lying bursted and broken on the ground."

That which PORTER calls a covered way and double rifle pits was along the foot of the bluff, and within short musket range of the bank of the river. The river was nearly on a level with the bank, and boats presented a fair mark. The lower fort was where a road ascended the hill to the interior. The forts had bombproof magazines. This rifle trench, nearly on the level of the narrow belt of plateau between the bluff and the river, and within what one of the navy officers calls pistol-shot of the river, was the most formidable part of the work to a force landing to carry the place by storm. The greater number might escape the shot from the batteries, provided these did not happen to sink the transports, but infantry in this secure trench could mow them down as fast as they could land. The line of rifle trench was held by a brigade, the greater part of the force being in reserve behind the top of the bluff.

The current of the river at Grand Gulf is swift, and strikes the shore. As many of McCLERNAND's corps as could be crowded into the barges and towing steamers, say 10,000, were to be held in readiness just out of range of the upper battery, and, when the gunboats had silenced the heavy guns, were to be towed down, packed in clumsy barges like sheep for the slaughter house, to make a landing under this fire, in the way that towed barges must in a rapid river.

While those troops stand thus bound for the sacrifice by the order of one impassive individual, let this paper pause to remark the immense work which they had done in the last thirty days. This review has too profound respect for the army profession to give praise to the commander of that fated corps, whom GRANT and SHERMAN describe as a "political General." Besides, in all the Vicksburg operation Gen. McCLERNAND gives so much trouble to GRANT and BADEAU as to excite sympathy for them. But in that corps, now destined to the sacrifice, were 20,000 volunteers from the Northwestern States—or so many of the 20,000 as had survived GRANT's swampordeal—who were serving their country for the love of it, and who had done a vast work in building roads and bridges for the army on a route of march and supplies, now drawn out to seventy miles.

They had started from Milliken's Bend without tents or baggage, with ten days' rations, and few cooking utensils. Through that wonderful military route of soft alluvium and swamp they had built up a road, which, now that the fiction of a navigable route had faded, was the sole road for the march and supply of an army of 50,000 men. Even the reticent allusions which GRANT and BADEAU make give ground for the belief that Gen. McCLERNAND did not exaggerate the work of his corps when he said in his address:

Your march through Louisiana, from Milliken's Bend to New Carthage and Perkins' Plantation, on the Mississippi River, is one of the most remarkable on record. Bayous and miry roads, threatened with momentary inundation, obstructed your progress. All these were overcome by unceasing labor and unflagging energy. The two thousand feet of bridging which was improvised hastily out of materials created on the spot, and over which you passed, must long remain a marvel.

Gen. McCLELLAN's whole army did greater labor than this on the Peninsula, and while astride the Chickahominy; but this work in the Mississippi swamps was all done by the soldiers of McCLERNAND's corps. And it was after they had been worked three months in digging canals and pulling sunken trees out of bayous and swamps, in undertakings which their intelligence told them had no chance of success. Yet when these volunteers at last were permitted to set foot on firm ground, they marched by night and fought by day, on scanty rations, with a gallantry that was irresistible. What real military enterprise could be called doubtful with such troops, directed by military intelligence?

BADEAU says that GRANT, "in order to appease the unappeasable ambition and conceit of his subordinate, had given him command of the advance." Thus had he assigned to McCLERNAND's corps the honor of making a road for the army through that wonderful route. Also that he had "charged him with an operation which, if successful, would have rendered McCLERNAND famous at once." That operation was now to be performed, and McCLERNAND's devoted corps stood ready for the sacrifice. It was to be done in the perfection of the military art, as practiced by GRANT and SHERMAN, which held that the first step of a reconnaissance of a fortified place is a general assault, and that the art of war has no way of judging whether an undertaking is in a military sense impossible, save by sacrificing an army in the attempt.

CHAPTER XIX.

LEARNING THE ART OF WAR BY GENERAL ASSAULTS—TAKING VOLUNTEERS AT THEIR WORD—BOMBARDMENT OF GRAND GULF—SHIPS AND FORTS—ARMY RESIGNATION TO INFERIORITY—BOTTOM GONE FROM THE PORT HUDSON PLAN—A NEW MOVEMENT.

In the history of the wars of the great Generals of Europe, it appears that the costly method of taking fortified places by storm is reserved for fortresses of great strategical consequence, under imperative circumstances, which make the object adequate to the inevitable sacrifice of soldiers. And these assaults are regarded by military men as so much beyond what a General may properly command men to do, that it is the practice to call for volunteers for the leading column, to receive the first fire, to whom special honor is awarded. And the military man can in general calculate whether the conditions in which the assault is to be made are such as to give reasonable promise of success to what brave men may be expected to do.

But in this fresh young country, where all

things are infused by the spirit of its geographical greatness, a commander forms a plan to escape from his second aborted campaign to another so remote and vague as to be indescribable, whose preliminary starting point depends upon landing troops from towed and crowded flatboats upon a narrow plateau in front of a thoroughly fortified place, to carry it by assault. This storming of Grand Gulf from the river had been reckoned upon at Milliken's Bend as a vital part of the Port Hudson plan, without any information as to its practicability, and without any of that knowledge of the situation which was attainable to any military man who made it his business to know. And in general, as at Chickasaw Bayou, in the siege of Vicksburg, at Kenesaw Mountain, Spottsylvania, Cold Harbor, Petersburg, and Richmond, to order a general assault on intrenchments was regarded as a proper tentative operation, in the nature of a reconnaissance; and the failure, with losses of from 2,500 to 7,000 men, without having hurt the enemy, was accepted as proof of the Commanding General's enterprise. These were the tactics which LINCOLN immortalized by the classic phrase, "pegging away."

But in our army all were volunteers. The common figure of speech for their volunteering was that they offered their lives to their country. Our greatest Generals accepted that figure of speech as reality. When young men rose up so spontaneously to serve their country for the love of it as to make an embarrassment of riches, and with an enthusiasm which was quite irregular in the regular army school, our Generals could afford a kind of tactics which consumed them liberally, and to seek fame and promotion by a standard which rated the greatness of generalship by the magnitude of the slaughter of their own men. Therefore do we see in the tactics of our greatest Generals that general assaults on fortified places were a sort of preliminary observation.

When on the one part is a people who have so little to do that as many as a million and a half—in all—volunteer to serve their country, just for the love of her; and on the other hand a professional army class whose rise in rank, pay, and honors is in proportion to their consumption of these, the life of a volunteer becomes very cheap. In the "effete" military powers, where men have to be forced into the ranks, or dearly enlisted by bounties, the tactics are naturally less consuming. The Port Hudson plan made the taking of Grand Gulf by storm an essential part, as it did the navigable route by a canal and unknown bayous. And the projector was as wise as to the possibility of one as of the other.

"The plan," says BADEAU, to take Grand Gulf, "was for the naval force to bombard and silence the batteries, and immediately afterward the troops were to land at the foot of the bluff and carry the works by storm. Accordingly 10,000 troops of the 13th Corps were crowded aboard the transports and barges, and moved down the stream to the front of Grand Gulf, at a point just out of range." This was on the 29th of April. "At 8 o'clock PORTER began the bombardment with all his ironclads, seven in number, and one ordinary gunboat. For five hours and twenty minutes he kept up a vigorous fire without intermission, running his vessels at times almost within pistol shot of the batteries. At twenty minutes past 1 o'clock the Admiral withdrew, the utter futility of his effort having been amply demonstrated." BADEAU says: "It would have been madness to attempt a landing under unsilenced guns like these." But there was that all along the front which would have been a thousand times worse to a landing force than those two batteries of thirteen heavy guns. Mr. HENRI COPPEE, author of "GRANT'S Campaigns"—whose book is Badeau to a considerable extent, but not so much so as BADEAU—intimates that it was fortunate that the navy did not succeed in silencing the great guns. Thus does it appear from one biographer that GRANT'S proverbial luck did again interpose to save him from the fatality of his plan.

The gunboats suffered much more in this bombardment than in running the Vicksburg batteries. They were badly battered, and several of them required extensive repairs to fit them for service. On three of them eighteen men were killed and fifty-seven wounded. This was probably greater than the enemy's loss, although the heavy guns of the navy must have been more than thrice as many as in the batteries on shore. As many as 3,000 rounds were fired by the navy. This action was an illustration of the feebleness of the idea which had taken deep hold in our regular army—that ships can take forts. There must have been a decrepitude in a professional army class who could so readily accept a theory of the imbecility of their own profession.

The theory that ships can take forts was the base upon which SCOTT had constructed his "anaconda plan," the main part of which was a gunboat fleet to go down the Mississippi. He had instilled this delusion deeply into LINCOLN. McCLELLAN imbibed it. HALLECK believed it, or professed to. It is an example of the wonderful intelligence which directed the war from Washington, that HALLECK, the General in Chief, thought that an expedition to open the Mississippi River was the most important expedition in the war. So he said to GRANT while he was fighting the swamps and bayous west of the Mississippi. And while BANKS had to take the field in West Louisiana to prevent the losing of the State, river and all, HALLECK was continually ordering him to go and help GRANT open the Mississippi River, as if to get one passage through would open the Mississippi, while the Confederate armies were unbroken in all the country on both sides of it. He ordered BANKS, and GRANT urged him, to drop all, and come up and help GRANT open the Mississippi; which, if BANKS had done, would have given up both Louisiana and the Mississippi River.

This feeble idea of the army that it could not resist ships, nor even such light shells as the river gunboats, pervaded all our military operations in the first two years of the war, and some of the most important of them to the end. It took McCLELLAN away from an interior line, and isolated him in a malarious peninsula; for he pleads that he expected the navy to silence the batteries at Yorktown and Gloucester Point, and that because they could not his surprise movement began with a month's siege. At Fort Donelson, GRANT, with double the force of the enemy, waited for Commodore FOOTE with four mailed gunboats to take the fort, and came near losing his army by his unguarded waiting. It was upon this delusion in LINCOLN's mind that gunboats could clear out forts, that McCLERNAND got a special commission to raise and command an expedition to open the Mississippi.

GRANT and SHERMAN, both educated at West Point, thought this commission to McCLERNAND to open the Mississippi by means of a fleet, so great an opportunity to him that it demoralized them, and one of them hastened back from a true military line to snatch the river expedition from him, while the other feebly waited to be driven back by the loss of his supplies. It would be unreasonable to impeach the military sense of LINCOLN or McCLERNAND, when SCOTT—the Great Captain—HALLECK, McCLELLAN, GRANT, SHERMAN, and a lot of others of that class which assumes to know all military knowledge, maintained the same notion of the superiority of navies to armies, yet the remark must be made that McCLERNAND was not a regular army General; he had not been trained in a school in which each follows the preceding, in a routine like pack mules in a string, and he ought to have known better than to have promoted a river opening expedition upon such an idea. The probability is that GRANT unwittingly took a bad job off his hands when he assumed command of the river opener.

GRANT's Port Hudson plan had assumed that the storming of Grand Gulf was as easily done as said. After all was over BADEAU put into his history, and GRANT confirmed, his faultfinding with McCLERNAND because he had not taken Grand Gulf before he got to the river, or got any means to cross the river. The taking of Grand Gulf by storm was the key of the Port Hudson plan, as the bayou navigable route was its base. And now this was found to be "madness," and the navigable base had dropped out.

Yet something must be done, and done quickly; for the line of supplies by a precarious road, through a hostile country, was now attenuated to seventy miles. At the best that army could not be supplied by it; and if the Confederates should turn their attention to it, the greater part of the army would be needed to keep it open. The next move—as BADEAU said of the failure of the Lake Providence plan—will serve "to demonstrate the fertility and variety of resources developed during this anomalous campaign." After the bombardment had failed, the transports were brought back to Hard Times, the troops landed, and in the night they marched down the river five miles below Grand Gulf to be Shroon's The transports ran past Grand Gulf in the night, the gunboats engaging the batteries again to cover them. And now on the next day a new movement was to be made, which, through the interposition of GRANT's proverbial luck, got turned around from a retreat into that which was indeed a movement,

CHAPTER XX.

THE DELIVERANCE—SUCCESSFUL CROSSING OF THE MISSISSIPPI—BATTLE OF PORT GIBSON.

On the 29th of April, says ADAM BADEAU, the failure of the naval cannonade of Grand Gulf having developed the idea that "it would have been madness to attempt a landing," and the gunboats and transports having passed down below, GRANT wrote to HALLECK: "I feel now that the battle is more than half over." Thus was the failure to take Grand Gulf by storm the more than half achievement of the battle.

On the 30th as many of the troops of McCLERNAND'S corps as with their artillery could be placed on the transports at a time were embarked at De Shroon's, and set out to find a landing on the east side of the river. The destination was as free as the familiar one of trading vessels—"For Cowes and a market." GRANT, says BADEAU, "had hardly hoped to get a footing anywhere north of Rodney," which is eighteen miles below Grand Gulf; and of the practicability of getting a footing there he had the same abiding trust in the unknown as in his bayou route of navigation, and in the taking of Grand Gulf by storm.

Here came to the rescue the nation's ever faithful friend, the slave. "That night information was procured [received] from a negro that a good road led from Bruinsburg, six miles below Grand Gulf to Port Gibson, twelve miles in the interior, and on high ground. When the embarkation began, it was with a view to steam down the river until land should be found; but this information being relied on, the first transports went direct to Bruinsburg, and found the negro's story correct." Such a deliverer of a great military plan from a drifting into the unknown ought to be mentioned more reverently.

Behold now the great Mississippi River opening expedition, which started in with 130,000 men and a great navy, now with its head brigade, like the nucleus of a comet, embarked on flatboats, and drifting down the Mississippi on a voyage of discovery, to find a lodgment from which Gen. GRANT might send 20,000 troops to Port Hudson to operate on the bowels of the river there; the rest of the great expedition stretching behind, like the comet's spreading tail, through De Shroon's, Hard Times, Richmond, Young's Point, Milliken's Bend, Helena, Memphis, to the active recruiting stations in the Northwestern States, all co-operating in the river opening operation!

Gen. McCLERNAND'S report divests the expedition of some of this romance by narrating that he and a party had reconnoitered down to opposite Bruinsburg, and had observed this landing. That report tells also of much scouting and reconnoitering all the way from Milliken's Bend to Smith's Plantation, New Carthage, Perkins', and so on down to Hard Times, De Shroon's, some of which were strange voyages of discovery; also of skirmishing dashes with parties of Confederates all along the route from Milliken's Bend, and of the necessity of incessant vigilance against their desire to immerse them by cutting the levees of the bayons. But this review prefers BADEAU and the more romantic account, with the negro as the savior of the army from the General's dilemma.

Happily the nucleus of the great comet found a dry landing at Bruinsburg undefended. And now, indeed, the battle for Grand Gulf, and likewise for Vicksburg, was "half over." For, once established on the east side of the river, GRANT was master of the situation, and, if he could not beat the enemy, he had no business to come. The topographical conditions were singularly favorable. Just below Grand Gulf the river diverges from the bluff line, leaving an interval of bottom, which widens to three miles. Down to where Bayou Pierre joins the river at Bruinsburg, this bottom had so recently emerged from the river flood that it was impracticable for even skirmishers. This information the writer got from a Confederate officer who tried it.

From Bruinsburg to Port Gibson, thirteen miles, the road is a little north of east. Bruinsburg, Port Gibson, and Grand Gulf make three points of a triangle. The road from Grand Gulf is seven miles. On this road BOWEN'S forces from Grand Gulf, which is northwest of Port Gibson, were coming; also from Vicksburg, by way of Hankinson's Ferry over the Big Black River, which fetched them by roads north-northeast of Port Gibson. The fortunate conjunction of the wet bottom along the river above Bruinsburg prevented direct interference from Grand

Gulf with the landing of troops, and BOWEN decided that at Port Gibson was the place to make the stand, for that would cover the roads both to Vicksburg and Jackson.

The length of the ferriage from De Shroon's was six miles, and the embarking and landing of troops and artillery is not a quick operation by such means; but by 4 p. m. McCLERNAND's column moved for the bluffs about three miles in the interior, reaching the upland before sunset, and pushing on in the night to reach Port Gibson, in time to prevent the enemy from destroying the bridges at that place over Bayou Pierre. At 1 o'clock a. m. the head of the column, nine miles from Bruinsburg, and four miles west of Port Gibson, struck a line of infantry and artillery; the head brigade deployed, returned and silenced the fire, and then rested till morning.

BOWEN's report shows that this was Gen. GREEN's force of about a thousand men, which had been sent forward into position the day before, and which thereby was enabled to choose its ground. The rest of BOWEN's forces were coming up during the night and next day. The Confederate line was on a range of hills running across two diverging and converging roads which parted about half a mile in front, and came together in the rear at Port Gibson, and were about two miles apart at the Confederate line.

BOWEN stated his number in a lumping way as 5,500. GRANT, two days after the battle, wrote HALLECK that it was 11,000. The matter is mixed by troops on the way from Vicksburg, and the absence of clear statement how many got into the engagement. BADEAU quotes GRANT's estimate, but does not give his own. The real number was probably between the two. The only rational object BOWEN could have in advancing to the fight was to hold GRANT until force enough could be brought up to beat or drive him back to his boats. In any other view his fighting was folly, and, to a very great General, with such an overwhelming number on the ground and coming up, exposed his small force to be cut off and captured. As the battle was fought, however, its tactical object was only to drive BOWEN from the ground.

McCLERNAND's report states that his movement to the attack was along the two diverging roads that led to the enemy's right and left, his reserves being where these two roads parted; that the first brigade of OSTERHAUS' division, at 5:30 a. m., encountered the enemy's right, and after an obstinate resistance drove them, when they fell back to cover and to a new and strong position. His second brigade came up and he attacked the new position, but found insurmountable obstacles in the nature of the ground, and decided that a front attack at that point was impracticable. It was now 2 p. m., and about this time J. E. SMITH's brigade of Gen. LOGAN's division came up, and attempted the same position with the same result; thus, he says, "attesting the correctness of Gen. OSTERHAUS' admonition on that point."

OSTERHAUS now demonstrated on the enemy's right center, and at the same time moved a strong force to his extreme right, and "personally leading a brilliant charge against it, routed the enemy, taking three pieces of cannon. A detachment of SMITH's brigade" (J. E. SMITH, LOGAN's division) "joined in the pursuit of the enemy to a point within a half a mile of Port Gibson."

Gen. McCLERNAND now takes up the operations on his right. "At 6:15 a. m., when sufficient time had elapsed to allow OSTERHAUS' attack to work a diversion in favor of my right, I ordered Gen. CARR to attack the enemy's left. Gen. BENTON's brigade promptly moved forward to the right of the main road to Port Gibson. His way lay through woods, ravines, and a light canebrake: yet he pressed on until he found the enemy drawn up behind the crest of a range of hills intersected by the road. * * * The hostile lines immediately opened on each other, and an obstinate struggle ensued."

STONE's brigade moved forward on the left of the road into an open field and opened on the enemy's left center. "The action was now general, except at the center, where a continuation of fields, extending to the front of my line for more than a mile, separated the antagonists. The enemy had not dared to show himself in these fields, but continued to press my extreme right, with the hope, as I subsequently learned, of crushing it, and closing his concave line around me." BOWEN's report shows that he made such an effort, and claims considerable progress in it. "Gen. HOVEY came up at an opportune moment, and reported his division to be on the ground." By the time HOVEY had formed his division near the fork of the two roads, SMITH's division came up, and HOVEY moved forward to the support of CARR's on the right.

In the execution of this order Gen. McGinnis' brigade moved to the right front, in support of Benton's, encountering the same obstacles that had been overcome by the latter. Col. Slack's brigade moved by the flank near the main road, and without much difficulty gained its proper position to the left of McGinnis. During the struggle between Benton's brigade and the enemy, the former had moved to the right to secure its flank, and left a considerable gap between it and Stone's, The gap was immediately closed up by a portion of Gen. Hovey's division upon its arrival upon the ground assigned to it. The enemy's artillery was only 150 yards in front, and was supported by a strong line of infantry, which, it was reported, had just been re-enforced, and was the occasion of the shout of the enemy distinctly heard about this time.

To terminate the sanguinary contest which had continued for several hours, Gen. Hovey ordered a charge, which was most gallantly executed, and resulted in the capture of 100 prisoners, two stands of colors, two twelve pounder howitzers, three cannon, and a considerable quanity of ammunition. A portion of Gen. Carr's division joined in this charge.

Then comes this pleasant incident: "About this time I heard that Maj. Gen. GRANT had come up from Bruinsburg, and soon after had the pleasure of meeting him on the field." Without doubt the pleasure was mutual. There is said to be no brotherhood so warm as that of brothers in arms. By this expression of pleasurable emotion does Gen. McCLERNAND ingeniously state the stage of the battle at the time when he first had the pleasure of the sight of Gen. GRANT. He continues:

Determined to press my advantages, I ordered Gens. Carr and Hovey to push the enemy with all vigor and celerity. This they did, beating him back more than a mile, and frustrating all his endeavors to make an immediate stand. * * * Returning to bring up the narrative of other operations. Gen. Smith's division came up to Shaeffer's about 7 a. m., and just before Gen. Hovey moved to the support of Gen. Carr. The four divisions of my corps were now on the field, three of them actually engaged, and the fourth eager to be. The last immediately moved forward into the fields in front of Shaeffer's house, and together with a portion of Gen. Osterhaus' division, held the center, and at the same time formed a reserve.

The second position taken up by the enemy on my right front was stronger than the first. * * * Having advanced until they had gained a bold ridge overlooking the bottom, Gens. Hovey's and Carr's divisions again encountered the enemy's fire. A hot engagement ensued, in the course of which, discovering that the enemy was massing a formidable force on my right flank, I ordered Gen. Smith to send forward a brigade to support that flank. Burbridge's brigade moved rapidly forward for that purpose; meanwhile Gen. Hovey moved his artillery on the right, and opened a partially enfilading and destructive fire on the enemy. The effect of these combined movements was to force the enemy back upon his center with considerable loss.

Here, finding a large concentration of forces, he renewed the attack, directing it against my right center. Gen. Carr met and retaliated it with both infantry and artillery with great vigor. At the same time Landram's brigade of Gen. Smith's division, re-enforced by a detachment from Gen. Hovey's division, forced its way through cane and underbrush and joined in Carr's attack. The battle was now transferred from the enemy's left to his center, and after an obstinate struggle he was again beaten back upon the high ridge on the opposite side of the bottom, and within a mile of Port Gibson. Gen. Stevenson's brigade of Logan's division came up in time to assist in consummating this final result.

The shades of night soon closed upon the stricken field, which the valor of our men had won and held, and upon which they found the first repose since they had left De Shroon's Landing twenty-four hours before.

So much for Gen. McCLERNAND. In his view he commanded, and his four divisions fought the battle, aided at the close by two brigades of LOGAN's division, one of which, J. A. SMITH's, tried to carry a position on the left, against OSTERHAUS' admonition, and failed, and a detachment of which "joined in the pursuit of the enemy," when OSTERHAUS made his final successful charge on the left; the other, Gen. STEVENSON's, "came up in time to assist in consummating the final result on the right."

BADEAU narrates that "the artillery fire was heard at the landing, eight miles off, and GRANT started at once for the front, arriving in the field at 10 a. m. on a borrowed horse [borrowed, a military term] and with no escort but his staff [also on borrowed horses]. He immediately assumed direct command." He narrates that "McCLERNAND was pressing the rebels vigorously on the right with the bulk of his force, but OSTERHAUS' division on the left had not been so successful * * * until two brigades of LOGAN's division in McPHERSON's corps appeared. * * * McPHERSON coming on the ground in person * *   this was about noon. GRANT at once directed him to throw JOHN E. SMITH's brigade to the support of OSTERHAUS, with instructions to advance on the left, and, if possible, outflank the enemy."

"GRANT and McPHERSON accompanied this brigade;" therefore "the movement was perfectly successful." LOGAN seems to disappear in the presence of so many commanders "in person." Thus was Gen. GRANT in command of the whole, and at the same time leading a brigade in a flank movement. "As soon as the position of the enemy could be definitely ascertained, and the ground sufficiently reconnoitered, a charge was made across the avine and on the rebel flank, simultaneously with a direct attack by OSTERHAUS in front. This combined effort soon drove the rebels from their position on GRANT's left, and sent them in precipitate retreat toward Port Gibson." And now it was before sunset. "Before sunset their right was completely broken and swept away."

The principal difference between McCLERNAND and BADEAU in this is that BADEAU has GRANT and McPHERSON, "in person," with a brigade, take the affair out of the hands of OSTERHAUS and his division, and make the decisive operation; while McCLERNAND has OSTERHAUS plan and carry out the finishing movement, assisted by a detachment from J. A. SMITH's brigade. BADEAU does not recognize LOGAN.

He narrates that "McCLERNAND, meanwhile, notwithstanding the determined gallantry and steady progress of HOVEY, CARR, and A. J. SMITH, was sending repeated messages to GRANT for re-enforcements on the right, but his wishes were only partly gratified." GRANT knew better than McCLERNAND whether he needed re-enforcements. GRANT's official report has this statement, and that McCLERNAND, even before LOGAN had arrived with his two brigades, wanted both LOGAN's and QUINBY's whole divisions.

But he says he had been over there, and "could not see how they could be used there to advantage." However, when the two brigades of LOGAN's division arrived he sent one (STEVENSON's) to McCLERNAND; but BADEAU says that before this "appeared on the right, the rebels had begun to withdraw, and the sight of fresh national troops added to their demoralization, although not to their discomfiture, as STEVENSON did not really become engaged." This gives to STEVENSON's brigade even less weight in the final consummation than McCLERNAND gives. But it supports GRANT's judgment that he knew better than McCLERNAND whether he needed re-enforcements, particularly when he had none to give him.

The battle was fought by McCLERNAND's corps of about 16,000, and two of LOGAN's divisions, making about 19,000, according to BADEAU. Except the difference made in the flanking movement on the left by one of LOGAN's brigades, by Gen. GRANT accompanying it in person—McPHERSON, LOGAN, and J. E. SMITH being also present in person—the most material difference in the accounts is that McCLERNAND fancied he was in command, and he reports all the dispositions and movements as if he were the god of the machine; whereas BADEAU says that at 10 a. m. GRANT assumed direct command, and then led in person a brigade in a flanking movement. The probability is that the most essential presence in person was that of the volunteers of the ranks, and their immediate officers, the Lieutenants, Captains, Majors, Colonels, and Brigadiers, especially the men in the ranks.

CHAPTER XXI.

THE DAY AFTER THE BATTLE—BRIDGE BUILDING—BOWEN'S MEAT—KILLED AND WOUNDED—THE WAY THE BATTLE WAS FOUGHT IN THE REPORTS — EMANCIPATION OF THE SOLDIERS FROM THE SLOUGH.

The "last order" of Gen. GRANT to Gen. McCLERNAND at night after the battle shows an expectation of a renewal next day, and of a possible night attack from the enemy. BADEAU quotes for admiration:

Push the enemy with skirmishers well thrown out until it gets too dark to see him. Then place your command on eligible ground wherever night finds you. Park your artillery so as to command the surrounding country, and renew the attack at early dawn. If possible, push the enemy from the field or capture him. No camp fires should be allowed, unless in deep ravines and to the rear of troops.

Camp fires would reveal their presence to the enemy. Such energy of orders, after a retreating foe, is more than half the battle. Says BADEAU:

Early on the morning of the 2d McClernand's troops, flushed with the success of the day before, and elated at the idea of being at last on dry land, with plenty of open country for operations, pushed into the town, finding no enemy but the wounded.

This elation of the troops at getting out of

the swamps strangely forgets the hardening and inspiriting effect which he had before ascribed to the swamp labors.

Grant immediately detached one brigade of Logan's division to the left, to engage the attention of the rebels there, while a heavy detail of McClernand's troops was set to work rebuilding the bridge across the South Fork. The break was more than 120 feet long, but was repaired with extraordinary rapidity, officers and men working up to their waists in water, and the houses in the neighborhood being torn down for timber.

No further pursuit was made till afternoon, when another division of McPherson's corps (Crocker's) had come up from the river, and this corps now came to the front, McClernand resting and falling to the rear. McPherson's report says of the above movement of one brigade to engage the enemy's attention on the left:

While waiting the construction of a bridge, Gen. Stevenson's brigade was moved down near the crossing of Bayou Pierre, on the Grand Gulf road, to engage the attention of the enemy, who were strongly posted on the hills on the northern side.

This position of the enemy, while they wanted only to retreat, is explained by Gen. Bowen's report, thus:

The enemy attempted no pursuit, and all crossed in safety to this side of Bayou Pierre, destroying the bridges behind us. Gen. Baldwin, misled by the burning of the railroad bridge, and by rumors that it was the suspension bridge, took the road due north through Port Gibson, instead of the Grand Gulf road, and unfortunately destroyed the bridge over the North Fork of Bayou Pierre, cutting me off from most of the meat, which had been sent between the two forks for safety.

I had sent a train around to bring it all here, and some of the wagons were cut off. They are coming in, however, and I expect none will be lost. I am endeavoring to get it over a ferry on North Fork, and if I do not succeed, shall at all events try to destroy it. I ordered all the commissary stores left in town (mainly corn) to be burned.

Thus was Bowen holding a bold rear to get away his meat, while Grant was engaging his attention to cover the building of the bridge. Badeau says: "While this was doing two brigades of Logan's division forded the bayou and marched on."

McPherson, however, shows that the two brigades made a detour to southeast three miles, to find a ford across South Fork, which gave them nine miles of marching to get to a point three miles advanced beyond Port Gibson. This was good marching, but through the several circumstances the pursuit did not begin till after 4 p. m., at which hour the bridge was ready.

The South Fork, running northwest, crosses, a mile northeast of the town, the road which runs northeast from Port Gibson, and keeps on the same course two miles further, to junction with North Fork, which running west southwest, crosses the same road five and a half miles northeast of Port Gibson.

While the pursuit pauses is a time to sum up the results of the battle. Bowen had made an orderly retreat from all but Badeau. He stated his losses at 448 killed and wounded, and 384 missing. His wounded fell into Grant's hands. The temptation to count these once as wounded, and again as prisoners, was so strong in this campaign as to make it pardonable to the historian. Grant's reports never descended to such a detail as the casualties. Badeau says they were 848 killed and wounded. McClernand's report states the losses of his four divisions in detail, making an aggregate of 803, and leaving 45 to Logan's two brigades. McClernand says two guns were taken; Grant wrote Halleck four; Badeau says six; these above two were counted from the field guns disabled and left at Grand Gulf.

Badeau gives all the credit to the gallantry of McClernand's division commanders. This is an instance of the radical difference between a real General and a mere volunteer General, who has taken it up by instinct. For in all of Gen. Grant's battles, as narrated by Badeau, Grant directs and carries out every movement in every part, division, brigade, and regiment, and his genius so pervades all parts that every detail of success is his own; while, on the other hand, ill fortune in any part is because of incompetency in subordinates. But although McClernand imagined that he had commanded in a successful battle, yet, being a mere volunteer, or political General, the success was gained in spite of him, by the gallantry of his Generals of divisions. All the accounts show the splendid gallantry of the soldiers of the ranks, and of their immediate officers. It was a stand up fight against brave troops, aided by a strong position, and the victory was won by valor, and not by tactics.

Whether, with at least twice the enemy's number, and with more arriving as fast as they could be ferried, to lose at the least as many killed and wounded—probably twice as many—as the enemy, who would have been forced to a precipitate retreat if his position had been turned, was as well as generalship could do, is not for this review to pronounce upon; for this review is simply historical, and has not the high ambition of military criticism. It was a question for Gen. GRANT, but it does not appear that the question how to use superior numbers to save his own troops entered much into Gen. GRANT's tactics. It came to be thought in our war that victories were great in proportion to the killed and wounded of our own men. Gen. McCLERNAND's report gave this opinion:

This, the battle of Port Gibson, on Bayou Pierre, was one of the most admirably and successfully fought battles in which it has been my lot to participate since the present unhappy war commenced. If not a decisive battle, it was determinate of the brilliant series of successes that followed.

As Gen. McCLERNAND claims to have arranged and directed the fighting of the battle, he may be accepted as the most competent judge; and he gives conspicuous credit to his subordinate Generals—a matter of detail which BADEAU habitually omits.

Gen. GRANT, however, gave to the whole of McCLERNAND's report of this campaign the following indorsement:

Respectfully forwarded. This report contains so many inaccuracies that to correct it, to make a fair report to be handed down as historical, would require the rewriting of most of it. It is pretentious and egotistical, as is sufficiently shown by my own and all other reports accompanying.

That Gen. GRANT has a severely critical judgment of what a fair report should be, to be handed down as historical, from which all egotism is eliminated, no reader of his matured conclusions in BADEAU's history can question.

For Gen. McCLERNAND, who narrates that he planned the battle, to set down in a public record that it "was one of the most admirably and successfully fought in which it has been my lot to participate," does carry the sound of egotism to the ear. Yet when it is considered that, besides Arkansas Post, which was his own, the only battles in which he had ever participated were those of GRANT, and that at Belmont GRANT had to excuse the affair by the very unfortunate plea of the lack of discipline of the troops he had long trained; that at Donelson McCLERNAND's division was doubled back, and WALLACE's with it, while GRANT was unaccountably absent, and that the only other battle was at Pittsburg Landing, it is found that his comparative ascription is exceedingly moderate.

But in spite of the killing and wounding of 848 brave men, the battle gave new life to the soldiers. Save to the survivors from Donelson, it was their first victory under GRANT. After their dreadful experience in the Slough of Despond it was emancipation. True, it was only a soldier's life still, in a campaign of great hardship, but it was their first taste of a soldier's life for at least six months—and such dreadful months! And the footing which they had now gained opened the way to success by the work of a soldier which every volunteer could see. And none of them doubted the result if led straight on to Vicksburg. No one but their Commanding General was in doubt, and that doubt was now to cause him a severe mental conflict.

CHAPTER XXII.

RETREAT OF THE ENEMY ACROSS THE BIG BLACK RIVER—THE PURSUIT—ENEMY LEAVE GRAND GULF—GRANT'S MENTAL STRUGGLE BETWEEN THE PORT HUDSON PLAN AND A FORWARD MOVEMENT.

In the afternoon of the 2d CROCKER's division, of McPHERSON's corps, had come up, and the bridge was done, and says BADEAU: "GRANT now ordered McPHERSON to 'push across the bayou and attack the enemy in flank, in full retreat through Willow Springs, demoralized, and out of ammunition.'" The way that GRANT's military intuitions could tell McPHERSON in what state to find the enemy is shown further along. He had found telegrams from BOWEN to PEMBERTON stating that "he had been compelled to fall back, his ammunition having become exhausted."

McPHERSON "started at once, and before night his two divisions had crossed the South Fork and marched to the North Fork, eight miles further on" (five and a half miles from Port Gibson). "They found the bridge at Grindstone Ford still burning, but the fire was extinguished and the bridge repaired in the night, the troops passing over as soon as the last plank was laid. This was at 5 a. m. on the 3d. Before one brigade had finished crossing, the enemy opened on the head of the column with artillery, but the command was at once deployed and the rebels soon fell back." And thus it continued all the way to Hankinson's Ferry, on the Big Black River, thirteen miles from Port Gibson, over which Bowen had crossed with all his troops and trains, including those from Grand Gulf.

Bowen had saved his bacon, and had made an orderly retreat from all but the "demoralizing" Badeau. At Willow Springs a road ran west to Grand Gulf, and Logan diverged on this road; but, after marching five miles, he heard that Grand Gulf was abandoned, and he then fetched a turn back into the road of pursuit north. The advance of the pursuit reached the bridge at Hankinson's Ferry at night, in time to save the bridge from the enemy's last men, who were then trying to destroy it. The conversion of this ferry to a bridge had been recent. The manner was told the writer hereof by a Confederate officer, in charge of a company of sharpshooters, who was far in the rear of the retreating column as a sort of rear guard, in the nature of skirmishers.

The two flatboats of the ferry had been placed end to end, and at that stage of the river they just spanned it. Bowen had found this bridge good enough for his artillery and wagons. By subsidence of the river the boats had become jammed between banks. The rear party could not move them, and they would not burn. To scuttle them was vain, as they would not sink, and could be easily patched up. The men cut levers from the woods and were trying to pry the end off. Their guns were stacked in the road, and part were working to dislocate the bridge, and others were washing their feet in the river or otherwise taking things easy, all unconscious of the approach of a party of "Federal" cavalry along the farms on the left bank of the river further down.

The river at the ferry makes a short bend round to northwest. Trees along the narrow bottom on the other side had veiled the coming of the cavalry, and when they emerged from this cover they were in a position to rake the rear of the bridge party, across a river so narrow that two flatboats spanned it. They quickly dismounted behind the trees, came forward, and opened fire.

The bridge party abridged the order of their going, and went at once. A causeway on the north side led from the ferry through a quarter or half a mile of bottom to the upland. This wooded bottom, from recent overflow, was a swamp. Into this cover the Confederates made a precipitate flank movement. From behind trees they returned the fire. Soon another "Federal" party came up the road with two guns, which were whirled about and let drive. This made their cover insufficient. When they emerged from the swamp, out of range, their Confederate gray was converted to the more indigenous butternut. Bowen meanwhile had bivouacked for the night, two miles ahead. Thus did Grant, the child of luck, come in possession of a bridge over the only obstacle on the direct road to Vicksburg.

McPherson's troops rested for the night and following days, from Hankinson's Ferry back to Willow Springs. Badeau relates that by this time Grant perceived that the Confederate "movements since the battle had all been made to cover the escape of the garrison" of Grand Gulf. "Accordingly, on the morning of the 3d Grant started from Willow Springs in person with one brigade of Logan's division, and a cavalry escort of twenty men, for the town." This start, however, was not till after McPherson's "gaining the crossroads" from the retreating enemy, which must have been late in the forenoon, and after Logan had taken that road. "On the way he learned that the rebels had abandoned all the country between the Big Black River and the Bayou Pierre," therefore he kept on with only the cavalry escort.

He "found the naval force in possession." The "cannon had been buried or spiked, while the garrison had begun its retreat at 8 o'clock the evening before." Badeau gives Grant's energetic and minute orders for the dispositions of his army for that night and following. McPherson was to hold the line from Hankinson's back to Willow Springs and beyond. McClernand was to "guard the roads in the rear," to "watch the enemy's movements far down the Bayou Pierre," and to "make a reconnaissance in that direction with one division." This employment of the larger part in guarding and far reconnoitering in the rear, after Grant had "learned that the rebels had already abandoned all the country between Big Black River and Bayou

Pierre," proves that the Holly Springs lesson had not been thrown away on GRANT.

GRANT'S tactics were still on the Port Hudson plan. Says BADEAU:

> Grant's intention was to collect all his forces at Grand Gulf, and get on hand a good supply of provisions and ordnance stores, and in the meantime to detach a corps to co-operate with Banks against Port Hudson, and so effect a junction of their forces.

The change of this plan from a retreat to an advance was to cost GRANT a severe mental conflict, which was even now shadowing him. The issue was the crisis of that campaign and of his military life. He had gained the long desired secondary base for the withdrawal to Port Hudson; shall he continue on that reverse movement or turn and go forward to victory?

He had uttered the Port Hudson plan to HALLECK and LINCOLN as from the ripened experience of his defeated swamp undertakings. He had reiterated the promise that, once at Grand Gulf, he would turn all his mind to "opening the Mississippi River," and would do it by sending a corps to BANKS. He had promised BANKS 20,000 men with such precision of time as would make him plan upon this his operations in his great department. The Port Hudson plan had played a strategical part to stop a gap—that is to say, a yawp of people in the rear. Shall he now abandon all his promises? And what if, having so abandoned, he should fail in the new plan!

On the other hand was the terrible temptation of a retreating enemy. The universal instinct is to pursue the flying. BADEAU says that GRANT'S great tactical rule was to let his "movements be governed by those of the enemy." The spirit of his soldiers had rebounded from the Slough of Despond, and they were eager to go forward. Great generals have said that the high spirit of troops inspires the commander. The indomitable spirit of these volunteers, which not all their dreadful swamp experience could crush, was enough to lift any commander above himself. BADEAU says that GRANT himself "felt the inspiration of success." The novel taste of victory had given him an awakening; like as the pet tiger, brought up from a kitten in the household, unconscious of his nature, experiences an illumination at the accidental taste of living blood.

But while this conflict raged, the forward movement waited from the night of the 3d till the 11th, during which the only movements were for convenience in "living off the country," and as BADEAU says with mysterious strategy, "were in the nature of developments." Meanwhile the Confederacy shook with desire, vastly transcending its ability of performance, to gather forces to crush the invader. Fortunately, living off the country was good; for the impossibility of feeding the army by supplies hauled from Milliken's Bend was already found. GRANT said: "We picked up all the teams in the country, and free Africans to drive them. Forage and meat were found in abundance through the country."

To SHERMAN, who, following in the gleaned part, was concerned for the future, GRANT wrote: "You are in a country where the troops have already lived off the people for some days, and may find provisions more scarce; but as we get upon new soil they are more abundant, particularly in corn and cattle."

The way of running supply boats past the Vicksburg guns had also been found to have too large a discount. The last that is told of this is that on the 30th "orders were issued to the Chief Commissary and Quartermaster of the command to prepare two more tugs to run the blockade, each with two barges in tow, and to load them to their full capacity with rations." BADEAU tells not what became of them. PEMBERTON'S report states that his guns sank two of them. Perhaps the fate of all by the time they had run Warrenton and Grand Gulf was too sad for utterance.

GRANT, at Grand Gulf, issued vigorous orders for the forwarding of supplies from Milliken's Bend. The base was changed from Bruinsburg to Grand Gulf, thus shortening the wagon route on the west side to sixty miles. He also wrote HALLECK, without any mention of future movement. After writing dispatches till midnight, BADEAU says, dramatically: "At midnight of the 3d he turned his back on the Mississippi River, and started for Hankinson's Ferry."

CHAPTER XXIII.

GEN. GRANT'S BATTLE BULLETINS—GENIUS OF BONAPARTE—ARRIVAL OF THE BIOGRAPHER—LIMITATIONS OF THE LAY REVIEWER OF MILITARY OPERATIONS.

From Grand Gulf Gen. GRANT wrote Gen. HALLECK a report of his operations since the 29th of April, giving this view of the battle:

On the following day the whole force with me was transferred to Bruinsburg, * * * and the march immediately commenced for Port Gibson. Gen. McClernand was in the advance with the 13th Army Corps. About 2 a. m. on the 1st of May, when about four miles from Port Gibson, he met the enemy. Some little skirmishing took place, but not to any great extent.

The 13th Corps was followed by Logan's division of McPherson's corps, which reached the scene of action as soon as the last of the 13th Corps was out of the road. The fighting continued all day and until dark, over the most broken country I ever saw. * * * It was impossible to engage any considerable portion of our force at any one time. The enemy were driven from point to point toward Port Gibson, until night closed in, under which it was evident to me they intended to retreat.

The pursuit was continued after dark until the enemy was met again by Logan's division, about two miles from Port Gibson. The nature of the country is such that further pursuit in the dark was not deemed practicable or desirable. On the 2d our troops moved into town without finding any enemy but the wounded.

Gen. GRANT in this does not seem aware that the battle was more than a heavy and protracted skirmish. He puts LOGAN'S whole division into a prominent place, although BADEAU says that only two of LOGAN'S four brigades came up, and only one of these got engaged.

In the matter of giving honor GRANT had this generous conclusion: "Where all have done so well it would be out of place to make invidious distinction."

After he had written this letter he wrote a telegram giving an enlarged view, making the battle general and decided, routing the enemy, and leaving out the circumstance of McCLERNAND's being in the advance. This would be that account which would go to the country:

We landed at Bruinsburg April 30, moved immediately on Port Gibson, met the enemy 11,000 strong four miles south of Port Gibson at 2 a. m., and engaged him all day, entirely routing him, with the loss of many killed, and about 500 prisoners beside the wounded. Our loss about 100 killed and 500 wounded.

The enemy retreated toward Vicksburg, destroying the bridges over the two forks of Bayou Pierre. These were rebuilt and the pursuit continued till the present time. Besides the heavy artillery at this place, four field pieces were captured certain, some stores, and the enemy driven to destroy much more. The country is the most broken and difficult to operate in I ever saw. Our victory has been most complete, and the enemy thoroughly demoralized.

By this ingenious arrangement the great and decisive battle and brilliant victory would go to the country, with the glory of it appropriated by a "We," while the modified battle and undecided result, with McCLERNAND in the advance, would go to HALLECK to fix McCLERNAND's status.

The war bulletin is a standing simile for truthfulness. CÆSAR's "Veni, vidi, vici" is the classic model upon which the finest war bulletins are only an expansion. That master of the art of war, BONAPARTE, was master of the art of war bulletins. Possession of the latter genius is presumptive evidence of possession of BONAPARTE's genius in the other.

In the appendix Gen. GRANT's military historian says he gives copies of all dispatches between GRANT and HALLECK during the entire Vicksburg campaign. This care for the completeness of the record enables the reader to perceive that the information given by the dispatches was of the same high order as that which invented the several plans of this "anomalous campaign."

This care for historical completeness brings next in the order of the record, following GRANT's improved account of the battle of Port Gibson, the following, which, although of but two lines, is greatest in consequences: "Gen. GRANT to Gen. L. THOMAS, Hankinson's Ferry, Miss., May 5, 1863. I have the honor to request that Capt. ADAM BADEAU, A. A. D. C., be ordered to report to me for duty on my staff." A divine poet has emphasized the slenderness of the thread on which future events are suspended. From this dispatch of two lines came the history, in three volumes, which is the authority of this admiring historical review. From this, Capt. ADAM BADEAU grew to be Gen. BADEAU. From a line of soft places in the army he evolved to the post of Consul General at London, which is held to be the softest place abroad in the gift of the government.

This soft seat, in the course of twelve years, enabled him to finish in elegant leisure his second and third volumes, and to have them duly revised by their illustrious hero. From thence he was transferred to the light and genteel occupation of Minister to Copenhagen. Thus does the great republic give the lie to the tradition of the old world despotisms, that an autocratic government, with pensions in its unlimited hands, is essential to the encouragement of literature.

Capt. ADAM BADEAU, A. A. D. C., was not a West Pointer—to use the military idiom—but his constant perception of the immeasurable difference between a volunteer and a West Pointer makes him almost one. Besides, his confidential relation to Gen. GRANT, on his staff, enriching his mind to write his military life, sharing, as it were, his bed and board—board, a dry metaphor—hearing from his own lips the maxims of the art of war, must have been a better military education than the mere rudiments taught at West Point.

The tradition holds that ADAM BADEAU had served a term in the noble profession of journalism, and that he acquired his facility in that elevated and impartial style which treats alike the most commonplace doings and the brightest achievements of his hero with the same superlative ascription, from practice in a rural journal, in the composition of descriptions of interesting natural and abnormal productions—mammoth squashes, cabbage heads of uncommon development, dreadful accidents, multitudinous births, misbegotten monsters, testimonial gifts of garden sauce (pro. sass) to the editor, fat lambs, majestic rams, prize bulls, swine who have carried to the ultimate the self-culture which is only the working of Nature's great law of the survival of the fittest, which develops alike the best pork of commerce and the greatest Generals.

The same tradition holds that his reverse style of stricture toward all of Gen. GRANT's subaltern Generals came also from the journalistic habit of critical animadversion upon the negative virtues of the contemporary editor over the way. Whether this tradition was fetched through the method of the scientific and theological people, to reason from effect back to cause, or whether it is strictly biographical, can not be material, as the result is the same; and this result is a work of great service to the student of the art of war in its highest reaches.

The military art hath the peculiar property that it is most abstruse and technical in the elementary parts, as the school of the soldier, the section, platoon, company, and so on, and grows more simple—or rather more in the line of general knowledge and general aptitude—in the higher branches of grand tactics and strategy. Thus one may be scholar, scientist, statesman, or editor of a daily journal, and yet not know how to do or command the facings, the manual of arms, the loading by twelve commands; how to give the commands to form line into column and column into line; how to give the orders or do the genuflections of that most abstruse part of a military training, the dress parade.

But the practice of the higher branches, the tactics by which battles are fought, or the strategy which plans campaigns, embracing the whole theater of war, is set forth by generals and historians to the understanding of the common mind. This draws the line between the military things, which the "lay" reader or commentator may understand, and the military things which are understood only by those technically educated.

Even ADAM BADEAU, who keeps to the view the impassable gulf between officers who were educated at the institute, and officers who were not, recognizes that the popular mind can comprehend the doings of stupendous strategy and grand tactics which he recounts of Gen. GRANT. When the military biographer himself sets forth exercises of the highest parts of military science for the admiration of the common people, it can not be presumptuous in the common mind to appreciate them. Thus doth the reviewer modestly, but firmly, assert his office.

CHAPTER XXIV.

GRANT, AFTER A LONG MENTAL STRUGGLE, DETERMINES TO ABANDON HIS PORT HUDSON PLAN AND TURN AGAINST VICKSBURG—THE DEBATE—BRACING TELEGRAM FROM SECRETARY STANTON—PRIVATIONS OF THE COMMANDING GENERAL.

With Grand Gulf in Gen. GRANT's possession, the way now lay open before him to carry out his Port Hudson plan. The impregnable rear intrenchments which he found would enable him to hold against the enemy from Vicksburg, while waiting with part of his army besieged, for the Port Hudson part to go, view, conquer, and return, fetching the deliverer BANKS with it.

Nothing was now needed to put this plan on the high road to success but the invention of some means of supplying the army, the finding of some means to get the 20,000 men to Port Hudson, and to get them back again, and a few other details. For there were not means to transport them by the river, and if 20,000 men were to start to march that distance in the enemy's country, they would hardly get there, and it was as unlikely that BANKS could fetch his troops up to Vicksburg. This clear way, and Gen. GRANT's long attachment to the Port Hudson plan, which was the cherished child of his own brains, made him very loth to give it up.

Besides, one more new plan might be the last feather to break the back of the long suffering confidence of HALLECK, LINCOLN, and STANTON. A fortunate decision seems to make much argument unnecessary; but BADEAU, out of his abundance, gives much argument against the Port Hudson plan. Most of the reasons are of the impracticability of the plan, which were as obvious as at Milliken's Bend as now, but which he represents GRANT as unaware of till he reached Grand Gulf by the rear. In this it is likely that BADEAU does GRANT but scant justice; for the military necessity to get away from Vicksburg by some way that should seem for the time to go forward, could not allow GRANT to consider any impossible things that were several weeks off.

BADEAU classes the reasons against the Port Hudson plan as the negative, the reasons for going toward Vicksburg as the positive, and he has such a wealth of negative reasons that he omits the small ones, to wit: that GRANT had not means to feed his army; nor to keep the part left at Grand Gulf from being cut off from its supplies, nor to get 20,000 men to Port Hudson without capture, or to get them back again. Among his negative reasons he gives the following two as especially decisive in effect:

First, "GRANT was now fifteen miles [in fact ten] on the road from Grand Gulf either to Jackson, Black River bridge, or Vicksburg. He could not afford to delay, much less to retrace his steps."

GRANT had not yet learned patience by delay; yet no one asked him to delay the march on Port Hudson. But Nature's strict economy ceases to nourish those parts which are disused. After Gen. GRANT had constantly exercised his army in the movements of the Holly Springs campaign, the Lake Providence, Chickasaw Bayou, and Steele's Bayou operations, and in a march of seventy miles to get away from Vicksburg—ever, like poor Joe in Bleak House, moving on—it had lost the use of the step retracing muscles.

Second, he had at this "crisis" (mental) received a letter from BANKS, stating that he could not be at Port Hudson before the 10th.

GRANT answered this letter on the 10th, showing that he could not have received it earlier than the 9th. Inasmuch as GRANT could not get 20,000 men to Port Hudson in less than a fortnight, if at all, it appears quite remarkable that in BADEAU's subsequent view, indorsed by GRANT, it was BANKS' inability to be there before the 10th that made GRANT resolve to turn his back on BANKS.

This also helps to find the time when this mental conflict determined. GRANT wrote BANKS, May 10, the following apology, in which, however, he said nothing of BANKS' being behind time:

It was my intention on gaining a foothold at Grand Gulf to have sent a sufficient force to Port Hudson to have insured the fall of that place, with your co-operation, or rather to have co-operated with you to secure that end.

Meeting the enemy as I did, however, I followed him to the Big Black, and could not afford to retrace my steps. I also learned, and believe the information to be reliable, that Port Hudson is almost entirely evacuated. This may not be true, but it is the concurrent testimony of deserters and contrabands. Many days can not elapse before the battle will begin which is to decide the fate of Vicksburg, but it is impossible to predict how long it may last. I would urgently request, therefore, that you join me, or send all the force you can spare, to co-operate in the great struggle for opening the Mississippi River.

The great playwright has given touching expression to Sir John Falstaff's knightly chagrin when he had sent Bardolph to the mercer for a new suit of satin bravery, with his own and Bardolph's names, and the mercenary dealer had sent back a request for better security:

I had as lief they would put ratsbane in my mouth as offer to stop it with security. I looked a' should have sent me two and twenty yards of satin, as I am a true knight, and he sends me security!

Alike rueful must have been the feelings of Gen. Banks, who, for more than six weeks, had been imminently promised 20,000 men by Gen. Grant, when in answer to a letter announcing his readiness for the co-operation he received this request to drop Louisiana and the Mississippi and fetch all his forces to Grant, "to co-operate in the great struggle for opening the Mississippi River."

During the time in which Grant had been engaged in his Port Hudson plan, and had been promising 20,000 men immediately to Gen. Banks, he had been enjoying an active experience. His force was 30,000 men when he took command, December 11, 1862, and he was assured of the co-operation of Grant at Vicksburg. The Confederates thought Louisiana our weak spot, and were active in West Louisiana and Texas, favored by a country which was almost inaccessible. To hold New Orleans, with its many protecting forts and approaches, required the larger part of his corps, so that his movable force was less than 14,000 men, while the Confederate force at Port Hudson was 18,000. Leaving the fort to the future, he had taken the field in the Atchafalaya country with considerable success. But he was recalled by an urgent call from Admiral Farragut to send a force to co-operate in recovering command of the river above Port Hudson.

This had been lost by the activity of some rebel gunboats, which sallied out from branch rivers and bayous, and which had captured the ram Queen of the West, and the gunboat De Soto, from Grant's navy. The Admiral declared it necessary to run the Port Hudson batteries, now very formidable, and Banks sent his troops to the rear to co-operate. The naval operation was costly.* The frigates Hartford, Mississippi, Richmond, and Monongahela, and the seagoing gunboats Albatross, Genesee, Kineo, Essex, and Sachem made the attempt. The Mississippi, the largest ship, was lost. The Hartford and Albatross got by. The rest dropped back variously hurt. And now Banks took the field again in West Louisiana, in co-operation with the navy, for which he was blamed by Halleck in his annual report, who thought that with his 14,000 men he should have besieged the fort—ascertained positively, afterward, to have had 16,000 men.

Aided by some light draught gunboats, which had now come from Porter's fleet, he followed Gen. Dick Taylor to the Atchafalaya, opened up that to the Red River, captured Alexandria and Fort De Russy, seized two rebel steamers, and destroyed eight, and three gunboats. These operations were accomplished by May 9, and now Gen. Banks was ready to co-operate with the 20,000 men promised by Grant to capture Port Hudson and open the Mississippi River. And now, May 12, he received Grant's letter of the 10th that, having succeeded at Grand Gulf, he could not send him the long promised army corps; but applying an emollient to his disappointment by asking him to come with all his force and join him in the great operation to open the Mississippi River.

In the military operations that are read of, when the two armies join issue, it is expected that the verdict will soon come. But Gen. Grant informs Banks that "many days can not elapse before the battle will begin which is to decide the fate of Vicksburg, but it is impossible to predict how long it may last;" as if it might be like freedom's battle, which, once begun, is bequeathed from bleeding sire to son.

To make the way entirely clear to Banks, Grant gave him the valuable information that Port Hudson was evacuated. Subsequently Banks found it sufficiently defended to resist an assault. Had Banks started on this chase he would have given up Louisiana and the Lower Mississippi to the Confederates. He had no means to transport his troops by the river, and the march by land would have been a march into captivity.

So much for the negative reasons. But Badeau says "the positive ones were of greater force, as they always were with this commander." He "had won a victory"—an unwonted sensation; "had gained a foothold on the high land and on the east bank that he had been five months striving to obtain;" "his troops were encouraged, and the enemy demoralized;" he "felt the inspiration of success;" "it was his nature in war always to prefer the immediate aggressive;" so "he determined that night to detach no force against Banks, but to begin operations against Vicksburg." He wrote this to Banks, dated the 10th. And now BADEAU says the matter was determined; but even after this the movements seemed tentative. BADEAU says they "were in the nature of developments."

Having finally cast off his Port Hudson plan, according to BADEAU, as the snake emancipates himself from his own skin, and determined to begin operations against Vicksburg, the next thing was to plan the operations. In this does BADEAU take the reader into the highest reaches of strategy, which will come in the next chapter. But before passing too far the order of events, the record should be brought up by giving the following dispatch, which honors Secretary STANTON's head and heart and other viscera, and which proves that the Assistant Secretary of War's impressions at GRANT's luxurious headquarters on one of the largest steamers of the chartered fleet, illuminated by the generous hospitalities of his staff and circle of Generals, had been duly transmitted to his chief:

Hon. E. M. Stanton to C. A. Dana, Esq.—(Cipher Telegram.)

WASHINGTON, D. C., May 6, 1863.

Gen. Grant has full and absolute authority to enforce his own commands, and to remove any person who by ignorance in action or any cause interferes with or delays his operations. He has the full confidence of the government, is expected to enforce his authority, and will be firmly and heartily supported, but he will be responsible for any failure to exert his powers. You may communicate this to him.

The authority was plenary, but the time inopportune; for the removal of McCLERNAND would reach the people on the heels of news of a victory in which he thought he commanded. But this was now only a question of opportunity, and the Port Gibson victory made it imperative.

Personal incidents in the lives of great men are those which oftenest remind us that we may make our lives sublime. BADEAU gives only its due prominence to an instance of Gen. GRANT's submission to privation in this "anomalous campaign."

He narrates that "while lying at Hankinson's Ferry the horses and personal luggage [he means baggage] of Gen. GRANT and his staff arrived at headquarters. Up to this time he and his officers had messed with any General near whose camp they happened to halt, riding borrowed horses [borrowed, a military term], and sleeping in the porches of the houses on the road. When he left Hard Times GRANT took no baggage [he means luggage] with him but a toothbrush."

This picture of GRANT's privation has elicited much admiration. A commanding General with no luggage (or baggage) but a toothbrush, and messing around on other officers! To avoid unwholesome thinking, BADEAU mentions the important fact that he borrowed a shirt of the navy at Grand Gulf. Yet each common soldier had his knapsack with all his luggage and baggage, which, like the immortal JOHN BROWN, he carried strapped upon his back as he went marching on; also his faithful companions, the musket, bayonet, and cartridge box with forty plump cartridges; likewise his haversack with three days' rations, which he was "ordered to make last five;" and although the weather was hot, yet so luxuriously were they provided that each carried on his shoulder an army blanket.

They had all this baggage and luggage with them wherever they went, in their marching by night and fighting by day, and when they slept, which was not cramped by the "galleries" of planters' houses, but was under heaven's broad canopy. So luxuriously were the common volunteer soldiers cared for, while their Commanding General, who had left luxury's lap to serve his country on the pay of a mere Major General, took no baggage (or luggage) with him but a "toothbrush," and had no place to lay his head save in the houses borrowed of the planters by the wayside.

CHAPTER XXV.

THE CAMPAIGN ARRIVES AT THE STAGE OF BRILLIANT STRATEGICAL OPERATIONS—THE DIRECT LINE TO VICKSBURG AND THE STRATEGICAL LINE—REASONS FOR THE LATTER—THE STRATEGICAL MARCH AWAY FROM THE ENEMY.

This history has now reached that stage of the Vicksburg campaign in which the strategy and operations raised Gen. GRANT's military fame to its zenith, and made him thenceforward the sun of our great army, round which all other Generals must revolve, and, in effect, the military dictator for the rest of the war.

Up to this point a degree of monotony was unavoidable in this history. Achievement is essential to make the story of a campaign interesting. ADAM BADEAU remarks that all of Gen. GRANT'S swamp operations were fruitless, save in their educating the Commanding General, and hardening and inspiring the troops. Education, although necessary, is not thrilling in narrative; but the campaign has now come to a stage of thrilling interest, in which a great opportunity, thrown in the Commanding General's way without his intention, inspired him to a series of operations which Gen. HALLECK, instructed by GRANT'S bulletins, and BADEAU, instructed by GRANT'S matured reflections, likened to the most brilliant, short, sharp, and decisive of BONAPARTE'S campaigns.

A distinct idea of the field of operations is essential to the understanding of the strategic movements now to be made. Attention to a few points of outline will enable the reader to carry it in mind as well as if he had the map before him. Hankinson's Ferry, now a bridge, on the Big Black River, was GRANT'S point of departure, and had been the place from which he dated as his headquarters since the 3d.

From Hankinson's Ferry due north, over the upland, to Vicksburg is fifteen miles. From Vicksburg due east to Jackson, to which was a railroad, is forty miles. From Hankinson's Ferry east-northeast to Jackson is forty-five miles. This boundary incloses the whole field of Grant's and Pemberton's operations. The outline is that of a long right angle triangle, the perpendicular side being from Hankinson's to Vicksburg, the base side from Vicksburg to Jackson, the hypotenuse from Jackson to the ferry; or say like a wedge, supposing the slant to be all on one side, the butt being at the ferry and Vicksburg, and the straight side from Vicksburg to Jackson. The following diagram gives the shape and proportion of the field of operations:

THEATER OF THE WAR.

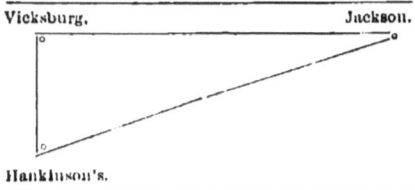

This is the theater of the war. The main natural feature crossing it is Big Black River, which, coming down southwest, crosses the railroad ten miles east of Vicksburg, and on down to Hankinson's Ferry, and to the Mississippi at Grand Gulf. Five miles east of Big Black, on the Vicksburg & Jackson Railroad, is Edwards' Station, soon to be historical. About seven and a half miles east of this is Champion Hill, soon to be called by the soldiers "the hill of death;" a little way east of this, Bolton Station; then, nearly nine miles east, Clinton; from there to Jackson is about nine miles. On diverging and converging roads from Hankinson's to Jackson, along the hypotenuse, are Rocky Springs, Utica, Cayuga, Auburn, New Auburn, Raymond, and Mississippi Springs. The diagram is on the direct lines. The actual distance from Vicksburg to Jackson by the railroad is forty-four miles; from Hankinson's Ferry to Jackson by the common roads near fifty miles. From Hankinson's to Vicksburg, or to the railroad in the rear of Vicksburg, there need not be more than a mile or two variation from the direct line of fifteen miles.

GRANT'S immediate base is at Hankinson's Ferry. His objective is PEMBERTON'S army, covering Vicksburg, its line of communication being the railroad to Jackson. A march of fifteen miles from Hankinson's Ferry would bring GRANT'S army upon this railroad, and compel PEMBERTON to come out to fight a battle for his communications or be shut up in Vicksburg without an effort. BADEAU says GRANT estimated PEMBERTON'S force at 30,000. GRANT was not subject to the military fault of underrating the number opposed to him. At Pittsburg Landing he sent word to BUELL that he was attacked by 100,000 men.

Of this estimated 30,000 GRANT reported that he had engaged 11,000 at Port Gibson, and had "entirely routed" and "thoroughly demoralized" them. The route direct to Vicksburg from Hankinson's had the line of bluff on the one hand, which, with the wet bottoms beyond, formed a rampart for the left flank and rear, all the way to Vicksburg. On the other hand, the Big Black River offered a natural intrenchment for the right flank and rear, all the way. The route would be over a rolling country of plantations and roads, and with no serious natural obstacles.

The route taking Warrenton by the rear, the Confederates would have to depart therefrom as soon as the march began. At Warrenton GRANT would strike the river a little way below the lower end of his canal across the tongue of land opposite Vicksburg, whereby the wagoning of his supplies from Milliken's Bend and Young's Point would be reduced to three miles, by a road now practicable. Thus a march of ten miles to Warrenton would fetch him back to his base of supplies and re-enforcements. This would relieve all the troops that were guarding the land route of sixty miles, round by way of Richmond to Hard Times, and would add these to his fighting force.

The defeat of PEMBERTON in a pitched battle, while covering Vicksburg, might be expected to carry with it the immediate fall of the place, without the dreadful labor and consuming of the army by a siege. Then GRANT could turn his army east, scatter the ineffectual force at Jackson, and make that his base of operations. Gen. J. E. JOHNSTON'S narrative shows that he expected GRANT to do this, and he said that GRANT'S occupation of Jackson was the loss of the State of Mississippi. It appears that at first GRANT contemplated the direct line; for he wrote SHERMAN, then at Grand Gulf, May 7: "If BLAIR was now up I believe we could be in Vicksburg in seven days." BLAIR had only two brigades, and was on the way from Milliken's Bend.

To march, however, from Hankinson's Ferry, fifteen miles, upon the communications of PEMBERTON'S army, covering Vicksburg, and decide the fate of the Confederate army and of Vicksburg in one battle, would be so direct and obvious that it could hardly be called anything higher than a grand tactical movement. It is what any General would do if he thought he could beat the opposing army. And in general, when a commander enters on an invading campaign, he thinks he can beat the enemy's army.

It is such a direct and obvious movement as BONAPARTE would have made, or FREDERIC the Great, but it would not be strategic in the highest degree. But to depart from a direct line of fifteen miles, and to march fifty miles to Jackson, lengthening it by zigzag marches to seventy, and then back, leaving the enemy covering Vicksburg—this is high strategy.

This is that which raised Gen. GRANT'S military fame to its zenith. In explaining this strategy, BADEAU takes the common mind into the uppermost realms of the military art. The general and overruling reason was in GRANT'S nature, as he has before stated: "It was his nature in war always to prefer the immediate aggressive." Therefore he went to Jackson and back, when the enemy was in his immediate front. But BADEAU has also an abundance of particular reasons.

BADEAU concedes the apparent advantages of the direct or tactical line, but he mentions a serious obstacle: "Apparently GRANT'S most natural course was to march direct upon Vicksburg, and at once begin the siege, or at least attack its garrison, should that come out to meet him. He was not more than twelve [ten] miles from Warrenton, and had only one formidable obstacle to encounter, the Big Black River, the line of which would probably be taken by any enemy opposing him."

The adage celebrates the short memories of truthful historians. After ADAM BADEAU has had GRANT for several days in possession of the crossing of the Big Black River, and after McPHERSON, on the 4th, had made a reconnaissance north along the west side of the Big Black, to within six miles of Vicksburg, and had found no enemy, he restores the Confederate army to the Big Black River, in front of GRANT, as a "formidable natural obstacle" which GRANT would have to encounter with the Confederate army holding it, if he went by the direct road.

The statement of this reason by ADAM BADEAU, approved by GRANT, is an indication of the abundance of reasons GRANT had for leaving a direct way of fifteen miles, and going around 150 miles to avoid the enemy at Vicksburg. The other reason is that Gen. GREGG was "collecting another force toward the east and north, of whose strength GRANT was not well informed." Therefore he resolved to go east "to drive eastward the weaker one" before the two could unite. Then he would seize Jackson, destroy the railroads there, and thus would have "Vicksburg and its garrison isolated from the would be Confederacy."

That no force arrived at Jackson or on the east till the 10th only distinguishes GRANT'S foresight in making the immediate objective of his plan a re-enforcement which might come on the east if he waited for it. That the Confederate forces at Vicksburg and Jackson, having the inner line, could unite by moving half the distance which GRANT marched to prevent them, might be a consideration in war as practiced in the old world;

but ADAM BADEAU says that GRANT's military methods were original; that "His mind, indeed, was never much inclined to follow precedents, or to set store by rules; he was not apt to study the means by which other men had succeeded; he seldom discussed the campaigns of great commanders in European wars, and was utterly indifferent to precept or example whenever these seemed to him inapplicable." And if he was "not apt to study" these, they were always inapplicable.

Therefore did GRANT determine to leave PEMBERTON on his flank, and to leave to him the inner line, while he himself went to Jackson to see if any troops were there, and to drive them eastward, then to return and gain a new base. The time when he determined upon this strategy is movable, like the time when he gave up the Port Hudson plan, beginning with midnight of the 3d, and reviving on the 10th, and renewed again on the 13th. And if it shall appear that the plan was constructed after the event, and that the movements followed GRANT's great principle of not fettering himself by any plan, "always expecting to be governed by the emergencies that were sure to arise," is it any the less exalting to his genius?

Can there be any higher effect of genius than to have "built wiser than you knew?" It shows an intuition transcending your own comprehension. If this be not genius, what is it? One need not have read Capt. Toby Shandy's narrative of his experience at the siege of Namur to find that history of battles by those who fought them is a progress of evolution. The poet or orator often has ideas above his comprehension. Gen. GRANT, with intuitional inspiration, may have made the several operations of this "anomalous campaign," "governed by emergencies that were sure to arise," and following his great role of letting his movements be governed by those of the enemy.

But when, in subsequent years, after the halo of developing narrative had gathered about these events, ADAM BADEAU wove them all into the web of a great strategical plan, is it not natural that Gen. GRANT should presume that this was what he designed from the beginning?

The great strategical movement upon PEMBERTON's army and Vicksburg, fifteen miles to the front, by a march away to Jackson, is about to begin.

CHAPTER XXVI.

GRANT ALONE—THE WHOLE WORLD OPPOSES HIS PLAN—LIKE ATLAS, HE STANDS UNMOVED—CUTTING HIS BASE—THE MARCH AWAY FROM THE ENEMY.

War history is prone to be tainted by the injustice of crediting secondary Generals with successes which were organized by the Commanding General's mind. Happily this history is free from such fault; for ADAM BADEAU narrates that the strategy of the operation against PEMBERTON at Vicksburg, by marching away to Jackson, was GRANT's alone, and was entered upon contrary to the views of all his general officers, and contrary to Gen. HALLECK's orders. There is great pathos in BADEAU's description of Gen. GRANT's lonely state, at this crisis, bearing all the weight of his plan:

So Grant was alone; his most trusted subordinates besought him to change his plans, while his superiors were astounded at his temerity and strove to interfere. Soldiers of reputation and civilians in high places condemned in advance a campaign that seemed to them as hopeless as it was unprecedented. If he failed, the country would concur with the government and the Generals. Grant knew all this and appreciated his danger, but was as invulnerable to the apprehensions of ambition as to the entreaties of friendship or the anxieties even of patriotism.

The way in which he came to be thus alone, bearing like Atlas this dreadful load, is, first, by means of a dissolving view, in which the Port Hudson plan melts into the Vicksburg plan, and the objections of SHERMAN and other military men and civilians to that are brought forward and hitched to this; second, by ingeniously extinguishing time and space, so as to fetch forward one of HALLECK's dispatches co-operative to the Port Hudson plan, and fitting it to the Vicksburg plan, and calling it a countermand. "And so GRANT was alone!" But he who could steal from GRANT the credit of the hypot cause and right angle plan of the campaign of 150 miles against PEMBERTON and Vicksburg, fifteen miles in front, is a more contemptible wretch than he who steals the golden trash which is slave to every holder.

So shadowy was left the military possession of the country north to the Ohio by GRANT's operations to open the Mississippi, that tele grams had to be sent round by Grand Gulf and the wagon route of supplies by way of Richmond to Milliken's Bend, and thence by convoyed steamboat to Cairo, to reach the telegraph. Therefore, while GRANT was vacillating between his Port Hudson plan of retreat and his opportunity to advance, HALLECK, in ignorance, was sending bracing co-operative dispatches to him and BANKS. ADAM BADEAU fetches forward one of these, which was faithful to GRANT'S Port Hudson plan, in ignorance of any other, and evolves it into a countermand of his Vicksburg plan, and thereby achieves his lonely pathos.

ADAM BADEAU views GRANT's plan of operation against PEMBERTON at Vicksburg, by the line of the hypotenuse to Jackson, and the base line back to Vicksburg, as the one that "presented the most absolute and splendid advantages; but it also presented difficulties and dangers sufficient to deter any but the most confident of commanders. To undertake it GRANT must not only advance between two armies, either of which was a formidable opponent" (one of these armies was GREGG'S, who by the 10th had a brigade), "and run the risk of their combining to crush him; but, more daring still, he would expose his only line of communication with the Mississippi to attacks from PEMBERTON. If he attempted to guard that line, he must weaken his moving column, so that it would be unsafe to cope with GREGG, now daily expecting re-enforcements from the South and East."

The General whose strategy leads him from the enemy's main army in his front to a flank march fifty miles away does appear to expose his communications, likewise his rear. Therefore, says ADAM BADEAU: "He at once decided to abandon his base altogether, to plunge into the enemy's country with three days' rations, trusting to the region itself for forage and supplies, and to the chances of victory to enable him to regain some point on the Mississippi, in spite of all the opposition of two hostile armies. * * * The utmost celerity of movement was indispensable not only to his success, but to his salvation."

That the General who marches 150 miles to fetch round to the objective fifteen miles in his front, needs celerity, seems undeniable; that when he marches fifty miles away from his base, and leaves the enemy's main army within fifteen miles of it, he exposes his communications, seems equally plain; and each enhances the wonderful strategy. But the words of the argument just quoted convey that GRANT'S design at this time was simply a raid, to destroy railroads and stores, and "to regain some point on the Mississippi in spite of all the opposition of two hostile armies." This may explain some of the enigmatical movements in "this anomalous campaign."

Gen. GRANT's act of cutting loose from his base of supplies is that which gave the charm of romance to this campaign, as it did to Gen. SHERMAN'S march to the sea. In each the achievement of marching away from a base of supplies was so dazzling as to eclipse the homely fact that it was a march away from the enemy. But the just measure of glory has not been given to Gen. GRANT's cutting away from his base of supplies, not even by ADAM BADEAU. This is because of the misconception that GRANT's base of supplies was at Grand Gulf.

If to cut his base to go fifty miles to Jackson, to operate on PEMBERTON at Vicksburg, was a brilliant achievement, then the greater brilliancy of cutting his base at Milliken's Bend, sixty miles further away, can be exactly calculated. At that place is where Gen. GRANT cut his base of supplies when he started on his Port Hudson plan. He expected to carry his base along by the canal and bayou navigation, but this had sunk away. He cut no base of supplies at Grand Gulf; for he took all he could get, and waited from the 3d to the 10th for more. He took all the teams with him that he could get up by that time, and was followed subsequently by a train of 200 wagons more. At Milliken's Bend was where the romantic feat of cutting loose from the base was performed, and the romantic objective of it was the retreat to Port Hudson.

On the 6th of May Gen. GRANT dispatched to HALLECK: "Ferrying land transportation (teams) and rations to Grand Gulf is detaining me on the Black River. I will move as soon as three days' rations are secured, and send the wagons back to Grand Gulf for more." While the main army was marching to the front, an army in the rear and a fleet of transports were hurrying forward supplies; yet now six days after the landing at Bruinsburg, and ten days after reaching Hard Times, GRANT'S troops, although spread out to "live off the country," had not three days' rations ahead.

In the same dispatch he said: "Information from the other side leads me to believe the enemy are bringing forces from Tullahoma. Should not ROSECRANS at least make a demonstration of advancing?" It appears, by Gen. J. E. JOHNSTON's report, that he and Gen. BRAGG agreed in the opinion that, in the then attitude of ROSECRANS, no forces could be taken from BRAGG without losing Tennessee; therefore, that ROSECRANS was rendering very effective co-operation to GRANT, while his waiting gave time enough to fetch BRAGG's forces against him, if they had been free.

The great movement of celerity is about to begin, but has not yet begun. For some mysterious reason there is hesitancy. Says ADAM BADEAU: "On the 6th GRANT ordered McPHERSON: 'Move one of your divisions to Rocky Springs to-morrow, leaving the others to occupy from your present headquarters to the ferry. On the approach of SHERMAN's advance order up the second.'" "Accordingly at 10 a. m. on the 7th" LOGAN's division moved, and was followed by CROCKER's to Rocky Springs, five miles east of Hankinson Ferry, "where they remained in camp till the 9th. On the 8th GRANT's headquarters were removed to Rocky Springs."

SHERMAN's corps had reached Hankinson's on the 8th, having that morning drawn three days' rations at Grand Gulf. Says BADEAU: "This day GRANT announced to HALLECK, 'Our advance is fifteen miles from Edward's Station, on Southern Railroad. All looks well.'" Edward's Station is on the Vicksburg & Jackson Railroad, and appears by the map to be twenty miles northeast of Rocky Springs. BADEAU says in a foot note: "This estimate was incorrect. Rocky Springs is full twenty-five miles from Edward's Station." But the statement served well enough for the time, and gave to HALLECK the idea of a vigorous forward movement, while GRANT was waiting for something. To discredit GRANT's statements that were good for the time seems reprehensible in ADAM BADEAU.

At this interesting point BADEAU has one of the most miscellaneous of the miscellaneous turns which regularly occur when the plan becomes involved, and when the reader's mind, strained by intense pursuit of the narrative, requires diverting. Inasmuch as when he resumes, a change of GRANT's plan has to be told and explained, and as a history of all this, up to the next change of plan, would make this chapter too long, the opportunity is taken to end the chapter here, rather than have to do it in the middle of a thrilling stroke of strategy.

CHAPTER XXVII.

BADEAU'S HARMONIOUS ASCRIPTIONS—A CRISIS IN THE STRATEGY BEFORE IT HAS MOVED—WAITING FOR RATIONS AND CEREBRAL DEVELOPMENTS.

All through Capt. ADAM BADEAU's three valuable volumns run little alternating strains, as if on parallel cleffs of the music staff, complementing each other like the parts of a vocal duet. And as in the operatic duet the parts may seem to be disputing and challenging to mortal combat, yet they harmoniously blend, so ADAM BADEAU's strains may seem contradictory, yet they are one in the harmonious end.

For example, one strain celebrates Gen. GRANT's farsighted sagacity, which discerns the end from the beginning, and shapes every particular and detail to that end; the complementing strain sings that he did never fetter himself with precise plans, but "always expected to be governed by the emergencies that were sure to arise"—the principle which was the guiding star of the life of the distinguished Wilkins Micawber.

Again, one strain celebrates the minuteness of Gen. GRANT's military mind, and tells how he gave orders not only to commanders of corps, but to their subordinates, the commanders of divisions, brigades, and regiments, also the quartermasters, commissaries, and wagon masters, how detailed and minute these orders were, reaching to the most rudimentary parts, as well as to grand tactics, such as directing a Major General, in moving upon the enemy, to put his wagon train in the rear rather than in front; the blending strain sings that "GRANT never gave express orders in advance; it was his custom always to await the contingencies of a campaign;" "he contented himself beforehand with giving orders for the earliest movements," leaving the rest to be "governed by the movements of the enemy."

In one strain Gen. GRANT so orders every part in general and detail, and his commanding "in person" so directs and pervades every division, brigade, and regiment that each succesful part is his own, and each part that is not successful is the blunder of a subordinate; in the counterpart he simply "indicates the great features of a campaign," or "the principal object of a battle," and leaves to each commander to choose his order of movement.

In one strain, "it was his nature in war, always to prefer the immediate aggressive;" "his strategy was always that of bringing to bear upon a certain point all the force he could command; he did not necessarily select the weakest point, but rather that which was vital, and, therefore, likely to be best defended; but he threw his entire strength upon this point, and repeated the blows until all was ended;" in the contralto part he surpasses all the great masters of the art of war by the surprising strategy of marching away from the enemy in his front, to hunt for future problematical detachments.

In one strain GRANT's rule of war is to disregard places, in order to make the destruction of armies his objective; in the counter strain his greatest strategical and tactical achievements are in so directing his line of operations as to fetch the opposing army into its strongest fortified places.

These are but examples of a long succession of these harmonious strains. To the unwonted reader they sound inconsistent. So, to the uncultured, WAGNER's overtures are discordant, while to the cultured ear they are wonderful harmonies. In like manner he who is attuned to ADAM BADEAU's consistency will have ceased to be perceptive of contradiction.

When ADAM BADEAU resumed the thread of his narrative, after the very miscellaneous turn at the end of the last chapter, a crisis had changed the complexion of GRANT's strategy. He relates that: "At Rocky Springs GRANT heard that the rebels were fortifying and concentrating at Edward's Station, about twenty-five miles off, on the Vicksburg & Jackson Railroad." What was a General to do in such a crisis? BADEAU tells what GRANT did. First "he determined to change the relative positions of two of the corps." McCLERNAND, on the right, was shifted over to the left, next the Big Black River; McPHERSON, on the left, was shifted over to the right; SHERMAN still in the center.

If the reader pays not strict attention he will lose his mental grip on one of the finest pieces of strategy in "this anomalous campaign." Continues BADEAU: "It was his intention now to hug the Big Black River as closely as possible with McCLERNAND's and SHERMAN's corps, and strike the railroad with them beyond Edward's Station, somewhere between that place and Bolton, forty or fifty miles from Hankinson's Ferry. Meanwhile McPHERSON was to move by way of Utica to Raymond, thirty-five miles from the ferry, and thence into Jackson, twenty miles further, destroying the railroad, telegraph, and public stores there; he was then to push west and rejoin the main force."

The ingenuity of this strategy, like the moral of Capt. John Bunsby's observations, will appear in the application of it, thus: "By these dispositions GRANT would avoid a battle with the main rebel army on the ground selected by PEMBERTON, * * * while at the same time he divided the enemy, interposing between PEMBERTON and the rebel forces at Jackson." Thus does Gen. GRANT's historian lay bare the most abstruse parts of the art of strategy, so that the common mind can understandingly admire.

Nothing can be plainer or more admirable. GRANT, at Rocky Springs, deciding it unwise to attack the enemy where he is concentrated and fortified, at Edward's Station, in his front, moves McPHERSON away by the flank in front of the enemy, to Jackson, and divides his army, from the Big Black River to Jackson, a distance of forty miles, in front of the enemy's center and strong position at Edward's Station, in order to "divide the enemy." Surely, according to ADAM BADEAU, the nation owes a statue to PEMBERTON.

And now it appears that all this enlightenment, and all this plan, came to GRANT after he moved to Rocky Springs, and heard there that PEMBERTON was fortifying and concentrating at Edward's Station, and that till now he had been following his great rule of fettering himself by no plan, but expecting to be "governed by the contingencies that were sure to" turn up. And even now he told no one of his new plan. BADEAU says he did not tell McCLERNAND, because he "feared to trust him with an independent expedition, which the movement against Jackson seemed likely to prove, and, therefore, put him on the left."

Nor did he tell SHERMAN and McPHERSON,

though BADEAU says that somehow they understood it; "the latter, especially, was aware that, if possible, he was to push on toward Jackson, though not without express orders." And it appears that GRANT did not tell himself; for at this juncture BADEAU digresses into the following glowing ascription to GRANT's genius in keeping himself free from plans, and seizing things as they turned up:

"These" (i. e., express orders) "GRANT never gave in advance. It was his custom always to await the contingencies of a campaign. None of his plans were so precise that he could not vary them; all allowed for the uncertain and unexpected movements of the enemy. After the great features of a campaign, or the principal object of a battle, was indicated, and the position of the troops at the outset determined, he contented himself beforehand with giving orders for the earliest movements, always expecting to be governed afterward by the emergencies that were sure to arise. Many of his most notable successes were inspired at the moment." Therefore he told no one, not even himself, that he was aiming at Jackson.

By this fine ascription, added to the description, it appears that GRANT, at Rocky Springs, on the 8th, 9th, and 10th of May, was waiting for the emergencies that were sure to arise."

Predominance of the memory stunts the creative faculty, and would make war history dull. What reader can desire that ADAM BADEAU, revised by GRANT, should be limited by plodding memory, when by emancipation from its fetters he can narrate on page 230 this change of plan, and this elaborate new strategy, formed on the 8th, at Rocky Springs, because PEMBERTON had selected, fortified and was concentrated at Edward's Station, and then can state in a foot note on page 241, this: "PEMBERTON did not arrive in person at Edward's till the 14th, but his troops were there the day before."

BADEAU relates that GRANT was practicing a stratagem to deceive McCLERNAND in this new arrangement by shifting him from the right to the left, and informing him that the enemy's main army was at Edward's Station, and that that was the objective. He says of the Jackson plan: "McCLERNAND was not informed of this intention at all. * * * McCLERNAND was sure always to claim the most important position or command, but as he was really nearer the great bulk of the rebel army, he had no reason to complain, supposing himself to be in the advance."

The Commanding General who carries along a very complex strategy to deceive the enemy as to his movements, and has at the same time to practice deep stratagem to deceive the commander of his principal corps as to his movements and plans, shows a double genius for war, and, as BADEAU observes of the bayou operations, "demonstrates the fertility and variety of devices developed during this anomalous campaign."

By turning forward to page 258 it will be observed that up to the 16th GRANT supposed that PEMBERTON was still keeping guard over Vicksburg, and that his raid was based upon that idea, expecting, as was said, in telling the original plan on page 220, "to regain some point on the Mississippi, in spite of all the opposition of two hostile armies."

After mature reflection upon the events of a campaign in which the instinct of genius was directed by "the emergencies which were always sure to arise," the great work of framing a comprehensive, foresighted, back-action, strategical plan by which all shall have come about as foreseen and foreordained, is a task which requires a high order of talent; and even the highest is liable to get affairs into an intricate state.

But this history follows ADAM BADEAU, indorsed by Gen. GRANT; and as their plan of the strategy, which was the most brilliant feature of this campaign, hinged, from the 9th, when GRANT was at Rocky Springs, on PEMBERTON's being concentrated and fortifying at Edward's Station, that part can not be left out until the development of BADEAU's history shall put it out. Therefore, for the present, PEMBERTON shall be where BADEAU and GRANT put him.

Resuming the thread of his narrative, after this glowing episode to the military genius which takes things as they come, BADEAU says: "McPHERSON marched on the 9th of May to a point seven miles west of Utica, and McCLERNAND to the Big Sandy River." Utica is ten miles east of Rocky Springs. Seven miles west of Utica would be three miles east of Rocky Springs. To Big Sandy Creek is by a road that forks to the northeast three or four miles from Rocky Springs. On the evening of the 9th McPHERSON was directed: "March your command to-morrow to water beyond Utica, provided you find it within six or seven miles of the place on the direct Raymond road."

McClernand was ordered May 9: "Move your command to-morrow on the telegraph road to Five Mile Creek. Instructions have been given to Gens. Sherman and McPherson to move so as to continue on the same general front with you." This was pushing McClernand to a line only ten miles from Edward's Station, where Grant had placed Pemberton, intrenched; the other two corps stretching off away from the enemy to southeast. Badeau makes the following explanation of the hesitancy of these movements in a campaign in which celerity to surprise and divide the enemy was declared essential to salvation: "All the movements thus far were preliminary merely, or of the nature of developments, the necessary supplies and ammunition for the march not having yet arrived."

The term developments is much used in military affairs, also in the sciences of phrenology and of the origin of species. The use here is in the sense common to the three. These movements were not to develop the position of the enemy, for Grant's plan was to shun that; not to develop his own army, for that had been developed in "living off the country," and had to be gathered up for a forward march; the waiting, therefore, as Badeau will presently show more plainly, was to develop in the head of the Commanding General an idea what to do next. Some movement of the enemy was necessary to this.

At this juncture, however, the waiting for supplies made convenient the waiting for cranial developments. Badeau tells with admiration the energetic orders which Grant issued on the 3d and 4th to hurry forward supplies from Milliken's Bend. On the 6th Grant had dispatched Halleck that he would move as soon as he got three days' rations. His army was living on a country which he said abounded in corn and cattle, and yet on the 9th he was still waiting to get three days' rations ahead. Since he landed at Bruinsburg the Confederates had now had nine days—since he passed below Grand Gulf eleven—to gather forces by their railroads, to unite with Pemberton. Luckily they had them not to bring, for Rosecrans was keeping Bragg.

A march of ten miles from Hankinson's Ferry to Warrenton would practically restore Grant to his base of supplies at Milliken's Bend. All the navy and transport fleet would follow him. The wagon part of his line of supplies across the tongue of land by his river-turning canal would be only three miles. Mahomet would not go to the mountain, therefore the mountain was coming to Mahomet in wagon loads around the bayou road of sixty miles to Hard Times, thence by boats to Grand Gulf, thence by wagon over a single bad road ten miles to Hankinson's Ferry, or twelve and fifteen miles to Willow Springs and Rocky Springs. This was the wonderful romance of cutting loose from the base of supplies to make an operation in which "the utmost celerity of movement was indispensable, not only to his success, but to his salvation."

In this crisis of the celerity, while Grant's "movements are in the nature of developments," waiting for something to turn up, is a favorable time to pause till the next chapter, which will positively and without reserve launch into that course of brilliant strategy and of celerity of operations which raised Grant's military fame to its zenith.

CHAPTER XXVIII.

THE REASONS FOR MARCHING AWAY FROM THE BASE OF SUPPLIES AND FROM THE CONFEDERATE ARMY—THE BATTLE OF RAYMOND.

Up to the 11th of May, says Adam Badeau, all the movements of Gen. Grant "were preliminary merely, or of the nature of developments, the necessary supplies and ammunition for the march not having yet arrived;" that is to say, he was marking time. He had landed at Bruinsburg April 30, and from that day the Confederacy divined his objective to be Vicksburg, and that Pemberton must be re-enforced. The battle of Port Gibson was fought on the 1st of May, and now on the 11th his army was but fifteen miles from that place, in an operation in which he says not only success but salvation depended on celerity.

His advance had reached Hankinson's Ferry, and secured that crossing of Big Black River, on the direct route to Vicksburg May 3. A reconnaissance next day to within six miles of Vicksburg found no enemy. A march of ten miles, which he could have made on the 4th or 5th, would fetch him to his base of supplies, and relieve the troops that were guarding the circuitous road of sixty miles to Hard Times, and the wagon transportation along that road and on the road from Grand Gulf to Hankinson's Ferry, on all of which a round trip could not be made in less than a fortnight.

A march of ten miles on the direct line to Vicksburg would as effectually connect him with his supplies and re-enforcements as he had been at Millikin's Bend. It would have supported his troops by regular rations for the hardships of the camp, the march, and the battle. It would have given the means of taking care of the sick of the campaign and the wounded of the battle, instead of leaving the sick and the stragglers of the forced marches to the hands of the enemy, and the cruelty of fighting a battle with no means to care for the wounded, and where they must be abandoned to the enemy by moving on; for this is one of the romantic features of a campaign which cuts loose from its base.

A march of not more than five miles from this secure base would fetch Gen. GRANT's army upon PEMBERTON's communications, and would force a battle which, in all military probability, would be decisive of the fate of that army and of Vicksburg. BADEAU, approved by GRANT, recognizes this, and has to fetch back PEMBERTON's forces to the possession of the Big Black at Hankinson's Ferry, to find a reason for GRANT's not taking this course. This prompt march and joining of the issue would have enabled GRANT to turn East, scatter all forces that might come, occupy Vicksburg, and thus effectually hold the State of Mississippi, instead of making a mere devastating raid on that place. And Jackson, as a base, was of far more importance than Vicksburg.

He had estimated PEMBERTON's force at 30,000, and had reported to HALLECK that he had routed and demoralized 11,000 of this number. PEMBERTON, keeping about 8,000 at Vicksburg, was able to bring into the field only about 17,000 men. Probably in all GRANT's army there was not, save Gen. GRANT, an able bodied volunteer who was not confident of the result if led directly upon the Confederate army. This was what every volunteer expected and was eager for. The reason why GRANT did not take this course is one of those things which are very hard to find out in ADAM BADEAU's history. Even with the advantage of framing a plan of campaign years after the event, the true reason for this march away from the enemy could not be set forth, save in self-contradictions.

Three reasons are given and contradicted:

1. That on the direct route to Vicksburg, GRANT would have to encounter the formidable obstacle of the Big Black River, with PEMBERTON holding it; whereas BADEAU says that GRANT held it from the 3d, and had reconnoitered across it to within seven miles of Vicksburg on the 4th. But, by making the march away to the east, GRANT gave to PEMBERTON this formidable line to meet him returning.

2. That at Rocky Springs on the 8th, 9th, or 10th, GRANT knew that PEMBERTON was concentrated and fortifying at Edward's Station, eighteen miles east of Vicksburg; where, as GRANT's orders on the 16th prove that up to that time he thought PEMBERTON was keeping guard over Vicksburg. In fact, as GRANT found out, two days late, PEMBERTON's army arrived at Edward's Station on the 13th, and he on the 14th.

3. That GRANT left a direct line of fifteen miles, which would have brought him upon PEMBERTON, and marched east to divide PEMBERTON from re-enforcements on the east; whereas this would be the very way to enable PEMBERTON to make such a junction, because this would relieve him from immediate fear for Vicksburg, and he and his re-enforcements could unite by marching not half so far as GRANT would have to march to separate them.

These reasons, invented after the events, are contradicted by their context. This straining of invention seems to concede that the actor in "this anomalous campaign" could not explain why he embraced a great opportunity by marching away from it.

Others are offered, which are contradicted by the nature of things, and which do not allow to BADEAU and his hero the possession of sound minds:

1. That to guard his rear from being attacked by a problematical future force from Jackson, GRANT, represented as then confronting PEMBERTON at Edward's Station, and fearful of attacking him, turned his rear to PEM-

BERTON, and offered him every chance to attack his rear, while his army was too widely divided for support.

2. That GRANT's great objective in marching away from PEMBERTON to the east was to divide the enemy; whereas at the time when BADEAU says he formed this plan there was no enemy on the east to be divided, and whereas his line of movement not only gave the enemy time and opportunity to unite, but widely separated his own army, in such a manner as, if PEMBERTON had been where he pretends, would have presented to him a great opportunity to attack GRANT in detail.

3. That GRANT, by dividing and delaying his army to destroy railroads, was doing anything to help the only rational objective of his campaign, the beating of PEMBERTON's army, or the capture of Vicksburg.

4. That GRANT cut himself away from his base of supplies for any military purpose; whereas, on the contrary, the direct march upon the enemy would be a march back to his base, and the march away from his base was a march away from the enemy.

5. That GRANT would turn and march away from PEMBERTON at Edward's Station, for the reason that PEMBERTON was there prepared, if he expected to fight him on his return, when he would have had time to be much more prepared.

6. That GRANT, who had before him the opportunity to reach his base of supplies by a day's march, and resting on that, to join issue with PEMBERTON, in a clear field, would march away from that opportunity and that base, and expect to fight a battle with PEMBERTON on his way back, in such position as PEMBERTON might choose, where GRANT would have no means to care for his wounded, and his rear would be exposed to the gathering Confederate forces.

The consideration of these and many other things that are revealed in BADEAU's narrative makes the course which Gen. GRANT took incompatible with the object of attacking the Confederate army, if he be allowed a strong mind and good military sense. BADEAU, revised by GRANT, does not mention in any of his explanations of the movement to the east, that GRANT intended to attack PEMBERTON. There is no sound of this till GRANT, at Bolton, gathering by forced marches to head off JOHNSTON in a race to the Mississippi, heard that PEMBERTON was advancing to attack him.

On the contrary BADEAU says:

He at once decided to abandon his base altogether, to plunge into the enemy's country with three days' rations, trusting to the region itself for forage and supplies, and to the chances of victory to enable him to regain some point on the Mississippi, in spite of the opposition of two hostile armies.

To regain "some point on the Mississippi!" To expect to fight PEMBERTON's army was to fight for Vicksburg, not to regain some point on the Mississippi. The expression "to regain some point on the Mississippi in spite of the opposition of two hostile armies," conveys to evade them and merely regain his supplies.

All of BADEAU's explanations leave unexplained the object of this march away from supplies and support, and away from the enemy, save that it was to destroy railroads. This explains the marching away from the base and the enemy, and explains many other things which will appear further along. But the march upon the Confederate army and upon GRANT's base of supplies was by one road, and that road he turned his back upon after waiting seven days for the Confederates to unite and re-enforce. On the other hand, the daringly romantic act of cutting away from his communications was to cut away from the enemy's army.

Up to the 11th the movements, BADEAU says, "were preliminary merely, or of the nature of developments." On the 11th GRANT "ordered McPHERSON, who was now beyond Utica, 'Move your command to-night to the next crossroads, and to-morrow with all activity into Raymond. * * * We must fight the enemy before our rations fail, and we are equally bound to make our rations last as long as possible.'" This history takes such fragments of GRANT's orders as BADEAU gives. Fight what enemy before the rations fail? He then expected no enemy at Raymond, and BADEAU says he had decided to shun PEMBERTON. Yet this order conveys that the fighting was to be all done before the three days' rations had failed.

The same order informed McPHERSON: "SHERMAN is now moving on the Auburn and Raymond road, and will reach Fourteen Mile Creek to-night. When you arrive at Raymond he will be in close supporting distance. I shall move McCLERNAND to Fourteen Mile Creek early to-morrow, so that he will occupy a place on SHERMAN's left. The Auburn road to Raymond diverged just beyond Rocky Springs to the left of the Utica road, the one which McPHERSON had taken. The general course of both roads was northeast. McCLERNAND was on another road further to the left, his left extending to the Big Black River. By these orders the general line of the front of the three corps would face a little east of north; McCLERNAND's front would be only six miles from Edward's Station; the right of the line fifteen miles from his left.

On the 12th, at 3:30 a. m., LOGAN's division moved toward Raymond, followed by CROCKER at 4. "At 11 o'clock LOGAN met positive resistance within two miles of Raymond. This was Gregg's brigade, which had arrived from Port Hudson. By this time PEMBERTON, whose main force had been till now west of Big Black River, covering Vicksburg, finding that GRANT was moving east, resolved to move his main army to the east of the Big Black, at Edward's Station, where GRANT would have to attack him, if Vicksburg was his object. He ordered the movements on the 12th, and on the same day ordered GREGG to await his opportunity to attack GRANT in the rear when GRANT attacked at Edward's Station. This outlying part of the plan was not very formidable, unless, indeed, GRANT made a great blunder when he countermarched Gen. LEWIS WALLACE's division of 8,000 men, and so kept it out of the battle, because it was coming in on the Confederate flank and rear at Shiloh.

LOGAN's division got into line of battle; CROCKER's formed the reserve:

Both sides of the road were occupied, and at 2 p. m. the whole line was ordered forward. Scarcely had the advance begun when the battle opened vigorously on the center and left center, where under cover of woods and ravines the rebels had moved a large portion of their force. McPherson, however, outnumbered Gregg two to one, and before Crocker's division had reached the field the enemy was beaten and in full retreat toward Raymond.

GREGG retreated in good order, although BADEAU demoralizes him as usual. McPHERSON states his loss as 69 killed, 341 wounded, 30 missing; the enemy's, 103 killed, 720 wounded and prisoners. The troops entered Raymond at 5 p. m., the enemy having gone on toward Jackson. Although it was a battle of a division and another supporting division against a brigade, estimated by McPHERSON at "between 4,000 and 5,000," and although Raymond was a place of no consequence, it figured in the bulletin all the same. GRANT dispatched HALLECK: "Raymond, Miss., May 14.—McPHERSON took this place on the 12th after a brisk fight of more than two hours."

McPHERSON took the place! Not LOGAN. When McCLERNAND's corps fought the battle of Port Gibson, GRANT's dispatch was that "we" did it, and in his report he made this generous observation: "Where all have done so well, it would be out of place to make invidious distinction."

CHAPTER XXIX.

A CHANGE IN THE STRATEGY—MARCH AWAY FROM THE ENEMY AGAIN TO PROTECT THE REAR—GEN. J. E. JOHNSTON ARRIVES—THE CAPTURE OF JACKSON.

The unexpected fight at Raymond caused a change in Gen. GRANT's plans. Says ADAM BADEAU:

The battle of Raymond, and the flight of the rebels to Jackson, confirmed Grant in the idea that a strong hostile force was on his right flank, and he at once determined to move his entire army in that direction, deflecting McClernand and Sherman from the course he had previously ordered them to pursue.

This appears to show that till now GRANT had been acting upon his great rule of letting the movements of the enemy govern his. But this application of it would keep him moving on after any detached force that had fled, the same beyond Jackson as to Jackson. BADEAU continues:

McPherson alone might not have been able to dislodge Johnston from Jackson, which was strongly fortified; and the destruction of that place as a railroad center was absolutely necessary, in order to deprive the rebels of its use in concentrating a force to interfere with Grant's future operations.

What future operations? The destruction of Jackson as a railroad center had no relation to a battle with PEMBERTON's army, nor with the immediate re-enforcing of that army, for the enemy could march as GRANT's troops did; and if Jackson had been "strongly fortified," GRANT, by this operation, would have achieved the brilliant strategy of placing his army, without supplies or communications, before a fortified place, which might hold him indefinitely, while he had exposed his rear to an army which he feared to face. Whatever the "future operations" were which made the destruction of Jackson as a railroad center absolutely necessary, they were not the destruction of PEMBERTON's army; for GRANT had marched away from the most favorable opportunity for that, and he could now join battle with that army in an hour or two, if it were at Edward's Station.

As before mentioned, BADEAU says that at this time GRANT was practicing a stratagem on McCLERNAND, to make believe that he was moving on Edward's Station, while in reality he intended to send McPHERSON and SHERMAN to Jackson, and then have McCLERNAND'S corps to follow. Playing this stratagem, GRANT continued: "You will then move to-morrow, to keep up this appearance, a short distance only from where you now are, with the three advance divisions, leaving the fourth, or SMITH's, in about its present position." Therefore, says BADEAU: "On the evening of the 12th of May the Army of the Tennessee occupied a line almost parallel with the Vicksburg & Jackson Railroad and about seven miles south of it."

McCLERNAND had a sharp skirmish by HOVEY's division, to gain Fourteen Mile Creek. GRANT had not expected any enemy at Raymond, and had instructed the several corps commanders to keep in connection with each other. His headquarters were at Dillon's, near the center of the line, which, on the 12th, was fifteen miles long. BADEAU relates that "Later on the 12th GRANT said to McCLERNAND, from Dillon's Plantation: 'Edward's Station is evidently the point on the railroad the enemy have most prepared for receiving us. I therefore want to keep up appearances of moving upon that place, but want to get possession of less guarded points first.'"

And now the campaign of celerity began. At a quarter past 9 on the evening of the 12th he directed McPHERSON to "move on to Clinton and Jackson at daylight in the morning." To go to Clinton was to diverge from the direct road to Jackson, eight miles to the northwest. Clinton is on the railroad, nine miles west of Jackson. SHERMAN's orders were changed at the same hour: "After the severe fight of to-day at Raymond, and repulse of the enemy toward Clinton and Jackson, I have determined to move on the latter place, by way of Clinton, and take the Capital of the State, and work from there westward."

And "work from there westward?" Does this sound of battle with PEMBERTON'S army? or of a raid away from it? "McPHERSON was ordered to march at daylight to Clinton. 'You will march at 4 a. m in the morning, and follow McPHERSON.'" Thus were two corps hurried off to Clinton. McCLERNAND was ordered: "Start with three of your divisions as soon as possible, by the road north of Fourteen Mile Creek, to this place (Dillon's), and on to Raymond." Thus were two corps sent northeast, and one southeast, and when these marches had been made, three of McCLERNAND's divisions would be fifteen miles from the other two corps, with their rear exposed to PEMBERTON's army, which on that day reached Edward's Station. McCLERNAND's report states that this day's march was the hardest of the campaign. And it was to no purpose but to countermarch more rapidly.

McCLERNAND's fourth division was ordered back to Auburn, thirteen miles southwest of Raymond, "to await the arrival of trains now on the road, and BLAIR's division, to conduct them to the army." BLAIR's division, the last of SHERMAN's corps to leave Milliken's Bend, was escorting a train of 200 wagons from Grand Gulf. Thus was the army divided before PEMBERTON, now, in fact, arrived on the 13th at Edward's Station (although GRANT did not find it out till the 16th), and thus were two of GRANT's three corps pursuing a Confederate brigade, which had fled toward Jackson, and the other was held divided as a reserve for the same operation.

Says BADEAU of the affair at Raymond: "PEMBERTON had been completely deceived by GRANT's maneuvers; supposing the object of the latter to be Edward's Station, he remained at that place with the bulk of his force awaiting an attack." But this is illuminated by a foot note on the same page, showing that PEMBERTON did not make his dispositions to advance to Edward's Station till the 12th, and by another further along, that his army did not arrive there till the 13th, and by the text further along showing that Grant did not know till the 16th that Pemberton had advanced to Edward's Station. Thus it appears that if any one was deceived it was not Pemberton.

Badeau says that through this deceiving of Pemberton, Grant "divided the rebels and beat them in detail." He says also: "It was fortunate that Grant acted with such promptness, for on the night of the 13th Johnston arrived at Jackson and took supreme command of all the rebel forces in the State, and he was a man of far more genius and energy than his subordinate." It was very fortunate, therefore, that before the terrible Johnston had arrived, Grant, who had reached Big Black Bridge (late the ferry) on the afternoon of the 3d, where he had fifteen miles to his front the Confederate army's vital position, and ten miles in that way his own base of supplies, had acted with such promptness and celerity that now on the 12th his corps that was furthest to the right had reached thirty miles, and driven a brigade, and his whole army had moved an average of twenty-five miles from Hankinson's, from the enemy's army, and from his base of supplies. If so much had not been accomplished by "promptness and celerity" before Johnston came, it is fearful to contemplate, in the light of Badeau, what might have been.

McPherson arrived at Clinton on the afternoon of the 13th, and went at destroying the railroad. He here found the before mentioned orders from Pemberton to Gregg. "Sherman had arrived at Raymond before McPherson left the town," and now Grant changed his orders again and directed Sherman, instead of following McPherson to Clinton, to "take the direct or southern road to Jackson. By night he had reached a position near Mississippi Springs, ten miles from Jackson." "During this day McClernand withdrew from his position near Edward's Station, where his pickets had been within two miles of Pemberton's army. One division of the 13th Corps was drawn up in line of battle, and behind this cover the remainder retired without embarrassment, the enemy discovering the movement too late to interfere."

Thus did Grant expose one corps of his army to the near presence of the enemy whom he thought too strong for his whole army to cope with. Thus did he turn his rear to the enemy's superior army, according to Badeau, in order to guard his future rear against a retreating brigade. Thus was he dividing his army before an enemy he deemed not prudent to attack, in order to divide the enemy. When McClernand came to withdraw his corps he found the enemy strong in his front. But fortunately for Grant, Pemberton had from the first resolved on a strictly defensive course, and was still adhering to it. And in all this Grant had "the confidence of his ignorance," for until the 16th he clung to his idea that Pemberton was west of Big Black River, keeping guard over Vicksburg.

Johnston reached Jackson on the night of the 13th, and found there Gregg's and Walker's brigades, about 6,000 men. He expected Gist's and Maxcey's brigades next day to raise his force to 11,000. Had Jackson been "strongly fortified," as Badeau says, a General could not have marched his army into a completer trap than Grant's, without supplies, with a strongly fortified place in front and Pemberton in his rear. But Johnston decided that the intrenchments were weak, faulty in location, and the whole town commanded by surrounding hills; therefore all the defense that was made was to cover his withdrawal.

McPherson, moving from Clinton at daylight, met the Confederate outposts five miles out from Jackson, on the northwest, and pushing on, found the enemy in position two and a half miles outside the city, northwest, where he prepared for action. Sherman, coming from Raymond, arrived on the southwest of the city. A gap of two miles was between the two lines. McClernand had now been marched about, so that one division was at Clinton, one at Mississippi Springs, one at Raymond, the other back at Auburn, the distance from Auburn to Clinton being twenty miles, and from Clinton to Mississippi Springs fifteen miles. Thus was Grant dividing his army to divide the enemy. These, says Badeau, together with Blair's and McArthur's divisions, still further away, "were all held in reserve"—the reserve of the operation against Jackson, where Johnston had 6,000 men, and was showing a front only to cover removal.

At 11 o'clock McPherson ordered an advance, the skirmishers met a strong fire, then a charge was ordered, and Crocker's division swept forward, drove the enemy out of the ravine, charged gallantly up the hill, when the enemy fled behind their works. The troops followed a mile and a half till they came in range of the artillery of the defenses of the city. Here two batteries were wheeled into position, the line reformed, skirmishers thrown out, and officers sent forward to reconnoiter. All these operations had occupied three hours.

SHERMAN, meanwhile, coming from Mississippi Springs, on the southwest, encountered no resistance save such as his skirmishers could drive, till after crossing a stream and emerging from the woods, "in front and as far to the left as could be seen, appeared a line of intrenchments; and the enemy kept up a brisk fire of artillery from the points enfilading SHERMAN's road." GRANT was with SHERMAN. He sent a party to the extreme right to reconnoiter. This party not returning, GRANT and his staff rode in the same direction, and found the way all clear into the town. The only remaining soldiers were some left to work the guns to the last moment.

McPHERSON's troops, about the same time, found that the enemy had left the place, and they moved forward into the town. McPHERSON sent STEVENSON's brigade to cut off the retreat, but it arrived too late. Says BADEAU: "McPHERSON considered STEVENSON's delay unnecessary, and blamed his subordinate." But a march to cut off a retreat which had got away undiscovered, requires uncommon marching legs.

The troops were in possession of the town by 3 o'clock, and raised the national flag over the State Capital. But, unhappily, it was only for a raid; whereas if they had been led upon the enemy's main army, instead of marching their legs off to shun it, they could have come as conquerors, to stay, instead of to take flight, and from this base to possess the State of Mississippi.

CHAPTER XXX.

THE BATTLE OF JACKSON—GEN. J. E. JOHNSTON'S DIVERTING COMBINATIONS—GEN. GRANT'S NEW PLAN—A RACE FOR THE MISSISSIPPI—UNPARALLELED COMBINED MOVEMENTS OF ALL ARMIES.

Gen. GRANT had started a dispatch to Gen. HALLECK early on the morning of the 14th, stating: "I will attack the State Capital to-day." Says ADAM BADEAU: "This was the first report GRANT had made since severing communication with the government." The same dispatch reported the capture of Raymond, which was the first action GRANT had to report since the severing.

From Jackson, May 15, GRANT dispatched: "This place fell into our hands yesterday, after a fight of about three hours. Gen. JOE JOHNSTON was in command. The enemy retreated north, evidently with the design of joining the Vicksburg force. I am concentrating my force at Bolton to cut them off if possible." The modesty of GRANT's bulletins has been much admired. They simply stated the great event, leaving the rest to the imagination. And upon a mere statement of the great event, with the terrible JOE JOHNSTON beaten, what imagination would conceive that JOHNSTON had but 6,000 men, and was anxious only to get away, while GRANT had two corps in the attack, and the other supporting?

And what imagination so barren as to suppose that the modest announcement that he had captured Raymond, by a battle, meant no more in a military sense than the capture of any other mile of country road?

In narrating the dispositions for the battle of Jackson, McPHERSON on the northwest and SHERMAN on the southwest, with a space of two miles between them, BADEAU says GRANT "made no effort to connect the wings, thinking it more important to hold the southern road and prevent the escape of the garrison in that direction." The success of this is stated four pages further along in this: "While this show of opposition was being made in SHERMAN's front McPHERSON was held long enough for the main body of the enemy to escape by the Canton road, on the northern side of the town, by which alone JOHNSTON could effect a junction with PEMBERTON."

Thus doth BADEAU make appear that GRANT's tactics exposed the army by dividing it in front of an intrenched enemy, to accomplish the object of forcing JOHNSTON to withdraw in the only way by which he could join PEMBERTON. Yet he had before stated that GRANT's great object in going away from PEMBERTON to Jackson was to prevent any forces there from joining PEMBERTON.

Between 3 and 4 o'clock in the afternoon Grant sent for his corps commanders, and gave them their orders at the State House. McPherson was to encamp one division inside the intrenchments, and the other between the battlefield and the city.

Sherman was directed to occupy the line of rifle pits at once, and on the following day to destroy effectually the railroad tracks in and about Jackson, and all property belonging to the enemy. He set about his work in the morning (15th) and utterly destroyed the railroads in every direction, north, east, south, and west, for a distance in all of twenty miles. All the bridges, factories, and arsenals were burned, and whatever could be of use to the rebels destroyed. The importance of Jackson as a railroad center and a depot of stores and military factories was annihilated, and the principal object of its capture attained. A hotel and a church in Jackson were burned without orders, and there was some pillaging by the soldiers, which their officers sought in every way to restrain.

ordered Gen. GIST, who was arriving from Port Hudson, to the east on the railroad, forty or fifty miles from Jackson, and Gen. MAXCEY, arriving with another brigade, to join GIST. He said in his letter to PEMBERTON:

This body of troops will be able, I hope, to prevent the enemy in Jackson from drawing provisions from the east.

And as to the two brigades which had marched north with him, he said:

And this one may be able to keep him from the country toward Panola.

Thus was GRANT's incredible genius for

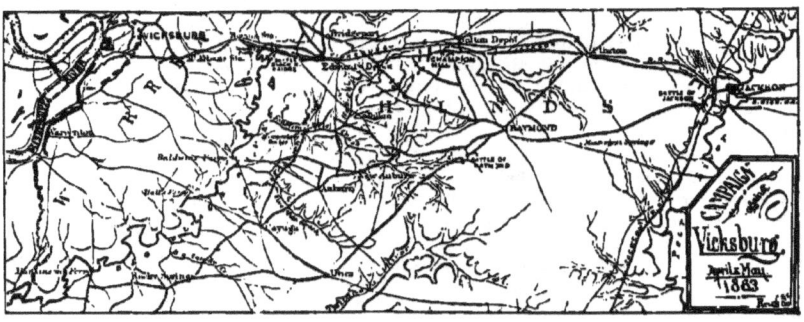

MAP OF THE FIELD OF THE WAR.

This was the destruction of that which a rational military course would have converted to the use of our army, and have made Jackson a military center as important in its relations to Mississippi and Louisiana as Chattanooga to Tennessee and Georgia. It was also the destruction of that which it was the nation's interest to have preserved, if the object of the war was to restore the National Union. But the military policy of shunning the Confederate army, to devastate places, made this campaign more like the ravaging of a horde of Tartars than the course of a war to save a nation.

In all the delusions of the three parties to "this anomalous campaign," the astute Gen. J. E. JOHNSTON seems to have been worst deceived. He could not believe that GRANT had come to Jackson merely for a devastating raid; he supposed he had come to stay, and to make that a base of military operations. Consequently, when he left the place he

missing his opportunity converted to strategy which neutralized the astute JOHNSTON. If he could have believed that GRANT was only upon a raid intending to avoid serious opposition, his course might have been widely different. Thus does genius build wiser than it knew, and thus was a wise soldier deceived by his unbelief that another could have so small a purpose for so great an army.

Before JOHNSTON had reached Jackson the Quartermaster in charge of the public property had begun to remove it. JOHNSTON decided the place indefensible. The reasons were not stated in the reports of the time, but are given in JOHNSTON's report of his abandonment of the place upon the second raid, which was made by SHERMAN after the surrender of Vicksburg. He says:

These [the defensive works], consisting of a line of rifle pits, prepared at intervals for artillery, extended from a point north of the town, a little east of the Canton road, to a point south of the town, within a short distance of Pearl River, and covered most of the approaches west of the river, but were badly located and constructed, presenting but slight obstacle to a vigorous assault. * * * Hills commanding and encircling the town, within easy cannon range, offered favorable sites for batteries. A crossfire of shot and shell reached all parts of the town, showing the position to be entirely untenable against a powerful artillery.

Perhaps an artillery fire from field guns, from the hills about Jackson, into the heart of the town for two or three days, would not have been worse than to let SHERMAN inside. The detention of GRANT for two or three days before Jackson, if JOHNSTON could have raised PEMBERTON from his defensive attitude, might have sent GRANT off precipitately in his returning raid. The commander who thought it imprudent to attack PEMBERTON alone, might be "demoralized" when he found PEMBERTON attacking his rear, and 11,000 men holding a fortified place in his front. But here again did GRANT's proverbial luck save him from his fatal devices. JOHNSTON, thinking GRANT was making a campaign instead of a raid, and that he wanted Jackson for a base, and would have it, "if it took all summer," gave it up to him without a struggle, and then set about cutting him off from supplies.

So JOHNSTON marched north, while the coming GIST and MAXCEY were directed to the east. JOHNSTON marched six miles on the Canton road on the 14th, and there encamped. He sent dispatches to PEMBERTON announcing the fall of Jackson, and the dispositions of GIST and MAXCEY and himself, to prevent GRANT from drawing supplies. He asked: "Can he supply himself from the Mississippi? Can you not cut him off from it? And above all, should he be compelled to fall back for want of supplies, beat him." The contrast between JOHNSTON's words and doings is quite striking. He then expressed this opinion for future guidance: "As soon as the re-enforcements are all up, they must be united to the rest of the army. I am anxious to see a force assembled that may be able to inflict a heavy blow upon the enemy."

Such an interest in the subsequent proceedings was laudable, and his expressions as to the future course were valuable to PEMBERTON. It gave him to understand that a considerable part of the coming re-enforcements had been disposed so as to prevent GRANT from drawing supplies from the east, and that JOHNSTON with the rest was doing that service on the north, and it declared for uniting the forces at some indefinite future. But while JOHNSTON was marching away from GRANT, he gave PEMBERTON valuable aid by exhortations to attack GRANT. On the 15th JOHNSTON moved north ten miles further to Calhoun Station.

Gen. GRANT got hold of one copy of JOHNSTON's dispatch to PEMBERTON, and it gave him an illumination. Says BADEAU: "It was apparent now that a concentration of the rebels was imminent." In the lives of great Generals remarkable incidents are always happening, which fetch them information in the nick of time to rescue from destruction. One of these now happened. It shows that stratagem played a part as extraordinary as strategy in this "anomalous campaign." BADEAU relates how, "some months before these events," a loyal man in Memphis, anxious to serve the national cause, had been drummed out of that place by HURLBUT for uttering seditious language and communicating with the enemy."

This patriotic person had been waiting his opportunity, and now he offered to carry JOHNSTON's dispatch to PEMBERTON, which BADEAU says was a dangerous task. Of course his offer was gladly accepted by JOHNSTON, and so the man fetched the dispatch straight to GRANT. By this far sighted provision GRANT, whose march away from the enemy had been to prevent their concentration, was now illumined with the idea "that a concentration of the rebels was imminent." And now the most energetic orders were issued to concentrate the army and head off JOHNSTON, who all this time was marching away to the north. Says BADEAU:

Accordingly that afternoon McPherson was directed to retrace his steps, marching early in the morning on the Clinton road toward Bolton, about twenty miles west of Jackson, and the nearest point where Johnston could strike the railroad. Grant also informed McClernand of the capture of Jackson, and ordered him to face all his troops toward Bolton: "It is evidently the design of the enemy to get north of us and cross the Big Black River, and beat us into Vicksburg. We must not allow him to do this. Turn all your forces toward Bolton Station, and make all dispatch in getting there. Move troops by the direct road from wherever they may be on the receipt of this order."

Gen. FRANK BLAIR had got to Auburn with his division of SHERMAN's corps, and a train of 200 wagons. Auburn is fifteen miles southeast of Bolton. BLAIR, too, was ordered most energetically to move in the same direction:

> Their design is evidently to cross the Big Black, and pass down the peninsula between the Black and Yazoo rivers. We must beat them. Turn your troops immediately to Bolton: take all the trains with you. Smith's division and any other troops now with you will go to the same place. If practicable, take parallel roads, so as to divide your troops and train.

This was the culmination of the splendid strategy of this campaign. and these its marches of greatest celerity. GRANT, supposing that PEMBERTON was still west of Big Black River covering Vicksburg, and that JOHNSTON'S movement was to join him, was issuing most energetic orders to concentrate his army to outrun JOHNSTON. He had marched away from PEMBERTON at Vicksburg to hunt for PEMBERTON'S re-enforcements in the east. At length he had found some. Behold, now, GRANT'S army, concentrating at Bolton by forced marches from the east, from the southeast, from the south, from the southwest, from distances severally of twenty, twelve, ten, and fifteen miles, to enter on a race with JOHNSTON'S 6,000 for the Big Black River.

To complete the military situation, PEMBERTON, at last, on that day, had concluded to act upon JOHNSTON'S suggestions to move so as to cut off GRANT from the Mississippi, and had begun to move southeast to attack his rear. Then was presented a scene which surpassed all that the great FREDERIC or BONAPARTE ever dreamed. Everybody was marching away from everybody, to every point of the compass.

GIST and MAXCEY, with 5,000 men, were marching fifty miles east of Jackson, to cut off GRANT at Jackson from drawing supplies from the east. JOHNSTON, with GREGG'S and WALKER'S brigades (6,000), was marching away north for the same purpose. GRANT, thinking PEMBERTON still west of Big Black River, was making forced marches to the northwest, to beat JOHNSTON in a race toward PEMBERTON. PEMBERTON was marching southeast to attack GRANT'S rear, thinking him moving on Jackson.

Following the method of the serial novel, this is a sensational place to end a chapter, with the promise of a crisis in the next.

CHAPTER XXXI.

TO REALIZE THE CAMPAIGNS OF THE MASTERS OF THE ART OF WAR—WHY A GENERAL IS GREATER THAN A MAN—SPLENDID MILITARY COMBINATION BROKEN UP BY UNTIMELY INFORMATION—ANOTHER GREAT STROKE OF LUCK.

Military authors have established the judgment that BONAPARTE was master of the art of war. The common mind accepts this judgment, but there is no realism in it. Comparatively few study BONAPARTE'S campaigns in such a way as to understand his mastery of the art. Thus the common mind has no means of knowing how much greater is the genius which masters the art of war than can find adequate scope in other affairs.

But when campaigns are planned, and battles fought, in our own country and generation, which military men, who have studied the great models, say rank with those of BONAPARTE, these give a practical demonstration of his achievements so that we can appreciate his genius, and so can measure the greatness of our own General who thus exemplifies the highest model. Thus when Gen. HALLECK—a military author—ranks GRANT'S campaign about Vicksburg with that of BONAPARTE about Ulm, and Capt. ADAM BADEAU, approved by GRANT, accepts this so far as it goes, but adds that BONAPARTE'S first campaign in Italy is needed to complete the parallel; the one being a campaign great in results achieved by strategy without battles; the other a campaign great in direct and rapid marches to battles, then he whose happy fortune was to live in the great civil war can have a realizing sense of the greatness of the genius of BONAPARTE and of the General whose achievements parallel a combination of BONAPARTE'S greatest.

The remark may be offered, on behalf of men in other walks of life, that no other profession or art has such conditions to inspire a transcending state of mind as those which surround the Commanding General. War is the grandest game played by man, and it lifts the leader above himself. The mere fact that 50,000 men are in his absolute command, to be sent to their death by his word, is alone enough to inspire a leader. How much more when through all this disciplined mass, organized into a solid force, ready to be precipitated at his command, runs an heroic spirit which had led these young men to leave happy homes to fight for country; when this solid mass of heroes naturally looks up to its Commanding General as a supreme being; when upon his plans they spring promptly to the forced march, and are only too eager to rush into the slaughterous combat; when literally the lives of 50,000 heroes, and all the brave deeds that heroism can do, are at his beck, and all their achievements are for his glory!

The military leader, therefore, is surrounded by influences which exist in no other business, and which ought to animate him with a genius transcending all that can be possible in other affairs. If it be true that man is the creation of the environment, the Commanding General of an army of American volunteers ought to be the greatest of heroes and of men. This reflection may solace those who think that inordinate honors are given to the profession of arms, and that there is injustice in conferring upon one man the honors and rewards for the achievements of all. In no war of history has the recognition been so entire that the success was gained by the genius of one man. BADEAU's history, approved by GRANT, justifies this; for although BONAPARTE was master of the art of war, it is allowed that he had the aid of a number of great Generals; but BADEAU states that in this campaign, which all declare to be the most brilliant of GRANT's military life, his plan was opposed by all his Generals and by the General in Chief, and that in his great Richmond campaign all his corps commanders had serious faults, and each one in turn was inadequate to his opportunity, GRANT alone being entirely great.

The end of the previous chapter was in the midst of an evolution of movements of armies as brilliant in strategic intelligence and execution as the evolving colors of the kaleidoscope. Comparison can go no higher than the highest model, and it may be said boldly that the several movements and designs transcended any of the operations of BONAPARTE or FREDERIC the Great. Gen. JOSEPH E. JOHNSTON had given up Jackson to Gen. GRANT. Thinking GRANT had come to stay, JOHNSTON had ordered 5,000 men fifty miles to the east to cut off GRANT from supplies from that direction, and was marching 6,000 to the north to the same end. Gen. GRANT, thinking PEMBERTON still west of the Big Black River, covering Vicksburg, and that JOHNSTON was moving to join him, was making forced marches from Clinton, from Jackson, from Mississippi Springs, from Raymond, and Auburn, west, northwest, and north to Bolton, to beat JOHNSTON in a race. PEMBERTON, who had come to Edward's Station, was marching southeast to attack GRANT's rear, thinking him still aiming at, Jackson.

How far they would have gone on these diverging lines is a question for conjecture, for on the next day, the 16th, PEMBERTON was turned about by receiving JOHNSTON's positive order, and GRANT by one of those "emergencies which are always sure to arise." PEMBERTON had found a bridge gone from a rain, and a ford impracticable on his direct route, and had been forced to make a detour, whereby he had not got far in his day's march, and next morning he received JOHNSTON's order, stating that he had left Jackson, and that the only way for them to unite was for PEMBERTON to march northward; so he countermarched.

GRANT had been turned about by one of those romantic incidents which are always happening in the histories of great Generals, bringing them rescuing intelligence in the nick of time. On the morning of the 16th two railroad workmen were brought into his headquarters who had passed through PEMBERTON's army, and, as appears, had been taken into PEMBERTON's confidence. BADEAU narrates:

At about 5 o'clock on this morning two men employed on the Jackson & Vicksburg Railroad, and who had passed through Pemberton's army the night before, were brought into Grant's headquarters at Clinton. He was wakened at once to receive the news. The men stated that Pemberton was at Edward's Station, fifteen or eighteen miles off, with eighty regiments of infantry and ten batteries of artillery. They estimated his whole force at 25,000 troops, still advancing.

This intelligence changed the face of things; the race with JOHNSTON was abandoned, and now the energetic orders that had been given for concentration to run with him were diverted to a movement to meet PEMBERTON, whose plan, these reliable men said, was to attack GRANT's rear. To SHERMAN, who was still at Jackson, finishing his work, GRANT dispatched:

Start one of your divisions on the road at once with their ammunition wagons, and direct the General commanding the division to move with all possible speed until he comes up with our rear, beyond Bolton. It is important that the greatest celerity should be shown in carrying out this movement, as I have evidence that the entire force of the enemy was at Edward's Depot at 7 p. m. last night, and was advancing. The fight may, therefore, be brought on at any moment; we should have every man in the field.

The other division was to follow as quickly as possible. "This dispatch reached SHERMAN at ten minutes past 7, and his advance division, STEELE'S, was in motion in one hour from that time." The following order was sent to BLAIR, who had been at Auburn when ordered to hasten to Bolton:

The enemy have moved out to Edward's Station, and are still pushing on to attack us with all their force. Push your troops on in that direction as rapidly as possible. If you are already on the Bolton road continue so; but if you still have a choice of roads, take the one leading to Edward's Depot. *Pass your troops to the front of your train, except a rear guard, and keep the ammunition wagons in front of all others.*

The italics of admiration in this order are BADEAU'S, and he considerately explains: "This last injunction was very necessary, as BLAIR was obliged to reverse his command, which would bring the wagon trains in front." In the course of practical military education Gen. GRANT had now reached the higher branches, and had learned that the wagon train in front is not the best formation for going into battle. But Gen. GRANT had none of that class exclusiveness which would withhold professional learning from a mere volunteer or "political General," so he freely communicated his developing military knowledge to Major General FRANK BLAIR, who had entered upon active service at the very incipiency of the war.

ADAM BADEAU ascribes very high qualities of clearness and particularity to Gen. GRANT'S army orders, and gives citations, of which this is an example. He refutes the current notion that Gen. RAWLINS wrote GRANT'S orders or dispatches; he says "they were his own composition," and that "none of his staff officers ever attempted to imitate his style," which may readily be believed. The minuteness of the orders which are cited as examples, and the diffusion of their force on elementary details, enhances the wonder that GRANT'S mind could also take in the general dispositions. BADEAU says that GRANT'S order book, of this campaign, is a great curiosity; his specimens support this ascription.

From this note of admiration of the military genius exhibited in Gen. GRANT'S orders, BADEAU continues his issuance of energetic orders to meet the emergency that had arisen from the two railroad laborers:

McClernand was now directed to assume command of Blair, and establish communication between him and Osterhaus at once, and to keep it up, moving forward cautiously. "Direct Maj. Gen. Blair to move with his division as soon as possible, moving on the same line by the first lateral road leading into the one on which Osterhaus is now marching."

This was a mistaken direction, as the road for BLAIR to take, and which he did take, was the southern, whereas Osterhaus was on the middle road; but McCLERNAND and BLAIR were more clear in the matter of roads than GRANT was in this flurry.

At forty-five minutes past 5 McPherson was also ordered forward to the support of Hovey: "The enemy has crossed Big Black with the entire Vicksburg force. He was at Edward's Depot last night, and still advancing. You will therefore pass all trains and move forward to join McClernand" (Hovey's division.) "I have ordered your rear brigade to move at once, and given such directions to other commanders as will secure prompt concentration of your forces."

Thus was McPHERSON also directed to put his trains to the rear. Continues BADEAU: "SHERMAN had evacuated Jackson by noon of the 16th, paroling his prisoners, and leaving his wounded on account of the haste of the movement. He marched twenty miles, reaching Bolton with his entire command the same day."

This is one of the romantic features of a campaign which cuts its base. McPHERSON reported 228 wounded at Jackson. SHERMAN had to abandon these to the mercies of the inhabitants of a town which he had devastated. Their next movement would be either to the unhonored grave or to a Confederate prison. The parole of his prisoners counted for nothing. Under the cartel they were released by this.

The situation, as now changed in consequence of the sudden illumination which GRANT had received from the two railroad laborers, may be understood by a brief recapitulation.

When GRANT ordered McPHERSON'S and

SHERMAN'S corps to Jackson, he reversed McCLERNAND'S position, and ordered three of his divisions severally to Clinton, to Raymond, and to Mississippi Springs to support the two corps operating on Jackson, scattering McCLERNAND'S corps in utter unconsciousness that PEMBERTON was now in his rear at Edward's Station. The fourth division he ordered on the back track to Auburn, where was Gen. FRANK BLAIR'S division and a train of 200 wagons. This appears to have been preparatory to the return of the raid to Grand Gulf, after he had broken up the railroad and the "railroad center."

But when GRANT conceived the remarkable idea that JOHNSTON had got the start of him, and was moving west to beat him by crossing the Big Black River and joining PEMBERTON, whom GRANT still supposed to be west of the Big Black, he ordered McCLERNAND to gather up his scattered divisions by forced marches to Bolton. They had just made very severe marches northeast, southeast, and south to divide, and now they had to countermarch by forced marches from the several points of the compass to concentrate at Bolton. Thus went the operation which was governed by "the emergencies that were always sure to arise."

OSTERHAUS' division of McCLERNAND'S corps, moving from Raymond, reached Bolton first at 9:30 on the 15th. HOVEY'S division came up from Clinton soon after. At this time GRANT'S race with JOHNSTON appears to have paused. McCLERNAND'S report says of the further operations of this day:

Both divisions were disposed to meet any attack that might come from the enemy known to be in front. During the day an active reconnaissance was pushed by Col. Mudd, Chief of Cavalry of my corps, up to the enemy's picket lines, and at some points beyond. * * * Every effort was made * * * to acquire familiar knowledge of the ground and roads for seven miles west of Edward's Station. It was found, three roads led from the Raymond and Bolton road to Edward's Station, * * * designated the northern, middle, and southern roads to Edward's Station, and united within some two miles of that point.

Night found Gens. Hovey, Osterhaus', and Carr's divisions, in the order stated, at the entrance to these several roads, prepared to receive a threatened attack, or to move forward upon converging lines against Edward's Station. Gen. Smith's division came up during the night, and bivouacked north of Raymond near Gen. Carr's. Gen. Blair's division of Gen. Sherman's corps bivouacked at Raymond.

This disposition of my corps but anticipated events.

Gen. McCLERNAND, in the above, speaks of dispositions to meet attack from an enemy known to be in front, but Gen. GRANT did not know of any enemy in front, nor order any dispositions to that end; for, according to BADEAU, he was thinking only of a race with JOHNSTON, and he supposed PEMBERTON still west of the Big Black River.

But the lucky outcome of all GRANT'S blind stumbling, and of McCLERNAND'S vigilance, was that on the night of the 15th McCLERNAND'S four divisions rested on or near to three roads, which, about two miles apart, ran west to Edward's Station, passing by and over Champion's Hill. Consequently, when GRANT, at Clinton, got out of bed at 5 o'clock on the morning of the 16th, to receive information from the two railroad laborers that PEMBERTON had crossed Big Black River, reached Edward's Station, and was "still advancing," intending to "attack his rear," McCLERNAND'S four divisions, and BLAIR'S division added, happened to be situated on the right roads for meeting PEMBERTON, either by waiting or advancing.

BADEAU prefers to have GRANT receive by the extraordinary accident of the well informed railroad laborers, four days after the event, his first information that PEMBERTON'S army had crossed the Big Black; and BADEAU is confirmed by GRANT. But Gen. McCLERNAND'S report infringes on the romantic accident by this:

During the evening of the 15th I received a dispatch from Maj. Gen. Grant advising me that the entire force of the enemy at Vicksburg had probably crossed the Big Black, and taken position at Edward's Station, and ordering me to feel the enemy without bringing on a general engagement, and to notify Gen. Blair what to do.

But this still leaves to the railroad laborers the communication to GRANT that PEMBERTON was advancing on the south to attack his rear—a piece of information which, as will be seen, governed his tactics of the battle.

McPHERSON had come up behind HOVEY from Clinton. SHERMAN was coming by the same road from Jackson. Thus, by a wonderful stroke of luck, the forced marching to all points of the compass, and the forced countermarching toward Bolton for a race with JOHNSTON, when stopped by GRANT'S new information, found the army well situated to meet the emergency that had arisen. The only drawback to GRANT's good luck was that his stratagem in maneuvering MCCLERNAND to the rear had fetched him to the front.

On this day was fought the bloody battle of Champion's Hill.

CHAPTER XXXII.

FULL DEVELOPMENT OF THE GRAND STRATEGY.

The progress of events in this history has more fully developed the strategy of the campaign, and has laid bare the object of the march away alike from GRANT's base of supplies, from the Confederate army, and from Vicksburg. That the plan was adapted to the object is well shown by BADEAU. The situation was especially favorable.

GRANT's plan was "to hug the Black River as closely as possible, with MCCLERNAND and SHERMAN's corps," while working his way up to destroy the railroad between Big Black River and Jackson. By this demonstration with his left he expected to divert PEMBERTON's attention to the guarding of the Big Black crossings all the way up from Hankinson's to the railroad crossing at Bovina Station, while he reached forward with his right to destroy the road.

Then, still having PEMBERTON west of Big Black River, GRANT could return and regain the river at Grand Gulf. BADEAU says vaguely, "regain some point on the Mississippi;" but there was no practicable point on the river, above Vicksburg, short of Memphis, save at Walnut Hills, close by Vicksburg, where he might connect with the fleet by way of the Yazoo. But is it likely that GRANT, having marched away from PEMBERTON's army and Vicksburg and his own supplies, when all were within his reach by two easy marches, would expect to make for Walnut Hills on his return, where he would have to expect to fight PEMBERTON's army in its strongest position, while his own, after all the consuming of the march, would be without supplies, and if repulsed would certainly be captured?

Such a supposition would suppose GRANT destitute of military or other sense. But below Vicksburg, if cut off from Grand Gulf, he would have a chance at Bruinsburg, and further below. When GRANT thought JOHNSTON moving north of him. "evidently to cross the Big Black, and pass down the peninsula between the Big Black and Yazoo rivers," he had cause for his alarm; for with such support at hand, PEMBERTON could turn the advantages of the line of the Big Black against GRANT all the way down to Hankinson's, and would have the inner line by which to cut him off from Grand Gulf.

The strategy had its designed effect on PEMBERTON up to the 12th. He divided his army, guarding the crossings of the Big Black, and keeping a vigilant guard over Vicksburg. At length, he thought that GRANT was aiming at the railroad at Edward's Station, and he moved to that place, issuing his orders for it on the 12th, but still guarding further down the crossings of the Big Black. His letter to JOHNSTON, May 12, from Vicksburg, defines the plan he was pursuing:

> The enemy is apparently moving his heavy force toward Edward's Depot, on Southern Railroad With my limited force I will do all I can to meet him. That will be the battlefield if I can carry forward sufficient force, leaving troops enough to secure the safety of this place. Re-enforcements are arriving very slowly, only 1,500 having arrived as yet. I urgently ask that more be sent; also that 3,000 cavalry be at once sent to operate on this line. I urge this as a positive necessity. The enemy largely outnumber me, and I am obliged to hold a large force at the ferries on Big Black, lest he cross and take this place. I am also compelled to keep considerable force on either flank of Vicksburg, out of supporting distance.

PEMBERTON's report charges his inability to cut off GRANT from the Mississippi soon after his landing at Bruinsburg, to the condition that he had been stripped of cavalry to send to BRAGG against ROSECRANS. However this may be, it is another instance that the attitude of ROSECRANS was giving important aid to GRANT. PEMBERTON narrates his advance to Edward's Station, and says: "On the evening of the 12th I moved my headquarters to Bovina to be near the scene of active operations. The command arrived at Edward's Depot on the 13th, and was placed in position, covering all the approaches from the south and east."

GRANT's reconstructed strategy, in BADEAU's history, sets forward the movement of the Confederate army to Edward's Station to the 8th or 9th. In the narrative of the events of the time, however, GRANT did not find it out till the 16th, when the two railroad laborers brought him the intelligence. A Bonaparte maxim holds that a General who understands his trade will know the enemy's force, positions, and intentions; but this is not essential in a plan which expects to be governed by "the emergencies which are always sure to arise." The change in Gen. GRANT's plan by the emergency that the two railroad laborers fetched him may be seen by referring back to BADEAU's statement, pages 239, 240, of what that plan was:

The battle of Raymond, and the flight of the rebels to Jackson, confirmed Grant in the idea that a strong hostile force was on his right flank, and he at once determined to move his entire army in that direction, deflecting McClernand and Sherman from the course he had previously ordered them to pursue. * * * Sherman's orders were changed at the same hour: "After the severe fight of to-day at Raymond, and repulse of the enemy toward Clinton and Jackson, I have determined to move on the latter place by way of Clinton, and take the Capital of the State, and work from there westward."

The intended "work" is shown by that which was done as soon as McPHERSON struck the railroad, which was at Clinton on the 13th, when, instead of pushing forward to the enemy, he "at once set about tearing up the railroad track and ties, bending the iron, burning bridges, and destroying culverts and telegraph poles and wires," in pursuance of the grand object of this operation, which BADEAU says was to leave "Vicksburg with its garrison isolated from the would be Confederacy."

Next to the present risk of that "immediate aggressive" course, which BADEAU says was GRANT's nature always, the great consideration which influenced him to leave a very promising opportunity to make a real campaign by first destroying PEMBERTON's army, and, on the contrary, to make a mere raid to destroy a railroad, was the intelligence which reached GRANT while in a vacillitating frame of mind at Hankinson's Ferry, of the consternation caused in the South by GRIERSON's cavalry raid from Memphis through Mississippi to Port Hudson. Says BADEAU:

At this time Grant learned the success of Grierson's raid, and the timely effect it was producing on the Southern people. The rebel newspapers were filled with accounts of the damage done, and this really daring exploit, unexampled at that period of the war, was magnified into proportions and importance greatly superior even to that which Grant had hoped.

That GRANT "had hoped" much more from this than a temporary cutting of communications, affecting impending military operations, and that he had formed in his mind an idea that raids were great moral and material effects to end the war, is set forth by BADEAU, page 188, in narrating GRANT's suggestion of this raid to HURLBUT at Memphis, February 13:

This movement was also intended to act as a diversion to Grant's new campaign [at that time the Yazoo Pass campaign], as well as to test the idea he entertained that the fortunes of the rebellion were waning, its armies becoming exhausted, and its supplies rapidly decreasing; that, in fact, men and stores were alike drawn to the outside, and the so called Confederacy itself was only a "hollow shell."

He adds that this raid had "a moral effect upon the population altogether unprecedented." Thus it appears that in GRANT's mind raids were greater military operations than campaigns and victories.

Thus does BADEAU show the processes which, after GRANT had gained the footing that had cost him six months of rapid consuming of a great army, made him turn away from his opportunity, and set out upon a raid. Thus was he going to march away from the Confederate army, to prove that the Confederacy was a "hollow shell." Thus by feeding his own army in the Confederacy was he going to prove that its "stores were drawn to the outside." And so the Confederacy was to be brought to terms, not by overthrowing its armies, but by evading them, and making raids to demonstrate that its armies were in the front and not in the rear, and, therefore, it was a hollow shell.

This raiding strategy makes clear BADEAU's statement that: "The utmost celerity of movement * * * was indispensable not only to his success, but to his salvation," and therefore he cut loose from his base; for if GRANT's plan had been to fight, first an army on the east, and then to turn on the one on the west, his line of operation would completely protect a line of supply, as in fact it did. This raiding idea explains BADEAU's statement that: "Believing that he would not be allowed to make the campaign if he announced his plan beforehand, GRANT did not now inform the General in Chief of what he contemplated." Also that it was fortunate that there was no telegraph nearer than Cairo, for: "Had the General in Chief been able to reach his subordinate, the Vicksburg campaign would never have been fought;" that is to say, the raid would not have been made; it had to be as clandestine in its start as it was in its military character.

That GRANT and BADEAU subsequently thought that a raid on a railroad, and even on Jackson, was not the highest improvement of GRANT's opportunity is shown by their posterior construction of a plan to take in the battle with PEMBERTON's army. This necessity is that which has given to this part of BADEAU's narrative its complex character. But this relieves Gen. GRANT from the alternative supposition, which would be utterly incompatible with his great genius, namely: that he made an exhausting march of his troops away from his own base and from PEMBERTON's army when the way was open and near to both, expecting to attack him on his return, at a time when PEMBERTON might be expected to hold the "formidable obstacle" of the line of the Big Black, and when GRANT's rear would be in air, exposed to the gathering Confederate forces.

Thus does the actual strategy, which was a raid, relieve GRANT from the alternative supposition of a serious campaign on a plan which would be about as plain a plan to shun a victory, and lead an army to destruction, as ingenuity could well devise. The strategy of the raid worked successfully for a limited time.

If followed up with celerity, it would probably have kept PEMBERTON west of the Big Black until GRANT had returned to Grand Gulf. It was for a time hesitating in execution. Then the affair on the road to Raymond drew GRANT away from his original plan. Then PEMBERTON crossed the Big Black, and took a position which compromised GRANT's return. GRANT, still ignorant of this, had started on a race with JOHNSTON. In the very act he was accidentally informed that PEMBERTON was marching to attack him in such a line as to cut off his regaining the Mississippi. Thus by a wonderful stroke of luck, which at the time seemed to him a catastrophe, he was forced into a fight which redeemed his operation from the character of a raid, and converted it into a real campaign, in which, of course, his troops were victorious, as they would have been if led directly upon the enemy. This stroke of luck again delivered GRANT from the fatality of his plan, and enabled BADEAU to construct a strategy which from the beginning embraced all these events.

CHAPTER XXXIII.

SITUATION OF CHAMPION'S HILL—THE SURPRISES WHICH BROUGHT PEMBERTON AND GRANT TO ISSUE THERE—THE HARD MARCHES OF THE EXPEDITION—SPLENDID QUALITIES OF THE VOLUNTEERS—THE PART THAT OFFICERS PLAY IN BATTLE.

A road running direct from Raymond west-northwest twelve miles to Edward's Station, for this operation is called the southern road. Champion's Hill is four miles east-northeast of Edward's Station. A road, called the middle road, forks from the southern road a mile and a half from Raymond, running more to the northwest, till it has diverged about two miles, when it runs nearly parallel with the southern road across the ridge, then converging to Edward's Station.

From the middle road, four miles from Raymond, a road forks and runs nearly north to Bolton Station, where it comes to the road which runs west from Clinton to Edward's Station, which is called the northern road. This road runs nearly west from Bolton to the north end of the ridge called Champion's Hill, when it makes a turn to south, running up and along the ridge for a mile, then turns west, down the ridge, to a junction with the middle road from Raymond to Edward's Station. Baker's Creek has its rise east of Champion Hill, between the middle and northern roads, runs northwest across the northern road and the railroad two miles east of Champion's Hill, fetches a circuit north of the hill to a southwest course west of the hills, and across the roads that run to Edward's Station. Confederate historians call the battle that of Baker's Creek.

PEMBERTON, on the afternoon of the 15th, moved his whole force from Edward's Station, southeast by the Raymond road, to attack GRANT's rear, to cut him off from Grand Gulf, supposing him to be still advancing on Jackson. Previous freshets had carried off the bridge on the direct Raymond road, two miles east of Edward's Station, and a present rain had made the ford impassible. PEMBERTON marched by the middle road till he had passed the creek on a bridge, and then he turned to the right, so as to strike the southern or Raymond road three and a half miles from Edward's Station. Here he rested for the night.

PEMBERTON said that the divisions of BOWEN and STEVENSON had been on the march till past midnight, and the men were fatigued, and as he desired to receive reports of reconnoissances in front, he did not issue orders to continue the movement early the next morning. At 6:30 o'clock he received a positive order from JOHNSTON as follows:

BANTON ROAD, TEN MILES FROM JACKSON, May 18, 1863, 8:30 o'clock A. M.—Our being compelled to leave Jackson makes your plan impracticable. The only mode by which we can unite is by your moving directly to Clinton, and informing me, that we may move to that point with about 6,000. I have no means of estimating enemy's force at Jackson. The principal officers here differ very widely, and I fear he will fortify if time is left him. Let me hear from you immediately. * * *

But McPHERSON had reached Clinton on the 13th, and HOVEY's division of McCLERNAND's corps on the 14th. On the 15th HOVEY had moved west from Clinton to Bolton, and McPHERSON back from Jackson through Clinton to Bolton, in pursuance of GRANT's peremptory orders to McPHERSON and McCLERNAND to concentrate at Bolton to head off JOHNSTON in a race for the Mississippi. Thus JOHNSTON, in ordering PEMBERTON to move to Clinton to effect a junction, was in the same blissful ignorance of GRANT's positions, movements or designs, that GRANT was of JOHNSTON'S and PEMBERTON's. This part of the campaign was as if all the gods of war were playing at blind man's buff. No mercy has been shown to PEMBERTON by either side; but to use GRANT's expression, adapted to the situation, "Where all have done so well it would be out of place to make invidious distinction."

Upon receiving this order, PEMBERTON says: "I immediately directed a countermarch, or rather a retrograde movement, by reversing the column as it then stood, for the purpose of returning toward Edward's Depot to take the Brownsville road, and then to proceed toward Clinton by a route north of the railroad." North of the railroad he could keep clear of GRANT's columns, and this was now the only way by which he could join JOHNSTON. But just as this reverse movement was beginning, the advance of A. J. SMITH's division of McCLERNAND's corps, moving west, by the southern road from Raymond, came upon the head of PEMBERTON's column, drove in its cavalry pickets, and opened with artillery, and a brisk artillery duel took the place.

PEMBERTON tried to continue his retrograde movement, but the pressure of the divisions of SMITH on the southern road and of OSTERHAUS on the middle road, compelled to form line of battle. The situation happened to be favorable for forming his line, since he must. Behind him a road ran north from the southern to the middle road and to a junction with the road over the ridge called Champion's Hill. A broken and wooded country in front of his center and right was a cover while making his formation. Champion's Hill, and the road over it made a natural fortress for his left, its north end jutting out bold and steep. LORING's division was on the right, BOWEN's the center, and STEPHENSON's the left, holding the ridge.

As has been told, GRANT's dividing, forced marching and forced countermarching of McCLERNAND's corps, in strange ignorance that PEMBERTON had moved east of the Big Black, and his starting the several divisions, together with BLAIR's, on a wild chase for JOHNSTON, had the extraordinary luck to bring these five divisions upon the three roads that run west to Edward's Station, passing around and over Champion's Hill, so that his surprise when the railroad laborers told him that PEMBERTON was east of the Big Black, and was advancing to his left and rear, found McCLERNAND's corps in as fine positions as GRANT could have devised if he had known what was going on.

HOVEY's division was on the northern road; CARR and OSTERHAU'S took the middle road; A. J. SMITH took the southern or Raymond road, on which also was Gen. FRANK BLAIR's division, now, in GRANT's strait, attached to McCLERNAND's command. No delay seems to have been made by these several divisions in turning from a chase north to a march west to battle, and they were now in positions to flank and envelop Champion's Hill, and capture PEMBERTON's army, as BADEAU shows further along. There must have been excellent marching qualities and facility of maneuver in all the troops of GRANT's army, to have been moved with such flexibility and celerity to the phases of his changing mind.

Not all of GRANT's movements in this expedition had been made with celerity. There had been waiting enough near Hankinson's to give the Confederates time to re-enforce PEMBERTON from BRAGG's army, if ROSECRANS' attitude had not prevented. BADEAU calls the round march from Bruinsburg to Vicksburg 200 miles. The main body of the army was about Willow Springs, and between that and Rocky Springs and Hankinson's, during the waiting, making the previous march not over twenty-five miles, and that after the new start 175 miles. As the distance by the roads is not more than 100 miles, this allows seventy-five miles for the zigzag marching upon the changing plans. But some of the marching was very hard. By singular fortune, most of the hardest marching was in movements which developing information showed to be unnecessary. Such was that of McCLERNAND's diverging divisions to support SHERMAN and McPHERSON against Jackson, which McCLERNAND's report says was the hardest march of the campaign. Such was the forced marching of two corps to concentrate at Bolton. And SHERMAN on the 16th marched his corps twenty miles, yet to no use in the battle.

The hardship of this marching was greatly increased by the lack of the regular rations and the absence of all shelter; and its labor was increased by having to make expeditions to gather food. Yet there was no flinching; But there was great hardship. Besides, the malaria of a life of six months in the swamps was not soon eliminated from the bones, if ever. This march had its continuous sinking of brave men to the sick list.

A notable fact is that BOWEN's report states that the men of TRACEY's brigade, which reached the field of Port Gibson during the battle, "were completely jaded and broken down with continuous marching;" that Gen. BALDWIN's "troops were so utterly exhausted that he could not get up in time;" that PEMBERTON's report states that after the march toward Dillon's the troops of two of the divisions were so fatigued that he did not order the march resumed early next morning; that JOHNSTON says, in his report of the time, when he was at Calhoun Station—which was a very crisis to PEMBERTON—"The Brigadier Generals representing that their troops required rest after the fatigue they had undergone in the skirmishes and marches preceding the retreat from Jackson, * * * I did not move on Saturday;" that thus all the Confederate troops were fagged by the marches, and yet there is no sound of flinching in our volunteers, nor sound of any allowance by Gen. GRANT for their fatigue.

Something more than a single directing brain is required to organize troops to such facility of movement, and such ability to stand hard marching on short rations, in carrying out the phases of genius, as evolved by the rising emergencies. Something more than one man's mind—great as it may appear in these operations—is required to create the qualities of troops who can stand such marches on insufficient food, with undiminished spirit for the battle. There must in the first place be a foundation in the character, spirit, intelligence, and pluck of the soldiers; in the second place, officers of the same qualities, in whom the soldiers have confidence, all the way from Lieutenants to Brigadiers, and particularly those officers who are present with the men on the march and in the battle.

A popular idea is that victories are made by a Commanding General, on a prancing horse, uttering, in the nick of time, an heroic sentence to the army, or else leading them at his horse's running speed into the enemy's ranks. Battle pictures carry this idea. Battle stories keep it up. The way that honors for successful war are concentrated is upon this idea. BADEAU's history is upon the same notion, varying only in form and detail. The Commanding General can not carry out the details of organization and discipline; but when he is skillful and thorough in these general parts of the organization of an army which he and no one else can supervise, his spirit will infuse all the details of organization and discipline. On the other hand, when the general parts are neglected by the Commanding General, the slackness pervades all the branches.

A striking instance of this neglect of the general formation of an army was seen at Pittsburg Landing, where the organization of the new regiments and brigades, under volunteer officers, was far better than the general army organization, and, indeed, had to be made in the face of the neglect of all that part of organization and preparation which belongs to the Commanding General. Gen.

SHERMAN himself bore testimony to an example of the other sort, in his report, in which he told that after waiting till about noon on the second day, while BUELL'S army on the left had begun the battle at daylight: "Here I saw for the first time the well ordered and compact columns of Gen. BUELL'S Kentucky forces, whose soldierly movements at once gave confidence to our newer and less disciplined men."

Gen. SHERMAN had to plead lack of discipline to excuse the disaster of the first day; yet in GRANT'S army on that field had been a number of troops as large as BUELL'S, who were not newer, and had seen as much service. The American volunteer took on discipline with aptitude, as soon as field operations showed him the bearing of it, and as soon as he came under a general organization which carried it out; and this without losing his intelligence, self-reliance, or spirit.

War history has not another exhibition of so great a combination of these qualities of discipline and individual spirit and spontaneous action as that when the Army of the Cumberland, ordered out of the line of intrenchments to make a demonstration to ascertain if BRAGG was withdrawing from Mission Ridge, formed its lines in what the gazing Confederates thought a parade, and then, in the same manner of a parade, moved forward and swept the astonished enemy from the strong fortification of Orchard Knob, and from the whole intrenched line to right and left, acquiring a new base, and essentially changing the conditions of the battle which came two days after.

Also when the same army, two days after, in perfect order but yet without orders, by a spontaneous movement, stormed Mission Ridge, and thus by an assault upon a place so difficult that a commander would not be justified in ordering it—an assault so incredible to the Confederate Generals that they were taken by surprise, and whose very spontaneousness made it irresistible, rescued the battle from Gen. GRANT'S plan, which, fatally mistaking the Confederate position, had expended the greater force of his combined army in that which he meant to be the decisive attack but which had entirely failed.

These are examples of the high qualities of discipline and individual spirit and self-reliance which distinguished the American volunteers, and made them the best soldiers in the world. A veteran officer of the regular army, who had served in two wars, testifying before the Committee on the Conduct of the War, said that in battle the only officers who can be any support to the soldiers are the officers who are with them, first the company officers; that if the soldiers have confidence in the firm discipline of these, it is a strong supporting influence, but that, after all, the men of the ranks do the fighting, from their own qualities. Yet military biography will continue to be written, as ADAM BADEAU has done it, and yet the honors of successful war will continue to be conferred, upon the idea of the battle pictures.

This history has now reached the bloody battle of Champion's Hill.

CHAPTER XXXIV.

THE BATTLE OF CHAMPION'S HILL.

Gen. PEMBERTON'S dispatch to Gen. JOHNSTON stated that his movement from Edward's Station was with 17,000 men. Through ADAM BADEAU'S misty figures it appears that Gen. GRANT had now concentrating upon PEMBERTON from 40,000 to 45,000 men. McCLERNAND'S corps was in the advance, with BLAIR added to A. J. SMITH on the southern, OSTERHAUS and CARR being on the middle, and HOVEY on the northern road, the roads being about two miles apart, thus making a front of four miles, the several divisions being connected across a difficult country by lines of skirmishers.

Gen. GRANT was at Clinton. SMITH'S division came first upon the enemy at 7:30 a. m., following up his skirmishers for half a mile, when an artillery exchange took place. This was with what had been the advance of PEMBERTON, who was now reversing his movement; but this affair, which, to Gen. SMITH'S mind, showed that the enemy was falling back, helped to keep in Gen. GRANT'S mind the impression that the Confederate tactics were to turn his left to get into his rear. OSTERHAUS' report says that, hearing this firing at 7:30, and his cavalry patrols reporting that "Gen. SMITH had engaged the enemy on the Raymond road, in order to co-operate with him, I advanced rapidly to a point where the road leaves the open fields and enters a very broken section of timbered land, behind which the enemy was formed apparently in very strong numbers."

This early engagement on GRANT'S left and center had an important influence on his imagination and conduct of the battle. HOVEY'S division, on the northern road, was in a less difficult country. McPHERSON's corps was following HOVEY. At 9:45 McCLERNAND got a dispatch from HOVEY that he had found the enemy strongly posted in front, that McPHERSON's corps was behind him, and asking whether he should bring on the battle. McCLERNAND informed GRANT of the situation. BADEAU states that GRANT's previous instructions to McCLERNAND were that "When these dispositions were made he was to feel the enemy with a heavy line of skirmishers, but not to bring on a general engagement unless certain of success."

Of course McCLERNAND, in an unknown country, before an enemy whose movement had surprised GRANT, could be certain of success before he began.

PEMBERTON had stopped to fight, in order to get away. He expected, as his report shows, to retreat that night. Champion's Hill was nothing to him but a place for the day's defense, and was nothing to GRANT. SHERMAN was coming by a more northern road. To the north of Champion's Hill was an open country to the road in the rear of PEMBERTON'S position. Also the southern road, on which were two divisions, ran to the rear of the ridge. The middle road ran through the Confederate center.

About 45,000 men were marching on 17,000 by a way in which they could turn and envelop the position, and either force the enemy to precipitate flight or to surrender. The situation was favorable in an extraordinary degree for achieving a great victory without slaughter. The sequel will show how it was improved.

BADEAU relates: "HOVEY sent back word to McPHERSON that he had met the enemy in force, strongly posted on the northern or Bolton road." Whereupon "McPHERSON dispatched to GRANT: 'I think it advisable for you to come to the front as soon as you can.'"

A foot note explains that "McPHERSON saw that a battle was imminent, and McCLERNAND was the ranking officer at the front," under whom he did not want to go into action. Therefore, he sent this urgent call to GRANT, who hastened to the front. And now the situation changed, and there was exhibited the important part which a Commanding General may play in a battle.

McPHERSON'S corps now moved up. Says BADEAU: "GRANT found HOVEY's skirmishers near the enemy's pickets. The troops were rapidly getting into line, and HOVEY could have brought on an engagement at any moment." He gives this description of Champion's Hill, and the Confederate line:

The enemy was strongly posted, with his left on a high wooded ridge called Champion's Hill, over which the road to Edward's Station runs, making a sharp turn to the south as it strikes the hills. This ridge rises sixty or seventy feet above the surrounding country, and is the highest land for many miles around. The topmost point is bald, and gave the rebels a commanding position for their artillery, but the remainder of the crest, as well as a precepitous hillside to the east of the road, is covered by a dense forest and undergrowth, and scarred with deep ravines, through whose entanglements troops could pass only with extreme difficulty.

This describes a natural fortress. Further along he narrates that the deep cut road running along the crest of the ridge, then turning and running across and down to the west, made an intrenchment for the Confederates when driven to and along the top.

'To the north the timber extends a short distance down the hill, and then opens into cultivated fields on a gentle slope toward Baker's Creek, almost a mile away. The rebel line ran southward along the crest, its center covering the middle road from Raymond, while the extreme right was on the direct or southern road. The whole line was about four miles long.

Upon this description of this peculiar ridge, standing up like a promontory above the surrounding country, with open fields around it on the north to the road to Edward's Station, and with the Raymond road turning it on the south, making a strong natural fortress, which could easily be turned and surrounded, BADEAU concludes: "Champion's Hill, on the rebel left, was evidently the key to the whole position;" therefore was the place to be attacked. This is upon the rule of the art of war that if the enemy has taken position for battle, you must find at what point he is best fortified, and attack there; for that is "the key to the whole position."

Hovey's division was disposed for the attack on the Bolton road (on both sides of it), and reached to the hillside and into the wooded ravine; two brigades of Logan's division were thrown to the right of the road, and almost to the rear of the enemy, while Crocker was still coming up in column on the road. But Grant would not permit the attack to begin until he could hear from McClernand.

Grant had heard from McClernand, and had given him instructions.

Says Badeau, of McClernand: "Staff officers were sent to him at once to push forward with all rapidity; but by the nearest practicable route of communication he was at least two and a half miles off." The kind of orders "to push forward with all rapidity" is told: "At fifteen minutes past 10, Grant sent him written orders: 'From all information gathered from citizens and prisoners, the mass of the enemy are south of Hovey's division. McPherson is now up with Hovey and can support him at any point. Close up all your forces as expeditiously as possible, but cautiously. The enemy must not be allowed to get to our rear. If you can communicate with Blair and Ransom, do so, and direct them to come up to your support by the most expeditious route.'"

This proves that Grant was still acting upon the information given him that morning by the two reliable railroad laborers, and that he thought that Pemberton's main force was moving upon his left flank and rear by the southern road. Upon this theory he informed McClernand, as above, that the mass of the enemy was south of Hovey, that is to say, in front of McClernand's other divisions; that Hovey was well enough supported by McPherson, and that McClernand, having the mass of the enemy on his hands, must move very cautiously, and see that the enemy did not get around his left to his rear.

The weight which this theory had on Grant's imagination is further shown by his orders to Ransom's brigade of Arthur's division of McPherson's corps, now coming up from Grand Gulf. Says Badeau: "Grant therefore directed Ransom to move his command so as to join the forces north of him, by the first road leading northward. 'Enemy are reported as having sent a column to our left and rear; avoid being cut off.'" All of Grant's conduct of this battle was under this delusion as to the situation. The orders to McClernand were of a tenor calculated to put him on the defensive, or at the best to make him very cautious, and to turn his attention to his left, to extend that, to prevent being outflanked, instead of pushing boldly forward, or extending northward to support Hovey.

This wholly reversed a plan which McClernand had formed; for he says in his report that he rode to Grant's headquarters early that morning to ask that McPherson support Hovey:

Urging, among other things, that if his corps should not be needed as a support, it might, in the event that I should beat the enemy, fall upon his flank and rear and cut him off. Assurances altogether satisfactory were given by the General, and I felt confident of our superiority on the right. I went forward with the center, formed by Osterhaus and Carr.

Thus did Grant order the battle defensively, under the belief that he was in danger of being taken in the rear, and cut off from return to Grand Gulf; and thus his attack on the Confederate left at Champion's Hill was to make a diversion from that danger. Badeau now begins the battle against the fortress of Champion's Hill:

Continuous firing had been kept up all the morning between Hovey's skirmishers and the rebel advance, and by 11 o'clock this grew into a battle. At this time Hovey's division was deployed to move westward against the hill, the two brigades of Logan supporting him. Logan was formed in the open field, facing the northern side of the ridge, and only about 400 yards from the enemy; Logan's front and the main front of Hovey's division being nearly at right angles with each other.

As Hovey advanced his line conformed to the shape of the hill, and became crescent like, the concave toward the hill. McPherson [Logan] now posted two batteries on his extreme right, and well in advance; these poured a destructive enfilading fire upon the enemy, under cover of which the national line began to mount the hill. [No enfilading fire could cover the movement of Hovey's crescent line up the end of the ridge.] The enemy at once replied with a murderous discharge of musketry, and the battle soon raged hotly all along the line, from Hovey's extreme left to the right of Logan; but Hovey pushed steadily on, and drove the rebels back 600 yards, till eleven guns and 300 prisoners were captured; and the brow of the height was gained.

When a division has stormed such a natural fortress, and has taken "the key to the whole position" by that which was equivalent to carrying strong intrenchments by assault, it might naturally be expected that the Commanding General, who was observing this, would have support at hand to carry this forward and make this "key" turn the whole position. But it was otherwise:

> The road here formed a natural fortification, which the rebels made haste to use. It was cut through the crest of the ridge at the steepest part, the bank on the upper side commanding all below, so that even when the national troops had apparently gained the road, the rebels stood behind this novel breastwork, covered from every fire, and masters of the whole declivity. Finding himself, however, in spite of this advantage, losing ground on a point so vitally important, the enemy now pushed re-enforcements rapidly; and when these arrived, rallied under cover of the woods, and poured down the road in great numbers on the position occupied by Hovey.
>
> For awhile Hovey bore the whole brunt of the battle, and after a desperate resistance was compelled to fall back, though slowly and stubbornly, losing several of the guns he had taken an hour before. But Grant was watching the fight on the first spur of the hill *under fire*, and seeing that the enemy was getting too strong for Hovey he sent in a brigade of Crocker's division, which had just arrived.

Hovey's report relates the same incident thus:

> Brigadier General Quinby's division, commanded by Gen. Crocker, was near at hand, and had not yet been under fire. I sent to them for support, but, being unknown to the officers of that command, considerable delay ensued, and I was compelled to resort to Gen. Grant to procure the order for their aid. Col. Boomer, commanding 3d Brigade of Quinby's division, on receiving the command from Gen. Grant, came gallantly up the hill; Col. Holmes, with two small regiments—10th Missouri and 17th Iowa—soon followed. The entire force sent amounted to about 2,000 men.

Badeau continues: "These fresh troops gave Hovey confidence, and the height that had been gained with fearful loss was still retained. The preponderance, however, was even yet in favor of the enemy." But Hovey's lack was more of battalions than of confidence, and he says:

> My division, in the meantime, had been compelled to yield ground before overwhelming numbers. Slowly and stubbornly they fell back, contesting with death every inch of the field they had won. Col. Boomer and Col. Holmes gallantly and heroically rushed with their commands into the conflict, but the enemy had massed his forces, and slowly pressed our whole line with re-enforcements, backward to a point near the brow of the hill. Here a stubborn stand was made.

To resume now Badeau's narrative at the point where Grant sent the re-enforcement:

> Meanwhile the rebels had made a desperate attempt on their left to capture the battery in McPherson's corps which was doing them so much damage; they were, however, promptly repelled by Smith's brigade of Logan's division, which drove them back with great slaughter, capturing many prisoners. Discovering now that his own left was nearly turned, the enemy made a determined effort to turn the left of Hovey, precipitating on that commander all his available force; and while Logan was carrying everything before him, the closely pressed and nearly exhausted troops of Hovey were again compelled to retire. They had been fighting nearly three hours, and were fatigued and out of ammunition; but fell back doggedly, and not far.

Outnumbered, fatigued, and out of ammunition, too, is reason enough. Continues Badeau:

> The tide of battle at this point seemed turning against the national forces, and Hovey sent back repeatedly to Grant for support. Grant, however, was momentarily expecting the advance of McClernand's four divisions, and never doubted the result.

Still, more battalions to Hovey, outnumbered and out of ammunition, might be as useful at the moment as Grant's never doubting the result.

But was Grant momentarily expecting this? Badeau continues:

> At thirty minutes past 12 he had again dispatched to McClernand: "As soon as your command is all in hand, throw forward skirmishers and feel the enemy, and attack him in force, if an opportunity occurs. I am with Hovey and McPherson, and will see that they co-operate."

So he was promising McClernand that he would see that Hovey co-operated; likewise McPherson. And McClernand, after he had got his men well in hand—which they had been since daylight—was to throw forward skirmishers and feel the enemy, and "if an opportunity occurred," to attack him in force. He was to wait for his opportunity.

Considering what was going on where Grant was, "under fire," his orders to McClernand seem almost too energetic and peremptory, indicating an undue excitement, or the glow of battle. Badeau says: "That commander, however, did not arrive." But as Grant, in answer to McClernand's inquiry whether McPherson would support Hovey and whether he should bring on the battle had sent the above order, following another, telling him that the mass of the enemy was in his (McCLERNAND's) front, aiming to turn his left, GRANT could hardly expect him "to arrive." And now, BADEAU continues:

Grant, seeing the critical condition of affairs, now directed McPherson to move what troops he could by a left flank around to the enemy's right front on the crest of the ridge. The prolongation of Logan to the right had left a gap between him and Hovey, and into this the two remaining brigades of Crocker were thrown. The movement was promptly executed; Boomer's brigade went at and into the fight, and checked the rebel advance till Holmes' brigade came up, when a dashing charge was made, and Hovey and Crocker were engaged for forty minutes, Hovey recapturing five of the guns he had already taken and lost.

BADEAU by this has made two affairs of the sending of BOOMER and HOLMES to HOVEY's aid, of which HOVEY makes but one. The middle is explained by CROCKER's report, which says that two regiments of Col. SANBORN's brigade were taken from the right to support Col. BOOMER, and that Col. HOLMES came after. CROCKER continues: "At this critical moment Col. HOLMES arrived in the field with two regiments * * * and proceeded * * * to the front, relieving Col. BOOMER, who by this time was out of ammunition." This situation on the left of HOVEY, and nearest to GRANT, was that which impressed him that "the position was in danger;" that is to say, that his right wing was in danger of being turned by its left and cut off.

BADEAU continues:

But the enemy had massed his forces on this point, and the irregularity of the ground prevented the use of artillery in enfilading him. Though baffled and enraged, he still fought with courage and obstinacy, and it was apparent that the national line was in dire need of assistance. In fact, the position was in danger.

This seems a remarkable achievement of generalship, with 45,000 men at hand, against 17,000, desiring only to retreat. And now comes another stroke of generalship. BADEAU goes on:

At this crisis Stevenson's brigade of Logan's division was moved forward at a double quick into a piece of wood on the extreme right of the command, the brigade moved parallel with Logan's general line of battle, charged across the ravines up the hill and through an open field, driving the enemy from an important position, where he was about to establish his batteries, capturing seven guns and several hundred prisoners. The main Vicksburg road, after following the ridge in a southerly direction for about a mile, to the point of intersection with the middle, or Raymond road, turns almost to the west again, running down the hill and across the valley where Logan was now operating in the rear of the enemy.

At length the battle, after slaughtering men for hours in assaulting a steep and broken hill, naturally so strong a position that practically it tripled the enemy's force, had stumbled upon a clear way around the head of the ridge by which PEMBERTON could be turned and captured. Continues BADEAU:

Unconscious of the immense advantage, Logan swept directly across the road, and absolutely cut off the rebel line of retreat to Edward's Station, without being aware of it.

But at this juncture, the essential part played by the Commanding General in this battle is again to be exemplified:

At this very juncture, Grant, finding that there was no prospect of McClernand's reaching the field [McC. was following Grant's instructions], and that the scales were still balanced at the critical point, thought himself obliged, in order to still further re-enforce Hovey and Crocker in front, to recall Logan from the right, where he was overlapping and outflanking the rebel left.

Had the national commander been acquainted with the country, he would, of course, have ordered Logan to push on in the rear of the enemy, and thus secure the capture or annihilation of the whole rebel army. But the entire region was new to the national troops [to Grant], and this great opportunity unknown.

And now comes a singular incident, reversing the usual effect. When LOGAN withdrew from this road, to march by a long circuit to HOVEY's left, then the Confederates became alarmed for the road, and gave up the fight. Says BADEAU:

As it was, however, the moment Logan left the road, the enemy, alarmed for his line of retreat, finding it, indeed, not only threatened, but almost gone, at once abandoned his position in front.

But there was a coincidence at the front:

At this crisis a national battery [Badeau is too delicate to say of Hovey's division—in fact three batteries] opened from the right a well directed fire, and the victorious troops of Hovey and Crocker pressing on, the enemy once more gave way; the rebel line was rolled back for the third time, and the battle decided.

But before this consummation an episode had come off, which had an important effect:

Before the result of the final charge was known, Logan rode eagerly up to Grant, declaring that if one more dash could be made in front, he would advance in the rear and complete the capture of the rebel army. Grant at once rode forward in person, and found the troops that had been so gallantly engaged for hours withdrawn from their most advanced positions, and refilling their cartridge boxes. Explaining to them the position of Logan's forces, he directed them to use all dispatch and push forward as rapidly as possible.

By this it appears that Grant was going to send Logan back to the road from which he had withdrawn him to re-enforce Hovey's left, and that he passed by commanding officers, and mingled with the soldiers, and explained the situation to them, and directed them to use all dispatch, and make another dash at the enemy. Badeau relates that then:

He proceeded himself in haste to what had been Pemberton's line, expecting every moment to come up with the enemy, but found the rebels had already broken and fled from the field. Logan's attack had precipitated the rout, and the battle of Champion's Hill was won. This was between 3 and 4 o'clock in the afternoon.

The attentive reader of this interesting battle narrative must here wonder what made the Confederates "break and fly from the field." Badeau's narrative makes out that Grant had withdrawn Logan from his attack on their left and rear, and that Hovey's troops had withdrawn from their most advanced position, and, as appears, were not engaged at the time, as they were "refilling their cartridge boxes," and that Grant went among them and explained Logan's position, and directed them to make one more assault, and then himself rode in haste toward Pemberton's line.

Such a suspension of the attack, and such a retiring movement, does not usually cause the strongly placed adversary to break and run. The only explanation suggested of the cause of the sudden turn of the battle to victory at this juncture is Grant's riding in haste at Pemberton's line. This would make at least one instance in which the victory was won, according to the battle pictures, by a careering Commanding General riding furiously at the enemy's ranks. Perhaps, however, by going back to the next preceding citation, and adding thereto Hovey's and Crocker's reports, and the fact that Logan continued to attack, an idea may be had of the cause of Pemberton's giving up the battle.

By referring back to Hovey's account of what followed when he had been re-enforced from Crocker's division, it will be seen that before the re-enforcement arrived his division had been forced to give ground, and that this continued thereafter till all had been driven back to the brow of the hill, where a stubborn stand was made. At this point Hovey relates that which was the turning point in this "key of the position:"

The irregularity of our line had previously prevented me from using artillery in enfilading the enemy's line, but as our forces were compelled to fall slowly back, the lines became marked and distinct, and about 2:30 p. m. I could easily perceive, by the sound of firearms through the woods, the position of the respective armies.

I at once ordered the 1st Missouri Battery, commanded by Capt. Schofield, and the 16th Ohio Battery under First Lieut. Murdock, to take a position in an open field, beyond a slight mound on my right, in advance of, and with parallel ranges of their guns with, my lines. About the same time Capt. Dillon's Wisconsin Battery was put in position; two sections of the 16th Ohio Battery on the left, the Wisconsin Battery in the center, and Capt. Schofield's on the right. Through the rebel ranks these batteries hailed an incessant shower of shot and shell, entirely enfilading the rebel columns.

The fire was terrific for several minutes, and the cheers from our men on the brow of the hill told of success. The enemy gave back, and our forces under Gen. McGinnis, Col. Slack, Col. Boomer, and Col. Holmes drove them again over the ground which had been hotly contested for the third time during the day, five more of the eleven guns not taken down the hill falling a second time into our possession. * * * Thus ended the battle of Champion's Hill at about 3 p. m.

But while this gives a reason for the retreat of the enemy which the common mind can understand, Adam Badeau's account of Grant's action at this crisis can be reconciled with it by taking in Crocker's report, which states that Col. Holmes' arrival at the front "relieved Col. Boomer, who by this time was entirely out of ammunition." It is probable, therefore, that it was to Boomer's men, while refilling their cartridge boxes, that Gen. Grant was explaining Logan's situation, while the rest of the line was dealing the finishing stroke to the enemy's line.

This explanation allows also for any effect in the final scene, which might have been wrought by Gen. GRANT, which riding at PEMBERTON'S line, if it had still been there.

The length to which this chapter has been drawn, rather than make a break in the midst of the battle, constrains to defer to another the summing up of the character and results of this terribly slaughterous conflict, the theory and tactics which distinguished it, and the part of the rest of the line therein, together with a glance at the conduct of the Confederate side.

CHAPTER XXXV.

THE INVETERED CONCEPTION UPON WHICH GRANT ORDERED THE BATTLE OF CHAMPION'S HILL—FIGHTING A BATTLE DEFENSIVELY AGAINST A RETREATING ENEMY—THE OTHER PARTS OF THE BATTLE—THE MURDEROUS NATURE OF THE ASSAULT ON THE RIDGE—HEROISM OF THE SOLDIERS AND OFFICERS OF THE LINE—THE DREADFUL LIST OF THE DEAD AND WOUNDED.

ADAM BADEAU'S narrative ignores the action in all that part of the line of four miles which was south of the point of the assault on the north end of the ridge, and he charges great delinquency on Gen. MCCLERNAND for not pressing the enemy and destroying his right. He says:

A vigorous effort on the part of McClernand would have accomplished the defeat by noon. * * * Or, later in the fight, Logan could have been kept in their rear, if McClernand had come up in time, and with all their retreat cut off, the enemy might have been forced to surrender in mass.

But, BADEAU'S narration shows that when GRANT reached the front at the north end of the ridge, he took charge of the battle and made a reverse change in MCCLERNAND'S dispositions; that his conduct of the battle was upon his idea that PEMBERTON'S main force was moving to MCCLERNAND'S left and rear—whereas it was trying to get away in the opposite direction; that at 10:15 he sent to MCCLERNAND this alarming order: "Close up all your forces as expeditiously as possible; the enemy must not be allowed to get to our rear;" to BLAIR a similar order, to RANSOM this: "Enemy are reported as having sent a column to our left and rear; avoid being cut off;" that even so late as 12:35, when HOVEY was storming the ridge, he sent MCCLERNAND a dubious, vague, cautionary order, calculated to keep him on the defensive, and his chief attention to his extreme left and rear; and that at the beginning he had separated HOVEY'S division from MCCLERNAND'S command, and had countermanded his order to keep in connection.

While thus issuing alarming orders to his center and left, calculated to keep all that part of the line on the defensive toward the extreme left and rear, GRANT promised this support: "I am with HOVEY and MCPHERSON, and will see that they co-operate." Thus was he seeing that, by assaulting the ridge, they co-operated with MCCLERNAND in preventing the enemy's main force from getting by the left to GRANT'S rear. This is the only theory that is given to explain the assault on the ridge.

By this strange misconception, it fell out that while PEMBERTON was fighting defensively to get a chance to retreat, GRANT was ordering the battle defensively to prevent PEMBERTON getting around his left to his rear, and that he thought necessary to order the desperate assault on the north end of the ridge, to "co-operate" with MCCLERNAND in preventing his left from being turned. And so, after HOVEY'S division had been engaged since 11 o'clock, in the dreadful slaughter which it suffered in storming the north end of the ridge, GRANT at 12:30 sent MCCLERNAND, two miles away, this vague, doubtful, timid, cautionary order, which MCCLERNAND'S report says was in reply to a message he sent, describing the position of things, and asking if he should "bring on a general engagement:"

As soon as your command is all in hand, throw forward skirmishers and feel the enemy, and attack him in force if an opportunity occurs. I am with Hovey and McPherson, and will see that they co-operate.

And he was seeing that they co-operated. HOVEY'S and LOGAN'S divisions had been co-operating for an hour in storming that deadly ridge, and a thousand brave men had fallen in co-operating with GRANT'S fears that four miles to the south he was being taken by the rear. Fortunately, the country has ADAM BADEAU'S account of this, approved by Gen. GRANT, else it would not be believed.

McClernand's report narrates further that Gen. A. J. Smith, on the Southern road, sent an aid to tell him that the enemy was not moving to the left or rear, and that he communicated this information to Grant, whereupon he received an order to attack. The precious time consumed by all this, when Gen. Smith was four miles from Grant, and a part of the country between was very difficult, may be estimated. At length this information got Grant out of the alarmed defensive policy for his center and left, with which he was co-operating by consuming Hovey's and Logan's divisions in storming an almost impregnable hill.

Grant's orders were enough to have neutralized McClernand's three remaining divisions and Blair's; but all this time brisk skirmishing was going on, and artillery exchanges and advances, along a front of four miles in a very difficult country, especially that on the middle road, and between that and Grant's position. Osterhaus and Carr were on this road, Carr in the reserve. Osterhaus' report gives this description of the ground, mentioning also the force of his division:

With this force of 2,704 men, I entered upon one of the most difficult terrains [grounds] for the passage of troops which can be imagined. A chaos of ravines and narrow hills, sloping very abruptly into sink hole like valleys, diverge in all directions. All is covered densely by trees and brush, except the public road, which winds its track in bizarre curves, and follows the hills and valleys without permitting at any point an open view of more than fifty or 100 yards.

This was a country in which a small force could retard the advance of an army. It was a country for the exercise of skill in pushing on, or for pushing men into such a bushwhacking slaughter as Grant's in the thicket of the Wilderness. Osterhaus' report shows that the affair was managed with skill, and the Confederate line pressed back without heavy loss on the national side, the loss of Osterhaus' division being 110 killed, wounded, and missing. The fact that there was not a butchery is instanced by Badeau as proof that there was no action. Badeau says that "15,000 men thus lingered under his (McClernand's) command, in the vicinity of the field, though moving on roads converging to the front. The force opposed to him was probably not greater than 6,000 or 7,000." Badeau conjures numbers on either side up and down to suit the occasion, unmindful of the other relations. When he comes to dispute Pemberton's report of his force at this battle, he makes it great enough to have outnumbered the scattered forces all along the line. And Badeau ignores the ruling part that Grant had magnified this force to McClernand, and had put him on the defensive.

In narrating Grant's riding alone at Pemberton's line, Badeau tells an incident which shows that McClernand's central divisions were pushing on:

Arriving now at the Raymond road, Grant saw on his left, and along the next ridge, a column of troops approaching, which proved to be Carr's division. McClernand was with it in person. To the left of Carr Osterhaus soon afterward appeared, with his skirmishers well in advance.

This was timely in meeting Loring's division, which, at length, moving by a rear road, had come up to help Stevenson on the ridge, but, being too late, was trying to protect the retreat.

The battle on Champion's Hill, on the Confederate side, was fought first by Stevenson's division, then re-enforced by one brigade from Bowen's division, and then by the other brigade. Pemberton called on Loring for help, but Loring said he was hard pressed; when he did come it was too late. Gen. J. E. Johnston gives the opinion that Loring was sufficiently engaged in resisting McClernand. A loss in Stevenson's and Bowen's divisions of 355 killed, 1,074 wounded, of which twenty-nine officers were killed and 105 wounded, attests the stubbornness of the resistance, as well as the heroic valor of the men who fought this resistance and all the advantages of that strong position.

Badeau, ignoring the rest of the line, says: "The battle was fought with McPherson's command and Hovey's division of the 13th Corps." Lest this might go to the credit of Hovey or McClernand, he adds: "Grant directing all of Hovey's movements himself in the absence of McClernand." He continues: "This hardest fought battle of the campaign cost him (Grant) 426 men killed, 1,842 wounded, and 189 missing. Hovey alone lost 1,200 men, one-third of his command. McPherson lost about 1,000 men." Perhaps none but a soldier can apprehend the nature of the fighting, the effect on the mind, and the destruction of military organization by the loss of one-third of a division in a battle.

Gen. HOVEY'S report expresses becoming feeling, and does justice to the soldiers and officers of this murderous assault:

I can not think of this bloody hill without sadness and pride; sadness for the great loss of my true and gallant men; pride for the heroic bravery they displayed. ° ° ° It was after the conflict literally the hill of death; men, horses, cannon, and the debris of an army lay scattered in wild confusion. Hundreds of the gallant Twelfth Division were cold in death, or writhing in pain, and with large numbers of Quinby's gallant boys lay dead, dying, or wounded, intermingled with our fallen foe. I never saw fighting like this. The loss of my division on this field was nearly one-third of my forces engaged.

Gen. HOVEY's report, alone, gives a list of the regiments and their commanders. In a nation where soldierly heroism is appreciated —where gratitude is not all expended on one man, the names of all the regiments engaged in the assault on Champion's Hill would be household words. HOVEY mentions those of his division as if the volunteers and their immediate volunteer officers did the fighting which BADEAU appropriates to GRANT by the statement that "GRANT directed all of HOVEY's movements himself." Both HOVEY's report and BADEAU's account show that GRANT's directing did not extend to the duty of supporting him by ordering up assistance. HOVEY's mention of his troops is here given in his own words:

Of the 29th Wisconsin, 24th and 28th Iowa, in what words of praise shall I speak? Not more than six months in the service, their record will compare with the oldest and best tried regiments in the field. All honor is due to their gallant officers and men, and Colonels Gill, Bryan, and Connell have my thanks for the skill with which they handled their respective commands, and for the fortitude, endurance, and bravery displayed by their gallant men.

It is useless to speak in praise of the 11th, 21th, 34th, 46th, and 47th Indiana, and 56th Ohio; they have won laurels on many fields, and not only their country will praise, but posterity will be proud to claim kindred with the privates in their ranks. They have a history that Col. Macauley, Col. Spicely, Col. Cameron, Col. Bringhurst, Lieut. Col. McLaughlin, and Col. Rayner, and their children will be proud to read.

His report, in narrating the progress of the battle, tells also of the service of the 1st Missouri Battery, Capt. SCHOFIELD; the 16th Ohio Battery, Lieut. MURDOCK, and Capt. DILLON's Wisconsin Battery in the crisis of the battle. Also this of the brigade commanders:

My brigades could not have been managed with more consummate skill then they were by Brigadier General McGinnis and Col. James R. Slack. Their services deserve the highest reward that a soldier can claim. ° ° ° The division lost in killed and wounded fifty-four officers, twenty-nine in the 1st Brigade, twenty-five in the 2d.

The effective force of the division was 4,180; the losses 211 killed, 872 wounded, 119 missing; total 1,202, in less than four hours.

LOGAN's report, while not giving a list of regiments and officers, gives the same honor to the men of the ranks and their line officers. The loss of his division was 374 killed and wounded, thirty-nine missing; in CROCKER's (QUINBY's) division 662 killed and wounded.

The aggregate loss in this assault of the ridge was 2,262. BADEAU says:

The losses were thus heavy from the nature of the ground. Grant was compelled to mass his men in order to charge, and in the ascent of the hill the fire from the rebel infantry into the serried ranks of the assailants was murderous.

Inasmuch as this was the great battle which redeemed GRANT's raid, and turned it into a campaign which raised his military fame to its zenith, and as such a battle should be an example for teaching the art of war, it is proper to examine the inquiry why GRANT, with more than double the enemy's force, sacrificed 2,262 soldiers in assaulting an almost impregnable point, which had roads and an open country running around it, and from which the enemy wanted only to get away.

CHAPTER XXXVI.

JUDGMENT ON THE BATTLE OF CHAMPION'S HILL, AS ESTABLISHED BY THE MATURED CONCLUSIONS SET FORTH BY GEN. GRANT AND HIS AUTHORIZED BIOGRAPHER.

The battle of Champion's Hill was the first battle which Gen. GRANT had commanded in person from its beginning, having all the ordering of the army, and the choice of time and place, since his battle of Belmont. It gives the measure of progress of two years of the work of the practical education of a Commanding General.

The circumstances, conditions, and ideas of this battle are so well revealed by ADAM BADEAU's narrative, that a simple summing up of these constitutes a complete judgment on the generalship. By taking this the reviewer can avoid all disputing criticism, and can let the whole question rest on the authority of the Commanding General and his authorized biographer. Their history sets forth the following facts and conclusions:

1. Gen. GRANT, up to the morning of the 16th, was ignorant that PEMBERTON's army had crossed the Big Black River, while in fact it had advanced to Edward's Station on the 13th; therefore all his railroad destroying and other diffusive operations were in the belief that PEMBERTON was west of Big Black River, keeping guard over Vicksburg.

2. Gen. GRANT, at 5 o'clock in the morning of the 16th, was surprised by the intelligence from two railroad laborers that PEMBERTON, with a force which these wonderfully informed persons estimated at 25,000, was at Edward's Station and advancing, with the "design to attack his rear," around his left.

3. Gen. GRANT was greatly alarmed by this intelligence, as was shown by the alarming orders he issued to SHERMAN, McPHERSON, McCLERNAND, BLAIR, and RANSOM.

4. Gen. GRANT's order and conduct of the battle, after he had come to the front, was upon his idea that PEMBERTON's main force was moving southeast into his rear, while in fact PEMBERTON was trying to retreat to the north. In this persistent delusion GRANT ordered the battle to be defensive, with extreme caution, on the center and left, embracing, BADEAU says, 15,000 men, and he ordered the assault on the head of Champion's Hill as a co-operation in the defense of his extreme left and rear.

5. Through open fields around the head of Champion's Hill was a clear way to a road in the rear of the ridge, which was the road of retreat from the hill, which, had GRANT known, he need not have assaulted the hill, but could have "thus secured the capture or annihilation of the whole rebel army."

6. Gen. GRANT, having reached the front about 10 a. m., still holding to his delusion that PEMBERTON's main force was on the offensive to his (GRANT's) left and rear, sent orders to McCLERNAND to make his dispositions accordingly, and then he, without reconnoitering the open country around the north end of the ridge, in ignorance that it could easily be turned, without waiting for SHERMAN's corps, without waiting even till all of McPHERSON's had come up, ordered HOVEY's division, supported by LOGAN's, to assault the most difficult point of the ridge.

These conclusions are all set forth by Gen. GRANT's authorized biographer, and are confirmed by Gen. GRANT's revision. The conclusions of Gen. GRANT and of his inspired biographer leave no room for dispute. They establish the judgment that the assault on Champion's Hill was unnecessary; that without any necessity of the situation save the fancied one of Gen. GRANT's delusion as to the enemy's movement, he sent the right wing of the army massed to an assault which must inevitably be to a great slaughter, and made a needless sacrifice of 2,262 brave volunteers, and a waste of the heroism of all, in consequence of a false conception of the situation, which was exactly the reverse of the true.

A striking example is given of the stuff of which military heroes are made, when all the glory of the heroism of 15,000 soldiers, sent to the slaughter, and of 2,262 volunteers slain or mutilated, is placed upon the head of the Commanding General whose strange mistake ordered this needless sacrifice. To this point the reviewer, and the conclusions of the hero and his biographer travel together, and thus the unpleasantness of disputing judgment is avoided.

But it must be remarked that this mistake as to the enemy's design does not give any rational meaning to the assault on the ridge. If the enemy had been on the offensive, as Gen. GRANT thought, advancing upon his left to get to his rear, the consuming of his right wing in assaulting the natural fortress of the north end of the ridge would be the most effective co-operation which GRANT could give to the enemy's purpose. If they had actually been flanking his left, he, being, as BADEAU represents, free from all incumbrance of a base or of communications, was in complete condition to turn their left by the open country around the head of the ridge called Champion's Hill. What he did would appear to be a co-operation with the enemy's purpose to turn his left, by himself destroying his right.

Gen. GRANT'S apprehension of danger of being taken in the rear was his controlling idea in ordering this action. It was persisted in, although when Gen. A. J. SMITH in the morning came in collision with the enemy they were falling back. The only explanation given by BADEAU is that the two railroad laborers told GRANT that PEMBERTON was moving to attack his rear. He narrates as a great blunder on the part of PEMBERTON, that he "proposed to fall on the communications of his antagonist, supposing these would be cut at Dillon's;" for he says: "What communications GRANT now had were with Jackson, and his face was turned toward Vicksburg, when PEMBERTON set out to attack his rear at Dillon's;" but in this he forgets his account of the alarming changes which GRANT made, and the alarmed orders which he gave, when, as he was hurrying all toward Bolton, he was told by the tramps that PEMBERTON was moving toward Dillon's to attack his rear.

Gen. J. E. JOHNSTON makes the same point against PEMBERTON, calling his movement on GRANT'S communications absurd in plan, because GRANT had cut loose from communications. But it is seen that when GRANT heard that PEMBERTON was so moving, it gave him such alarm for the safety of his army as to control all his action, and cause him to subject it to that which BADEAU describes as almost a defeat, and which did make a terrible sacrifice. Reflection will show that there was a more positive cause for this alarm than the word of the accidental railroad laborers, in GRANT'S situation, and in that state of the mind which is embraced by the military term morale.

The alarm was inevitable from the nature of the raid, which had abandoned the base of supplies and the line of retreat, and had trusted to getting back by avoiding any serious battle, when surprised by the fact that the army which it had avoided was advancing to cut off its return. To be cut off was destruction. Even a drawn battle would be danger of surrender. BADEAU, in describing the plan, said it risked the loss of the whole army. No other reason can be given for GRANT's marching away from both his base and from PEMBERTON's army, than that he did not feel able to attack it; and now, when far away from his base, he heard that that army was advancing across the line of his return.

If he thought, when on his base, he had reason for moving away from that army, how much greater reason had he for alarm when he thought that army was advancing to attack him by a line upon which defeat would make sure the destruction of his army. The situation was enough to account for the loss of a self-possession which was not at any time founded upon an intelligent comprehension of the whole situation, but was rather from a slow apprehension. The shock must necessarily be very great when GRANT, with his mind bent on concentration to the north to pursue JOHNSTON, thinking PEMBERTON west of Big Black River, suddenly heard that PEMBERTON's whole army had crossed the Big Black, had reached Edward's Station, and was still advancing upon a line to cut off his return.

Gen. GRANT'S order to McCLERNAND, dated at 12:35 p. m., shows that the part which he was ordering HOVEY and McPHERSON to take was to co-operate with McCLERNAND in repelling PEMBERTON's imagined movement to GRANT's left and rear. This is all the reason given for the Champion's Hill slaughter. In the same description he says: "To the north the timber extends a short distance down the hill, and then opens into cultivated fields on a gentle slope toward Baker's Creek, almost a mile away." This creek fetched a circuit and ran west of the hill to the south. He says further, the road which ran up the hill "turned almost to the west again, running down the hill and across the valley," and that when GRANT recalled LOGAN he had "swept directly across the road, and absolutely cut off the rebel line of retreat to Edward's Station."

He says further that if the opportunity offered by this road had been known to GRANT, and embraced, he could have "thus secured the capture or annihilation of the whole rebel army." The only excuse which he gives is this: "But the entire region was new to the national troops, and this great opportunity unknown." Thus, while the glory and reward of the victories of the national troops centered on GRANT's head, the responsibility for his ignorance of the situation, which sent them to butchery, is diffused over "the national troops."

Troops under command have no means to acquire knowledge of the region they are operating in; that is the part of the Commanding General. He must be eyes and brains to the army. If he understands even the rudiments of his profession, he has an organization that acquires knowledge of the country which is the field of operations. The most elementary teachings of the art of war are that a reconnaissance to ascertain the enemy's situation, and the best line for operations, should precede an attack. It is the more vital when the enemy is found in a position which appears at the first glance to be naturally very strong.

The enemy was waiting in front of GRANT on an eminence that stood up above the surrounding country, and around which was an open country to a road at the rear, which was their way of retreat. GRANT could choose and did choose his time to attack. He acted as if he had all the knowledge of the situation that he wanted. BADEAU's account shows that if any sort of reconnaissance for information had been made it would have found that the hill could be easily turned. Consequently he shows that Gen. GRANT neglected the simplest rudiments of the part of a Commanding General when he sent this army of heroes to the unnecessary slaughter.

As it it were fated by Gen. GRANT's proverbial luck that he should leave nothing undone that the mistakes of a Commanding General could do to destroy his army. BADEAU relates that GRANT, in the very crisis of the battle on the ridge, sent an order recalling LOGAN from the right, where he had advanced across the enemy's road of retreat, to fetch him around to add to HOVEY's left— an order which, if carried out, would have left the battle to be begun anew, under the influence of a repulse all along the line.

By this omission of the simplest duties of a General, Gen. GRANT not only made this sacrifice of his own soldiers, but he permitted the bulk of PEMBERTON's army to escape, to subject the volunteers to the consuming work of a siege, and the further repeated slaughter of assaulting the recuperated enemy in fortifications. Such was the costly course of the practical education of a General. But while thus costly to his soldiers, it had the remarkable fortune to him that his honors were increased in proportion to the unnecessary sacrifice of his heroic men.

CHAPTER XXXVII.

THE LOSSES AND GAINS OF THE BATTLE—TACTICS OF THE PURSUIT—GIVING THE ENEMY FREE PASSAGE TO VICKSBURG—HEROIC CHARGE OF THE VOLUNTEERS AT BIG BLACK BRIDGE.

Among the other brilliancies of generalship of the battle of Champion's Hill, BADEAU states this:

Only the celerity of the movements which have been described prevented the junction of the rebel armies; for as has been seen, Pemberton was actually moving to join Johnston when Grant came up and attacked him.

And the way that GRANT's celerity came to prevent it, was that he thought PEMBERTON was moving southeast to his rear, in an opposite direction from JOHNSTON.

Gen. PEMBERTON's report says:

Had the movement in support of my left been promptly made when first ordered, it is not improbable that I might have maintained my position, and it is possible that the enemy might have been driven back, though his vastly superior and constantly increasing numbers would have rendered it necessary to withdraw during the night to save my communication with Vicksburg.

This confirms the judgment summed up from BADEAU's statements—namely, that the assault was an unnecessary sacrifice, and that PEMBERTON's army might then and there have been captured, and all the consuming of men by the siege have been saved.

Gen. PEMBERTON's report states that STEVENSON and BOWEN had both told him they could not hold their positions, and "large numbers of men were abandoning the field on STEVENSON's left" before he ordered the retreat, which was to the Raymond road, over Baker's Creek; and that "although a large number of men had shamefully abandoned their commands, and were making their way to the rear, the main body of the troops retired in good order." His report states his loss as 1,420 killed and wounded, 2,195 missing. BADEAU, with a pen more deadly than musketry, says "the enemy's loss was estimated at between 3,000 and 4,000 in killed and wounded."

In the enemy's advantage of position their loss shows the stubborn character of the fighting. HOVEY reported 300 prisoners taken under fire, and 400 after the battle, and eleven guns under fire; LOGAN, eleven guns under fire and 1,300 prisoners. Hovey's Division, and one brigade of McPherson's corps, remained on the place, which the soldiers christened "The Hill of Death," to care for the dead and wounded, and were none too many for that dreadful duty; the rest started in the pursuit, but were too tired to go far that night.

McClernand's other divisions came to the front in the pursuit, but the retreating army, as was always the case, was able to go as fast as the pursuing. At the crossing of Baker's Creek, Loring chose to part company with the rest of Pemberton's army without a formal farewell. He made a detour to the southwest, and after much straggling reported at Jackson with 5,778 men. Gen. Stevenson says he arrived about sunset at the ford on Baker's Creek, and found there Bowen's division, and they held the ford, although the enemy was crossing further up the creek, waiting for Loring to come; but not only did he come not, but one of his brigades, which was near, moved of. He abandoned twelve guns.

Bowen and Stevenson resumed their retreat, crossing the railroad bridge (now planked) at Big Black after midnight. Pemberton says "the entire train of the army was crossed without loss." Badeau, as usual, says "the rout of the rebels was complete." The divisions of Carr and Osterhaus reached Edward's Station about 8 p. m., and at 3:30 in the morning of the 17th resumed the pursuit. In six miles they came upon 4,000 Confederates strongly posted at the east end of the bridge over Big Black River. The position was strongly intrenched. Pemberton says the object in holding it was to enable the still looked for Loring to cross.

The river at this place makes a bend like a horseshoe, the open part to the east. Across this open part run a bayou, which formed a natural ditch to the rifle parapet a mile long. Trees and brush growing in the bed of the bayou had been felled to obstruct the way. It was defended by eighteen guns and 4,000 men, as many as could be used at the parapet. Along the front were cleared fields from 400 to 600 yards in width, across which open and level space an assaulting column would have to move. Carr's division, with Lawler's brigade on its right, invested the place on the right, Osterhaus' division on the left. Gen. Smith's division came up and joined the left. They found it a difficult place. Osterhaus was wounded early, and had to transfer the command to Gen. A. E. Lee.

Gen. Sherman had left Jackson on the 16th, marching twenty miles to Bolton that day and night, and starting again at 4:30 next morning for Bridgeport, two and a half miles north of Edward's Station. Blair, after the battle of Champion's Hill, had been ordered to join him by way of Edward's Station. Says Badeau: "This arrangement brought Sherman's whole corps together at the most favorable position for crossing the Big Black River, and turning the enemy's left flank." But Gen. Grant seems not to have thought of any movement for turning the enemy, so long as they held a fortified place to be assaulted; or of cutting off their retreat to Vicksburg; for his tactical aim seemed to be to give them a free passage into Vicksburg.

Pemberton says: "So strong was the position that my greatest, almost only, apprehension was a flank movement by Bridgeport or Baldwin's Ferry, which would have endangered my communications with Vicksburg." Further along he says: "The enemy by flank movement on my left by Bridgeport, or on my right by Baldwin's or other ferries, might reach Vicksburg almost simultaneously with myself, or perhaps interpose a heavy force between me and that city." Thus did he show what an opportunity was opened to Grant by Pemberton's attempting to hold a position on the Big Black.

Badeau quotes this as evidence that "the rapidity and strangeness of Grant's maneuvers had evidently affected the imagination of his antagonist," as if, after Pemberton had witnessed Grant's assault on Champion's Hill, his imagination must be affected indeed if he thought that Grant would undertake any flanking or cutting off movement, so long as in his front there was a fortification for assault. Thus were the troops of Carr's and Osterhaus' divisions left to attack this strong fortification. There was no lack of alacrity on their part.

A brisk interchange of artillery and musketry was kept up during most of the forenoon, with but little change of the situation save that Gen. Lawler, on the right, had moved these regiments and a battery into a copse of underwood north of the railroad, about 300 yards in front of the parapet, extending from the road to the river. At length it became evident that other tactics must be used, and an assault was resolved on. As this was made by LAWLER'S brigade, the account is taken from his report. The heroic character of this charge, and its exhibition of the qualities of the volunteers and of volunteer officers calls for a more particular and just narration than BADEAU gives:

During the greater part of the forenoon a heavy but ineffectual musketry firing was kept up by the enemy upon my men, briskly responded to by our sharpshooters. Late in the forenoon, finding it impossible to press further forward along the river bank toward the enemy, as I had intended, Col. Kinsman, 23d Iowa Volunteers, proposed to charge at once the enemy's works, and drive them out at the point of the bayonet, and asked my consent to the same. Foreseeing that a charge by a single regiment, unsustained by the whole line, against fortifications as formidable as those in his front could hardly be successful, * * * I determined that there should be a simultaneous movement on the part of my whole command.

Accordingly, the 21st Iowa Volunteers, Col. Merrill, was ordered to charge with the 23d, the 11th Wisconsin Volunteers following close upon them as a support, and the 22d Iowa, Col. William M. Stone—which had in the meantime crossed the field and taken position on the river bank on the right of the 11th Wisconsin—was ordered to move out into the field and act as a reserve force. Two guns of the Peoria Battery, and one 20 pounder Parrott, belonging to the 1st Wisconsin Battery, were in position in the field actively at work upon the enemy and doing good service.

In addition orders had been sent to the 49th and 69th Indiana Volunteers—two regiments which had been sent from Osterhaus' division to my support early in the forenoon—to send forward at once two companies of skirmishers to attract the attention of the enemy from the movement on the right, and as soon as the charge should be commenced, to move promptly forward to its support. Orders were further given that the men should reserve their fire until upon the rebel works. Finally the regiments that were to lead the charge were formed, with bayonets fixed, in the edge of the woods on the river bank.

All things being in readiness, the command forward was given by Col. Kinsman, and at once his noble regiment sprang forward to the works. The 21st, led on by Col. Merrill, moved at the same instant, the 11th Wisconsin closely following. Through a terrible fire of musketry from the enemy in front and a galling fire from his sharpshooters on the right these men dashed bravely on. Kinsman fell dangerously wounded before half the distance was accomplished. Struggling to his feet he staggered a few paces to the front, cheered his men forward, and fell again, this time to rise no more, pierced through by a second ball.

Col. Merrill, the brave commander of the 21st Iowa, fell wounded early in the charge, while gallantly leading his regiment against the enemy. Immediately Lieut. Col. Glasgow placed himself at the head of the 23d, and Maj. Van Anda led on the 21st. Undismayed by the loss of their Colonels * * * the men of the 23d and 21st Iowa, and the 11th Wisconsin Volunteers pressed onward nearer and nearer to the rebel works, over the open field, 500 yards, under a wasting fire, and up to the edge of the bayou. Halting there only long enough to pour into the enemy a deadly volley, they dashed forward through the bayou filled with water, fallen timber and brush, on to the rebel works with the shout of victors, driving the enemy in with confusion from their breastworks and riflepits, and entering in triumph the rebel stronghold.

Hurrying forward the 49th and 69th Indiana and 22d Iowa Volunteers, I sent the two Indiana regiments to the support of my left, and ordered the Iowa regiment to move against the extreme left of the enemy's works, where they, several hundred strong, still held out, while the 11th Wisconsin Volunteers was directed to occupy the ground between the enemy and the bridge, and thus cut off their retreat. The movement was successful. The rebels broke and fled before the 22d Iowa, and fell an easy prey to the 11th Wisconsin Volunteers. Those of the rebels who were not captured hastened to make good their retreat over the bridge.

As the result of this successful charge we may with justice claim that it gave our army entire possession of the enemy's extended line of works, and with them their field artillery, eighteen pieces in ell; a large quantity of ammunition, thousands of small arms, and 3,000 prisoners. * * * But this brilliant success was not accomplished without considerable loss; fourteen killed, and 185 wounded in the space of three minutes, the time occupied in reaching the enemy's works, attest the severity of the fire to which my men were subjected.

The total loss in this battle was twenty-nine killed, 242 wounded.

Gen. LAWLER makes special mention of regimental and company officers, and closes with this handsome tribute to the men of the ranks:

Finally I can not close my report without expressing my admiration for the brave men of the ranks, to whose steadiness and determined courage is in a great measure due the glory of the brilliant and decisive victory of Big Black River Bridge. To them I return my warmest thanks.

Lest this affair should reflect any credit on the general commander, McCLERNAND, BADEAU minutely remarks: "LAWLER had received no orders to make his gallant charge. He and his men deserve all the credit of its success." GRANT was too far away to appropriate it.

The charge routed the Confederates. PEM-

BERTON says "it soon became a matter of sauve qui peut." There was, besides the railroad bridge, which the enemy set on fire, a bridge made of a dismantled steamboat turned athwart the stream. Many of the fugitives were unable to gain either bridge, and rushed into the river, in which some were drowned. Many surrendered. This was the last stand made, and the unlucky PEMBERTON and his troops, now pretty thoroughly "demoralized," wended their way, with much straggling, but unmolested, to Vicksburg.

CHAPTER XXXVIII.

PEMBERTON RETREATS INTO VICKSBURG—DEMORALIZATION OF HIS TROOPS—SHERMAN'S FRESH CORPS ARRIVES IN FRONT OF VICKSBURG NEXT MORNING—SHERMAN HALTS—THE OBJECTIVE A SIEGE—GRANT AND BONAPARTE—THE STRONGHOLD OF VICKSBURG.

Gen. PEMBERTON's report states that after the rout at the battle of Big Black River Bridge the condition of his army was such, besides the liability to be flanked and cut off from Vicksburg, that nothing remained but to retire the army within the defenses of Vicksburg, "to reorganize the depressed and discomfited troops." The retreat was not harassed. McPHERSON and McCLERNAND were detained building bridges. SHERMAN had reached Bridgeport by noon of the 17th, where BLAIR had already arrived. BLAIR had the only pontoons, and was laying them. Two divisions passed over that night.

PEMBERTON's forces reached Vicksburg on the night of the 17th. BADEAU gives a description of their condition, referring to "a rebel narrative of the siege by H. S. ABRAMS:"

Late on a Sunday night the main body of the vanquished forces began pouring into the town. Neither order nor discipline had been maintained on the march; the men were scattered for miles along the road, declaring their readiness to desert rather than serve again under Pemberton. The planters and population of the country, fleeing from the presence of the victorious enemy, added to the crowd and the confusion; and the inhabitants of the city awoke in terror to find their streets thronged with fugitives—one vast uproarious mass, in which, with shrieking citizens and timid women and children, were mingled the remnants of Pemberton's dismayed and disorganized army. And these were the troops that were now the reliance of Vicksburg.

According to PEMBERTON's report this picture is much overdrawn, but it gives GRANT's idea of the condition of the forces when they reached Vicksburg. Upon the heels of this demoralized army came Gen. SHERMAN with a fresh corps that had not been in any of the fighting:

Starting at break of day on the 18th, Sherman pushed rapidly on, and by half past 9 o'clock the head of his column had struck the Benton road, three and a half miles from Vicksburg. He thus commanded the Yazoo River, interposing a superior force between the rebels in the town and their forts on the Yazoo. His advance now rested until the whole command should close up.

The Confederates had already abandoned the batteries on the Yazoo bluffs. Here came off this interesting scene:

Grant was with Sherman when his column struck the Walnut Hills. As they rode together up the the furthest height, where it looks down on the Yazoo River, and stood upon the very bluffs from which Sherman had been repulsed six months before, the two soldiers gazed for a moment on the long wished for goal of the campaign—the high, dry ground on the north of Vicksburg, and the base of their supplies. Sherman at last turned abruptly round and exclaimed to Grant: "Until this moment I never thought your expedition a success. I never could see the end clearly until now. But this is a campaign; this is a success, if we never take the town."

"This is a campaign!" A stroke of that which seemed alarming adverse fortune had lifted the expedition from a raid away from the enemy to a campaign upon the enemy; and now it was a campaign, even if they never took the town, but merely reached the supplies. BADEAU is magnanimously commiserating to SHERMAN, as a zealous subordinate, but as always apprehensive, and as needing GRANT's directing mind and confidence. He excuses SHERMAN by the plea that he "had seen the dangers of this venturesome campaign so vividly that his vision was dimmed for beholding success." In a foot note, page 282, he further pleads that "SHERMAN had not been present at any of the victories of this campaign except Jackson [where he said SHERMAN did none of the fighting], he therefore had not felt that splendid confidence which only those who engage in successful battle know."

On no rule of Gen. GRANT's tactics did he place so much stress as that, when the enemy were beaten and retreating, was the time to throw in the utmost energy, to pursue and destroy them. He complained bitterly of ROSECRANS for that, after his hard fought repulse of VAN DORN at Corinth he did not destroy him in the pursuit. He told HALLECK and STANTON to hold on and not promote Gen. GEO. H. THOMAS, after the battle of Nashville, until he saw whether THOMAS was energetic in the pursuit. BADEAU reflects on THOMAS for not in person following the pursuit from Mission Ridge.

Where the line of retreat is open, the retreating army can march faster than the pursuing, and in such a country as ours, where pursuit is confined to roads, in most cases through woods, a small rear guard can obstruct the pursuing army. Nothing ever came of these pursuits that compensated for the fatigue and loss of soldiers, already exhausted by the battle and its preceding labors and nervous strain. GRANT'S pursuit had not harassed PEMBERTON'S troops. But here the "remnants of PEMBERTON'S dismayed and disorganized army" had retreated into a town where they could retreat no further; and here was a corps of fresh soldiers, and GRANT and SHERMAN "in person."

Now, if ever, would seem to be the time to push into Vicksburg, while the troops were dismayed and disorganized, and the whole town was in a panic. But at this crisis these great Generals indulged in a mutual admiration scene, and pronounced this a real campaign, even if they never took the town. And so this corps waited all the rest of the day, while the disorganized and dismayed Confederates were recovering their organization, courage, and confidence, and were strengthening their intrenchments and placing their guns.

At this point Gen. GRANT'S biographer, as if the campaign had gloriously terminated in getting the Confederate army into a place whose fortifications quadrupled its force, and restored its morale, pauses in the history to sound a pean to the brilliancy of the strategy, and the splendor of the results, and to compare this with two of BONAPARTE'S brightest campaigns, rather to BONAPARTE'S disparagement. In a foot note he remarks how the history of BONAPARTE was repeating itself in GRANT. In the text he notes that the repeating was with several improvements, original to GRANT:

The following extracts from Napoleon's proclamation to his soldiers after his first great Italian campaign illustrates how curiously history repeats itself: "Soldiers! in a fortnight you have gained six victories, taken twenty-one pairs of colors, fifty-five pieces of cannon, several fortresses, and conquered the richest part of Piedmont; you have made 15,000 prisoners, and killed or wounded more than 10,000 men. * * * Destitute of everything, you have supplied all your wants. You have gained battles without cannon, crossed rivers without bridges, made forced marches without shoes, bivouacked without brandy, and often without bread. The republican phalanxes, the soldiers of liberty alone, could have endured what you have endured. * * * The two armies which so lately attacked you boldly are fleeing affrighted before you; the perverse men who laughed at your distress, and rejoiced in thought at the triumphs of your enemies, are confounded and trembling."

BADEAU says that in this operation GRANT "separated forces twice as numerous as his own," thus proving that in the hands of the truly great the pen is mightier than the sword. Not content with showing that GRANT'S strategy was unparalleled, he goes on to make out that the "rebel movements" were so blundering that no skill in strategy or tactics was needed by the national commander to beat them.

He repeats his tale of GRANT'S great stratagem in deceiving PEMBERTON at Edward's Station on the 10th, by turning away toward Raymond, forgetting that he has told that PEMBERTON did not move to Edward's Station till the 13th, and that GRANT was surprised by intelligence of it on the 16th.

But this strange operation of going away from the enemy and from his supplies upon a raid, and all the hardships of the forced marching, with short rations, a distance which BADEAU makes out to be 175 miles, all the fighting in the unmeaning operations at Raymond and Jackson, and the unnecessary sacrifice at Champion's Hill, had resulted in giving the enemy an impregnable place to protract the resistance, and to subject our troops to the dreadful labors of a siege in the hot season in that unhealthy region, and to further sacrifice by vain assaults, ordered upon the calculation that volunteers were cheap, and that generalship was enhanced by their lavish consumption. The time had not yet come for glorification of the generalship.

The general mind has no conception of the severity of the labors imposed on a besieging army, and of the incessant dangers of a service which has none of the inspiration or honors of a battle. The siege of Vicksburg was against an intrenched line of eight miles, along ridges fronted by ravines with steep declivities. The besieging line of intrenchments was ten miles. Justice to the troops engaged in this siege, and largely consumed in it, requires a description of the ground, which will give an idea of the difficulties to which GRANT had brought his army, as if this was a triumph of strategy. BADEAU takes it from the report of the engineers:

The ground upon which Vicksburg stands is supposed by some to have been originally a plateau, four or five miles long and about two miles wide, and 200 or 300 feet above the Mississippi River. This plateau has been gradually washed away by rains and streams, until it is transformed into a labyrinth of sharp ridges and deep irregular ravines. The soil is fine, and when cut vertically by the action of the water, remains in a perpendicular position for years, and the smaller and newer ravines are often so deep that their ascent is difficult to a footman. The sides of the declivities are thickly wooded, and the bottoms of the ravines never level, except when the streams that formed them have been unusually large.

At Vicksburg the Mississippi runs a little west of south, and all the streams that enter it from the east run southwest. One of these empties into the river five miles below the city, and the dividing ridge that separates two of its branches was that in which the rebel line, east of Vicksburg, was built. On the northern side of the town the line also ran along a dividing ridge between two small streams that enter the Mississippi just above Vicksburg: these ridges are generally higher than any ground in their immediate vicinity.

Leaving the Mississippi on the northern side of Vicksburg, where the bluffs strike the river, the line stretched back two miles into the interior, crossed the valleys of two small streams, and reached the river again below at a point where the bluff falls back from the Mississippi nearly a mile. Here the works followed the bluff up the river for a mile or more, so as to give fire toward the south on any troops that might attempt an attack from that direction by moving along the bottom land between the bluff and the Mississippi.

The whole line was between seven and eight miles. * * * It consisted of a series of detached works on prominent and commanding points, connected by a continuous line of trench or rifle pit. * * * They were placed at distances of from seventy-five to 500 yards from each other. * * * The ravines were the only ditches, but no others were needed, trees being felled in front of the whole line, and forming, in many places, entanglements which, under fire, were absolutely impassable. * * * The difficult nature of the ground * * * rendered rapidity of movement and unity of effort in an assault impossible.

North of the railroad the hills are higher, the wood denser, and the line naturally stronger, but south of that road, although the ridges were lower and the country cleared, "the ground was still rough and entirely unfitted for any united tactical movement," and the artificial works were stronger.

The whole aspect of the rugged fastness, bristling with bayonets, and crowned with artillery that swept the narrow defiles in every direction, was calculated to inspire new courage in those who came * * * from their succession of disasters in the open field. Here, too, were at least 8,000 fresh troops who, as yet, had suffered none of the demoralization of defeat.

Yet, to have maneuvered PEMBERTON's demoralized troops into this impregnable place, and into this re-enforcement of near 8,000 men, is to BADEAU a great achievement of GRANT's generalship, setting him above BONAPARTE. For this had he marched away from the enemy, when a march fifteen miles to the front would have restored him to his base of supplies, and have forced PEMBERTON to join issue with him in the open field. And this issue the volunteers of GRANT's army would have met with alacrity and entire confidence.

CHAPTER XXXIX.

THE FIRST ASSAULT—THE REPULSE—THE ART OF STORMING INTRENCHMENTS.

Gen. GRANT, on the 19th, ordered a general assault on the works of Vicksburg. He ordered the corps commanders to "push forward carefully and gain positions as close as possible to the enemy's works, until 2 o'clock p. m.; at that hour they will fire three volleys of artillery from all the pieces in position. This will be the signal for a general charge along the whole line." This method of assaulting fortifications has the merit of giving due notice to the defenders, and of taking no advantage of them by unexpected movement.

An interval of thirty-six hours behind strong works, spent in restoring discipline, placing guns and strengthening works, may radically change the condition and spirit of a beaten army. That which BADEAU describes as a horde of stragglers as they poured into

Vicksburg at midnight of the 17th was in a very different condition when Grant, with Sherman's corps, had paused in the vicinity of the works from the morning of the 18th till the afternoon of the 19th. Badeau says: "When Sherman's troops rushed up, thinking to march easily into Vicksburg, they found not only the ramparts were difficult, but the defenders had got new spirit, and were once more the men who had fought at Donelson, and Shiloh, and at Champion's Hill."

Badeau deems necessary to find excuses for the assault, and to claim that, although it was repulsed, it got compensation for the sacrifice of men in the gain of knowledge of the situation. He says: "The troops were buoyant with success and eager for an assault, and their commander believed himself justified in an attempt to carry the works by storm." The troops were as buoyant and eager on the morning of the 18th, when it may reasonably be supposed that Pemberton's troops had not recovered from such a state of dismay and disorganization as Badeau describes; and the eagerness of troops to assault neither excuses the loss of the favorable time by the Commanding General nor relieves him from the responsibility of ordering it without intelligence.

Badeau pleads further that Gen. Grant thought the enemy completely demoralized. From this it appears that he was unconscious that the morale of troops may be quickly restored by the protection of strong fortifications, before which a following army hesitates. Also that "he underestimated Pemberton's numbers, supposing them to be about 12,000 or 15,000 effective men." If so, he halted Sherman's fresh corps, which must have been as much as 12,000, before about an equal number of beaten troops. But Grant estimated Pemberton's number when it was advancing on him at 25,000, and he would hardly reckon that Pemberton had left Vicksburg without a garrison.

The compensating gains in knowledge by the assault were these:

But although unsuccessful, the operations of this day were important to Grant. The nature of the enemy's works and their approaches, the character of the ground, and the unusual obstacles by which it was encumbered, together with the policy of the defense, all became known; while the national lines were advanced, positions for artillery selected, and the relations of the various parts of the army were fully established and understood. It was clearly seen, from the knowledge thus obtained, that to carry the works of Vicksburg by storm was a more serious undertaking than had been at first supposed.

So much progress gained in the work of the practical education of a Commanding General, at a cost of only some 600 or 1,000 volunteers, seems beggarly cheap. By sending a line of brave men upon a line of intrenchments, to be shot down under conditions where they could not get more men into the assaulting line than the enemy had behind the works to oppose them, Gen. Grant had acquired that knowledge of the situation which a previous reconnaissance could have found. He had also learned "the policy of the defense," and that it was to defend.

He had also learned by this cheap lesson "that to carry the works of Vicksburg by storm was a more serious undertaking than had been at first supposed." Further along will appear that the same lesson in the same conditions had to be repeated at a larger cost of volunteers.

Badeau describes the conditions and the assault:

There was slight skirmishing on various parts of the line from early morning, and everywhere the troops were deployed and put into position. * * * At the appointed hour Blair advanced in line, but the ground on both sides of the road was so impracticable, cut up in deep chasms, and filled with standing and fallen timber, that it was impossible for the assaulting parties to reach the trenches in anything like an organized condition. The 13th United States Infantry was the first to strike the works, and planted its colors on the exterior slope; its commander, Capt. Washington, was mortally wounded, and seventy-seven men out of 250 were either killed or wounded. Two volunteer regiments reached the same position nearly as soon, and held their ground, firing upon every head that presented itself above the parapet, but failed to effect a lodgment or even penetrate the line. Other troops also gained positions on the right and left, close to the parapet, but got no further than the counterscarp (the outer slope of the bank). Steele's division, on Sherman's extreme right, was not close enough to attack the main line, but carried a number of outworks, and captured a few prisoners.

Thus was begun and ended the assault. Parts of the line clung for some time to the outer slope of the parapet, in a mere murderous exchange, with no other possible result, or fell back to rear cover, keeping up a scattering fire until night covered their withdrawal. The nature of the ground was such that it was impossible to bring troops upon the works in any solid formation. There could be no massing of a column for assault, nor for its support. In the least difficult places it was an assault in line, and in most a much broken line, and this against a line of at least equal number, covered by intrenchments. All the conditions which make an assault of works possible were absent; all that make it impossible were conspicuously present, and could be as well known before as after the assault.

The assault was to be general, but McPherson's corps did not arrive in front of Vicksburg till after nightfall of the 18th, and it had to move forward and find positions along the ravines and ridges on the 19th. BADEAU says of this corps:

The roughness of the country prevented any decided advance, except by Ransom's brigade, which made a brief but unsuccessful attempt to carry the works in its front. McClernand, having more ground to march over than either of the others, was still at early dawn four miles from Vicksburg: but his troops were deployed at once, batteries were put in position, and opened on the rebel line, and by 2 o'clock the whole corps was advanced as close to the enemy's works as the irregular ground would allow.

Thus doth it appear that Gen. GRANT ordered a general assault of the Vicksburg fortifications when only one of his three corps had got near enough to reconnoiter them; when McPherson's corps had yet to approach and explore for positions in very difficult ground, and when the other corps was four miles away. Meanwhile Gen. GRANT was giving the enemy due warning by his demonstrations for half a day of what was coming. BADEAU states the result with innocent unconsciousness of its obvious reflection:

The extreme steepness of the acclivities, the strength of the works, and the vigorous resistance everywhere made, all rendered necessary to move with circumspection; so that without any fault or hesitation on the part of either troops or commanders, night had overtaken the national forces before they were really in a condition to obey the order of Grant, except at the point where Shereman had reached the works, but failed to make any serious impression.

Such is the power which a Commanding General possesses over the lives of his soldiers! Such the supremacy which military organization gives to the mind of one man, over the better minds of hundreds of other officers! ADAM BADEAU's account is sufficient to show that the assault was ordered in a situation which made it certain to be a vain slaughter. And ADAM BADEAU's account is approved by Gen. GRANT.

The part of McCLERNAND's Corps, however, was not so insignificant as BADEAU represents. McCLERNAND's report states that his command was in readiness at 4 a. m., and by 6.30 had reached a long hill, between which and the enemy's line of works was a creek and a series of deep hollows, and many ridges running out from the enemy's works to the narrow valley of the creek. From this hill he opened artillery fire, engaged the Confederate skirmishers, and moved forward across the creek to the hills on the other side.

"By 2 o'clock, with great difficulty my line had gained half a mile, and was within 800 yards of the enemy's works. The ground in front was unexplored, and commanded by the enemy's works, yet at the appointed signal my infantry went forward under such cover as my artillery could offer, and bravely continued a wasting conflict until they had approached within 500 yards of the enemy's lines, and exhaustion and lateness of the evening intermitted it. An advance had been made by all the corps, and the ground gained firmly held, but the enemy's works were not carried. A number of brave officers and men fell, killed or wounded, and among the latter Gen. LEE, who had signalized his brief command with equal activity, intelligence and gallantry."

Gen. GRANT made no report of this operation at the time. He vaguely mentions it in his general narrative dated July 6. BADEAU simply says: "No report was made to GRANT of the losses of this assault. They were estimated by him at fewer than 500." Gen. GRANT's reports rarely mentioned his losses. He had a munificent spirit in his expenditure of men which did not stoop to such reckoning. An affair which demanded that troops should march into certain destruction, and which killed and wounded, according to GRANT's belittling estimate, 500 volunteers, seems to have been thought unworthy of any report. SHERMAN tells very briefly the assault in his report of May 24 to GRANT. Gen. BLAIR lumps his losses in this with those of the assault of May 22.

According to Gen. GRANT's authorized historian, to have found out the several things of the situation, which he itemizes, which intelligent reconnaissance and scouting could have found out as well, and which it is the business of a Commanding General to find out before ordering an assault, was worth the sacrifice of 500 volunteers; worth all the discouragement to the troops which is inevitable from an heroic assault repulsed. And with this was the greater discouragement of intelligent soldiers and their officers, in the consciousness that they had been blindly sent to the massacre by an order to do that which ordinary military sense would have known to be impossible.

The art of war is not so poor that it has no means of finding out whether an assault is practicable save by a vain slaughter. The conditions which make an assault of works practicable are well understood. Nobody expects a line to carry intrenchments held by an equal line. The Commanding General who orders this, orders a sacrifice of his own men. The rule is accepted that a line of breastworks triples or quadruples the defensive force of the line of soldiers; a higher parapet still more. To make an assault practicable, the assaulting column must be massed so as to overcome by sheer numbers this advantage. It must be so supported that no losses which the defenders can inflict while it is passing over the intervening space can reduce it below the required preponderance of numbers.

It is expected that an assaulting column will lose heavily in a short time. It must be so massed and supported that it can stand this loss, and by its impetus can come quickly to a hand to hand issue. And as it pours over the works it must be supported by a larger column to meet any gathering resistance. Thus when assaults are ordered on military rules, although a severe loss in the head of the column is inevitable, yet in general the casualties in a successful assault are not great in number.

But an assault of strong intrenchments which can be approached only through very difficult ground, which requires the assaulting troops to file into line, and to assault in line, and even in a much broken line, is a sheer sending of soldiers to the sacrifice, and this is known as well before as after. This blind assault was the beginning of that course of generalship which sent a veteran, disciplined, and heroic army against intrenchments to be slaughtered in one dull succession, without strategic or tactical skill, until the number thus butchered without a single success made the most appalling list that modern war has known, save in the retreat from Moscow.

CHAPTER XL.

THE SECOND ASSAULT—FURTHER PURSUIT OF KNOWLEDGE OF THE SITUATION BY THE SLAUGHTER OF BRAVE VOLUNTEERS—A GRAVE DISPUTE BETWEEN GENERALS.

Gen. GRANT's biographer states that the sufficient compensation for the sacrifice of men in the assault of the 19th was the knowledge gained of "the nature of the enemy's works and their approaches, the character of the ground, and the unusual obstacles by which it was encumbered, together with the policy of the defense." Gen. GRANT proceeded to improve this acquirement of knowledge by ordering another assault on the 22d, under the same conditions, save that McPHERSON's and McCLERNAND's corps got into their positions before it began.

During the 20th and 21st the army was getting into places, opening communications between the several corps and with the river for supplies, securing and distributing rations and other necessaries, of which it had become destitute, bringing up means of shelter, which it had not seen since leaving Milliken's Bend in March, and getting such other supplies as were required by its greatest necessities. The hospital and stores at Grand Gulf were moved up to Warrenton, which was convenient to the base at Milliken's Bend; Warrenton, which GRANT could have reached by a day's march from Hankinson's Ferry, was now made the base of supplies for the left wing of the army, and so continued through the siege. Skirmishing was going on with the enemy's outposts during these two days, but without any near approach to the fortifications.

Vicksburg was not yet invested. The length of its circuit of works is stated by BADEAU as eight miles. When invested he says the investing line of works was twelve miles. The three corps, at the time of the assault of the 22d, had a front of not more than four miles. There was an open space of four miles between McCLERNAND's left and the river below Vicksburg; also a gap between McPHERSON's and McCLERNAND's corps. The army was without any covering works. GRANT was giving PEM-

BENTON the same opportunity that he gave the Confederates at Donelson, when he extended his line around that place, without cover, for two days, exposing it to a sortie by an equal force.

Gen. GRANT ordered a simultaneous attack to begin at 10 a. m. Admiral PORTER brought down his mortar boats and gunboats and kept up a bombardment and cannonade from noon of the 20th, through the 21st, day and night, till the assault began. It had no perceptible effect on the defenses, but it drove the citizens to dig caves in the hills for shelter. Skirmishers and artillery began all along the line of the army at an early hour. Vicksburg was encircled with a storm of fire, but it does not appear to have hurt the fortifications or their defenders. All of the army artillery was of field guns, save six thirty-pounder Parrotts in MCCLERNAND'S corps. It was not near the works, and, except these Parrott guns, it made no perceptible breach.

BADEAU gives a particular account of the attack by SHERMAN'S corps, adopting SHERMAN'S narrative in his report. He gives this as an example of the rest, and it briefly shows what the soldiers were required to do. SHERMAN'S main attack was by the Graveyard road, which ran along an inferior ridge across great ravines toward the line of intrenchments; but as it approached the works it turned to the left, running parallel with them for some distance, closely swept by musketry from the parapet. Says BADEAU:

Its general direction was perpendicular to the rebel line; but as it approached the works it bent to the left, passing along the edge of the ditch of the enemy's bastion, and entering at the shoulder of the bastion. The timber on the sides of the ridge and in the ravine had been felled so that an assault at any other point in front of the 15th Corps was almost impossible. The rebel line, rifle trench as well as small works for artillery, was higher than the ground occupied by the national troops, and nowhere between the Jackson road and the Mississippi on the north could it be reached without crossing a ravine a hundred and twenty feet below the general level of the hills, and then scaling an acclivity whose natural slope was everywhere made more difficult by fallen trees and entanglements of stakes and vines.

Such was the situation for an assault. A ravine 120 feet deep, with steep sides, tangled with felled trees, and stakes, and vines, to be crossed to reach the enemy's parapet, which crowned the higher bank. This ravine, crossed by a single road, on an inferior cross ridge; this road, enfiladed by the guns of the bastion, and as it neared the works turning so as to be swept broadside by musketry at short range. No other way by which to approach the works to make other attacks, or to support an attack by this road, than by crossing this great ravine, and climbing the acclivity, through the entanglement of fallen timber, to scale the parapet in the face of a line of infantry behind it, as strong as the storming line could be under such conditions.

To send brave men to the assault, under such conditions, was to send them to certain failure and certain death. Military sense could know this as well before as after. But volunteers were cheap. A volunteer "storming party" of 150 men carried boards and poles to cross the ditch, followed at a small interval by EWING'S brigade; this by GILES SMITH'S and then KILBY SMITH'S, making BLAIR'S division. At the minute the storming party dashed forward on a run, followed by the 30th Ohio in the lead of EWING'S brigade, the artillery meanwhile playing on the bastion which commanded this road. At the right point a double rank of the enemy rose up behind the parapet in every part that commanded the road, and poured a concentric fire on the head of the column which consumed it.

Says Gen. SHERMAN in his report:

It halted, wavered, and sought cover. The rear pressed on, but the fire was so terrific that very soon all sought cover. The head of the column crossed the ditch of the left face of the bastion and climbed upon the exterior slope, where the colors were planted, and the men burrowed in the earth to shield themselves from the flank fire. The leading brigade of Ewing being unable to carry that point, the next brigade of Giles Smith was turned down a ravine, and by a circuit to the left found cover, formed line, and threatened the parapet about 300 yards to the left of the bastion; and the brigade of Kilby Smith deployed on the off slope of one of the spurs, where, with Ewing's brigade, they kept up a constant fire against any object that presented itself above the parapet.

Thus the leading brigade had sought near cover from this concentric fire which consumed the head of the column, and the other two had turned off into the ravine for cover, from which the only way to renew the attempt to storm the works was by climbing the acclivity through the obstructions, and then scaling the parapet behind which its double rank of defenders was secure. Enough had been done to demonstrate the impossibility of the attempt; enough to vindicate the valor of the soldiers; enough of sacrifice of brave men for naught. But the murderous contest was not to stop here. Gen. SHERMAN'S report continues:

About 2 p. m. Gen. Blair reported to me that none of his brigades could pass the point of the road swept by the terrific fire encountered by Ewing's, but that Giles Smith had got a position to the left, in connection with Gen. Ransom, of McPherson's corps, and was ready to assault. I ordered a constant fire of artillery to be kept up to occupy the attention of the enemy in our front. Under these circumstances Ransom's and Giles Smith's brigades charged up against the parapet, but also met a staggering fire, before which they recoiled under cover of the hillside.

BADEAU says of this second attack:

The ground over which they passed is the most difficult about Vicksburg. Three ravines cover the entire distance between the Graveyard and Jackson roads, and opening into one still larger, rendered this portion of the line unapproachable, except for individuals. Nowhere between these points could a company march by a flank in anything like order, so broken is the ground, and so much was it obstructed by the slashing which had been made by felling forest timber and the luxurious vines along the sides of the ravines * * *

The troops pushed on, and in the blazing sun sought to reach the enemy's stronghold; but, like the column of Ewing, they became hopelessly broken up into small parties, and only a few, more daring than the rest, succeeded in getting close enough to give the rebels any serious cause for alarm. But these were met by a staggering fire, and recoiled under cover of the hillside. Many a brave man fell after he had passed through the difficulties of the approach and reached the rebel line. The foremost were soon compelled to crawl behind the logs and under the brows of the hills, where they waited for single opportunities to bring down the enemy as he showed himself along the parapet or in the rifle trench.

Gen. STEELE'S brigade, which was SHERMAN'S right, had a less difficult country to cross, but a cleared valley instead of the precipitous ravines, exposed his troops "for three-quarters of a mile to a plunging fire from every point of the adjacent rebel line. The distance to pass under fire was not less than 400 yards, and though the obstacles to overcome were less, the exposure to fire being greater, made the result here the same as the assault on SHERMAN'S left. By 2 o'clock it was evident that the national forces could not reach the rebel fortifications at any point in SHERMAN'S front in numbers or order sufficient to carry the line, and all further operations were suspended."

The line of works in front of McPHERSON'S corps followed the line of the high ridge nearly north and south; "they were strongly constructed, and well arranged to sweep the approaches in each direction." The only road to them "was completely swept at many points by direct and cross fires." In LOGAN'S division LEGGETT'S brigade was on the road, supported by JOHN E. SMITH'S brigade; STEVENSON'S brigade in the ravines and on the slopes to the south. At the appointed time all moved forward. BADEAU tells the result:

Their order of battle, however, was weak from the nature of the ground—columns of regiments not greater than a platoon front, battalions by the flank, in columns of fours, or regiments in a single line of battle, supported by troops in position, and covered by skirmishers.

Notwithstanding the bravery of the troops, they became broken and disorganized by the difficult nature of the ground, and the fire of the enemy from trench and parapet; and they, too, were compelled to seek cover under the brows of the hills along which they had advanced. John E. Smith was thus checked by the crossfire of artillery commanding the road. * * * Stevenson was somewhat protected by the uneven nature of the ground. * * * His advance was bold, and had nearly reached the top of the slope in his front, but being only in line, and, therefore, without any great weight, unsupported by columns or heavy bodies to give it confidence or momentum, it also failed.

QUINBY'S division was McPHERSON'S left. BADEAU says: "QUINBY'S troops moved out, but the enemy's line in their front being a strong re-entrant [turning by an angle inward] no great effort was made by them. At this time they were simply useful from the menacing attitude they held." Neither McPHERSON nor any of his Generals made any report of this assault; at least none was forwarded to the War Department. The reason will appear further along.

McCLERNAND'S corps held the left of the line —first A. J. SMITH'S division, then CARR'S, then HOVEY'S. BADEAU'S description makes the ground of the same difficult character, deeply cut up by ravines, but less encumbered with timber, save in HOVEY'S front. McCLERNAND'S report says:

Five minutes before 10 o'clock the bugle sounded the charge, and at 10 o'clock my columns of attack moved forward, and within fifteen minutes Lawler's and Landrum's brigades had carried the ditch, slope, and bastion of a fort. Some of their men * * * rushed into the fort, finding a piece of artillery, and in time to see the men who had been serving and supporting it escape behind another defense commanding the interior of the former. All of this daring and heroic party were shot down except one, who, recovering from the stunning effect of a shot, seized his musket and captured and brought away thirteen rebels, who had returned and fired their guns.

This captor was Sergeant Jos. GRIFFITH, 22d Iowa, who for this was promoted by Gen. GRANT to be First Lieutenant.

The colors of the 130th Illinois were planted upon the counterscarp of the ditch, while those of the 48th Ohio and 77th Illinois waved over the bastion. Within fifteen minutes after Lawler's and Landrum's success, Benton's and Burbridge's brigades * * * carried the ditch and slope of another heavy earthwork, and planted their colors upon the latter. * * * Capt. White, of the Chicago Mercantile Battery, carried forward one of his pieces by hand quite to the ditch, and, double shotting it, fired into an embrasure, disabling a gun in it ready to be discharged, and scattering death among the rebel cannoneers. A curtain connected the works forming these two points of attack.

Here, he says, "for more than eight long hours they maintained their ground with deathlike tenacity." OSTERHAUS' and HOVEY's troops, forming the column of assault on the left, had more difficult ground to pass over, and a longer march under fire. They "pushed forward under a withering fire upon a more extended line until an enfilading fire from a strong redoubt on their left front and physical exhaustion compelled them to take shelter behind a ridge. * * * Their skirmishers, however, kept up the conflict." The enemy now massed troops to drive the four brigades from the points they had gained in the works, and McCLERNAND sent to Gen. ARTHUR, who was coming up from Warrenton, asking for help, also to Gen. GRANT, advising him of the situation.

As this part of the affair runs into an unhappy dispute, in which it is alleged by Gen. McCLERNAND that because of GRANT's tardiness in supporting him he lost the ground in the enemy's works from which Vicksburg might then have been taken; and on the other hand it is alleged by Gen. GRANT that Gen. McCLERNAND claimed to have carried

[On page 100, for "outer slope of the bank," read "outer side of the ditch."]

important points in the enemy's works, which in fact were not important, and that thereby he caused the principal part of the sacrifice of men, the controversy is too great to be taken up in this chapter.

CHAPTER XLI.

THE CONTROVERSY OVER THE SECOND ASSAULT ON VICKSBURG—VOLUNTEERS CONSUMED BY JEALOUSIES OF GENERALS.

After the assault by SHERMAN's and McPHERSON's corps had failed, and while that of McCLERNAND's corps was persisting, an unhappy controversy was made by Gen. GRANT, which he alleges doubled the sacrifice of men, without any chance of gain. Inasmuch as the sacrifice in this affair is admitted by BADEAU to be 3,000, and was, in fact, nearer 4,000, a blunder which caused one-half so many is worthy of historical examination.

Gen. McCLERNAND's report states that within fifteen minutes of the time when the troops moved forward at the signal, LAWLER's and LANDMAN's brigades had carried the ditch, slope, and bastion of a fort; that some of the men rushed into the fort, the occupants taking flight, but returning and shooting down all but Sergeant GRIFFITH, who brought away thirteen of the enemy, surrendered to him. BADEAU states that sixteen surrendered to GRIFFITH, to escape the fire from both sides, the Confederates in the rear, the Nationals on the outer parapet, and that four of the surrendered were shot by the enemy as they were following GRIFFITH to the Union lines.

McCLERNAND's report states further that simultaneously "BENTON's and BURBRIDGE's brigades rushed forward and carried the ditch and slope of another heavy earthwork, and planted their colors upon the latter," and that Capt. WHITE, of the Chicago Mercantile Battery, "carried forward one of his pieces by hand quite to the ditch, and double shotting it, fired into an embrasure, disabling a gun in it ready to be discharged, and scattering death among the rebel cannoneers," and that "a curtain connected the works forming these two points of attack."

BADEAU's history, indorsed by Gen. GRANT, states a carrying of a part of the intrenchments substantially as is stated by Gen. McCLERNAND, but says it availed nothing because these were commanded by other works in the rear. The Confederate official reports refute the supposition of commanding works in the rear, and show that they regarded their line as dangerously broken. Gen. GRANT, on that night, wrote Gen. HALLECK, "We have possession of two of the enemy's forts." In his letter two days later he accuses McCLERNAND of misleading him as to the facts. Gen. GRANT's testimony, therefore, may be set aside as neutralizing itself.

This was a possession of two forts or redans in the line of fortifications, and of a rifle parapet connecting them, which now turned them against the enemy. It was such an entrance as makes an assault of fortifications successful if properly supported. That it could not be properly supported by heavy following columns was because of Gen. GRANT's plan for the operation, which ordered simultaneous assaults all along the line, and the line was attenuated by being drawn out as much as four miles. Storming a place held by an army of 18,500 men, none of these storming lines could have been supported if it had entered the place.

McCLERNAND's corps had lost heavily in battles since crossing the river. With this, and sickness and detachments, including the most of HOVEY's division left behind at Champion's Hill, the number now before the works was not above 10,000. It had to extend beyond the point of safety to guard against flanking on the left, between which and the river was a space of four miles. Gen. GRANT's order was to assault simultaneously all along the line. It was made in this attenuated manner by McPHERSON's corps, behind which GRANT stood, and by SHERMAN's corps. McCLERNAND's corps followed the same fatal order, and was all engaged. McCLERNAND's position during the attack was at the Parrott six gun battery, which had breached the line which his troops carried. He sent to Gen. GRANT this note, dated 11 a. m.:

I am hotly engaged with the enemy. He is massing on me from right and left. A vigorous blow by McPherson would make a diversion in my favor.

Gen. GRANT's report says he received this at 12, and that he responded in this remarkable manner: "I directed him to re-enforce the points hard pressed from such troops as he had that were not engaged." This was the same as to direct him that if he wanted re-enforcements he might re-enforce himself. But McCLERNAND had not directly asked re-enforcements, but had suggested that a vigorous blow by McPHERSON would prevent the enemy's massing on him from right and left, McPHERSON's and SHERMAN's attacks having ceased. Gen. GRANT narrates that as soon as he had sent this remarkable answer, he made this remarkable movement: "I then rode around to SHERMAN."

The reply which McCLERNAND received was this, dated 11:50: "If your advance is weak, strengthen it from your reserves or other parts of the line." This is interesting as an example of the great mind which a Commanding General can bring into the conduct of a battle, but it had little relevancy to McCLERNAND's need or suggestion. Gen. GRANT's report states that: "The position occupied by me during most of the time of the assault gave me a better opportunity of seeing what was going on in front of the 13th Army Corps than I believed it possible for the commander to have." If so it seems strange that he should leave so slightly a place upon receiving such a call from McCLERNAND.

GRANT's position was a mile and a quarter from this action; McCLERNAND's at a battery which had breached these works; but if GRANT had the superior view which he alleges, then, while this conflict was going on, while the national flag was on the parapets of two forts in the line, and the attack from McPHERSON's and SHERMAN's corps had ceased, or was only keeping up a skirmishing fire, when he received this appeal from McCLERNAND he answered it with a rebuff, and then rode away in an opposite direction, as if to put himself as far as he could from McCLERNAND's call.

Gen. SHERMAN, in his Memoirs, relates:

After our men had been fairly beaten back from off the parapet, and had got cover behind the spurs of ground close up to the rebel works, Gen. Grant came to where I was, on foot, having left his horse some distance to the rear. I pointed out to him the rebel works, admitted that my assault had failed, and he said the result with McPherson and McClernand was about the same.

He could speak advisedly for McPHERSON, but having left his view of McCLERNAND's action when the national flag was flying on the enemy's works, which was the sure sign of a desperate conflict raging, and when McCLERNAND had appealed to him for support, he could not say advisedly that the assault of McCLERNAND'S corps had failed; he could only state his own determination in the matter.

Gen. GRANT'S report states that just as he had reached SHERMAN:

I received a second dispatch from McClernand, stating positively and unequivocally that he was in possession of and still held two of the enemy's forts; that the American flag then waved over them, and asking me to have Sherman and McPherson make a diversion in his favor.

Gen. SHERMAN says in his Memoirs, the writing was "to the effect that 'his troops had captured the rebel parapet in his front,' that 'the flag of the Union waved over the stronghold of Vicksburg,' and asking him (Gen. GRANT) to give renewed orders to McPHERSON and SHERMAN to press their attacks on their respective fronts, lest the enemy should concentrate on him (McCLERNAND)."

By these quotation marks Gen. SHERMAN assumes to give McCLERNAND'S words. SHERMAN'S report told it in this manner, increasing the captured forts to three:

Gen. McClernand's report to Gen. Grant read that he had taken three of the enemy's forts, and that his flags floated on the stronghold of Vicksburg.

Gen. McCLERNAND'S real dispatch, as attested, was as follows:

We have gained the enemy's intrenchments at several points, but are brought to a stand. I have sent word to McArthur to re-enforce me if he can. Would it not be best to concentrate the whole or a part of his command at this point? P. S. I have received your dispatch. My troops are all engaged, and I can not withdraw any to re-enforce others.

Then followed this:

We are hotly engaged with the enemy. We have part possession of two forts, and the stars and stripes are floating over them. A vigorous push ought to be made all along the line.

This seems different from "stating positively and unequivocally that he was in possession of two of the forts," as Gen. GRANT'S report says, or that he had "taken three of the enemy's forts, and that his flags waved on the stronghold of Vicksburg," as Gen. SHERMAN'S report says. And Gen. McCLERNAND'S statement that he had "part possession of two forts," and the further decorative statement that "the stars and stripes are floating over them," is abundantly supported by the reports of the officers engaged in the assaults, and is substantially admitted by BADEAU'S narrative.

GRANT'S report makes the remarkable argument that this partial possession of the works "could give us no practical advantage unless others to the right and left of it were carried and held at the same time;" which is to say that in storming fortifications, to carry one part is of no consequence unless all are carried at the same time. This, like all the ordering of this affair, is an original theory in the art of storming fortifications.

Gen. GRANT'S report goes on to state that from where he had been he could not see McCLERNAND'S "possession of the forts, nor necessity for re-enforcements, as represented in his dispatches, and I expressed doubts of their correctness." But, he continues:

I could not disregard his reiterated statements, for they might possibly be true; and, that no possible opportunity of carrying the enemy's stronghold should be allowed to escape through fault of mine, I ordered Quinby's division * * * to report to McClernand. * * * I showed his dispatches to McPherson, as I had to Sherman, to satisfy him of the necessity of an active diversion on their part, to hold as much force in their fronts as possible. The diversion was promptly and vigorously made, and resulted in the increase of our mortality list fully 50 per cent., without advancing our position or giving us other advantages.

Gen. SHERMAN narrates in his Memoirs:

Gen. Grant said, "I don't believe a word of it," but I reasoned with him that this note was official, and must be credited, and I offered to renew the assault at once with new troops. He said he would instantly ride down to McClernand's front, and if I did not receive orders to the contrary by 3 o'clock p. m., I might try it again. Mower's fresh brigade was brought up under cover, and some changes were made in Giles Smith's brigade, and punctually at 3 o'clock p. m., hearing heavy firing down along the line to my left, I ordered the second assault. It was a repetition of the first, equally unsuccessful and bloody. The same thing occurred with McPherson, who lost in this second assault some most valuable officers and men without adequate result.

Meanwhile what had become of Gen. GRANT, who had started for McCLERNAND'S position to prove his dispatches false? It appears that he did not go there, but returned to his posi tion at McPherson's center, for he relates that he showed McClernand's dispatch to McPherson, and his subsequent dispatches to McClernand are dated "Field Signal Station." Gen. McClernand, in a letter to Gen. Halleck reviewing Grant's report, gives the following dispatches which he received from Grant after the events narrated above:

FROM FIELD SIGNAL STATION.

To Gen. McClernand:

McArthur advanced from Warrenton last night. He is on your left. Concentrate with him, and use his forces to the best advantage.

FROM FIELD SIGNAL STATION.

To Gen. McClernand:

Sherman and McPherson are pressing the enemy. If one portion of your troops are pressed re-enforce them from another. Sherman has gained some successes.

This instruction that "if one portion of your troops are pressed," the commander should re-enforce them from another portion that is not pressed, shows the fineness to which the art of war has been brought by a government military institute; also the important part which a Commanding General may perform in communicating great military instruction to his corps commanders in the crisis of battle

Grant's next dispatch was the following:

MAY 22—2:30 P. M.

General: I have sent a dispatch to you saying that McArthur left Warrenton last night; was about half way to the city this morning at 1 a. m. Communicate with him, and use his forces to the best advantage. McPherson is directed to send Quinby's division to you if he can not effect a lodgment where he is. Quinby is next to your right, and you will be aided as much by his penetrating into the enemy's lines as by having him to support the columns you have already got. Sherman is getting on well.

Gen. McClernand had not asked for reenforcements from any save McArthur's division, then coming up from Warrenton. Grant's dispatch, next above, shows that he proposed to first send Quinby's division to the assault, and, if that failed, to send it to support McClernand. Yet in making his case against McClernand he alleges that the attempts had all failed, and had shown that it was impossible to storm the Confederate works. But it appears that he changed his mind, and did not order Quinby to the assault, but sent him to support McClernand.

This remarkable conduct of Grant in riding away from McClernand's call, and in vacillating between riding back to McClernand's position to prove his dispatches false, or ordering a renewal of the assault without that, had consumed time which would have made his re-enforcements to McClernand of no avail in any possible event.

Gen Grant next received the following answer from McClernand, dated at 3:15 p. m.:

I have received your dispatch in regard to Gen. Quinby's division and Gen. McArthur's. As soon as they arrive I will press the enemy with all possible dispatch, and doubt not that I will force my way through. I have lost no ground: My men are in two of the enemy's forts, but they are commanded by rifle pits in the rear. Several prisoners have been taken who intimate that the rear is strong. At this moment I am hard pressed.

But time was flying during this discordancy. Quinby's division did not reach McClernand's position till near night; McArthur's not till next day. Says McClernand's report:

Col. Boomer's and Sanborn's brigades of Gen. Quinby's division, much exhausted, came up, but before either of them could be fully applied—indeed before one of them was entirely formed—night set in, and terminated the struggle. Col. Boomer early fell while leading his men forward, lamented by all. Meanwhile the enemy, seeing Quinby's division moving in the direction of my position, hastened to concentrate additional forces in front of it, and made a sortie, which was repelled. About 8 p. m., after ten hours' continuous fighting, my men withdrew to the nearest shelter and rested for the night, holding by a strong picket most of the ground they had gained.

But a history of this assault would be incomplete without a glance at the Confederate reports. These give some light on the subject of this controversy.

CHAPTER XLII.

ORGANIZED SLAUGHTER OF HEROIC VOLUNTEERS—ATTEMPT TO SHIFT THE RESPONSIBILITY—CRIMINATION TO COVER THE REAL AFFAIR.

The Confederate officers had views of the importance of the lodgment of a part of McClernand's corps in their line of fortifications. Gen. PEMBERTON's report says: It was of vital importance to drive them out. Gen. STEPHENSON's report has this:

The work was constructed in such a manner that the ditch was commanded by no part of the line, and the only means by which they could be dislodged was to retake the angle by a desperate charge. * * * A more gallant feat than this charge has not illustrated our arms during the war.

Brigadier General LEE was in the immediate command of that part of the line, but died without making a report. Col. DOCKERY, commanding a brigade of the reserve, says: "While on the way to Gen. MOORE's lines, a courier from Brigadier General LEE to Gen. GREEN reported that Gen. LEE's line had been broken by the enemy." Col. WAUL, of the Texas Legion, who organized the force which retook the works, says:

Alive to the importance of the position, Gen. Lee issued and reiterated orders to Col. Shelley, commanding the 23d Alabama, and Lieut. Col. Pettus, commanding the 46th Alabama, who occupied the fort, to retake it at all hazards, offering the flags to the commands capturing them. After several vain attempts they refused to volunteer, nor could the most strenuous efforts of their chivalric commander urge or incite them to the assault.
Gen. Lee then directed the Colonel of the legion to have the fort taken. He immediately went there, taking with him one battalion of the legion to aid or support the assailants, if necessary, informing Capt. Bradley and Lieut. Hagan, who respectively commanded the companies that had previously been sent as a support to the garrison. These gallant officers not only willingly agreed, but solicited the honor of leading those companies to the assault. * * * Three of Col. Shelley's regiment also volunteered. * * * This feat, considered with the accompanying circumstances, the occupation by the enemy, the narrow pass through which the party had to enter, the enfilading fire of musketry and artillery they had to encounter in the approach, the unwillingness of the garrison, consisting of two regiments, to volunteer, and permitting the flags to float for three hours over the parapet, the coolness, courage, and intrepidity manifested, deserve highest praise for every officer and man engaged in the hazardous enterprise.

Gen. GRANT's accusation admits that if McCLERNAND's troops had gained such a lodgment in the fortifications as he reported, then it was GRANT's duty to order the attack renewed by the other two corps, although he knew that it would only repeat their sacrifice against impregnable works. To the "layman" the thought is suggested whether this is the art of war. If McCLERNAND's troops had taken this part of the intrenchments, then Gen. GRANT takes to himself the responsibility for ordering a repetition of an assault which he then knew would be a slaughter without carrying any works at that part of the line. This Confederate testimony supports McCLERNAND in all that he reported, and more.

Gen. GRANT's accusation of McCLERNAND caused him to bring the testimony of the officers that led the attack, and of their immediate commanders, to prove that all the possession of the intrenchments that he claimed was gained. The testimony is from officers of many battles and gallant charges. It is abundant to prove that Gen. McCLERNAND received official dispatches of this progress from the officers engaged, besides being in a position from which he could see the operation; that all the possession that he reported to GRANT was gained, and more, and that the officers who led the assault which carried these works thought the way open to Vicksburg, if they had been supported in force.

This historical review need not give this testimony. The statement that it is conclusive is entitled to acceptance, when it is fully confirmed by the Confederate official reports, unbiased by this dispute, which show that a part of the line of fortifications which had been held by two regiments was in possession of the national troops for more than three hours; that the Confederate regiments which had been driven from this part of the fortifications could not be rallied to retake them, as Col. WAUL says, "Permitting the (National) flags to float for three hours over the parapet."

The official reports of Confederate officers, and the testimony of the National officers actually engaged, show that McCLERNAND's report to GRANT was within the reality of his occupation of the intrenchments. Gen. GRANT concedes that if McCLERNAND's troops had such a lodgment as he reported, then it was his (GRANT's) duty to support it by a renewal of the assault by SHERMAN and McPHERSON, which he says doubled the losses for the day, and, in another way of stating it, makes the cause of most of the loss. As the situation is proved to be just as McCLERNAND reported to GRANT, does not GRANT's admission that this new assault would be necessary in such a situation, take to himself the responsibility for ordering it, or at least share it with McClernand?

To the attentive reader it is obvious that this crimination is to cover up the real matter. What meaning was there in this assault of a strongly fortified line, if when any part was carried and the way opened, it could not be supported by masses so as to enter? Could it be supposed that this simultaneous attack along a line of at least four miles would simultaneously walk over the works, and that then the Confederate army would throw down its arms? Upon no other expectation could Gen. Grant assume that the storming of a fortified place by simultaneous attacks from a line stretched out more than four miles, in a very rough country, and utterly unable to strengthen one part from another, could be successful.

Did Gen. Grant think now as Badeau represents that he did in the first assault, of which he says: "When Sherman's troops rushed up, thinking to march easily into Vicksburg, they found not only the ramparts were difficult, but the defenders had got new spirit, and were once more the men who had fought at Donelson, and Shiloh, and at Champion's Hill" For "Sherman's troops" read Gen. Grant; for the troops knew better; but Gen. Grant had tried this "walkover" once.

In assaulting a fortified place, it is thought that the great part is to effect an entrance, and that when this is gained success is in hand; but it appears that in Gen. Grant's method of storming, to gain an entrance on one side is nothing, for his line is too thin to adequately support it anywhere.

Did the possession of the enemy's line, which McClernand reported to Grant, make further success practicable by such support as McClernand called for, or by the renewed assaults which Grant ordered? Conceding that McClernand held all that he reported, did that make possible a further success by his corps, which justified Grant in ordering the other corps to repeat an assault on impregnable works, and repeat the sacrifice of men, merely to make a diversion to support McClernand? Gen. Grant assumes that it did. Gen. Sherman takes the same sanguinary view. These two great soldiers appear to think the chance of technically making McClernand responsible, sufficient for the sending of these fated volunteers to the slaughter.

Both these great soldiers concede that what McClernand called for and more, and the assaults which they ordered, knowing they would double the bloody business, were right, if McClernand held what he reported. That he did hold it is proved beyond honest dispute. This makes Gen. Grant responsible for the operation which he ordered as a diversion to support McClernand. It makes him at least as responsible as McClernand; for he knew the situation. It makes him responsible in chief for doubling the sacrifice of men, after he knew that the works in front of Sherman and McClernand could not be carried; for McClernand could not have known this, nor could he fairly be held to require, for diversion, an attack so real as to double the sacrifice of men.

Is the art of war so poor as this work of dogged butchery? Is there any theory of war, as taught at the military institute, which required two-thirds of the army to be sent again to the sacrifice before impregnable fortifications, to make a diversion for the other third, because it had effected a lodgment in a part of the works which it could not support by a force sufficient to enter the place? Gen. Grant, if he may be accredited with a mind up to the ordinary level, knew the whole situation. He knew that from a line so extended as his army was, no column of attack could be supported with force adequate to enter the place when it had opened the way.

He knew that McArthur was not near, and that McClernand could get no additional force adequate to enter the place at the time when he ordered the assault repeated. He knew that several hours would be spent while Quinby was moving to McClernand's position. He knew that Vicksburg was held by an army which from the center could reenforce any part of its line, or could mass for a battle inside the fortifications, and that if any further success had been possible by prompt support of strong force where the assault had opened the way, or by other operations for diversion, it had been made impossible by the waste of hours, during which the Confederate army had abundant time to concentrate to recover their broken line, while he was riding away from the sound of the battle.

Vicksburg was not simply a fort, held by a limited garrison, enveloped by overwhelming numbers, its strength consisting chiefly in its walls, and lost as soon as these were entered;

it was an army intrenched with a circuit of strong fortifications along its front of eight miles, having the advantage of a short inner line, by which its reserves could be massed for any point, while GRANT's army was extended on a great circuit, from which concentration and mutual support were impracticable.

Upon the testimony of Confederate and National officers it may be said that if the successful storming of the works by parts of LAWLER's and LANDRUM's brigades could have been promptly supported by a heavy force, it could have entered the place, and that this, following up the panic stricken regiments that had been driven from the works—the attack being at the same time pressed on the other parts of the line—would have been very dangerous to PEMBERTON's army. Its complete success may be said to be as probable as military undertakings can generally be, when the chance is regarded as sufficient to justify the attempt; but it must also be said that in the dispositions which had been made of the army previous to this attack, and in the way that GRANT ordered it to be made, it was impossible to support any successful column adequately to enter the place, after it had opened the way.

On the other hand, there is as much certainty as can usually be foregathered in intelligent military undertakings, that when the momentum of this attack had been expended by reaching the works, and McCLERNAND was unable to presently support it by a heavy force, the time had gone by when the success could be carried further by anything which it was practicable to do. Still more inevitable was this failure when hours had passed, and the attack by the other two corps had long ceased, leaving the Confederate General free to direct his reserves to this quarter.

Lieut. Col. STONE, commanding the 22d Iowa, which entered the works, says: "Had we been re-enforced at any time before 12 m. by a fresh brigade, I have no doubt that the whole army could have gone into Vicksburg." As he received a wound at that time, he was unable to say further. This, however, means that the way was open for the whole army to go into Vicksburg. But the army was not there to enter, and its dispositions were such that no adequate force could be massed to enter anywhere. The ordering of the assault supposed that the whole line of four miles would march over the line of works.

The conduct of Gen. GRANT is the strangest part of this affair. While the battle was going on in the enemy's intrenchments, which he says he could see, and when he had been informed by McCLERNAND of the situation, he rode away, leaving the action suspended where he was, and going to SHERMAN, where it was also suspended. If McCLERNAND's further success had been otherwise possible, this conduct of the Commanding General made it impossible. If he had not determined the event, he could soon have judged for himself what should be done by riding to McCLERNAND. The distance to that part of the line where the battle was raging was no greater than to SHERMAN's part, where it had ceased. But the Commanding General, as if refusing to know McCLERNAND's situation, as if he had determined the event in his own mind, rode away from the battle, leaving these troops to be sacrificed, as if for succeeding in a desperate assault when SHERMAN and McPHERSON, in his own presence, had failed.

Is it possible that any one having such knowledge of the general situation as lay before the Commanding General's eye could believe that another attack of the fortifications by SHERMAN's and McPHERSON's corps, after 3 o'clock p. m., could enable McCLERNAND's troops to enter Vicksburg? Whatever chance there was of success was determined by Gen. GRANT's riding away from McCLERNAND's call while his troops were in the Confederate works, and keeping the rest of the army inactive for several hours. His order of another assault upon the fortifications after that was the sending of a gallant army to the slaughter, to no intelligent purpose, and with no possibility of gain.

This crimination is only a diversion from the real affair of the organized fatality of this assault. If a successful assault of those fortifications had been possible, it was made impossible by the dispositions of the army to invest so great a line, for which its numbers were inadequate, and by the order to assault from such an extended line a fortified army. This made it impossible to adequately support any column which should enter the fortifications. GRANT and BADEAU admit that the storming of the works was impossible, but BADEAU pleads that GRANT could not know this till he had tried the second time—could not know the strength of the works, the difficulties of the approach, nor that the Confederate soldiers would fight so well. This seems a plea of military incompetency for the Commanding General.

CHAPTER XLIII.

THE COMMANDING GENERAL CONCEDES THAT THE VOLUNTEERS DID ALL THAT HEROISM COULD DO, BUT SAYS THE UNDERTAKING WAS AN IMPOSSIBILITY—HIS EXCUSES FOR HIS FATAL ORDER—INFALLIBILITY OF MILITARY SCIENCE.

Gen. GRANT's formal report of the operations of the Vicksburg campaign, dated July 6, gave credit to the soldiers for the gallantry of the attack, and stated that the failure was because the strength of the fortifications, the difficulties of the ground, precluding any approach in strong columns, and the number of the defenders, made a successful assault impossible, and that the result would have been the same if his own army had been ever so much greater.

He wrote: "The assault was gallant in the extreme on the part of all the troops, but the enemy's position was too strong, both naturally and artificially, to be taken in that way." This does justice to the valor of the troops, and exonerates them from responsibility for this sacrifice of the army for nothing. He continues: "At every point assaulted, and all of them at the same time, the enemy was able to show all the force his works would cover." Thus the defenders could show a stronger line behind the rifle parapet and batteries than the assaulting army could bring up to them, through the difficult approaches.

He also argued by the following that greater numbers on his side could not have changed the result: "Each corps had many more men than could possibly be used in the assault, over such ground as intervened between them and the enemy. More men could only avail in case of breaking through the enemy's line or in repelling a sortie." Forasmuch as they did not break through the enemy's line, he regards it of no consequence that more men were not there to avail. This seems to show a sagacity in the ordering of the assault which had foreseen that it would nowhere enter the line of fortifications, and, therefore, had wasted no energy in providing force to follow it up.

Gen. McCLERNAND's report, which was made earlier, stated that two of his assaulting columns did break through the enemy's works, and that he had not adequate force to make this entrance avail. But Gen. GRANT's report was made to refute that. It showed also that the ordering of the assault, and the dispositions of the army were upon the conclusion that the enemy would make no sortie, and therefore men would not be required to meet that. Fortunately the enemy did not, save that the force which had been gathered to retake the works in McCLERNAND's front, and the further force which he says was concentrated because of QUINBY's movement, did make a sortie which caused considerable loss.

The average citizen has profound veneration for the military art. He is taught to believe it a system of absolute theoretical principles, which are taught at the military institute, by which the graduate can forecast military operations with an approximation to the exactness of science, and without which education no amount of experience in war can make a soldier other than an empirical bungler, whose success, if he ever makes any, is a matter of chance. To shake popular beliefs is always evil; for not alone is the particular tradition shaken, but this tends to weaken popular faiths in all things.

But the average citizen, reading Gen. GRANT's award to the gallantry of the soldiers in this assault of his ordering, and his unqualified declaration that the natural and artificial strength of these fortifications was such that a successful assault was impossible, and that the result could not be otherwise if he had had ever so many more men, is constrained to inquire whether military science has no other means of finding out that fortifications are impregnable to assault save by sending an army upon them to be destroyed.

Such fortifications are not hidden. This was a line of eight miles, along the highest projections. In a great part of the way they crowned the steep banks of deep ravines, which enabled the constructors to dispense with the outer ditch. They were further strengthened by redans, lunettes, and redoubts at the angles, and at places to command any ground that was practicable for an approach in formation. This line of fortifications was the most conspicuous feature in that region. Under cover of parallel ridges and of the thickets in the ravines, scouts and reconnoitering officers could observe the works.

Could not military science judge whether it was practicable to carry these fortifications by storm? Could the military art do no better than to sacrifice near 4,000 heroic volunteers, to find out what could be told by an intelligent reconnaissance? Was it necessary to order assaults all along the line of four miles, to try the strength of the works? If this be so, is the art of war, as taught at the institute, the infallible science that is popularly believed? If this be the only way to find that fortifications are impregnable to assault, is there such an unassailable height as is assumed between the officer of the special schooling and the officer of general education, general capacity, and of as much experience in war?

BADEAU says that "GRANT had in his various columns about 30,000 men engaged." Gen. PEMBERTON'S report states that at the beginning of the siege he had 18,500 effectives. ["To man the entire line I was able to bring into the trenches about 18,500 muskets."] GRANT'S army was extended as much as four miles. This extension, and the nature of the country, made it impracticable for one army corps to support another. The reports show also that neither of the three corps was so concentrated that in case of any part entering the works, it could be adequately supported to advance.

The previous disposition of the army for the attack, and the ordering of it from a line so extended, against a line of fortifications which covered an army, was upon the plan that the assaulting lines were to march over them simultaneously. After Gen. GRANT had tried this, he amply declared that they were impregnable. Had generalship no other way to find out this? Can it be said, upon his own account, that even by this terrible sacrifice he had proved that the enemy's line could not be broken by assaults in the manner that fortified places are usually assaulted, by massing at one or two points, and masking these by other demonstrations?

Reports of both Confederate and national officers show that the enemy's line was broken in McCLERNAND'S front. The previous dispositions of the army and Gen. GRANT'S order of the assault show that it was impossible to support this adequately to enter the place. Gen. GRANT said this possession of the Confederate works was of no use unless others to right and left were carried. This still further shows that the ordering of the assault all along the line was upon the theory that the whole line was to simultaneously march over the fortifications, after a cannonading fanfare, which made no impression save to give notice of what was coming.

Gen. GRANT'S biographer makes a formidable array of excuses for the ordering of this assault.

1. He felt that a resolute assault from the advanced positions obtained on the 19th would succeed, if made with proper vigor and co-operation.

Previously, in stating the compensations got for the sacrifice by the assault of the 19th, the principal item was this: "The nature of the enemy's works, the character of the ground, and the unusual obstacles by which it was encumbered, together with the policy of the defense, all became known." That knowledge was obtained by the sacrifice of something less than 1,000 men; but now something less than 4,000 had to be sacrificed to obtain the same knowledge.

2. He believed * * * he could reach the rebel works in sufficient order and with weight enough to break through before any serious loss could be inflicted by the enemy.

This is the way he improved the knowledge gained by the first assault. But he found that he could not reach the works with any heavy columns, nor, as BADEAU says, make "any tactical movement."

3. In addition to these tactical considerations, it was known that Johnston was at Canton, with the troops that had escaped from Jackson, re-enforced by others from the East and South; that accessions were daily reaching him, and that every soldier the rebel government could gather up in all its territory would doubtless soon be sent to Johnston's support. In a short time he might be strong enough to attack Grant in the rear, and possibly, in conjunction with the garrison, raise the siege.

The alleged grand strategy of Gen. GRANT'S march away from PEMBERTON'S army at Vicksburg, and from his base of supplies, both of which could be reached from Hankinson's Ferry by a march of fifteen miles, was that in this way he could scatter all forces that could be gathered on the east, seize Jackson, destroy the railroads that center there, and thus, said BADEAU: "Troops as well as stores would be cut off, and Vicksburg with its garrison isolated from the rest of the would be Confederacy."

This movement away from the enemy and the objective place, to first make impossible any aid from the east, so as to pen up PEMBERTON in Vicksburg and have his own way with him, was the whole of the grand strategy, as reconstructed after the event. It was upon this that BADEAU, approved by GRANT, declared that this movement equaled a combination of BONAPARTE'S first Italian campaign, and of his campaign about Ulm. Yet now only three days after his rapid march had reached Vicksburg, he determined that this desperate assault of impregnable fortifications was necessary because JOHNSTON might quickly be upon him.

If, when he had reached Hankinson's Ferry on the 3d of April, and on the 4th had reconnoitered to within six miles of Vicksburg, and he could have connected with his base of supplies by a march of ten miles to Warrenton, and within fifteen miles could have forced PEMBERTON to fight in the open country or lose his communications and be shut up, he had taken this course, he could not be more in danger of JOHNSTON or of any other interference from the east than he now pleads as an excuse for this sacrifice of his army by assaulting impregnable fortifications.

In fact, JOHNSTON did not reach Jackson till the 13th of April, and then he had but 6,000 troops. Thus it appears by BADEAU's apologies that GRANT's grand strategy of marching away from the objective and from his supplies, defeated itself, and that in his view JOHNSTON was now more dangerous, after all of GRANT's forced marching of his army, on short supplies, to extinguish him before tackling Gen. PEMBERTON and Vicksburg.

4. Possession of Vicksburg, on the contrary, would enable Grant to turn upon Johnston and drive him from the State; to seize all the railroads and practical highways, and effectually secure all territory west of the Tombigbee River before the season for active campaigning in this latitude should be past.

This is a further showing that the grand strategy had begun the campaign wrong end first. These were the grand advantages that were before Gen. GRANT when he reached Hankinson's Ferry, and which he marched away from, and marched his army a month further into the sickly season, and then compassed the dreadful labor and hardship of a siege, when it was probable that the issue would have been decided by a battle in the field, if he had marched directly upon PEMBERTON's army. At last the grand strategy has to confess that it turned everything wrong end first.

5. Finally the troops themselves were impatient to possess Vicksburg. ° ° ° The temper of the army, after its triumphant march, was such that neither officers nor men would have worked in the trenches with any zeal until they became certain that all other means had failed. ° ° ° So, although Grant certainly expected to succeed, he felt now as he did at Belmont, that there was a moral as well as a military necessity for the assault. The spirit of the men demanded it, and to this spirit every real commander will defer; or rather, with this spirit his own will be sure to be in unison.

So the useless and bloody assault has to be charged to the soldiers, as was the Commanding General's ignorance of the country at Champion's Hill. Near 4,000 of them must be killed and wounded to take down their spirit enough to make them work in the trenches, and for moral effect. Doubtless the blood letting was sufficient for their spirit and morale. Between butchery and digging siege trenches, they chose the trenches. The volunteers had no voice; but the country knows what they were, and how high their intelligence. They knew of one bloody assault, and the skirmishers knew these fortifications. Does any one suppose them such senseless machines that they did not know that this order was to send them to destruction without any hope of success?

MCCLERNAND says the order of the assault "was deemed not only by me, but by all my general officers who spoke to me upon the subject, as unfortunate, and likely to bring disaster upon us rather than the enemy." He says that on the previous day, when GRANT announced his purpose to assault, he volunteered the suggestion of a "concentration of our forces against one or two points, and not the dispersion of them into a multitude of columns," and that SHERMAN's remark was "that it was a question of how many men he was willing to lose." This is characteristic of Gen. SHERMAN's theory of war, but it does not show that he approved the attempt. Yet the accounts all show that officers and men went to their death with the same pluck as they would if they had thought this a sane military undertaking. BADEAU'S apologies continue:

6. The only possible chance of breaking through such defenses and defenders was in massing the troops, so that the weight of the columns should be absolutely irresistible. But the broken and tangled ground, where often a company could not advance by flank, made massing impossible; and this could not be known in advance.

Thus, after Gen. GRANT had made one assault for information of the works, and had been before Vicksburg three days, he could not know, before this second assault, that the nature of the ground in front of the fortifications made the massing of columns of assault impossible. This plea of ignorance of so simple a matter, and one which involved the destruction of his army, is calculated to shake popular faith in the infallibility of military science, as taught at the institute.

Furthermore, he was excusable because he did not suppose the Confederate troops would fight. BADEAU, in reciting the gain of information by the assault of the 19th, itemizes that "the policy of the defense had now become known." It was obvious that the policy of the defense was to defend. He says also of that pursuit of information: "When SHERMAN'S troops rushed up, thinking to march easily into Vicksburg, they found not only the ramparts were difficult, but the defenders had got new spirit, and were once more the men who had fought at Donelson, and Shiloh, and at Champion's Hill." But it appears that GRANT had to learn the policy of the defense by another lesson, for BADEAU says he could not have known beforehand that the Confederates would fight, and he dates back to Big Black Bridge, thus:

7. The rebels, too, had not shown [in the week preceding the assault any of the determination which they displayed behind their earthen walls at Vicksburg; the works at Big Black River also were impregnable if they had been well defended, and Grant could not know beforehand that Pemberton's men had recovered their former mettle any more than he could ascertain, without a trial, how inaccessible were the acclivities, and how prodigious the difficulties which protected these invigorated soldiers.

This list of excuses confesses the fatal ordering of the assault, and it states so many of the essential things which Gen. GRANT did not know of the situation that it leaves but a narrow margin for the essential things which he did know, when he spread out his army and sent it in thin formations against a line of fortifications which he says was impregnable to any assault. This has a tendency to confound the popular idea of the infallibility of military science, and to impeach the popular practice of giving all the glory and rewards for the victories and slaughter of the volunteers to the Commanding General. All this, however, fails to show that by an intelligent reconnaissance, concentration, and a properly ordered assault the army could not even then have carried Vicksburg by storm.

CHAPTER XLIV.

THE LOSSES BY THE ASSAULT—ROMANCE OF WAR BULLETINS—THE WAY POPULAR HISTORY OF THE VICKSBURG CAMPAIGN WAS MADE—LEAVING THE WOUNDED TO DIE AND THE DEAD UNBURIED.

The casualties in SHERMAN'S and McPHERSON'S corps by the assault of the 22d are not shown by the official reports. McCLERNAND'S report gave his as 1,487. Subsequently McPHERSON'S letter to GRANT, complaining of McCLERNAND'S congratulatory order to his command, mentioned the loss of his corps in the assault as 1,218. SHERMAN'S corps had been less reduced than the other two by battles, and he describes his assault as heavy, resolute, and repeated.

Reckoning SHERMAN'S loss as great as McPHERSON'S, would make the total 3,923; if as great as McCLERNAND'S, the total 4,192. On that evening Gen. GRANT wrote the following dispatch to Gen. HALLECK, in which the intelligent reader will have an idea of the relation which Gen. GRANT'S war bulletins bore to the events:

Vicksburg is now completely invested. I have possession of Haine's Bluff and the Yazoo, consequently have supplies. To-day an attempt was made to carry the city by assault, but was not entirely successful. We hold possession, however, of two of the enemy's forts, and have skirmishers close under all of them. Our loss was not severe. The nature of the ground about Vicksburg is such that it can only be taken by a siege. * * * What shall I do with the prisoners I have?

In the hand which writes war bulletins the pen is mightier than the army's assault. "Vicksburg completely invested!" Between his left and the river below Vicksburg was a space of four miles. The attenuation of the army for the assault had not even the excuse that it was in order to invest the place. BADEAU says the investment was not completed till the 11th of June. In like manner GRANT wrote this, of the skipping advance of his approaches, which had not yet begun: "The approaches are gradually nearing the enemy's fortifications. Five days more should plant our batteries on their parapets." The following month of hard labor by a great army did not plant the batteries in dangerous proximity to their parapets.

The assault "not entirely unsuccessful!" But "we hold possession of two of the enemy's forts." This seems to reinstate McCLERNAND's troops in the two forts, for this bulletin only, which, for other purposes, he denied that they had entered. "Have skirmishers close under all of them!" BADEAU says of the end of the action:

"The hillsides were covered with the slain, and with unfortunates who lay panting in the hot sun, crying for water which none could bring them, and writhing in pain that might not be relieved."

And there they lay for three days, the dead to rot unburied, and the helpless wounded to die because the Confederate works and outer pickets and sharpshooters commanded the ground, and GRANT would not ask permission to succor the wounded and bury the dead.

Something near 4,000 killed and wounded, yet this bulletin told the country that "our loss was not severe." The greatest quality of this great soldier was his imperturbability in the slaughter of his own soldiers. What thought the intelligent volunteers of the severity of the loss, whose comrades were thickly strewn, dead and wounded, before the enemy's intrenchments, the dead unburied, the wounded abandoned, "crying for water which none could bring them, and writhing in pain that might not be relieved?" Were they so imbruted that they had no feeling, when they knew that this sacrifice was a blunder of generalship?

This bulletin was the official report that would first go to the country, and would make popular history, which the truth could never overtake. This is the way that war history was made in the Vicksburg campaign.

Two days later, on the 24th, Gen. GRANT wrote a revised version of the assault. In this he stated the loss at 1,500—less than half the truth; but he charged it to McCLERNAND. He gave this fine definition of the result: "Our troops were not repulsed from any point, but simply failed to enter the works of the enemy."

He continued: "At several points they got up to the parapets of the enemy's works, and planted their flags on the outer slope of the embankment, where they still have them." Not repulsed, but simply failed to enter! Their flags still on the enemy's parapets, two days after the assault, but still he was unable to succor the wounded or bury the dead. He continues:

The loss on our side was not very heavy at first, but receiving repeated dispatches from Maj. Gen. McClernand, saying that he was hard pressed on his right and left, and calling for re-enforcements. I gave him all of McPherson's corps but four brigades, and caused Sherman to press the enemy on our right, which caused us to double our losses for the day. They will probably reach 1,500 killed and wounded. Gen. McClernand's dispatches misled me as to the facts, and caused much of this loss. He is entirely unfit for the position of corps commander, both on the march and on the battlefield. Looking after his corps gives me more labor and infinitely more uneasiness than all the remainder of my department.

That McCLERNAND's corps gave Gen. GRANT great trouble and uneasiness, and greatly occupied his mind, in all the Vicksburg operation, beginning in the Holly Springs movement, is sufficiently obvious in BADEAU's narrative; but it appears that in this particular action Gen. GRANT had no trouble or uneasiness about McCLERNAND, for when he sent a message that he was engaged in the enemy's works and "hotly pressed," GRANT rode away in an opposite direction, where the action had ceased. The rest of this report was a narration of his achievements by the interior movement and of those now in his hands, which, as they were written by the same hand that wrote the dispatch concerning the assault, were not diminished in the telling.

For two days the dead and dying of GRANT's heroic soldiers of the assault lay on the slopes before the Confederate works, and he made no sign. He could not bury the dead nor care for the wounded without Gen. PEM-

BERTON's permission, and to ask this would disclose to the country a situation quite different from that in his bulletin. At length, on the 25th, Gen. PEMBERTON sent this note:

Two days having elapsed since your dead and wounded have been lying in our front, and as yet no disposition on your part of a desire to remove them being exhibited, in the name of humanity, I have the honor to propose a cessation of hostilities for two and a half hours that you may be enabled to remove your dead and dying men. If you can not do this, on notification from you that hostilities will be suspended on your part for the time specified, I will endeavor to have the dead buried, and the wounded cared for.

To this Gen. Grant replied at 3:30 p. m. appointing 6 p. m. as the time for the cessation of hostilities. BADEAU, in a foot note, defends GRANT against PEMBERTON's imputation of inhumanity, for he says the impossibility of relieving those wounded "was occasioned by PEMBERTON's troops." He says also that this suffering of the wounded was only the fate of war:

The wounded suffer frightfully after every battle, and the party which is repelled is always unable to bestow attention on those whom it leaves on the field.

But GRANT's report to HALLECK denied that the assault was repelled; he said it only failed to enter the works, and was still at the threshold.

BADEAU does not allow humanity to Gen. PEMBERTON in this proposal to permit GRANT to care for his wounded and bury his dead; he conveys that PEMBERTON had another object in it—namely, to escape a pestilence bred by the stench of these dead Union volunteers. He says:

For two days the unburied corpses were left festering between the two armies, when the stench became so intolerable to the garrison that Pemberton was afraid it might breed a pestilence. He therefore proposed an armistice. * * *

Gen. PEMBERTON had another stratagem in this, and this reveals a fine stratagem on GRANT's part. Continues BADEAU:

The offer was promptly accepted, and the rebels also availed themselves of the opportunity to carry off the dead horses and mules that lay in their front, and were becoming very offensive to the besieged. These were the animals that Pemberton had turned loose from the city, and driven over the lines from want of forage. They were shot wherever they were seen by the sharpshooters from the besieging army, that the stench arising from their putrefaction might annoy the enemy.

As it turned out, however, the stink was the solace of GRANT's wounded soldiers, left to die amid this carrion, and to add thereto the stench of their own rotting. As three days had elapsed since the action ceased, the caring for the wounded had been much reduced. Gen. PEMBERTON had before issued an order that the ammunition in the cartridge boxes of the Union dead should be carefully gathered in. From this it may be presumed that they were also stripped under cover of night.

But the wounded could not be brought away nor the dead buried without the enemy's permission. To Gen. PEMBERTON it was a matter of war etiquette that the side which needed such permission should ask it. To Gen. GRANT, to ask it would admit to the nation in his rear that the Confederates held the battleground, and would reveal a situation very different from that represented by his bulletins. Thus this abandonment was his military necessity, and humanity to his own heroic volunteers had to give way to his own necessity in order that the history of the Vicksburg campaign might be rightly written in the public mind.

CHAPTER XLV.

THE SIEGE—IMMEDIATE FEAR OF JOHNSTON IN THE REAR—SACRIFICING OTHER OPERATIONS TO RE-ENFORCE GRANT—THE DREADFUL LABORS OF THE SIEGE.

Two bloody assaults having satisfied Gen. GRANT that the fortifications of Vicksburg could not be stormed, he put his army to the work of investing the place, and of approaching it by trenches, saps, and mines, and the other engineering works of a siege. The Confederate line of works, BADEAU says, was eight miles long, and the national intrenched line twelve miles, and he says GRANT had now about 40,000 men.

The present force was inadequate to the investment. There was still a space of four miles between GRANT's left and the river, through which Gen. PEMBERTON might have escaped, or have debouched upon GRANT's left, while the army, yet unintrenched, was so extended in a rough region that mutual support of its several corps was impracticable. But Gen. PEMBERTON's experience had subdued his spirit. Besides, from the beginning he had resolved on a defensive course. His movement to attack GRANT's rear at Dillon's, was because of JOHNSTON's urgency, and against his own views. And now, when JOHNSTON took the military ground that the place was of little consequence, and that he should let that go and save the army, PEMBERTON took the opposite view that the place was the essential thing. In this he coincided with the ideas of GRANT, HALLECK, LINCOLN, and STANTON.

The army was poorly equipped for a siege of such immense labor. It was much worn by the hardships and privations of the march, and had suffered heavily by battles and sickness. Large re-enforcements were needed to invest the place, and to fortify their own lines against sorties. Generals HURLBUT and PRENTISS were ordered to strip GRANT's department to send forward "every available man that could possibly be spared." And now Gen. GRANT, whose great strategy in marching away from Vicksburg and PEMBERTON's army to Jackson was to finally extinguish all interference from the east, began to sound the alarm that JOHNSTON was threatening him in the rear, which he kept up to the end of the siege.

Admiral PORTER sent "a brigade of amphibious and useful troops at his disposal, known as the Marine Brigade, to debark at Haine's Bluff, and hold the place until relieved by other forces."

A division from HURLBUT, under Brig. Gen. KIMBALL arrived June 3. On the 8th Brig. Gen. SOOY SMITH arrived with a division, and was placed at Haine's Bluff. Says BADEAU:

Herron's division [from the "Army of the Frontier"], the strongest in the combined army, arrived from Schofield's command on the 11th of June; and by the wise prevision of the General in Chief two divisions of the 9th Corps, under Major General Parke, were diverted from their march to East Tennessee [from Burnside's command], and arrived before Vicksburg on the 14th of the same month.

Thus, responsive to GRANT's unceasing alarms, did HALLECK, STANTON, and LINCOLN strip other departments, and cripple more important operations to increase GRANT's army for the siege which had been his own tactical objective.

Thus was the long wanted movement into East Tennessee—whose occupation now in co-operation with ROSECRANS' Chattanooga campaign, was of much greater military importance than Vicksburg, suspended at a time when it was essential to the true military movement down the center of the Confederacy. And while thus contracting GRANT's lines in the northern part of the Confederacy, and giving up important places to the enemy's possession, and suspending a co-operating movement which was essential to ROSECRANS' campaign, in order to carry out a siege of a single place, STANTON treated all of ROSECRANS' calls for troops and arms and cavalry as excuses for delay, and at length declared that he would not give him another man, and ordered him peremptorily to march. So far was carried this policy of giving up all to make sure the taking of this place, that Gen. BANKS was ordered to drop all and come to the help of GRANT, which, had he done, would have lost the lower river and Louisiana—a military possession of tenfold more importance than Vicksburg.

Gen. LANMAN's division arrived on the 24th of May, and was placed defensively on the Hall's Ferry and Warrenton roads, south of the place. HERRON's division arrived on the 11th of June, and took possession on the left. Then LANMAN moved up, and to the right, connecting with McCLERNAND's left, "and for the first time the investment became complete."

The plan of the siege was to work up to the fortifications by means of trenches and underground approaches, into near positions, for another general assault; this from a line which BADEAU says was twelve miles, and against a line of eight miles. Like the assaults, the besieging approaches were along the whole line, and the object of them another assault along the whole line. The mind can have but a faint conception of the immensity of the work of siege approaches against a line of fortifications of eight miles, in a region of singular difficulties to the besiegers, of which Gen. GRANT wrote to HALLECK: "The position is as strong by nature as can possibly be conceived of, and is strongly fortified."

The besieging army is also besieged. Extended in a circuit to invest a place which is held by an army, it is exposed to sorties from the center; therefore it must be intrenched all along its line, and must be ever vigilant. Thus the besieging army has double labor, intrenching itself and trenching upon the place. The trench approaches have mostly to be done by night. In general the conditions of such works are unhealthy, and the hardships great, but these were unexceptionally so in the ravines about Vicksburg, where the fiery heat of the sun by day, the dampness of the nights, the scarcity of water, and the most irksome labor, told heavily on the health and spirits of the Northern volunteers.

They did not realize so vividly as BADEAU the grandness of the strategy whose objective was a siege, and had made an exhaustive march on a circuit to achieve this consummation. ADAM BADEAU airs a vocabulary of siege terms in describing the manner of the work, as if he had lately learned them. The details of the work are not necessary to this historical review, which concedes all the magnitude of the labor which BADEAU asserts, and also its uselessness, and, in a great degree, aimlessness, save as a preparation for another general slaughter, which, happily, was saved by the shortening of PEMBERTON'S supplies, and by his idea that he could get better terms by giving to GRANT the theatrical coup of a surrender on the 4th of July.

In these siege approaches all along the line, the whole army was encamped in the near ravines, so as to be "as close to the enemy's works as shelter could be found; most of the camps were within 600 yards of the rebel parapet." This proximity made the fire of pickets and sharpshooters incessant. Roads had to be opened in the rear for supplying the several parts of the army, and inner roads and covered ways to connect the several camps. Timber had to be cleared away for digging the approaches. In the list of mighty labors BADEAU mentions eighty-nine batteries, not all in the first line, but advanced from time to time. He describes the construction of these as complete in detail, with all the technical terms thereunto belonging.

These batteries were connected by a line of rifle trench, which was advanced with them. These were constantly occupied by sharpshooters during the daylight, and by guards and advanced pickets during the night. Also, wherever an advanced cover for a man could be found a sharpshooter was placed. Alike for the style of the works and the style of the biographer, these specimens are quoted:

The style of the work in the batteries was varied, depending on the material that could be obtained at the time. In some cases the lines were neatly revetted with gabions and fascines, and finished with substantial plank platforms; while in others a revetting of rough boards or cotton bales, was used, and the platforms were made of timber from the nearest ginhouse.

The embrasures were sometimes revetted with cane, and sometimes lined with hides taken from beef cattle. * * * In all close batteries the gunners soon found the necessity of keeping the embrasures closed against rifle balls by plank shutters, sometimes swinging from a timber across the top of the embrasure, sometimes merely placed in the embrasure, and removed in firing. In close approaches the sap was generally revetted with gabions, empty barrels or cotton bales, but sometimes left entirely unrevetted, for when the enemy's fire was heavy, it became difficult to prevent the working parties from sinking the sap as deep as five or even six feet, when, of course, revetting became unnecessary.

Material for gabions was abundant, grapevines being chiefly used, though this made the gabions inconveniently heavy, the vines being too large. Cane was also used for wattling, the joints being crushed with wooden mallets, and the rest of the cane split and interwoven between the stakes of the gabion. The cane made excellent fascines, and was frequently used in this way. At first some difficulty was found in making saprollers which should be impervious to minie balls, and yet not too heavy to use on the rough ground over which the sap must run. Two barrels, however, were placed head to head, and the saproller was then built of cane fascines, wound around this hollow core.

This extract from much of the same sort shall suffice to show the elaborate details of the siege works, and the author's aptitude with the terms. These were the lighter parts; the main work was the digging. Thus did all these labors and the daily game of single killing go on along this line of twelve miles. At first the Confederates opposed the works with artillery; but soon they ceased, partly to husband their ammunition, and partly because familiarity gave them an idea that there was no present danger from the approaches. After a time the opposition by musketry fire slackened, the besieged having a short supply of percussion caps. Says BADEAU:

The aim of the rebels seemed to be to await another assault, losing in the meantime as few men as possible. This indifference to Grant's approach became, at some points, almost ludicrous. The besiegers were accustomed to cover the front of their night working parties by a line of pickets, or by a covering party, and while these were not closer than a hundred yards, the enemy would throw out his pickets in front. At one point the rebel pickets entered into a regular agreement with those of the besiegers not to fire on each other at night, and as most of the work in a siege is done at night, this arrangement was eminently satisfactory to the working parties.

On one occasion the picket officer was directed to crowd his pickets on the enemy's, so as to allow the working party to push on another parallel. In doing this the two lines of pickets became intermixed, and, after some discussion, the opposing officers arranged their lines by mutual compromise, the pickets in places not being ten yards apart, and in full view of each other.

This gives the Confederate soldiers' idea of the danger of GRANT's siege approaches. Nor is there anything to show that they underrated it, or had any reason to fear the result of another general assault from these nearer lines.

Thus was the army expended in this dreadful work along a line of twelve miles, in a burning sun by day and in the damps of the ravines by night, in the most unhealthy conditions, and in the most dispiriting labors that can be imposed on gallant soldiers; all of which, save the intrenching of themselves, were to be useless, and all of which were for an ultimate aim which would be another vain slaughter. Save that the besieged army may be short of provisions, its hardships are less than of the besiegers. Its intrenching is mostly done. Its line of fortifications occupies the high ground; and its holding of them is in a less unhealthy situation than that of the besiegers.

The following description of the condition of the besieged, save the matter of food, and save that the labor of the besiegers was vastly greater, needs but little modification to describe that of the devoted volunteers of GRANT's army:

The privations and exposures of the men were telling on their health and spirits. The miasmatic exhalations of the swamps, rising through the hot atmosphere of June, enveloped and penetrated their weary frames, exhausted by the long series of disastrous marches and incessant bivouacs. * * * Their numbers were reduced by casualties, but far more by disease. Thousands were tossing and groaning in the hospitals, with none of the delicacies and little of the attention that the sick require [The women of Vicksburg did not neglect the sick soldiers]; while those in the trenches were hardly better off.

Scorched by the sun, drenched by the rain, begrimed with dirt, for water was far off, and time more precious still, * * * those weary, but heroic, rebels defended the citadel whose fall they believed would be the fall of the Confederacy. Those who fought them the hardest could not, and did not, fail to recognize their splendid gallantry and thorough devotion to an unrighteous cause.

That this description is alike applicable to GRANT's better fed, but more severely worked and more unhealthily situated army, is obvious from the inevitable conditions, and is further shown by Gen. GRANT's statement to Gen. HALLECK, even after the army had been inspirited by the capture of Vicksburg, that it was now greatly exhausted, and "entirely unfit for any duty requiring much marching."

CHAPTER XLVI.

GEN. GRANT'S ALARM FOR HIS REAR—TO GIVE UP LOUISIANA FOR VICKSBURG—THE MIGHTY WORKS OF PICKAX AND SPADE—GEN. JOHNSTON'S INABILITY—IMMOBILITY OF HIS SUBORDINATES—GRANT'S OBJECTIVE STRICTLY LOCAL.

Gen. GRANT's strategic march away from Vicksburg and the Confederate army, to scatter any gathering forces on the east, so that he might have PEMBERTON's army "isolated from the would be Confederacy," had entirely failed in its purpose, as has been seen; for according to BADEAU not only did the fear of JOHNSTON in his rear constrain him to sacrifice his army in a vain assault on the Vicksburg intrenchments, but he was in continual apprehension of this, and was not at any time re-enforced enough to quiet his uneasiness.

On the 25th he wrote Gen. BANKS, asking him to come and help take Vicksburg. On the 31st he wrote HALLECK this alarming statement:

It is now certain that Johnston has already collected a force from 20,000 to 25,000 strong at Jackson and Canton, and is using every effort to increase it to 40,000. With this he will undoubtedly attack Haine's Bluff, and compel me to abandon the investment of the city, if not re-enforced before he can get here.

On the same day he received a letter from BANKS asking for 10,000 men to help him take Port Hudson, to which he answered that with this number, or even half so many taken away: "I should be crippled beyond redemption."

HALLECK telegraphed June 2:

Yours of the 24th is received. I will do all I can to assist you. I have sent dispatch after dispatch to Banks to join you. Why he does not I do not understand. His separate operating on Port Hudson is in direct violation of his instructions. If possible send him this dispatch. My last dispatch from him was May 4.

BANKS had invested Port Hudson, whose possession was as important to the possession of the Mississippi River as Vicksburg, to say nothing of all Louisiana, which this order virtually required him to abandon. It appears fortunate that communication with BANKS was so remarkably infrequent. GRANT, however, sent him HALLECK's dispatch.

Another instance of the alarm which GRANT's fears of JOHNSTON created at Washington, and of the jolted state of the heads there, is shown in LINCOLN's telegram to GRANT, as follows:

WASHINGTON, D. C., 6:30 P. M., June 2, 1863.
Are you in communication with Gen. Banks? Is he coming toward you, or going further off? Is there or has there been anything to hinder his coming directly to you by water?

In fact there had been nothing to hinder, save that even the armed ships could not pass the guns at Port Hudson, and that to come was to abandon Louisiana. June 3 GRANT telegraphed this: "JOHNSTON is still collecting troops at Canton and Jackson. Some are coming over the railroad, and all the country is joining his standard."

June 8, GRANT dispatched to HALLECK. "It is reported that three divisions have left BRAGG's army to join JOHNSTON. BRECKINRIDGE is known to have arrived." Gen. J. E. JOHNSTON's narrative shows that BRECKINRIDGE's division and 2,000 cavalry were all that he received from BRAGG's Army of the Tennessee, making 8,100, or 7,939 "effective." His report shows that his force during the siege was not raised beyond about 24,000 men, and these greatly crippled by the want of transportation. In JOHNSTON's report is a noteworthy statement of the time prior to his coming to PEMBERTON's help, and to Gen. GRANT's emerging from the swamps west of the Mississippi. He states that from the time of his arrival at Tullahoma "until the 14th of April Gen. PEMBERTON's reports, all by telegraph, indicated that the efforts of the enemy would be against Gen. BRAGG rather than himself, and looked to the abandonment of his attempts at Vicksburg."

JOHNSTON cites this from PEMBERTON: "I am satisfied ROSECRANS will be re-enforced from GRANT's army. Shall I order troops to Tullahoma." His report shows also that he decided, as he telegraphed the Secretary of War: "To take from BRAGG a force which would make this army fit to oppose GRANT, would involve yielding Tennessee." For himself he decided that BRAGG's holding of Tennessee against ROSECRANS was more important than to raise the siege of Vicksburg, but in reply to the urgency of the War Department, he threw on it the responsibility of reversing this judgment. He said in a telegram of June 12: "It is for the government to decide between this State and Tennessee."

This gives the relative importance which Gen. J. E. JOHNSTON placed on Vicksburg, and on the line then threatened by Gen. ROSECRANS. It shows, also, the important part which ROSECRANS' position and attitude exercised on the Vicksburg operation. Neither GRANT nor the Washington authorities appreciated these military elements.

To prevent JOHNSTON's approach from the east, expeditions were sent as far as Big Black River to destroy all bridges, and everything that could be of use to an army. Gen. BLAIR, with 12,000 men, was sent up the Yazoo. The expedition "moved along the Yazoo about forty-five miles," destroying on its return "all stock, forage, roads, and bridges," thus "preventing JOHNSTON from moving upon Vicksburg in that direction, and from drawing supplies from the region between the two rivers."

On BLAIR's return another force was sent up to watch the crossings of the Big Black River from Bridgeport, and complete the devastating of the country. GRANT's order said: "It is important that the country be left so that it can not subsist an army in passing over it. Wagons, horses, and mules should be taken from the citizens, to keep them from being used for the Southern army." GRANT dispatched to HALLECK "I will make a waste of all the country I can between the two rivers."

Trouble now began on the west side of the Mississippi, where GRANT still had a base of supplies at Milliken's Bend, and a post at Richmond, and where he had to keep forces to prevent the Confederates from re-enforcing and supplying Vicksburg from that side. On the 7th of June a Confederate force, which BADEAU states as 3,000, attacked Milliken's Bend, which "was successfully defended by black and white troops under Brig. Gen. DENNIS, ably assisted by the gunboats Choctaw and Lexington." GRANT re-enforced DENNIS with a brigade, with orders to drive the enemy beyond Richmond. A subsequent dispatch from GRANT to HALLECK, dated June 27, disclosed an attempt of military philanthropy to the colored people, which was disastrous to them. It contained this pregnant mention: "I may have to abandon protection of the leased plantations from here to Lake Providence, to resist a threatened attack from KIRBY SMITH's forces."

The reader can take in the full purport of this. The plantations which the owners had abandoned had been leased to the colored people as if they were secure in the protection of the army. These were now left to the tender mercies of their masters, aided by Confederate troops. Yet, after this experience, Gen. SHERMAN repeated the same cruel benevolence on the Savannah River.

Apprehensive that he might be forced to raise the siege, Gen. GRANT prepared Haine's Bluff as a place from which, as BADEAU says, the National forces "could still concentrate for a new effort either against the city or its means of supply. The orders were to fortify it so that it could be held against a sudden movement by 10,000 men, and be capable of giving protection to at least 40,000."

This fortification required a line of several miles of rifle trench, and five batteries on commanding points. GRANT informed SHERMAN on the 11th that if Haine's Bluff should be besieged, "you will be detached temporarily from your command here to take command of Haine's Bluff." This contemplated the singular predicament of besieging Vicksburg, and besieged at Haine's Bluff.

On the same day Grant said: "It is evident the enemy have brought large re-enforcements from Bragg's army, and I can not think it is with any other design than to raise the siege of Vicksburg."

He had now 10,000 or 12,000 men at Haine's Bluff, but ordered both McPherson and Sherman to hold part of their forces in readiness, in case that place should be besieged.

He also gave "detailed instructions" to McCLERNAND to govern him in such an emergency. "On the 22d positive information was received that JOHNSTON was crossing the Big Black River, and intended marching immediately on GRANT." Gen. GRANT thereupon formed an army of the rear from the several corps, which amounted to nearly half of Gen. GRANT's army, and placed SHERMAN in command. But this was not enough, and this army of the rear was set at work in a like colossal labor to fortify a line to the Big Black River, which is ten miles from Vicksburg. Says BADEAU: "A line of works was now constructed from the Yazoo to the Big Black River, quite as strong as those which defended Vicksburg, so that the city was not only circumvallated, but countervallated, as well."

A circumvallating line of intrenchments of twelve miles, pushing its approaches along the whole line by trench and sap and mine and new batteries, constructed with all of BADEAU's vocabulary of technical terms! A "countervallating" line of fortifications of several miles at Haine's Bluff! Another countervallating line of intrenchments of ten miles to Big Black River, "quite as strong as those which defended Vicksburg." Thus merrily went the pickax and the spade, in the work of the siege which had been the objective, and in the fear of JOHNSTON, who in the first instance was to be finally disabled from interfering with Vicksburg by GRANT's preparatory march to Jackson.

Still was GRANT in a state of alarm. Says BADEAU:

Grant's position, however, was at this time peculiar, if not precarious. He was again between two large rebel armies; besieging one, he was himself threatened with a siege by the other; while if both combined to assault him from different sides, it seemed quite possible that the garrison of Vicksburg, that splendid prize for which he had been so long struggling, might even yet elude his grasp.

Meanwhile what was JOHNSTON doing? The forces which had been divided at Jackson had been united; also LORING's division, by the 23d of May. By the 4th of June BRECKINRIDGE's division and some other troops had arrived, raising his force, according to his report, to "about 24,000 infantry and artillery and 2,000 cavalry," this force "deficient in artillery, in ammunition for all arms, and field transportation." "The draft upon the country had so far reduced the number of horses and mules that it was not until late in June that draft animals could be procured."

JOHNSTON, BRAGG, and the Confederate Government decided that to take troops from BRAGG, in the then attitude of ROSECRANS, would be to yield up Tennessee. The Confederacy had not the forces in any other quarter to re-enforce JOHNSTON to cope with such an army as GRANT now had. To strengthen his army to rescue PEMBERTON, JOHNSTON sent orders to Gen. GARDNER to evacuate Port Hudson and join him, but this was not obeyed. On the 23d he received a dispatch of the 21st from GARDNER, that he was threatened by the movement of BANKS, and asking re-enforcements. Thereupon JOHNSTON repeated his orders for the evacuation, saying: "You can not be re-enforced. Do not allow yourself to be invested. At every risk save the troops, and, if practicable, move in this direction." This dispatch did not reach GARDNER, Port Hudson being now invested.

When Gen. PEMBERTON had been compelled to fall back to Big Black River Bridge, he informed JOHNSTON of his disaster and of his apprehension that he would be compelled to fall back still, and that if so, his position at Snyder's Mills (Haine's Bluff) would be untenable. He added: "I have about sixty days' provisions at Vicksburg and Snyder's. I respectfully await your instructions." JOHNSTON replied on the same day, the 17th:

If Haine's Bluff be untenable, Vicksburg is of no value, and can not be held. If, therefore, you are invested in Vicksburg you must ultimately surrender. Under such circumstances, instead of losing both troops and place, you must, if possible, save the troops. If it is not too late, evacuate Vicksburg and its dependencies and march to the northeast.

This was military judgment as to the value of Vicksburg, and prescience as to the result. But Gen. PEMBERTON took a different view of the value of Vicksburg, and he had already retired with its lines when he received this order, which he says came to him about noon of the 18th, while engaged with several general officers in an inspection of the intrenchments, and that at the same moment the enemy was reported to be advancing by the Jackson road. But of the propriety of this order he says:

The evacuation of Vicksburg! It meant the loss of the valuable stores and munitions of war collected for its defense, the fall of Port Hudson, the surrender of the Mississippi River, and the severance of the Confederacy.

POLLARD says that PEMBERTON had confidential instructions from President DAVIS, upon which he disobeyed JOHNSTON's order. PEMBERTON continues, in his report:

I believed it in my power to hold Vicksburg. I knew and appreciated the earnest desire of the government and people that it should be held. * * * As long ago as the 17th of February last, in a letter addressed to his Excellency, the President, I had suggested the possibility of the investment of Vicksburg by land and water, and for that reason the necessity of ample supplies of ammunition, as well as of subsistence, to stand a siege. My application met his favorable consideration, and additional ammunition was ordered.

Thus had Gen. PEMBERTON decided beforehand that it would be better to risk his army, invested in the place, on the chance of the siege being raised from without, than to let go the place and save his army. PEMBERTON wrote JOHNSTON on the 18th, that he had laid his instructions before a council of war of all his general officers, and that "the opinion was unanimously expressed that it was impossible to withdraw the army from this position with such morale and material as to be of further service to the Confederacy."

Thus were Gen. JOHNSTON and his beleaguered subordinates playing at cross purposes, he holding that the interior was the great objective, and the army more important than places, and striving to concentrate that; they holding that places were the vital part, and permitting themselves to be shut up in them, and so losing both the army and the places, and laying open the interior. In this they seemed to think themselves supported by a power higher than Gen. JOHNSTON. From the time when Gen. PEMBERTON retreated into Vicksburg, and announced his decision to stay until the siege should be raised from without, and Gen. JOHNSTON's order to Gen. GARDNER to evacuate Port Hudson, found him invested by Gen. BANKS, JOHNSTON's expectation did not rise higher than a movement against the besieging army at Vicks burg, co-operative with one by PEMBERTON to fight his way out. But his correspondence with PEMBERTON was uncertain, and that commander does not appear to have had any positive idea of co-operating in such an attempt. The decision which he and his Generals made on the 18th, that it was impossible to withdraw the army from Vicksburg with such morale and material as to be of further service to the Confederacy, had much more reason now that the place was invested.

The action of PEMBERTON and GARDNER made JOHNSTON'S relief of either Vicksburg or Port Hudson impracticable at the beginning, and the arriving additions to GRANT'S army made it more hopeless as time went on. In no other way than by moving BRAGG'S army in mass could the Confederacy have JOHNSTON strong enough to raise the siege of Vicksburg. As to an attempt to relieve Port Hudson, JOHNSTON'S report says:

> The want of field transportation rendered any movement for the relief of Port Hudson impossible, had a march in that direction been advisable. But such a march would have enabled Grant (who had now completed his strong lines around Vicksburg) to have cut my line of communication and destroyed my army, and from the moment that I put my troops in motion in that direction the whole of Middle and North Mississippi would have been open to the enemy.

In this, as in the rest of Gen. JOHNSTON'S reports, it will be observed that he took a radically different view of the objective and scope of Gen. GRANT'S operation from that taken by GRANT. JOHNSTON supposed that GRANT'S objective was to take and occupy Mississippi, and that his taking of Vicksburg was only as a means to that end. Hence he spoke of it from the beginning as an operation which embraced the State. This idea governed his dispositions of his troops when GRANT took Jackson. His military mind could not comprehend that all this mighty operation had no aim beyond the place of Vicksburg, and that it intended nothing in the interior but devastating raids. He resisted the pressure from the Richmond government, to sacrifice his little army in a desperate attempt to save Vicksburg, because he regarded the interior as of more importance; and because, as a military man, he supposed that the interior was the real objective of the Vicksburg campaign.

CHAPTER XLVII.

DEVELOPMENT OF THE GRAND STRATEGY OF THE SITUATION—SUFFICIENT CAUSE FOR GRANT'S ALARM FOR HIS REAR—WHAT PROTECTED HIM FROM DESTRUCTION BY BRAGG'S ARMY—WHAT MIGHT HAVE BEEN IF THE WAR HAD A PLAN—THE END OF GEN. M'CLERNAND — A HAPPY DELIVERANCE.

Gen. GRANT'S authorized biographer states that when he began the work of the siege, after the second assault, he "had now about 40,000 men for duty." This means the number present for duty, which is in general much less than the number on the muster rolls.

Additional forces continued to arrive. BADEAU mentions 21,000 from GRANT'S department; "HERRON'S division, the strongest in the combined army, from SCHOFIELD'S command," and two divisions of the 9th Corps, "diverted from their march to East Tennessee." By this time, says BADEAU, "GRANT'S force amounted to about 75,000 men;" but all these corps, added to 40,000 effectives, must have made considerably more than this number. Gen. J. E. JOHNSTON'S report gave 24,000 infantry and 2,000 cavalry as his whole force after he had received all the troops that it was thought prudent to draw from BRAGG'S army. Gen. PEMBERTON, after he had retired within the Vicksburg lines, stated to Gen. JOHNSTON that his whole effective force for manning the lines was 18,500.

It appears that GRANT'S effective force was at any time as great as that of JOHNSTON and PEMBERTON combined. His situation must have been very faulty if their separation by his army made them more dangerous. By the middle of June GRANT'S force was twice as great as that of both JOHNSTON and PEMBERTON. Yet his alarm for his rear did not cease, nor the dreadful labor which this imposed on the troops, in fortifying for defense, and in pushing forward sap, mine, trench, and batteries preparatory to another assault along the whole line.

This alarm was not without sufficient reason, and the reason exhibits the false military position into which GRANT had brought his army, by abandoning the interior, and taking his army around to the edge, where it was isolated from all other operations; where, instead of co-operating, it demanded that other operations be suspended or crippled to help him besiege a single side place; where it gave up to the Confederacy all the communications and resources of the interior, and all the advantage of uniting these armies to fall upon him while thus held indefinitely at bay.

The hideous humor of the conduct of the war, and of the relative value placed on military operations, and of the history made at that time, has a broad illustration in the circumstances that GRANT had succeeded by what was thought a most brilliant movement in placing his army in an isolated position, where he saw that if BRAGG should come it would be routed; that Gen. ROSECRANS' position, which he held against the urgency of GRANT, HALLECK, and STANTON, was that which saved GRANT's operation from failure, and enabled him to capture Vicksburg, and so become the autocrat of the army.

All this is clearly shown by GRANT's incessant alarm because of BRAGG's army, and by Gen. J. E. JOHNSTON's statement that the attitude of Gen. ROSECRANS was that which prevented the Confederate chieftains from drawing forces from BRAGG's army, to raise the siege of Vicksburg. All this proves the military discernment of Gen. ROSECRANS, who resisted, when GRANT and HALLECK and STANTON, in their panic, wanted to push him forward unprepared, in order to relieve GRANT. He showed that it would risk both armies, and this is evident. Outside of Vicksburg were forces which if united would greatly outnumber his. If he had pushed forward and met a reverse, the united Confederate Army could then turn and crush GRANT.

But while he had not a force large enough for an advance, the Confederates thought his advance imminent. Thus secure in his threatening position he held BRAGG's army, and thereby delivered GRANT from a perilous situation, and enabled him to end a destructive campaign in the siege and capture of a place which was magnified to the making of his military and political fortunes.

But Gen. GRANT's military vision was focused on a side place. In his single idea that all should be concentrated on that, he could not perceive that Gen. ROSECRANS was protecting him from BRAGG's army. His consciousness of the isolated and faulty situation to which he had brought his army by leaving the interior, to head off McCLERNAND, allowed no cessation to his fear of BRAGG and JOHN-

STON, to his calls
works. Starvation
him, but because
interior he though
and he was inten
the whole line, un
success no more pr

This Confederat
which was vital
the importance of
of Gen. ROSECRA?
might have beer
in the interior,
supporting or
CRANS' campaign.
GRANT's departme
could have formed
Confederacy could
government could
CRANS another ad
could have made
Such a campaign
have made Vicksl
consequence.

What a wonderf
was that which u
in the several de
autagonistic: as i
much success as
ment commander
permitted Gen.
which had 130,000
from a line to the
and from all sup
any other militar
and neutralize
crippling all othe
a year, making the
disaster to anot
suming an incre
teers, giving up
munications in
the objective of a
and achieving not
in ending the war

This was the wa
of men had to
the rebellion, whi
decisive evidence
.This was the way
jected to the cons
civil war for four
and such troops,
had been directed
could have ende

way that patriotic volunteers, the most gallant soldiers the world ever saw, who were pushed into incessant hardships and slaughter, as if they were of no value, were robbed of the glory which they so dearly earned, by military incompetency, not in their immediate officers, but in the great chiefs, who assumed to know all of the art of war, but whose ideas of its general conduct could rise no higher than detached departments and devastating raids or disjointed campaigns upon local places.

During the dreadful work of the siege, to wit, on the 18th of June, the ax which Gen. GRANT had held suspended over the neck of McCLERNAND, by warrant of Secretary STANTON'S telegram of May 6, was let fall, and GRANT removed him from the command of the 13th Corps, and appointed Gen. ORD in his place. Thus was GRANT'S principal objective of the Vicksburg campaign at last achieved. The attentive reader will remember that while GRANT was at Hankinson's Ferry, he received through Mr. CHARLES A. DANA, Assistant Secretary of War for observation in the field, a cipher telegram authorizing him to remove any officer who stood in his way, and the reader will readily comprehend that this remarkable plenary authority did not come without much intriguing of Gen. GRANT against McCLERNAND.

The time, however, was inopportune. Mc-CLERNAND'S corps had just made a most arduous march from Milliken's Bend to Hard Times, scattering the Confederate detachments, and building a road for the rest of the army; had then made the forced march to Port Gibson, and beaten the enemy, which secured the success of the Vicksburg operation. As it was GRANT'S first success since Donelson, and as it would not be easy to keep McCLERNAND'S name from going to the country with it—although GRANT never mentioned it—the news of his removal from command would not seem to the country a fitting accompaniment.

But as the campaign went on the conditions grew more unfitting. BADEAU relates that GRANT designedly shifted the army round so as to put McCLERNAND from the right to the left while McPHERSON and SHERMAN moved on JACKSON, but this brought McCLERNAND to the front, when the two tramps informed GRANT that Gen. PEMBERTON had crossed the Big Black and was coming to attack him. In this way one of McCLERNAND's divisions came first to Champion's Hill, and although GRANT sent it to the slaughter as if that were his objective, it gained a victory. Then, through GRANT'S wonderful luck, McCLERNAND'S corps came upon the enemy's strong position at Big Black River bridge and carried it by storm, which was the most brilliant action of the whole campaign.

By another stroke of GRANT'S wonderful luck, McCLERNAND'S troops alone made a lodgment in the Vicksburg fortifications in the assault of the 22d, and the intelligence of their partial success so alarmed GRANT that he rode off to the other end of the line. All this kept putting the opportunity for removing him further away; but at last Mc-CLERNAND made it with his pen—another example that, in the hand of a great General, the pen can do that which the sword has failed to do. McCLERNAND issued a congratulatory address to his command, recounting its deeds in the Bonaparte style, and this was printed in some newspapers in the North.

BADEAU narrates the affair with great solemnity, and it was conducted with the solemnity and form of a rehearsed plan. He says.

On the 17th of June Grant received formal and official communications from both Sherman and McPherson, couched in the strongest and most indignant language, and complaining of a congratulatory order issued by McClernand to his corps on the 30th of May.

The address was in the Bonapartish style which military men in general affect, but it did not in fact overstate the doings of the corps. As a whole these had been distinguished.

Gen. SHERMAN'S letter alleged that the publication of this address was a violation of the order which forbids the publication of all official letters and reports. The particularly offensive part is in the following:

On the 22d, in pursuance of the order of the Commander of the department, you assaulted the enemy's defenses in front at 10 o'clock a. m., and within thirty minutes had made a lodgment and planted your colors upon two of his bastions. This partial success called into exercise the highest heroism, and was only gained by a bloody and protracted struggle. Yet it was gained, and was the first and largest success achieved anywhere along the whole line of our army.

For nearly eight hours, under a scorching sun and destructive fire, you firmly held your footing, and only withdrew when the enemy had largely massed their forces and concentrated their attack upon you. How and why the general assault failed, it would be useless now to explain. The 13th Army Corps, acknowledging the good intention of all, would scorn indulgence in weak regrets and idle recriminations. According justice to all, it would only defend itself.

If, while the enemy was massing to crush it, assistance was asked for by a diversion at other points, or by re-enforcement, it only asked what in one case Gen. Grant had specifically and peremptorily ordered; namely, simultaneous and persistent attacks all along our lines until the enemy's outer works should be carried; and what, in the other, by massing a strong force upon a weakened point, would have probably insured success.

This was too much; yet the reflection was not on SHERMAN and McPHERSON and their troops, but on the Commanding General. It even arraigned the ordering of the assault. Perhaps Gen. McCLERNAND expected that this would finish his command. Perhaps he thought, inasmuch as his corps had been the advance in most of the labors, marches, and battles since leaving Milliken's Bend, and had not been mentioned in GRANT's bulletins, save to deny to it any credit in this assault, and to charge most of the slaughter on him, while GRANT was incessantly making charges against him in an underhand way to HALLECK, that he would now have his say for once, and get it before the country, whatever the consequences. Who can deny that in fair play something was due to himself, and still more to the soldiers of his command, who were put under the ban of the Commanding General because he and his army circle were resolved to break down McCLERNAND?

The letters of SHERMAN and McPHERSON were very indignant, and showed much personal hostility to McCLERNAND, but their indignation was not pertinent to the real offense, which was to GRANT rather than to them. BADEAU relates that GRANT sent to McCLERNAND a peremptory demand for a copy of the congratulatory order, and thereupon removed him from command, stating this to HALLECK as the cause, and adding: "I should have relieved him long since for general unfitness for his position." Thus was the army relieved of an internal conflict which occupied GRANT's mind rather more than the Confederate enemy. Thus were the other two corps relieved from the bad example of the presence of a ranking commander of an army corps who was not of the Military Institute.

The reviewer can shed no tears over the removal of Gen. McCLERNAND. It was necessary that he should go. His rank placed his troops under a cloud, which their successes only darkened. Notwithstanding his good fortune in action, in all this operation, beginning at Arkansas Post, the general result of his appointment to a high command had been unfortunate. His river expedition had demoralized Gen. GRANT in a campaign in the interior, and had drawn him from the true military line to the disastrous river operation, to prevent McCLERNAND. A campaign was sacrificed in order to beat him, and the consequence was the consumption of a great army in the Mississippi swamps, and an operation which was the inversion of all military rules, which made Vicksburg at last a barren victory.

One of his divisions had fallen by separation under the immediate command of Gen. GRANT at Champion's Hill, and he had seen what came of it. In Gen. GRANT's bulletins no credit could be gained by McCLERNAND's troops while he was in command. His removal was therefore a military necessity; the successes of his corps, in which it had been singularly fortunate, made the necessity only the more imperative.

CHAPTER XLVIII.

CONTINUATION OF THE SIEGE—THE ART OF SIEGE MINING—THE DEATH HOLE—TACTICS OF BUTCHERY—THE ART OF WAR TO LOSE THE MOST MEN—THE DREADFUL BOMBARDMENT—STARVATION—THWARTED EXPEDITION TO RELIEVE VICKSBURG FROM THE WEST SIDE—JOHNSTON AT LAST GETS READY TO MOVE—THE END AT HAND.

By the 30th of June 220 guns were in position against the Vicksburg fortifications. These, however, were nearly all field guns, and the effect of their fire on the intrenchments by day was quickly repaired by night. One battery of heavy guns on the right was furnished and manned by the navy.

In McCLERNAND's corps was a battery of six 30-pounder Parrott guns. An attempt was made to put in battery the guns of the sunken gunboat Cincinnati, near the river above the town, when "it was hoped that the town might be reached from this point and much damage done," but although much digging was done to prepare this battery, the want of sling-carts to transport the guns through the bottom delayed its completion until the capitulation. The Confederate forces made but little use of their artillery to resist the siege approaches, and the musketry "was sparingly used in comparison with that of the besiegers." "The aim of the rebels seemed to be to await another assault, losing in the meantime as few men as possible. This indifference to GRANT's approach became at some points almost ludicrous."

The Confederates reckoned that they could repulse another assault as before, and that the raising of the siege from the outside, or starvation on the inside, would settle the affair before GRANT's digging became dangerous. Ammunition was not scarce with them, save percussion caps for muskets. Various devices were used to smuggle in these. But while little damage was done to the fortifications or their defenders by the investing batteries, great damage was done to the town by the bombardment from mortar boats of the navy, which were made fast to the further side of the tongue of land opposite Vicksburg. These sent their shells into the middle of the city, driving the inhabitants to caves for shelter. Seven mortars were dropping their bombs into the populous part of the town day and night, to which were subsequently added heavy guns in position.

On the 25th of June an extensive mine, on the Jackson road, in McPHERSON's front was fired. It extended thirty-five feet from the starting point, and branched into three, in all which 2,700 pounds of powder were placed; this backed by cross timbers and sand bags. Gen. GRANT's telegram to HALLECK gave this result:

Yesterday a mine was sprung under the enemy's most commanding fort, producing a crater sufficient to hold two regiments of infantry. Our men took immediate possession and still hold it. The fight for it has been incessant, and thus far we have not been able to establish batteries in the breach. Expect to succeed.

This and BADEAU's more detailed narrative give an idea of the aim of mining in this siege, from which it appears that the object was not to make a practicable opening for assault and entering the place, but to make a crater, commanded by a high and unscalable bank on the enemy's side, into which to send our troops with a rush, to be butchered in a huddle, with no expectation of results, save to kill a few of the enemy in exchange for many. Says BADEAU:

The crater was cone shaped, and entirely exposed to field projectiles or loaded shells thrown by hand; but McPherson's men rushed into this gulf, lighting and throwing grenades in return. The enemy, however, from his higher position, could throw ten shells to their one, and in nearly every case could see to direct them with deadly effect; indeed, the rebels had only to lay the lighted missiles on the parapet and roll them down.

No systematic attempt could be made to carry the enemy's work, or to take possession of his parapet and run boyaux [trenches] along the exterior slope, yet all night long parties of men, fifty, sixty, or eighty at a time, stood in the crater, along its sides, not shaped into banquettes [meaning with no cover], and fired at the enemy they could not see; for after the first hour the rebels ceased to appear on the parapet at all, contenting themselves with the use of grenades. After awhile feathered grenades were given to the National troops, and thrown inside the line with some effect, but many of these failed to explode, and were hurled back by the rebels with terrible results.

Boxes of field ammunition were also brought out by the enemy, who lighted them by portfires and threw them by hand into the crater. Nearly every one took effect, killing and wounding sometimes half a dozen men. The crater was called by the soldiers "the death hole," but the ground that had been gained was held through all the horrors of the night.

The "lay" reader has to inquire if the object of siege mining is to make a death hole for our own soldiers, and whether this sending our own volunteers into a slaughter pit, for the chance that for ten of them one of the enemy may be killed, is war.

This hole of death is an example of a system of butcher tactics which became chief in the war, and came to be received as the art of war. It was a brutal reckoning that whereas the North could raise three soldiers to the South's one, the sacrifice of our three to their one was progress in the war. The common idea of generalship became degraded to these tactics of "death holes," and "hills of death," and of sending gallant volunteers to the slaughter against intrenchments, thinking a commander great in ratio to his destruction of his own men. Strategy, tactics, and manœuver were contemned, and he became greatest who pitched his army into the slaughter, without skill, and then pitched in again in the same blind manner until his army was consumed.

The most prominent historian of the war gave to this horrible system the name of "the tactics of attrition." It came to be set forth as a principle of the art of war that it was a matter of killing so many men, and that the side which had most men had most to be killed, and it made little difference how it was done. Gen. SHERMAN expressed this with interesting candor in his reasons, in the United Service Magazine, for the unguarded state of the army at Pittsburg Landing, and, in his memoirs, for the assault at Kenesaw, and again in his address at the meeting of the Society of the Army of the Potomac at Hartford, June 8, 1881, when he justified the operations of Gen. GRANT from the Rapidan to Cold Harbor by this principle:

War is an awful game, and demands death and destruction. A certain amount of fighting—of killing—had to be done, and the banks of the Rapidan and Mattapony were as good a place for it as those of the James and Appomattox.

But if war is only a matter of unskilled butchery, why have a military institute to teach it? And if this be all of war, is there an impassable gulf between the professional and the volunteer? Can we expect to always have such conditions in our wars that we can afford to sacrifice three of our soldiers to do for one of the enemy, and therefore can afford to contemn all the art of war.

Having failed to make the mine practicable for anything but "the death hole," another mine was begun, which was exploded on the 1st of July. This appears not to have had any aim save to kill any Confederate soldiers that happened to be near at the explosion. The Confederate report says a ton of powder was fired in this. BADEAU says:

The result was the demolition of an entire redan, leaving only an immense chasm where the rebel work had stood. The greater portion of the earth was thrown toward the national forces, the line of least resistance being in that direction. The rebel interior line, however, was much injured, and many of those manning the works were killed or wounded. But no serious attempt to charge was made, the result of the assaults on the 25th having been so inconsiderable.

Gen. BENJAMIN F. BUTLER might find some satisfaction for the ridicule which educated officers heaped upon his Fort Fisher powder ship, in this mining by Gen. GRANT's direction, whose first great performance was to make a "death hole" where the safe enemy could butcher GRANT's soldiers, and the next was to see the earth fly. But this appears to have been thought the art of war in a siege, or BADEAU continues:

From this time forward the engineers were kept constantly and busily employed mining and countermining on different portions of the line.

Gen. GRANT reported to HALLECK on the 27th that JOHNSTON expected 10,000 re-enforcements from BRAGG. This was a mistake. JOHNSTON was in active correspondence with the Richmond government, which was urging him to act, while he was protesting that he had not more than half the force necessary, and that to make the attempt on GRANT's army with such a force would be destruction. And he said: "The defeat of this little army would at once open Mississippi and Alabama to GRANT." JOHNSTON could not believe that Vicksburg was the sole objective of all of GRANT's mighty campaign; he supposed that he wanted that for a base from which to occupy Mississippi.

Gen. PEMBERTON sent to JOHNSTON that he ought not to attempt anything with less than 40,000 men; this in co-operation with PEMBERTON's forces. It was, in fact, impracticable to arrange such co-operation, for it required correspondence in time, and correspondence was slow, difficult, and uncertain. JOHNSTON's whole force was about 26,000 men, but it was lacking in equipment and transportation. When he came, all the military materials were at Vicksburg and Port Hudson. "Artillery had to be brought from the East, horses for it, and field transportation procured in an exhausted country; much from Georgia, brought over wretched railroads." Thus he said: "I have not the means of moving."

Gen. JOHNSTON had written Gen. PEMBERTON on the 14th of June that all he could attempt would be to save the garrison, and that to do this exact co-operation was indispensable; that "by fighting the enemy simultaneously at the same point of his line you may be extricated;" that his own communications could best be preserved by operating north of the railroad, and asking him to state what point would be best for him. Gen. PEMBERTON answered this on the 21st, proposing that, with due notice, JOHNSTON should move by the north of the railroad, drive in the enemy's pickets at night, and at daylight next morning engage him heavily with skirmishers, occupying him during the entire day, and that on that night he, PEMBERTON, would move by the Warrenton road to Hankinson's Ferry.

He further required JOHNSTON to send to Hankinson's a brigade of cavalry, with two field batteries, to build a bridge there and hold that ferry; also to hold Hall's and Baldwin's ferries to cover his crossing at Hankinson's. By this JOHNSTON was to attack on the north, where were the intrenchments of Haine's Bluff, and to the Big Black River, while PEMBERTON moved out to the south. And this required pretty strong detachments from JOHNSTON's forces to keep PEMBERTON's way clear over the Big Black River. Gen. JOHNSTON answered this on the 22d, stating that Gen. RICHARD TAYLOR had sent Gen. E. K. SMITH to co-operate with PEMBERTON on the west side of the Mississippi, to throw in supplies, and to cross with his forces, if expedient and practicable. He added:

I will have the means of moving toward the enemy in a day or two, and will try to make a diversion in your favor; and if possible, communicate with you, though I fear my force is too small to effect the latter. * * * If I can do nothing, rather than surrender the garrison, endeavor to cross the river at the last moment, if you and Gen. Taylor can communicate.

Gen. PEMBERTON's report relates that about the 30th of May the meat ration was reduced one-half, but that of sugar, rice, and beans was largely increased, and chewing tobacco was impressed and issued to the troops. "This had a very beneficial influence." By the 12th of June, says Gen. PEMBERTON:

About this time our provisions, particularly of meat, having become nearly exhausted, Gen. Stoneman was instructed to impress all the cattle in the city, and the chief commissary directed to sell only one ration per. diem to any officer. He was also instructed to issue for bread equal portions of rice and flour, four ounces of each.

By this the reduction of the bread ration one-half came on top of the reduction of the meat ration.

On the 15th he wrote JOHNSTON: "Our men have no relief, and are becoming much fatigued, but are still in pretty good spirits. I think your movement should be made as soon as possible. * * * We are living on greatly reduced rations, but I think sufficient for twenty days yet." To the mortar bombardment were now added several very heavy guns, in position on the peninsula, the fire of which, PEMBERTON says, was very destructive. On the 19th he wrote: "I hope you will advance with the least possible delay. My men have been thirty-four days and nights in trenches without relief. * * * We are living on greatly reduced rations. What aid am I to expect from you?" Under date of June 22, his report says:

About this time, our stock of bacon having been almost exhausted, the experiment of using mule meat as a substitute was tried, * * * and I am gratified to say it was found by both officers and men not only nutritious, but very palatable, and in every way preferable to poor beef.

By the latter part of June, says BADEAU, taking from a Southern narrative of the siege:

Flour was $5 a pound, or $1,000 a barrel, rebel money; meal, $140 a bushel; molasses, $10 and $12 a gallon; and beef (very often oxen killed by the national shells and picked up by the butchers), was sold at $2 and $2 50 by the pound. Mule meat, sold at $1 per pound, was in great demand. Many families of wealth had eaten the last mouthful, and the poorer class of non-combatants was on the verge of starvation.

There was scarcely a building that had not been struck by shells, and many were entirely demolished. A number of women and children had been killed or wounded by mortar shells, or balls, and all who did not remain in the damp caves or hillsides were in danger.

The hospitals, which were now a large feature, had to take their chances with the other houses in the unceasing bombardment. Starvation was swiftly bringing the surrender of a place which was impregnable to all of GRANT's ill ordered assaults, saps, mines, and batteries. Gen. PEMBERTON, on the 22d, wrote JOHNSTON suggesting that he should propose terms to Gen. GRANT for the surrender of the place, but not of the troops. He added that his men were much fatigued by being constantly in the trenches, and were living on very reduced rations, but still, if there was hope of ultimate relief, they would hold out for fifteen days longer.

The difficulty of communication may be seen in the date of JOHNSTON's answer to this —the 27th. He said:

Gen. E. K. Smith's troops have been mismanaged, and have fallen back to Delhi. I have sent a special messenger urging him to assume direct command. The determined spirit you manifest, and his expected co-operation, encourage me to hope something may yet be done to save Vicksburg, and to postpone both the modes of extricating the garrison. Negotiations with Grant for the relief of the garrison, should they become necessary, must be made by you. It would be a confession of weakness on my part, which I ought not to make, to propose them. When it becomes necessary to make them, they may be considered as made under my authority.

The bearer of this dispatch was captured. Forasmuch as Gen. Johnston had now no expectation of an increase of his own force, this encouragement that Vicksburg might at last be saved depended on Gen. RICHARD TAYLOR's sending a force to break the investment west of the river, and throw in supplies. It is reasonable to suppose that with these the defense might have been prolonged indefinitely, and a very large diversion of GRANT's forces to the west side made necessary. But Gen. BANKS had Port Hudson now in the same strait as GRANT Vicksburg, and Gen. TAYLOR was trying to relieve that place. Thus divided between the two, he relieved neither. This gives a further illustration of the strange military idea of GRANT, HALLECK, STANTON, and LINCOLN, that BANKS should abandon the Lower Mississippi, and come and help GRANT besiege Vicksburg. Had he done so, not only would Louisiana and the Lower Mississippi have been lost, but it is unlikely that Vicksburg would have been taken.

Gen. GRANT, in his letter to HALLECK, explaining why he could not protect the leased plantations west of the Mississippi, stated:

Besides the gun boats, negro troops, and six regiments of white troops, left west of the Mississippi River in consequence of these plantations being there, I sent an additional brigade from the investing army, and that at a time when government was straining every nerve to send me troops to insure the success of the enterprise against Vicksburg. All this has not been availing.

But it appears that the colored troops, chiefly, repulsed an attack on his base of supplies at Milliken's Bend, and that this force, which he calls detached because of the leased plantations, defeated a promising expedition in the nick of time, for throwing supplies into Vicksburg.

Gen. JOHNSTON states that on the 28th, having procured the necessary supplies and field transportation and artillery equipment, and a serviceable floating bridge, the army was ordered to march next morning toward Big Black River. He says "the effective force was a little above 20,000 infantry and artillery, and 2,000 cavalry." Reconnaissances, "to which the 2d, 3d, and 4th of July were devoted," convinced him that no attack was practicable north of the railroad; he therefore "determined to move on the morning of the 5th by Edward's depot to the south of that road." On the 3d a courier from Gen. PEMBERTON arrived, having left Vicksburg on the 28th of June. He had been so near capture as to think necessary to destroy his dispatches. JOHNSTON sent back by him to PEMBERTON the following, dated the 3d:

Your dispatches of 28th were destroyed by messenger. He states that Gen. Smith's troops were driven back to Monroe. This statement and your account of your condition make me think it necessary to create a diversion, and thus enable you to cut your way out, if the time has arrived for you to do this. Of that time I can not judge—you must, as it depends upon your condition. I hope to attack the enemy in your front on the 7th, and your co-operation will be necessary. The manner and the proper point for you to bring the garrison out, must be determined by you, from your superior knowledge of the ground and distribution of the enemy's forces. Our firing will show you where we are engaged. If Vicksburg can not be saved, the garrison must.

An operation, requiring such exact and prearranged co-operation, between forces widely separated by the opposing army, and whose interchanges of intelligence were so slow and uncertain, was impracticable. The bearer of this dispatch was captured. Meanwhile that was going on between GRANT and PEMBERTON which made JOHNSTON's movement unnecessary just as he had gotten ready to begin.

CHAPTER XLIX.

PREPARING FOR ANOTHER ASSAULT—THE CAPITULATION—THE PLAY OF UNCONDITIONAL SURRENDER—MARRING A GREAT EVENT BY SMALL PERSONAL MOTIVES—THE PETTY DISPUTE—THE TERMS OF CAPITULATION—STRATEGEM TO DEMORALIZE PEMBERTON'S TROOPS.

By the 1st of July the trenching had reached such a stage that BADEAU says "little further progress could be made by digging alone, and GRANT accordingly determined to make the final assault on the morning of the 6th of July." Not that the "siege approaches" had reduced, or expected to reduce, any part of the fortifications, but that the trenches would enable "columns of fours" to debouch at points near to the enemy's works.

As before, the assault was not to be by massing troops on particular points, but was to be a general line attack on the fortifications, or as much of a line as could be made by debouching from the trenches in columns of fours. BADEAU narrates communications between the pickets which showed that the Confederate soldiers expected this assault with confidence. Whether this was to be the final assault was problematical. But assuming it to be certain, BADEAU includes among the terrors now hanging over Vicksburg the ancient custom of giving license to mercenary troops upon the disarmed soldiers and the inhabitants of a town taken by assault. He goes on:

To crown all, after a few more contractions of the coil, another mighty assault would bring the enemy immediately beneath the walls, when, covered by their works, and more numerous than the besieged, the assailants, in every human probability, would storm the town, and all the unutterable horrors to which fallen cities are exposed might come upon the devoted fortress.

But although BADEAU was revised by Gen. GRANT, this must be taken as a flight of rhetoric; for it is not likely that he had any thought of making the rapine, slaughter, and ravishment of the inhabitants of Vicksburg, nor even the slaughter of the garrison, the prize of the soldiers in a successful assault; and even if he had, the volunteers would not have accepted such a reward.

In the middle ages the mercenary troops were given unbridled license in a town taken by assault, after a formal demand for surrender had been refused. The British still practice this in their wars in Asia. But it is no part of civilized warfare, and is a shame to England. The imagination must be truculent which can suppose that the volunteers would have given rage to the passions of killing, pillage, and "the unutterable horrors" on the defenseless inhabitants, or on the overpowered soldiers of Vicksburg, if that place had been taken by storm. Gen. PEMBERTON, having about 18,000 soldiers in the lines, and the fortifications unbroken, had good ground to believe that he could repulse an assault as before, and to decline a summons to surrender. Under the circumstances such a refusal would be no reason for savage measures, if GRANT had carried the place by storm. But no mention is made that GRANT intended even the formality of a summons to surrender.

Gen. PEMBERTON's report narrates: "By the 1st of July I became satisfied that the time had arrived when it was necessary either to evacuate the city and cut my way out, or to capitulate upon the best attainable terms." He therefore addressed a communication to each of the division Generals, STEVENSON, FORNEY, SMITH, and BOWEN, requesting them to inform him as to the condition of their troops, and their ability to make the marches and undergo the fatigues necessary to accomplish a successful evacuation. The substance of the answers was that the troops were not in condition for such marching, and for the fighting which might be expected, and that the attempt would result in the destruction of a large part of the troops that made it.

Thereupon, July 3, Gen. PEMBERTON addressed to Gen. GRANT the following:

GENERAL: I have the honor to propose to you an armistice of —— hours, with a view to arranging terms for the capitulation of Vicksburg. To this end, if agreeable to you, I will appoint three commissioners to meet a like number to be named by yourself, at such place and hour to-day as you may find convenient. I make this proposition to avoid the effusion of blood, which must otherwise be shed to a frightful extent, feeling myself fully able to maintain my position for a yet indefinite period. This communication will be handed you under a flag of truce by Maj. Gen. John S. Bowen.

To this, in the course of two hours, was sent the following answer:

GENERAL: Your note of this date is just received, proposing an armistice for several hours for the purpose of arranging terms of capitulation through commissioners to be appointed, etc. The useless effusion of blood you propose stopping by this course can be ended at any time you choose by an unconditional surrender of the city and garrison. Men who have shown so much endurance and courage as those now in Vicksburg will always challenge the respect of an adversary, and I can assure you will be treated with all the respect due to prisoners of war. I do not favor the proposition of appointing commissioners to arrange terms of capitulation, because I have no terms other than those indicated above.

The greatness and dignity of this affair was now belittled by motives of personal vanity and popular clap-trap, which caused a truculent demand that was not in earnest, a pitiful dispute in the small effort to put upon Gen. PEMBERTON the humiliation of asking a reopening of negotiations after this refusal of all terms save unconditional surrender. The incitement to this may be seen by a reference to a previous surrender.

When Gen. GRANT returned from Commodore FOOTE's gunboat, and found that for half a day a furious battle had been raging by a sortie of the army of Fort Donelson, and that more than half of his army had been driven back, he sent this word to Commodore FOOTE, whose boats had all been disabled in attacking the fort the day before:

A terrible conflict ensued in my absence, which has demoralized a portion of my command, and I think the enemy is much more so. If the gunboats do not appear it will reassure the enemy, and still further demoralize our troops. I must order a charge to save appearances. I do not expect the gunboats to go into action.

Before his army had been hurt he had dispatched Gen. HALLECK that he would have to intrench, for he said: "I fear the result of an attempt to carry the place by storm with new troops."

Feeling this way before the disaster, the situation now looked badly. But Gen. C. F. SMITH formed a storming force of Gen. LAUMAN's brigade, resolved on something more than to save appearances. He led it in person, animating the "new troops" by his example, and they carried by storm a part of the fort which was the key to the position. Here they and their gallant veteran commander lay on the frozen ground without shelter, fire, or overcoats through the long night. In the morning Gen. BUCKNER hoisted the white flag, and sent a messenger to Gen. GRANT, proposing an armistice till 12 o'clock and the appointment of commissioners to arrange terms of capitulation. To refuse this peremptorily was proper; for GRANT could not know that the time would not be used as a ruse in order to mass troops to drive out the assaulting force. He now rose with the occasion, and sent back this answer:

No terms except unconditional and immediate surrender can be accepted. I propose to move immediately upon your works.

Gen. BUCKNER's situation—his two superiors having fled with all the troops that could get away in the night—was such that he was compelled to surrender unconditionally. In the great rejoicing over this great victory, Gen. GRANT's answer to BUCKNER was celebrated as if it, and not Gen. SMITH's leading and Gen. LAUMAN's brigade, had made the capture. That the surrender was unconditional was thought to be more than the victory. The initials of Gen. GRANT's name became popularly interpreted as Unconditional Surrender GRANT. Secretary STANTON, then wrestling with the much preparing Gen. McCLELLAN, wrote a letter to the editor of the New York Tribune, in a strain of great religious exaltation, conveying that the whole art of war was contained in GRANT's answer to BUCKNER, saying:

We may well rejoice at the recent victories, for they teach us that battles are to be won now, and by us, in the same and only manner that they were ever won by any people, or in any age since Joshua, by boldly pursuing and striking the foe. What, under the blessing of Providence, I conceive to be the true organization of victory and military combination to end this war, was declared in a few words by Gen. Grant's message to Gen. Buckner: "I propose to move immediately on your works."

Therefore did the vanity of playing a part up to the popular name of Unconditional Surrender GRANT lead him to make this peremptory refusal to negotiate for the capitulation of a place which he had twice assaulted, with great slaughter of his soldiers; whose fortifications were intact, and which had 18,000 men to defend them, and while he thought that the threatening situation on both sides of the Mississippi compelled him to assault again, with the certainty of repeating the slaughter of the 22d of June, and with no certainty of any other result.

The nature of this refusal of terms can be appreciated by reflecting on the probable consequences if Gen. PEMBERTON had taken Gen. GRANT at his word, and he had sent his troops to death in another assault. Does not BADEAU's history place GRANT in the situation of choosing the further sacrifice of his own soldiers, in order to play up to his popular sobriquet? Then followed an unseemly dispute over the unseemly question who it was that made the proffer of further negotiation, or of a mediation to get Gen.

GRANT to relent his implacable temper. BADEAU's version is this:

Bowen was received by Gen. A. J. Smith, and expressed a strong desire to converse with Grant; this, however, was not allowed; he then suggested that it would be well if Grant and Pemberton could meet. Grant, therefore, sent a verbal message that if Pemberton wished to see him, an interview could be had between the lines, in McPherson's, at 3 o'clock that afternoon.

He sent this verbal message with the above written answer. Thus was the demand for unconditional surrender coupled with the written promise of generous treatment, and with a consent to see PEMBERTON to talk over the matter.

BADEAU's narrative of the interview fetches this great affair down to a play of bluff. GRANT went to the place of meeting, between the lines, with Gens. ORD, McPHERSON, LOGAN, and A. J. SMITH, and several of his staff; PEMBERTON with Gen. BOWEN and Capt. MONTGOMERY. BADEAU narrates:

The two Generals shook hands, and Pemberton inquired what terms of capitulation would be allowed him. Grant replied: "Those that had been expressed in his letter of this morning;" whereupon Pemberton haughtily declared: "If this were all, the conference might terminate, and hostilities be resumed immediately." "Very well," said Grant, and turned away.

According to BADEAU's narrative Gen. GRANT thus chose to send his army to another assault upon these fortifications rather than grant any terms of capitulation, and he, by his peremptory manner, cut off all further negotiations. Gen. PEMBERTON's version is different; but Gen. GRANT, who revised BADEAU's narrative, is entitled to his version, whatever the reflection. BADEAU goes on:

But Gen. Bowen then proposed that two of the subordinates present should retire for consultation and suggest such terms as they might think proper for the consideration of their chiefs. Grant had no objection to this, but would not consider himself bound by any agreement of his subordinates. He, himself, must decide what terms were to be allowed. Smith and Bowen accordingly went a little way apart, while Grant and Pemberton walked up and down between the parapets conversing.

Even by BADEAU's account it thus appears that Gen. GRANT's refusal to consider any terms but unconditional surrender had now limbered down to a consent to let commissioners consult about conditions.

Gen. PEMBERTON's report narrates that he understood from BOWEN that GRANT desired a personal conference, but upon arriving on the ground:

I soon learned that there was a mutual misunderstanding in regard to the desire for this interview, and therefore informed Gen. Grant that if he had no terms to propose other than were contained in his letter, the conference could terminate, and hostilities be resumed immediately. After some further conversation, he (Grant) proposed that Gen. Bowen and Capt. Montgomery, and two of his staff officers, Maj. Gens. McPherson and Smith, should retire, consult, and suggest such terms as they thought proper for our consideration. After some conversation between these officers, we parted, with the understanding that Gen. Grant would communicate with me by 10 o'clock, and about that hour the following letter was received.

Here is a flat difference as to who proposed the personal interview, and who proposed the commissioners of conference, and Gen. PEMBERTON's statement has the corroboration of the result, which is wholly contradictory to the ground which BADEAU says that GRANT took. Gen. PEMBERTON, in 1875, wrote a letter to Col. JOHN P. NICHOLSON, of Philadelphia, giving his version of the interview. This states that the misunderstanding as to GRANT's having expressed a desire for an interview was his, and was satisfactorily explained; that after GRANT had repeated that he had no other terms but his first, and PEMBERTON had declared that the fighting would go on, it was GRANT that proposed a conference, and that they parted, GRANT consenting that as he had rejected PEMBERTON's proposition, it was his part to make one, and agreeing to send one that night.

BADEAU's further narrative seems to corroborate PEMBERTON in this. He says:

After some discussion it was agreed that Grant should send his terms to Pemberton before 10 o'clock that night. * * * Grant returned to his quarters, and, for the only time in his life, held what might be called a council of war. He sent for all his corps and division Generals on the city front, and received their opinions as to the terms which should be allowed to Pemberton.

It would not accord with BADEAU's measure of GRANT's great mind if he did not in this take a view greatly higher than his subordinates. It pleases BADEAU, approved by GRANT, to represent Gen. GRANT in this as implacable toward the Vicksburg army, and as demanding severer terms of surrender than other men could rise to. Accordingly, he says:

> With one exception (Gen. Steele), they suggested terms that Grant was unwilling to sanction, and their judgment was not accepted. The following letter was written instead, and forwarded to Pemberton.

But GRANT's letter was so different from his original demand as to make that appear a defeated attempt to play the bully. It offered these liberal terms: 1. To march in one division as a guard. 2. All officers and men to be paroled, and to march out, all to have their clothing, officers their side arms, field, staff, and cavalry officers one horse each. 3. Any required amount of rations and cooking utensils to be taken from their own stores, and thirty wagons for transportation.

These terms were generous, but not too generous under the circumstances. But to start in insolently with the refusal to talk of any terms but unconditional surrender, and then to come down to this proposition, was to thrust into a great military event the tactics of the Cheap John auctioneer. PEMBERTON received this at 10 o'clock p. m. of July 3, and in the same night sent an answer, accepting the terms in the main, but asking these amendments: 1. The garrison to march out at 10 o'clock on the 4th, and surrender by stacking arms in front of the works, then GRANT to take possession. 2. Officers to retain personal property. 3. Rights and property of private citizens to be respected.

The manner in which PEMBERTON proposed to make the surrender was much more spectacular than that of GRANT's propositions. It was as if he thought a scene of laying down arms would make it more imposing. GRANT accepted this, but declined any enlargement of the private property allowed to officers, or to bind himself as to the private property of citizens. Gen. PEMBERTON gave as his reason for proposing to surrender on the 4th of July that he thought "the vanity of our foes" would lead them to give better terms for a capture which would be such a celebration. It appears that both sides were expediting the negotiations all night to this spectacular end, and by 8 o'clock a. m. of the 4th, PEMBERTON's formal acceptance was received by GRANT, the surrender to be made at 10 o'clock.

But BADEAU narrates that during the livelong night Unconditional Surrender GRANT was not limiting himself to a negotiation of conditions with Gen. PEMBERTON, but was at the same time carrying on a negotiation through the Confederate pickets to corrupt PEMBERTON's troops. He says:

> During that night Grant sent instructions to Ord and McPherson to put discreet men on picket, and allow them to communicate to the enemy's pickets the fact that in case of surrender both officers and men would be paroled and allowed to return to their homes.

Not only paroled by him, but discharged from Confederate authority.

CHAPTER L.

THE SURRENDER—GRAND ENTRY OF THE NATIONAL TROOPS—THE GENERAL'S BULLETIN—THE TROPHIES—THE NOT VALID PAROLE—THE NUMBER PAROLED—HOW IT WAS SWELLED—THE MILITARY IMPORTANCE OF THE CAPTURE OF THE PLACE.

At 10 o'clock on the 4th of July, 1863, a ceremony took place which, to the volunteers who had survived this dreadful campaign, must have seemed the reward of their hardships, which, to the chiefs, brought glory and promotion, and whose announcement caused extravagant joy throughout the country. The defenders of Vicksburg marched outside of their lines and stacked their arms, while the national volunteers stood on their parapets in silence, observing the ceremony.

This triumph had cost the national volunteers dearly, and in the course of the whole campaign, sickness, wounds, and death had deprived of the view of this closing scene a larger number than the surrendered. The capitulation was a severe mortification to the Southern troops, but no dishonor. They had yielded to starvation that which superior force had tried in vain to take, and they had received honorable terms. The place which had been the object of all the hardships, sacrifices, and heroism of a great army for nearly a year was now gained.

Gen. LOGAN's division then entered the town. BADEAU says it was entitled to this honor of being first, because it "was one of those which had approached nearest to the rebel works," and "had been heavily engaged in both assaults." The column marched to the Court House, upon which the 48th Illinois placed its flag. Gen. GRANT and staff rode at the head of the column. "He went direct to one of the rebel headquarters," and entered, and, BADEAU says, was coldly received. He had an interview with PEMBERTON. BADEAU says that PEMBERTON now requested GRANT to supply the garrison with rations, and when GRANT asked him how many would be needed, PEMBERTON replied: "I have 32,000 men."

GRANT then rode to the landing to exchange "congratulations with Admiral PORTER on the flagship, but returned to his old camp at dark." His quarters were not removed to Vicksburg till the 6th. That night he announced the capitulation to the government in these words: "The enemy surrendered this morning. The only terms allowed is their parole. This I regard as a great advantage to us at this juncture. It saves probably several days in the capture, and leaves troops and transports ready for immediate service." GRANT had now become convinced that the conditional was better than the unconditional surrender.

A week was taken in making the paroles and other arrangements, and then the garrison, except the sick, marched out into the Confederacy. Gen. HALLECK sent to GRANT the following, July 8:

I fear your paroling the prisoners at Vicksburg without actual delivery to a proper agent, as required by the seventh article of the cartel, may be construed into an absolute release, and that these men will immediately be placed in the ranks of the enemy. Such has been the case elsewhere. If these prisoners have not been allowed to depart, you will retain them until further orders.

Before this was received, BADEAU says, the prisoners had left Vicksburg. Upon this point BADEAU makes a plea that GRANT was "obliged to parole and discharge his prisoners" by the terms of the cartel, and he quotes these terms as if proving it; but they prove that paroles were not to be held valid by either side unless the prisoners were reduced to actual possession, and were then formally delivered up to the other, at stated places, and to the authorized agent. One of these places was Vicksburg; but as GRANT had captured that, there was no Confederate authority there to which to deliver his prisoners.

Unquestionably Gen. HALLECK's statement of the conditions of the cartel was correct, and his view that if the Confederate authorities should hold strictly to the terms, they could place these paroled men in the ranks without exchange. The common report of the time was that this was done, and that among the forces gathered to resist the march of Gen. ROSECRANS were many of the paroled Vicksburg army. This is a matter which is not easy to find out at this time. It could not be expected to be found in Confederate reports, and BADEAU's treatment of this parole question is a plea of defense, and the defense is the false plea that "GRANT was therefore obliged to parole and discharge his prisoners" by the cartel.

The number of men surrendered is stated by BADEAU as 31,600, but he says "the number actually paroled was 28,892;" that "709 refused to be paroled, and were sent North as prisoners." To make up the rest he estimates that "many hundreds died in the hospitals before the paroling could be completed, and over 1,000 escaped, or concealed themselves, or, disguised as citizens, avoided being paroled." But the number actually paroled was 28,892, and the conditions were such as to make a parole desirable, instead of a thing to avoid. BADEAU states the captures as 105 field guns and sixty-seven garrison guns.

The history written by CHARLES A. DANA and GRANT's Chief Engineer, WILSON, says: "The rebels surrendered 21,000 effective men, and 6,000 wounded in hospital, besides over 120 guns of all calibers." Captured guns are cherished trophies, but more when captured on the field of battle than when surrendered by starvation. The difference between the surrender of men paroled and the number stated by Gen. PEMBERTON in his report as his effective force at the beginning of the siege, namely, 18,500, and in his dispatch to Gen. J. E. JOHNSTON after the two assaults, namely, 18,000, needs remark. BADEAU takes the number which he says PEMBERTON stated to GRANT as requiring rations, and from that he calculates back that PEMBERTON pursued a course of understating his force at Edwards' Station and Champion's Hill.

A lumping statement of numbers, however, made for rations to the hungry, may have been a liberal one. BADEAU has to guess at the unknown to make out 31,600, after he has stated all that were paroled. To suppose that PEMBERTON would make a false report of his force to Gen. JOHNSTON, when he was anxious for JOHNSTON to co-operate for his relief, would be unreasonable; also, a false report of his force would be swiftly challenged by JOHNSTON and the War Department. At the beginning he stated his effective force as about 18,500. Subsequently he stated his losses during the siege as about 1,000. But it will be supposed, as a matter of course, that all the citizens and sojourners in the town who were able to bear arms were made to help the defense.

BADEAU, taking from "a rebel narrative of the siege," describing the retreat of PEMBERTON's army into Vicksburg after the rout at Black River Bridge, says: "The planters and population of the country, fleeing from the presence of the victorious enemy, added to the crowd and the confusion." Every man in the Confederacy, between the ages of eighteen and thirty-five, was under conscription, and if permitted to be at home to work his farm or attend to other business, he was detailed to this. The men over this age were enrolled as "State troops." With all this PEMBERTON could place in the trenches every man in Vicksburg able to bear arms.

In the answers of PEMBERTON's Generals to his questions whether their troops were in a condition to make the attempt to fight the way out of Vicksburg, Maj. Gen. M. L. SMITH wrote: "There are about 3,000 men in my division, including State troops." In another part of the letter he mentions the regulars as 2,000. He said: "Out of the 3,000 only about 2,000 are considered reliable in case we are strongly opposed and much harassed." With the enrollment of all the men in Vicksburg who were able to bear arms, it is reasonable to suppose that PEMBERTON could increase his number of 18,500 effectives to 21,000 nominally in arms when he surrendered.

Besides, the service of the Confederate troops, since the national army had emerged from the swamps, had been severe, their losses in battle large, and they endured the hardships of campaigning with less stamina than the Northern volunteers. Such a list of sick and wounded as might reasonably be calculated would account for the number stated by DANA's history, as "21,000 effective men," including "State troops," and "over 6,000 in hospital," thus leaving the correctness of PEMBERTON's report that he had 18,500 effective men when first besieged in Vicksburg.

These 18,500 regular troops who were effective when GRANT began the siege, deducting their losses during the siege, were the effective regular force lost to the Confederacy by this siege and capture. Besides this was the large number of sick and wounded of the regular force, of whom the number stated by DANA as 6,000 was probably no exaggeration, making between 24,000 and 25,000 of the regular Confederate soldiers. The capture of the sick and wounded did not diminish the present Confederate strength, and they were a burden to us; but as many as survived would count in exchange.

POLLARD, the Southern historian, whose general candor is conceded by GREELEY's history, says: "The numbers which surrendered at Vicksburg were 27,000 men, with three Major Generals and nine Brigadiers, upward of ninety pieces of artillery, and about 40,000 small arms. Weakness from fatigue, short rations, and heat, had left thousands of the troops decrepit. Six thousand of them were in hospitals, and many of them were crawling about in what should be convalescent camps."

Citizens, armed for the defense, and State troops, made up the rest to the number stated by DANA and WILSON as 27,000, or to the number stated by BADEAU as actually paroled, namely, 28,892. It was Gen. PEMBERTON's duty to return for parole all that had borne arms in the defense, and the parole was sought for. Such of the planters and business men as were under the conscription, but were detailed to attend to their business, were glad to be paroled, because it was an indefinite furlough to them. The citizens and State troops desired it for the same reason. The Confederate soldiers wanted it because it relieved them from the terrible duty in the field, and seemed a promise of visiting their homes.

These conditions, aided by the present destitution and government rations, combined to enlarge the paroled list to a number greatly beyond the effective force surrendered, and to make the captures on the national side far greater than the loss of effective forces on the Confederate side. The authorities at Washington seemed to judge military results by the inventory of the surrendered, and to think a capture of a town by the work of starvation, after a campaign of two seasons, a greater military result than a victory in a pitched battle, such as that of Gettysburg, which effectually disabled LEE's hitherto invincible army as an offensive force, while the Confederate army in the West had yet to be encountered in the field.

The importance of the capture of a place, however, is not to be measured by its trophies in guns and flags, nor even by the number of soldiers surrendered. They who consider the object of war will hardly say that the capture of these men and guns was a sufficient military object for the occupation of all the force of GRANT's department for two campaigning seasons, and all the consuming of men and means thereby. No military power could afford to make war upon such terms. The importance of the taking of Vicksburg was not in the number of men or guns surrendered, but in its military position, as a commanding place lost by the adversary, or as a commanding place gained by us for further operations.

If the capture of Vicksburg had neither of these military consequences; if its loss did not lay open the Confederacy to a further campaign from this point of vantage; if it was not to us a base for a line of operations to the heart of the Confederate power in the western zone of the war, then the Vicksburg campaign would have no military meaning, and the capture not only would not be worth a tithe of the immense cost in men and other resources, but it would not redeem the course of disaster which had abandoned an interior campaign on a true military line, to bury an army in the Mississippi swamps. Further along we shall see the military consequences of this capture of a place which was thought to have fatally dismembered the Confederacy.

CHAPTER LI.

THE SURRENDER OF PORT HUDSON—A VICTORY IN SPITE OF ORDERS—SHERMAN'S MARCH ON JACKSON—VICKSBURG THE FINALITY OF THE CAMPAIGN—THE WAY KEPT OPEN FOR JOHNSTON TO RETREAT—DEVASTATION—THE ISOLATION OF GRANT'S ARMY AT VICKSBURG.

Gen. BANKS had been prosecuting the siege of Port Hudson with great energy, and the garrison had been reduced to extremity. Hearing of the surrender of Vicksburg, and finding no promise of relief from either Gen. J. E. JOHNSTON on the east, or Gen. RICHARD TAYLOR on the west, Gen. GARDNER surrendered on the 8th of July. And now, says BADEAU: "The attempted Confederacy was cut in twain, and, in the forcible language of LINCOLN, 'The father of waters rolled unvexed to the sea.'"

The capture of Port Hudson was the completion of an intelligent and successful operation west of the Mississippi, which was vital to the possession of Louisiana and of all the lower river. It had been carried out with a comparatively small force. BANKS had but about 10,000 men to besiege Port Hudson, held by over 7,000, and he was more imminently threatened by Gen. RICHARD TAYLOR than GRANT was by Gen. J. E. JOHNSTON. The possession of Port Hudson was as important to the "cutting of the Confederacy in twain," and the unvexed flow of the father of waters, as Vicksburg. The siege had been pushed with the utmost energy and by two assaults, and the garrison was nearly exhausted.

Gen. GARDNER surrendered 6,408 men, of whom 455 were officers. In the brief campaign west of the Mississippi, and in this conclusion at Port Hudson, Gen. BANKS' troops had captured 10,584 men, 73 guns, 6,000 small arms, three gunboats, eight other steamboats, besides cotton, cattle, and other supplies. And now this strong fort was taken, which commanded the navigation of the Mississippi as much as Vicksburg did. Instead of having now to begin the work of taking Port Hudson, which would have been the case if GRANT and the Washington authorities had had their way in calling BANKS off to help GRANT take Vicksburg, with probably the work of recovering Louisiana to begin anew, Louisiana was firmly in our possession, the last Confederate stronghold on the Mississippi captured; the Confederacy had suffered a heavy loss of men and munitions and supplies; the "Confederacy was cut in twain, and the father of waters rolled unvexed to the sea, and BANKS was ready for an operation which the administration was now very anxious to enter upon in Texas. All this had given essential co-operation to GRANT's taking of Vicksburg. Yet all this success was slighted by the Washington authorities, and BADEAU treats it as a consequence of GRANT's capture of Vicksburg.

Before PEMBERTON had proposed negotiations, SHERMAN had been placed in command of the army of the rear, formed to resist JOHNSTON. On the night of the 4th, GRANT ordered ORD and STEELE to join SHERMAN, making about 40,000 men, and ordered him: "Drive JOHNSTON from the Mississippi Central Railroad; destroy the bridges as far north as Grenada with your cavalry, and do the enemy all the harm possible." In another order he said: "I want you to drive JOHNSTON out in your own way, and inflict on the enemy all the punishment you can. I will support you to the last man that can be spared."

These orders gave Gen. GRANT's view of the objective of the Vicksburg campaign, and of the military value of the capture of that place. They showed that it had not been sought as a commanding base for further operations, but that the mere occupation of Vicksburg was the ultimate object of the whole campaign, which contemplated nothing further in that quarter save devastating raids. All of Gen. J. E. JOHNSTON's course proves that his limited mind could not rise to the height of GRANT's generalship; for he thought that GRANT wanted Vicksburg as a base for operations to possess the State of Mississippi.

He was incapable of believing that GRANT could spend such a force merely to capture a town. Believing that he intended this as a base for an interior movement into the very heart of the Confederacy, and the navigation of the river having before been lost, through FARRAGUT's fleet and the running of the Vicksburg guns, he held that the place was of little military importance to the Confederacy, and that the great necessity was to save the army to protect the interior from the invasion which he supposed would follow the capture of this place.

Thus did these two greatest military men of their respective sections—the one regarded as the greatest strategist and tactician of the Confederacy, the other as the greatest General of the nation, and rated by his authorized biographer as greater than BONAPARTE—take opposite views of the objective and opportunities of GRANT's campaign; JOHNSTON thinking that the great operation was to follow the capture of Vicksburg; GRANT making that his final objective.

JOHNSTON fell back to Jackson, before which place SHERMAN arrived on the 9th. JOHNSTON's narrative says of the fortifications, which had been made under PEMBERTON's orders:

These works, consisting of a very light line of rifle pits, with low embankments at intervals to cover field pieces, extended from a point north of the town, and a little east of the Canton road, to one south of it within a short distance of Pearl River, and covered the approaches to the place west of the river. These intrenchments were very badly located and constructed, and offered very slight obstacle to a vigorous assault.

Reports of JOHNSTON's officers led him to believe that the want of water would compel SHERMAN to make an immediate assault, and he disposed of his troops to meet that. But he says: "Instead of attacking as soon as it came up, as we had been hoping, the Federal army intrenched and began to construct batteries." He continues:

Hills within easy cannon range, commanding and encircling the town, offered very favorable sites for Federal batteries. A crossfire of shot and shell reached all parts of the town, showing that the position would be untenable under the fire of a powerful artillery. Such, as it was ascertained, was soon to be brought to bear upon it.

On the 11th JOHNSTON telegraphed President DAVIS that it was impossible to 'hold the place against a siege, and that unless the enemy attacked he must, or else abandon the place, and that to attack would expose the army to destruction. Gen. SHERMAN narrates in the memoirs:

We closed our lines about Jackson; my corps (15th) held the center, extending from Clinton to the Raymond road; Ord's (13th) on the right, reaching Pearl River below the town, and Parke's (9th) the left, above the town. On the 11th we pressed close in, and shelled the town from every direction. One of Ord's brigades (Lauman's) got too close, and was very roughly handled, and driven back in disorder. Gen. Ord accused the commander (Gen. Lauman) of having disregarded his orders, and attributed to him personally the disaster and heavy loss of men. He requested his relief, which I granted, and Gen. Lauman went to the rear, and never regained his brigade. He died after the war, in Iowa, much respected, as before that time he had been universally esteemed a most gallant and excellent officer.

Gen. JOHNSTON's narrative tells this affair as on the 12th. The "memoirs" paid little heed to accuracy in dates or other facts. JOHNSTON says:

On the 12th, besides the usual skirmishing, there

was increased fire with artillery, especially by batteries near the Canton road, and those immediately to the south of that to Clinton. The missiles fell in all parts of the town. An assault, though not a vigorous one, was made in Breckinridge's front. It was quickly repulsed, however, by the well directed fire of Slocomb's and Cobb's batteries, and a flank attack by the skirmishers of the 1st, 3d, and 4th Florida, and 47th Georgia regiments.

The enemy lost about 200 prisoners, the same number killed, many wounded, and the colors of the 28th, 41st, and 53d Illinois regiments. The attacking troops did not advance far enough to be exposed to the fire of Breckinridge's *line.*

On the 13th the Federal lines had been so extended that both flanks rested upon Pearl River. Col. A. C. Fuller, of Lieut. Gen. Pemberton's staff, arrived from Vicksburg, and informed us of the terms of the capitulation. * * * He stated also that at the time of the surrender about 18,000 men were reported fit for duty in the trenches, and about 6,000 sick and wounded in the hospitals. And the estimates for rations to be furnished to the troops of the garrison by the United States Commissary Department were based on a total of 31,000 men.

JOHNSTON learned from his scouts on the 14th that a large ammunition train had left Vicksburg by the Jackson road. On the 15th he telegraphed President DAVIS that the enemy had begun a siege, which he could not resist. A cavalry attempt to intercept the train failed. The state of the batteries indicated that all would open on the town on the 17th; therefore JOHNSTON evacuated the place on the night of the 16th. He says: All public property, and the sick and wounded, except a few not in condition to bear removal, had been carried to the rear, to Brandon, and beyond. The army marched to Brandon by two roads, destroying behind it the bridges by which it crossed Pearl River.

JOHNSTON gives his loss in Jackson as seventy-one killed, 504 wounded, twenty-five missing. Belated soldiers who left the town at 7 or 8 o'clock informed him that apparently the enemy had not then discovered its evacuation.

SHERMAN continues his narrative thus:

The weather was fearfully hot, but we continued to press the siege day and night, using our artillery pretty freely, and on the morning of July 17 the place was found evacuated. Gen. Steele's division was sent in pursuit as far as Brandon (fourteen miles), but Gen. Johnston had carried his army safely off, and pursuit in that hot weather would have been fatal to my command.

JOHNSTON's narrative tells this:

Two divisions of Federal infantry and a body of cavalry drove our cavalry rear guard through Brandon on the 19th, and returned to Jackson on the 29th. The object of the expedition seemed to be the destruction of the railroad bridges and depot, to which the outrage of setting fire to the little town, and burning the greater part of it, was added.

Gen. SHERMAN, with a force which, effectively, was more than twice as great as JOHNSTON's, and with all of GRANT's army to draw from, had found JOHNSTON facing him at Jackson. He had consumed seven days in intrenching and in an aimless, tentative kind of "close pressing," which exposed his troops to a sortie; had gotten considerably hurt by the flanking of one of his divisions; he was gathering ammunition for shelling the town, when at last JOHNSTON marched out by the east where all was open.

The whole operation by this superior force was as if the place were the objective, and the tactics to have JOHNSTON leave it. Meanwhile SHERMAN was literally carrying out GRANT's order: "I want you to drive JOHNSTON out in your own way, and inflict on the enemy all the punishment you can." Instead of disposing of his army to capture JOHNSTON's, or to bring it to battle in the field by marching upon its communications, he was encouraging it to depart, and was devoting his chief energies to the work of destroying property. Says BADEAU:

The work of railroad destruction went on vigorously, while regular parapets of earth and cotton were constructed in front of the lines. * * * Meanwhile Sherman sent out expeditions to the right and left, destroying the railroads in every direction—cars, locomotives, turntables, and shops, as well as tracks and bridges. * * * Some of his troops traversed as far as sixty miles, marking their whole route with devastation.

Of the evacuation he tells:

All night Sherman heard the sound of wagons, but nothing that indicated evacuation, for the picks and shovels were at work till midnight; but at dawn of day it became evident that the enemy had withdrawn across Pearl River. All the material of war had been removed in advance of retreat, by means of the railroad running east.

Of the work of SHERMAN at Jackson, JOHNSTON narrates:

The Federal army remained only five or six days at Jackson, but in that short time it destroyed all of the town so closely built that fire could communicate from house to house; its rear guard left the place for Vicksburg on the 23d.

BADEAU says with more comprehensiveness: "He remained two or three days completing the work of destruction."

Summing up the grand results, BADEAU says:

> They drove Johnston fifty miles, and left him in full retreat; they destroyed the great arteries of travel, which alone could enable him to reassemble troops and molest Grant's possession of the Mississippi, and they so exhausted the country through which they passed that no army could exist there again, during that season, without hauling its supplies. The campaign was a fitting supplement to the conquest of the Mississippi, and, indeed, was necessary to perfect the achievements of Grant. Sherman's whole loss was less than 1,000 men.

SHERMAN's tactics had kept open the way of JOHNSTON's retreat, with all the material of his army. He had made his grand objective the destruction of a railroad center whose occupation by our army, Gen. JOHNSTON said, would have brought the fall of the State of Mississippi. He had destroyed a place and material which a rational and comprehensive military plan would have converted to our means. All of his destruction was, in fact, of resources available to us. He had devastated a fruitful country, leaving it destitute, as if it were not our own, and we were not carrying on war to restore the Union, but were a horde of Tartars invading civilization.

All this was in pursuance of a plan which made the possession of Vicksburg the finality; all this devastation to make the Confederates unable to fetch troops to molest GRANT in Vicksburg. Having facilitated JOHNSTON's withdrawal with his army and material; having made a desert, and called it war, Gen. SHERMAN says he returned, reaching camp on the 27th near the Big Black River, "with the prospect of a period of rest for the remainder of the summer." Thus was GRANT's army, after it had achieved its objective, as completely isolated from all other armies, and as completely neutralized as to any co-operation or influence on other operations as when it was involved in the swamps west of the Mississippi. In respect to all interior campaigns, it had simply changed places with PEMBERTON's army.

CHAPTER LII.

A GALLANT OFFICER ELECTED SCAPEGOAT—THE VICKSBURG CAMPAIGN ARRIVED AT ITS ULTIMATE OBJECTIVE—CUTS ITSELF OFF FROM ALL SEQUENCE—THE CONFEDERACY CUT IN TWO AND ITS BACKBONE BROKEN—GRANT SITS DOWN TO WAIT FOR IT TO DIE.

The last previous chapter mentions the peremptory dismissal of Gen. LAUMAN, of Iowa, from the command of his brigade, by Gen. SHERMAN, at the demand of Gen. ORD, who charged him with the blame for the loss suffered by his brigade by a flank attack of the enemy, while the whole line was pressing upon the intrenchments of JACKSON. Gen. LAUMAN's high services, although only a volunteer General, warrant the reviewer in noticing this arbitrary execution, which terminated a distinguished military career in disgrace, at the hour of triumph.

It was Gen. LAUMAN's brigade that redeemed GRANT's disaster at Fort Donelson, and got him promotion by an assault which carried one part of the fort, and made the other untenable. This was after GRANT had waited with his army for the gunboats to take the fort, and they had all been disabled in the attempt; after he had dispatched Gen. HALLECK that he should have to intrench and enter upon a "protracted siege;" for, says he: "I fear the result of an attempt to carry the place by storm with new troops." And he was intending to wait for the fleet to go back and repair and return.

Also, this storming of the fort was carried by LAUMAN's brigade after the Confederate army had made a sortie, which had driven back the entire right wing of GRANT's army, and then WALLACE's division, in a fierce battle which raged from dawn till noon, while GRANT was absent on Commodore FOOTE's gunboat. It was made after GRANT had sent word to Commodore FOOTE that a fierce conflict had demoralized a portion of his command, and that if the gunboats did not appear, it would "reassure the enemy, and still further demoralize our troops," and that "I must order a change to save appearances."

Under all these "demoralizing" and disastrous conditions did LAUMAN's brigade make the assault, which not only saved appearances, but redeemed the disaster, saved the Commanding General, and set him afloat on the flood tide to fortune. It is unnecessary to say that such soldierly work is not done without that previous organizing and training which give to soldiers confidence in themselves, in each other, and in their officers. Such work is not done by "raw troops," and this brigade had been ripened by discipline and service.

If Gen. GRANT, who, before his army was hurt, distrusted its ability to carry the fort by storm, and who, after his army had been badly hurt, ordered the attack only to save appearances, was glorified to the skies, because the assault succeeded, what should be the measure of merit to Gen. LAUMAN, who trained the troops that stormed the fort, and who, with Gen. C. F. SMITH, led them into the enemy's works? The soldierly qualities of this brigade, which enabled it to do this work of veteran troops, had not been acquired without a good soldier for a commander, nor without much service.

This service had continued through all the discouragements and hardships of the Vicksburg campaign, and now in the hour of triumph this gallant officer was sent to the rear in disgrace. What was the special fault of Gen. LAUMAN in an operation which, with twice JOHNSTON's force, had permitted him to retire at his leisure, after having inflicted a sharp punishment? Gen. SHERMAN had stretched his army from the river above Jackson to the river below, and was "pressing in," whatever that may be. He narrates in his memoirs:

> On the 11th we pressed close in, and shelled the town from every direction. One of Ord's brigades (Lauman's) got too close, and was very roughly handled and driven back in disorder. Gen. Ord accused the commander, Gen. Lauman, of having disregarded his orders, and attributed to him personally the disaster and heavy loss of men. He requested his relief, which J granted, and Gen. Lauman went to the rear and never regained his brigade. He died, after the war, in Iowa, much respected, as before that time he had been universally esteemed a most gallant and excellent officer.

GEN. J. E. JOHNSTON's narrative, which is given in the previous chapter, tells this affair as on the 12th, which was the third day after SHERMAN had arrived in front of the Jackson lines, and shows that LAUMAN's brigade was struck in flank by four regiments. As there is on file, no report of ORD or SHERMAN of the Jackson operation, this is the sum of the information given to the public on this case of summary execution upon a distinguished volunteer officer. Gen. LAUMAN died unheard, and nobody but Gen. ORD knows what were the orders which Gen. LAUMAN disregarded.

The dangerous operation of spreading an army around a fortified place held by an army is not a new thing in war, although our commanders appear to have had to learn it by dear experiment. Gen. GRANT experienced it at Fort Donelson, in a disaster which LAUMAN's brigade turned into a crowning victory to GRANT. Gen. SHERMAN experienced it at Atlanta, where his loose tactics exposed successively two wings of his army to attack by superior force where he could not support them, and where it was only by heroic fighting against superior numbers that his army was saved from destruction. He was engaged in a like dangerous operation at Jackson, with tactics equally loose, and whose object is not made clear by his narrative, and was probably as vague in the orders.

The fact that LAUMAN's brigade was struck in flank and rear, so that about 200 of his men were forced to surrender, serves to show that SHERMAN's pressing line was not continuous. In the previous operation against Jackson, by MCPHERSON's and SHERMAN's corps, when the right and left were extended to the same points south and north of the town, BADEAU states that there was a gap of two miles between the two corps. The extent of this line must have been as much as five miles. It is not easy to understand how LAUMAN's brigade could be taken in flank and rear in such force, and that too before it had reached the enemy's line—which JOHNSTON's narrative shows to be the case—if there had not been a great gap in SHERMAN's pressing line.

He says on the 11th we pressed close in and shelled the town from every direction; again: "We continued to press the siege, using our artillery pretty freely," and so on till the 17th, when they found that JOHNSTON had departed. What was the object in pressing close in along this extended line? Was it not tentative to see if there was a weak spot where an assault might make a lodgment, or if a pressure all along the line would not expedite JOHNSTON's departure? The place was not besieged, for it was not invested. All on the east was open, and SHERMAN was pressing on the west to induce JOHNSTON to go. Meanwhile SHERMAN had sent back for heavier artillery and ammunition for shelling the town.

In this pressing close in by a line of four or five miles, which probably had great gaps, which did not intend a serious attack, it may have been difficult for a subordinate General to know just how strong a pressure he was to make, and Gen. ORD's orders may have partaken of the vague and tentative quality of this operation. Naturally Gen. LAUMAN, in case of doubt, would take the most enterprising course, although that would be the opposite of the way that ORD solved doubt at Iuka. But this extended pressing-in operation was a very dangerous one, and exposed the superior army to be fatally struck by a sortie from the fortified place.

The loss to LAUMAN's brigade was a small matter for that army, compared to what it was exposed to by such a way of operating against an army in a fortified camp. The arbitrary dismissal of LAUMAN looks like the appointment of a scapegoat, which might not be confirmed by inquiry. The confounding of all the properties of merit and justice in our war, by the infallibility and absolute power allowed to a certain class, and the irremediable disabilities kept upon all the rest of the army, has an exemplification in this summary disgrace of so distinguished an officer as Gen. LAUMAN, at the demand of Gen. ORD, for alleged disregard of orders which in the indefinite nature of the operation could not be made definite, and because his brigade happened to be the one hurt by the enemy in a dangerous operation which exposed the army to such sorties as at Donelson and Atlanta.

But suppose Gen. LAUMAN did err, was it a thing unheard of in Gen. GRANT's campaigns? If he erred, it was forward, not backward, as GRANT and ORD at Iuka, and, therefore, his error ought to be the more pardonable. Was it military propriety to dismiss such an officer unheard at the demand of ORD? Was it for Gens. GRANT and SHERMAN to pronounce such a sentence on a distinguished soldier, after their experience of the danger of spreading out an army before a fortified place at Donelson, and before their experience of the same at Atlanta, at Petersburg, and Richmond? Was this charge of pressing too far forward, in an operation whose generalship exposed the army to destruction, so fatal a fault that Gen. GRANT could not pardon it in the officer whose brigade had rescued him from disaster, and set him on the high road to all his fortunes?

With the surrender of Vicksburg, the driving of JOHNSTON's army beyond Jackson, the destruction of that place and of the railroads in all directions, and the devastation of the country, to the end of making it a desert in which an army could not find subsistence in operating against GRANT at Vicksburg, the campaign of GRANT's army ended. The possession of the river, which was declared to be acquired by the surrender of Vicksburg and Port Hudson, was the ultimate military objective. The destruction of Jackson and of the railroads, and the devastating of the country, was GRANT's decision against making Vicksburg and Jackson a base for a campaign to the interior, and it voluntarily destroyed the means for such a campaign.

Gen. SHERMAN returned and encamped between Big Black River and the Mississippi, and a Confederate cavalry division followed to the east bank of Big Black River, and remained in observation. The capture of Vicksburg had no military sequence. SHERMAN says in the memoirs: "GRANT's army had seemingly completed its share of the work of war, and lay, as it were, idle for a time." The military powers of all the earth must wonder at the magnitude of the war resources of a nation which could thus afford to have one great army rest at Vicksburg, as if its share of the work of the war were done, while in the interior of the West another army, lesser in number, and having to protect a long railroad line of supplies, was making a campaign from Murfreesboro to Chattanooga, and the Confederate forces east and west were thus left free to concentrate against it.

But there were military figures of speech which were potent in the war. One of these was the backbone of the rebellion, which we kept on breaking; which was declared broken at Donelson, and again at Corinth, and which was now pronounced finally broken by the surrender of Vicksburg. Another was that by getting possession of the Mississippi we had cut the Confederacy in two. It was held that the Confederate military body could no more live than the animal body, when cut in halves. At any rate, the campaign had reached its ultimate, and had no sequence, and if the Confederacy refused to die when its back was broken and it was cut in two, it was a contumacy so contrary to nature that military tactics could not be expected to provide against it.

Gen. J. E. JOHNSTON, however, argued to his government that when our armed ships passed Port Hudson the Confederacy lost control of the navigation of the Mississippi; still more when our gunboats ran the batteries of Vicksburg, and that that place had thus ceased to have any great military importance. Thus had the Confederacy in fact been cut in twain long before. The extent of the river and its multitude of branches made the preventing of the crossing of troops and supplies impossible. Thus in HOOD's campaign against Gen. GEO. H. THOMAS, in December. 1864, do we read of Gen. GRANT's apprehension that the trans-Mississippi Confederate forces would join Gen. HOOD, as one of the reasons for his order to supersede Gen. THOMAS for delay.

And now, forasmuch as in one part of the severed Confederacy PRICE and MARMADUKE continued in vitality in Arkansas, so that GRANT had to send 5,000 men to re-enforce Gen. SCHOFIELD on that line, and Gen. RICHARD TAYLOR in West Louisiana, became very active, in the face of Gen. BANKS, re-enforced by the 13th Corps (late MCCLERNAND's), and was able to hold West Louisiana and Texas till the end of the war, against two formidable expeditions; and, in the other severed part, BRAGG gathered a superior force against ROSECRANS' advance, while GRANT's army was reposing on its completed work, it appears that the Confederacy unconscionably refused to recognize the moral results of the tactics of the campaign, but continued to show the same vitality when cut in twain, and with its back broken, and that it was on our side that the energy and strategy of this great army had been so completely expended that the campaign had no sequence.

CHAPTER LIII.

THE FINISHED CAMPAIGN—DISTRIBUTION OF THE ARMY—ITS ISOLATION FROM THE THEATER OF THE WAR—GRANT WANTS TO MOVE ON MOBILE—SINGULAR NOTION OF CONCENTRATION ON VITAL POINTS—GRANT ORDERED TO RE-ENFORCE ROSECRANS, AND THEN TO TAKE COMMAND—BEGINS WITH A GRACEFUL ACT.

As soon as Gen. GRANT had pronounced the Vicksburg campaign finished, he proceeded to divide up his army, and to send a part to Gen. BANKS, 5,000 men to Missouri, to send back the 9th Corps to BURNSIDE, in East Tennessee, and to dispose of the rest for garrisoning the river, and for rest from its hard labors. In this dispersing, which usually is a sad finale to a General, he showed an alacrity as if this were the sealing of the completion of the campaign, or as if apprehensive that his worn out army might be ordered to another.

Such apprehension might be reasonable, for the military propriety of GRANT's army's co-operating with ROSECRANS by a movement from Vicksburg and Jackson, or of part of it being sent to re-enforce ROSECRANS, then seeking to bring Gen. BRAGG to action, was so evident as to suggest itself to the whole country. Gen. GRANT, before the capture of Vicksburg, had been generous in promises to Gen. BANKS to send him troops as soon as he had taken that place. A few days after the surrender, although Port Hudson had also surrendered, and Gen. BANKS' present strait was over, Gen. GRANT, says BADEAU, "offered to send him 'an army corps of as good troops as ever trod American soil; no better are found in any other.'"

BADEAU states that immediately after the capture of Jackson, GRANT sent to BANKS HERRON's division, whose number he now gives as 4,000. When it reached Vicksburg to complete the investment, he said it was the largest division in the combined army. Subsequently he sent ORD's corps, the 13th, lately MCCLERNAND's. SHERMAN's narrative says: "ORD's corps (13th) was sent down to Natchez and gradually drifted to New Orleans and Texas." As to the disposition of his own corps SHERMAN says: "It being mid-summer we did not expect any change till the autumn months, and accordingly made ourselves as comfortable as possible."

On the 18th of July GRANT announced to

HALLECK the capture of Jackson and the completion of the Vicksburg campaign, and suggested this: "It seems to me now that Mobile should be captured, the expedition starting from some point on Lake Ponchartrain. There is much sickness in my command now, from long and excessive marching and labor." HALLECK answered: "Before attempting Mobile, I think it will be best to clean up a little. JOHNSTON should be disposed of, also PRICE and MARMADUKE, so as to hold line of Arkansas River."

SHERMAN had reported to GRANT, and GRANT to HALLECK, that JOHNSTON had been disposed of; that "He is now in full retreat east. SHERMAN says most of his army must perish from the heat, lack of water, and general discouragement;" but HALLECK did not understand this easy method of destroying armies by bulletin, and he assumed that JOHNSTON's army was still to be disposed of. And although the capture of Vicksburg and Port Hudson was said to have possessed the Mississippi, and thus to have cut the Confederacy in two, HALLECK assumed that no military consequences were to follow, but that JOHNSTON in one-half, and PRICE and MARMADUKE in the other, had yet to be disposed of in the usual way.

HALLECK continued, as quoted by BADEAU:

This will enable us to withdraw troops from Missouri. Vicksburg and Port Hudson should be repaired so as to be tenable by small garrisons; also, assist Banks in clearing out Western Louisiana. When these things are accomplished there will be a large available force to operate either on Mobile or Texas. Navy is not ready for co-operation; should Sumter fall, then ironclads can be sent to assist at Mobile.

Upon this, BADEAU makes the remarkable commentary:

This strategy was in accordance with Halleck's habit of scattering his forces and energies upon comparatively unimportant objects, leaving the great and decisive aims to be accomplished last. He seemed to be unable to appreciate the fact that if the main objects of the war are gained, the lesser ones were sure to follow; or even the purely military maxim that strategic points of the highest consequence should be first secured.

Thus it doth appear that to withdraw GRANT's army from the interior, and devote it for nearly a year to the capture of Vicksburg, which had no tactical or strategical sequence, and then to take it around by sea to capture Mobile, separating it as widely as possible from the great interior campaign then on foot, was concentration upon the main objects and great strategic points. To the reviewer these great Generals appear to be able rivals in the tactics of avoiding co-operation of the armies, scattering forces, and devoting energies to comparatively unimportant places.

BADEAU states that "on the 24th of July GRANT renewed his suggestion: 'It seems to me that Mobile is the point deserving the most immediate attention,' and on the 1st of August he telegraphed to HALLECK: 'Mobile can be taken from the Gulf Department with only one or two gunboats to protect the debarkation. I can send the necessary force. With your leave I would like to visit New Orleans, particularly if the movement against New Orleans is authorized.'" The permission was not granted, nor the movement authorized; but GRANT soon after went to New Orleans, ostensibly to confer with Gen. BANKS about the Red River expedition, and BADEAU states that from there he renewed his solicitation for the movement on Mobile.

As the campaign of ROSECRANS progressed, Gen. GRANT seemed to grow more urgent to take his army to a remote point. The authorities at Washington, however, had resolved that Gen. ROSECRANS should be left to his chances with such force as he had, and were not intending nor desiring to re-enforce him, although his forward movement was attenuating his forces to guard his lengthening line of supplies. As to Gen. BANKS, they were desirous that he should move with a strong force into Texas, lest the French Emperor should be tempted to add that to the empire he was founding in Mexico.

While GRANT was urging HALLECK to permit an expedition to Mobile, he was also stating that his army was too much worn out for any other movement. Thus says BADEAU, quoting GRANT's dispatch to HALLECK:

The troops which had been engaged in the various operations of the campaign and siege of Vicksburg were now greatly exhausted, and "entirely unfit for any duty requiring much marching," but "by selecting any duty of immediate and pressing importance," said Grant, "it could be done."

Thus their exhaustion was so peculiar that it unfitted them for any marching campaign in the interior, but did not unfit them for an expedition further into a tropical climate in midsummer, with the probability of another siege.

True, the 13th Corps, which had borne as much of the hardship and sickness of the Mississippi swamp operations, and of the fighting, the labors, and dangers of all the campaign and the siege as any other, was sent off on a very severe marching campaign at midsummer in the malarial lowlands of West Louisiana, which was about as hard an ordeal as troops exhausted by previous hardship and labor could be subjected to; but it is probable that a penance was still owing by them for the sins of their late commander.

BADEAU states that at New Orleans GRANT renewed his solicitation on the 25th of September, and again a complaining solicitation on the 30th, and that HALLECK answered him again on the 13th of October, stating that "there were certain reasons which I can not now explain, which prevented such an attempt." Yet BADEAU states also that on the 22d of September, GRANT, who had then returned to Vicksburg, received HALLECK's dispatch of the 15th, ordering this: "All the troops that can be spared in West Tennessee and on the Mississippi River should be sent without delay, to assist Gen. ROSECRANS on the Tennessee River. * * * Information just received indicates that a part of LEE's army have been sent to re-enforce BRAGG:" also that on the 28th he wrote HALLECK: "I am now ready for the field, or any duty I may be called on to perform."

At last the Washington authorities had awakened to the situation, which had been inevitable to the common sense, which was that the brunt of the war was left to fall on Gen. ROSECRANS; that east of the mountains no operation was going on to prevent the re-enforcement of Gen. BRAGG from LEE's army by the short inner line; that in the west Gen. GRANT's great army had been taken out of the theater of the war, and was wielding no co-operative aid or influence, and was too remote to bring succor before the crisis of the campaign; while all Middle and West Tennessee and Kentucky, save where occupied by ROSECRANS' forces, was open to Confederate raids up to the Ohio River.

The authorities at Washington awoke to that which was before evident, but awoke too late. Nor was the sending of LONGSTREET's corps from LEE to BRAGG the first reason why they should not have permitted an army to lie isolated and idle at Vicksburg, while ROSECRANS was making the campaign from Murfreesboro into the heart of the South, where all knew that the Confederates would use every effort to concentrate forces to defeat him. HALLECK's first telegram was September 13. So shadowy had become the military possession in GRANT's department, north to the Ohio, that there was no telegraph nearer than Cairo. The dispatch was brought thence by steamer, and BADEAU tells this strange incident: "The messenger to whom this package was intrusted failed to deliver it promptly."

This dispatch was: "All of Major General GRANT's available force should be sent to Memphis, thence to Corinth and Tuscumbia, to co-operate with Gen. ROSECRANS." Strange that the messenger to whom this package was intrusted neglected to deliver it till the 25th. BADEAU says it was delayed ten days between Cairo and Memphis. As related above, HALLECK telegraphed again on the 15th, and BADEAU says this was received at Vicksburg on the 22d. The first troops embarked on the 27th. The battle of Chickamauga was fought on the 19th and 20th. On the 3d of October GRANT received a request from Secretary STANTON to come to Cairo and report from there by telegraph.

Conscious of what was in the wind, GRANT departed immediately with all his staff and headquarters. At Cairo he received a telegram from STANTON to proceed with staff, etc., for immediate operations in the field, to the Galt House at Louisville, Ky., where he would meet an officer of the War Department with instructions. At Indianapolis he met Secretary STANTON with an order creating a new military division, embracing all between the Alleghanies and the Mississippi, except such as was occupied by Gen. BANKS, and placing GRANT in command, subordinating the Department of the Cumberland, commanded by ROSECRANS, and the Department of the Ohio, commanded by BURNSIDE. The history of GRANT by DANA and WILSON states that his request, on being appointed to this command, was that ROSECRANS should be removed from command of the Army of the Cumberland, and Gen. GEORGE H. THOMAS put in his place. There came a time when he was even more desirous to put Gen. THOMAS out of the way.

CHAPTER LIV.

THE GREAT EXPECTATIONS OF THE TRADE THAT FOLLOWED THE FLAG—THE WAY IT FED THE ENEMY—THE FATHER OF WATERS BECOMES A CHANNEL OF SUPPLY TO THE CONFEDERACY—THE FOND VISION OF RECONSTRUCTION—GEN. SHERMAN'S STATESMANSHIP—A SUDDEN AWAKENING.

In the popular rejoicing over the capture of Vicksburg, and the generous magnifying of that military achievement, there was a large ingredient of thrift, in the expectation that it would open the way to trade in the South. Much cotton had been kept in the South by the obstructions to its export; the war had greatly raised the price of cotton, and the North had an abundance of goods and of products which the people of the South greatly needed.

The trade was very profitable; the more so because the necessity for having military protection, and the assistance of army transports and teams, made it in the nature of a privilege to the favored. Always were a sufficient number of persons whose commercial character rose above the prejudices of the war, to go between the belligerent parties in carrying on this trade, and it found means of softening military commanders to it, and of procuring favors in the way of protection and transportation. By December, 1862, the greenback price of cotton had risen to sixty-eight cents a pound; by December, 1863, to eighty-four cents; in 1865 it reached $1 20. The price of tobacco rose enormously. These articles being inconvertible within the Confederate lines, and being converted to such value by reaching the national lines, there were fortunes to be quickly made by those who could get favors from the Treasury agents and from military commanders, and large means for corrupting these.

There was a popular sentiment of the time, in the form of words that "trade follows the flag," which had a noble, national, and patriotic sound, making trade the sealing of the restoration of States to the Union. Secretary CHASE emphasized this fine sentiment; the agents of the Treasury Department were instructed to advance it, and were not loth; and so a horde of traders followed the flag, and it came about that with the establishment of the army at Vicksburg, Port Hudson, and Natchez, there was a large influx of traders, desirous to complete the work of restoring that region to the Union. That enterprising and cosmopolitan people, the Israelites, found themselves the chosen race in this, as always, alike by their commercial genius, their exemption from national prejudices, and their domicile on both sides, having equally the confidence of both parties.

BADEAU says that Gen. GRANT was from the first opposed to this trade, and that he demonstrated to the administration that it furnished supplies to the enemy, and enabled them to continue the war. He argued that whereas more than half the cotton was the property of the Confederacy, as soon as we permitted our traders to buy, this Confederate cotton would become nominally the property of whatever persons were allowed to trade in it, and thus it would bring supplies directly to the Confederate Government. But BADEAU says that GRANT was overruled, and that trade was opened, first within certain lines, and subsequently without any military limits, the trader giving a bond and receiving a permit.

GRANT said:

If trade is opened under any general rule, all sorts of dishonest men will engage in it, taking any oath or obligation necessary to secure the privilege. Smuggling will at once commence, as it did at Memphis, Helena, and every other place where trade has been allowed within the disloyal States, and the armed enemy will be enabled to procure from Northern markets every article they require.

BADEAU says that it so came about; trade was opened, "and the consequences predicted by GRANT followed rapidly." Thus was the singular consequence that the capture of Vicksburg and the recovery of the Mississippi River, which had cost so many lives and so much treasure, became a source of supply to the enemy.

Gen. GRANT could refer with emphasis to his previous observation of the corrupting influence of this trading with the enemy, for in the first Vicksburg campaign, called the Holly Springs campaign, when he was at Oxford, Miss., he found a necessity to issue the following general orders:

[A.]

HEADQUARTERS 13TH ARMY CORPS,
DEPARTMENT OF THE TENNESSEE,
OXFORD, Miss., Dec. 17, 1862.

General Order No. 12.

1. The Jews, as a class, violating every regulation

of trade established by the Treasury Department, are hereby expelled from the department.

2. Within twenty-four hours from the receipt of this order by post commanders, they will see that all this class of people are furnished with passes, and required to leave; and any one returning after such notification, will be arrested and held in close confinement until an opportunity occurs of sending them out as prisoners, unless furnished with permits from these headquarters.

By order of   MAJ. GEN. U. S. GRANT.
(Official.)
JOHN C. RAWLINS, Assistant Adjutant General.

[B.]

HEADQUARTERS, HOLLY SPRINGS, Dec. 18, 1862.
General Order No. 8.

By the order of Maj. Gen. U. S. Grant, all Jews are hereby expelled from the Department of the Tennessee. The Provost Marshal will at once give this notice to all Jews of this post, and see that they are provided with passes to leave the department; and all found here after the lapse of twenty-four hours will be arrested and placed in close confinement. No passes will be given to these people to visit headquarters of the Army of the Tennessee for the purpose of making personal application for trade permits. By order.   R. C. MURPHY,
Col. 8th Wis. Vol. In., Com'g Post.
Capt. N. G. Lane will see to the faithful execution of the above order.

The President rescinded this order, because of its invidious particularity; but the order and Gen. GRANT's remonstrances expressed the result of his observations of the working of this trade, under Treasury permits, and of the special genius which that enterprising people have for improving such opportunities. Indeed, the records of the Superior Court of Cincinnati show that one of that favored race, a leading merchant of Cincinnati, sought to ingratiate himself into special favor of the very Commanding General, for this trade, by making a partner of a very near relative—a partnership made public by a suit to recover the equal share in the venture, which was agreed to be set off for influence.

Gen. GRANT wrote from his headquarters at Vicksburg, July 21, 1863:

My experience in West Tennessee is that any trade whatever with the rebellious States is weakening to us to at least 33 per cent. of our force. No matter what the restrictions thrown around trade, if any whatever is allowed it will be made the means of supplying to the enemy what they want. Restrictions, if lived up to, make trade unprofitable, and hence none but dishonest men go into it. I venture to say that no honest man has made money in West Tennessee in the last year; yet many fortunes have been made during that time.

Mr. SHUCKERS, in his life of Mr. CHASE, says:

It is probably no exaggerated estimate that from the beginning to the end of the war, the surreptitious traffic thus carried on reached, at the least, an aggregate of two hundred millions of dollars.

This is of the trade besides that authorized by regular permits. Gen. CANBY, writing from New Orleans in 1864, said that the Confederate armies both east and west of the Mississippi, during the preceding twelve months, had been largely supported by this unlawful traffic, and that its inevitable result must be to give strength and efficiency to the Confederate army equal to an addition of 50,000 men. He said there were ten thousand men within our lines who were stimulated into active opposition to the successful prosecution of the war by the cotton trade, and that in order to save the cotton in the Confederate lines they gave the enemy warning of our military expeditions.

This contraband trade created many of the fortunes which were made in the war, which established the demoralizing tradition that the war was profitable to the Northern people. Our Commanding Generals testified against it, but between the arguments on the other side, and the sentiment that trade follows the flag, and the constructive regulation of it by bonds and permits, the trade went on in large proportions, and thus was presented the paradox that the acquirement of that river which was thought an irretrievable disaster to the Confederacy, became a valuable channel of Confederate supplies.

Gen. GRANT made his strong protest, and then rested the case, saying that no views of his own should prevent his executing orders from those in authority. It was an abominable traffic, in its supplying means to resist our armies, and in that its profits went chiefly to the disloyal and dishonest; but there was no way of preventing this but by total prohibition, and by arresting every person found within the lines without military business. Our government was not equal to that, and the affair was further embarrassed by the circumstance that the expectation of trade had greatly magnified the importance of recovering the Mississippi.

There was also a fond belief that the taking of Vicksburg would cause the Southwestern States to recognize that the Confederate cause was lost, and would lead to a movement for their restoration to the Union. SHERMAN's report of the desperate state into which he had driven JOHNSTON's army beyond Jackson, and GRANT's report of the disbandment of PEMBERTON's paroled troops, giving up the Confederate cause, and carrying disaffection to their homes, nourished this notion. As if the fighting were done, and the work of pacification were now in order, Gen. GRANT, in giving instructions to SHERMAN to issue supplies to the inhabitants who had been left destitute by our devastation, said:

It should be our policy now to make as favorable an impression upon the people of this State as possible. Impress upon the men the importance of going through the State in an orderly manner, refraining from taking anything not absolutely necessary for their subsistence while traveling. They should try to create as favorable an impression as possible upon the people, and advise them, if it will do any good, to make efforts to have law and order established within the Union.

Thus, after our army had been ordered to destroy everything that could subsist man or beast between Jackson and the Mississippi, it was transformed from ravening wolves to political doves, to preach the gospel of the Union.

ADAM BADEAU, in telling of the fatal blow given to the Confederacy by the taking of Vicksburg, says:

The country in the rear of Vicksburg was full of paroled soldiers, swearing they would not take up arms again if they were exchanged. Pemberton was reported to have but 4,000 men left together. The army that was paroled, said one, was virtually discharged from the rebel service. Thousands crossed the Mississippi and went West; many begged a passage to the North, and quite a number expressed a strong anxiety to enter the national service; but this, of course, was not allowed. Johnston's army also was greatly demoralized, and the men deserted by thousands. Even a political movement was started by citizens, west of Pearl River, to bring Mississippi back into the Union.

In the same mood of glorious fruition, Gen. HALLECK, August 29, wrote "Gen. SHERMAN, stating that the question of the reconstruction of Louisiana, Mississippi, and Arkansas, was now to come up, and that not only the length of the war, but our ultimate and complete success, will depend on his solution."

He desired to have the opinions of the Generals to lay before the President to preclude those of "gassy politicians in Congress." He had written BANKS, who had answered fully. He had also written Gen. GRANT, who had not answered. He desired SHERMAN to consult GRANT and McPHERSON, and write him unofficially, so that it need not go on file, but that he could use it with the President.

Such an appeal for a comprehensive opinion on affairs of statesmanship could not be made in vain to Gen. SHERMAN. The letter, dated September 17, occupies six and a half fine print pages in the memoirs. Its breadth of comprehension, and the keynote of its policy, may be judged by this in the fore part:

That part of North America known as Louisiana, Mississippi, and Arkansas is, in my judgment, the key to the whole interior. The valley of the Mississippi is America, and, although railroads have changed the economy of intercommunication, yet the water channels still mark the lines of fertile land, and afford cheap carriage to the heavy products of it.

The inhabitants of the country on the Monongahela, the Illinois, the Minnesota, the Yellowstone, and Osage are as directly concerned in the security of the Lower Mississippi as are those who dwell on its very banks in Louisiana; and now that the nation has recovered its possession, this generation of men will make a fearful mistake if they again commit its charge to a people liable to misuse their position, and assert, as was recently done, that because they dwell on the banks of this mighty stream they had a right to control its navigation. I would deem it very unwise at this time, or for years to come, to institute in this quarter any civil government in which the local people have much to say.

The latter went on to describe truly the social and political conditions of the Southern people, which made free government an absurdity, and to argue the necessity of keeping them in a state of pupilage, under military authority, until all traces of war were effaced, and the conditions made suitable for the restoration of local government, administered by the local people. It was a letter of wise statesmanship, whose wisdom has been confirmed by our sorry experiment of reconstruction. President LINCOLN paid it the compliment of reading it carefully and of asking HALLECK to telegraph SHERMAN for permission to publish, which SHERMAN refused. President LINCOLN also paid it the compliment of acting directly opposite to the advice of the letter, in his policy of reconstruction.

But while the military authorities at Washington, and the Generals on the Mississippi, had laid aside the sword, and put on the robe of the statesman, and were gathering in the political fruits of the campaign which had cut the Confederacy in two,' and broken its backbone again, they were awakened from their fond dreams of the political reconstruction of a broken up confederacy by intelligence that Gen. BRAGG, with an army recruited from the dispirited and demoralized West, and re-enforced by LONGSTREET'S corps from the East, confronted ROSECRANS south of the Tennessee, and that a great battle was at hand, and the army of the Department of the Tennessee was far away, and exercising no influence whatever in the war.

CHAPTER LV.

WHAT IT COST IN TIME, MEN, AND MONEY—ITS GRAND RESULTS—COMPLETE SEPARATION OF GRANT'S ARMY FROM THE THEATER OF THE WAR—THE CENTRIFUGAL MILITARY PLANS, AND HOW THEY NEUTRALIZED VICTORIES AND ORGANIZED DEFEATS.

The time, men, and means consumed in the Vicksburg operation are essential elements in estimating the value of that great achievement. The time may fairly be rated as nearly a year, beginning with an army disciplined and seasoned by much service. The calling of Gen. HALLECK to the chief command at Washington in July, 1862, left Gen. GRANT in command of the Department of the Tennessee, and pursuing the defensive policy. Gen. BUELL, in the Department of the Cumberland, had been ordered to turn his energies and forces to an expedition to occupy East Tennessee.

If the military plans of the two sections had been made to fit into each other, with the object of prolonging the war, they could not have better served the purpose. While the Army of the Department of the Tennessee was keeping to the defensive, and the Army of the parallel Department of the Cumberland was reconstructing railroads, preparing for its diversion to East Tennessee—one condition of which, by Gen. HALLECK's order, was that the Memphis & Charleston Railroad, running near a hundred miles along the enemy's front, should be restored and made a line of supplies—the Confederate army, under Gen. BRAGG, was improving the opportunity by a strong concentration and offensive campaign to the Ohio River.

In this defensive policy, SHERMAN was at Memphis, and GRANT's headquarters were at Jackson, Tenn.; but GRANT was not in connection with SHERMAN, although a railroad ran from Memphis to Jackson by way of Lagrange. His only way of communication with SHERMAN was by the rear to Columbus, Ky., and from thence by the Mississippi to Memphis. While Gen. BRAGG's march to the Ohio River was going on in the Department of the Cumberland, the only operations of importance in the Department of the Tennessee were the concerted movement against Gen. PRICE at Iuka, which culminated September 19—in which that part which was under GRANT and ORD strangely omitted to act its part in the concert, letting PRICE march away from their front to fall on ROSECRANS—and the decisive repulse of VAN DORN's attack at Corinth, October 4, by the troops under command of Gen. ROSECRANS—a victory which, according to BADEAU, was the occasion of much dissatisfaction to Gen. GRANT, and for which, as appears from BADEAU's representation, he thought he ought to be the one promoted, instead of ROSECRANS, and ROSECRANS disgraced.

But this decisive repulse disabled Gen. VAN DORN for further offensive operations for some time, and as it was the first decisive victory in that army since Fort Donelson, it was an excellent preparation for active operations by our troops. On the 16th of October HALLECK's general order made some rearrangement of the departments, and, BADEAU says, enlarged GRANT's command. In the same month he received large re-enforcements from the Northwestern States, and on the 26th he proposed to HALLECK a concentration for an advance, saying: "I think I would be able to move down the Mississippi Central road, and cause the evacuation of Vicksburg." From the month of October, at the latest, the occupation of the Army of the Tennessee in the Vicksburg operation may be dated, even if all the previous time of organizing and preparing be left out of the account. It was at the last of September, 1876, when a part of that army left Vicksburg to go to the relief of ROSECRANS' army at Chattanooga.

The Confederate force which Gen. GRANT had to encounter in the field and in the siege of Vicksburg has been given in its order in this review. That Gen. PEMBERTON would understate his force to Gen. J. E. JOHNSTON, or JOHNSTON to PEMBERTON, is improbable. He was not able to bring to the field at any time a force greater than half of that which GRANT had in the raid to Jackson. His force in all the Department of Mississippi and East Louisiana, reaching to the gulf, and including Gen. GARDNER'S division at Port Hudson, which March 31, 1863, had a total present and absent of 22,827, was little more than half as great as BADEAU mentions as in the Department of the Tennessee when GRANT began the Vicksburg operation in October, 1862.

The Confederate official report of March 31, 1863, of the troops of PEMBERTON's department, including, as above, GARDNER'S troops at Port Hudson, and the 1st Military District under Brig. Gen. RUGGLES, the 4th Military District under Brig. Gen. ADAMS, and the 5th Military District under Brig. Gen. CHALMERS, and 2,337 Mississippi State troops, present and absent, gives the following grand total: Present for duty, officers and men, 48,759; aggregate present, 61,485; aggregate present and absent, 82,398.

Gen. SHERMAN, in his memoirs, states that Gen. GRANT had abundant force for the interior campaign. BADEAU states the force in GRANT's department as 130,000 men. GRANT, November 8, informed SHERMAN that he was strong enough to handle PEMBERTON'S force "without gloves," and without SHERMAN's aid. To this great army was subsequently added a gunboat fleet, and a great fleet of steamboat transports, most of which were kept in constant attendance on the army during its swamp operations. During the siege of Vicksburg, the 9th Corps—a fresh corps, organized for the expedition to East Tennessee—was added to GRANT's army; also HERRON's division from the Department of the Missouri, which BADEAU mentions as the strongest division in the combined army.

Whether recruits were added in detail during the campaign does not appear from the records, but aside from these, the Vicksburg operation absorbed a great army, and was enormously costly in the naval part, in which part there was also much destruction of vessels and stores, and an enormous consumption of large ammunition. The cost of the stores destroyed by VAN DORN at Holly Springs was estimated by him at four millions; by BADEAU it is belittled to the bagatelle of a million. The true value was probably between the two figures, either of which shows great preparation of stores for the interior campaign. Gen. GRANT wrote to Gen. HALLECK, after the surrender of Vicksburg, that the army was so used up by hardship as to be unfit for any operation requiring much marching. The number of men consumed in the campaign can not be found without going through all the surgeons' returns, and these are not complete.

The officers' reports of casualties give only those of battles. Gen. GRANT's reports rarely descended to such detail as the loss of men, and when they did, it was only to a part of the actual loss. The number of soldiers consumed by disease in all the Vicksburg operation will never be known. To lose more by disease than by battles is not uncommon in campaigns; what, then, may be estimated of a campaign which, after the Holly Springs failure, began by sinking the army for three months in the flooded Mississippi bottoms, where the soldiers had to lay logs to support their beds above water, and by working them in the water in the most unhealthy and dispiriting labors.

Contemporary reports of the dying of the soldiers in that swamp habitation, and in those swamp labors, caused a popular demand for Gen. GRANT's removal. The number of men which BADEAU states as all that GRANT could bring to the siege of Vicksburg, by stripping his department, shows that a large number had disappeared. BADEAU mentions the levee for miles "furrowed its whole length with graves," and that "the troops were thus hemmed in by the burial places of their comrades." Gen. McCLERNAND mentions the heavy reduction of his corps by sickness from the swamp labors. In various ways there are materials for a rational estimate that the number of soldiers consumed in the whole operation was much greater than the number killed, wounded, and captured of the enemy.

Other campaigns which have been at the last successful may have consumed more of the offensive army than of the enemy, although, as the offensive is always supposed to be the superior force, such a loss does not show brilliant generalship; but it is not usual for a General to begin an offensive campaign by sticking his army helplessly in a malarious swamp, and making its chief losses in that way. Nor did convalescence restore to sound health such of the sick as survived. Not only they, but the most of those who did not succumb, got the poison of that malaria planted in their bodies for the rest of their lives.

But when the conditions oblige a General to consume his army heavily in attacks in an offensive campaign, his plan expects to gain thereby successes and strategic positions which shall either be decisive of the war or an advantageous base for further operations; but the finality of the Vicksburg campaign placed the army out of the field of war. It isolated that army from all other operations, leaving the Confederate armies free to concentrate against the army in the parallel department. And, as regards all the theater of the war, it left GRANT's army—to use his own phrase—"bottled up." GRANT knew not which way to turn to give his campaign some sequence. In any rational military plan his army should be co-operating or joined with that of ROSECRANS, on which the whole weight of the war was now left to fall. GRANT evidently feared that this would be ordered, and therefore he urgently solicited leave from HALLECK to divert his forces to another exterior operation on Mobile, at the same time hedging against the military use of his army by saying that it was so used up as to be unfit for any service requiring much marching.

The Confederate Government thought Vicksburg a place of great military importance, and its loss a heavy disaster. The national government thought the same, and glorified its capture accordingly, overlooking all its dreadful cost. Gen. J. E. JOHNSTON thought the place of but little military importance, since both it and Port Hudson had failed to keep control of the river. Even when in our hands, with all our gunboats, we could not prevent the Confederates from crossing forces and supplies—so little significance had this much vaunted cutting of the Confederacy in two. The statements of Gen. GRANT, Gen. CANBY, and of Secretary CHASE's biographer show that our recovery of the Mississippi, and our practice of the line sentiment that trade follows the flag, made the river a great channel for supplies to the Confederate army. Gen. CANBY estimated the aid thus given to the Confederate army as equivalent to 50,000 men.

Thus the loss of Vicksburg had a large compensation to the Confederacy by enabling it to convert its cotton into supplies for its armies, while it had no military sequence to GRANT's army, and left it where it exercised no material or moral influence on the war, while the real campaign, on a true military line, was going forward under Gen. ROSECRANS, and by a wonderful combination of scattering policies the Confederate armies east and west were left free to concentrate against it. The success in making one of our armies pull away from another army, and in diverting armies from co-operation in movements on the vital part, was so complete as to indicate the work of brilliant genius. But in all the war there was not so complete a performance of this off-pulling, isolating policy as when Gen. GRANT halted in his march near the Yallabusha, and by his irresolution lost his great accumulation of stores, retreated, abandoned the interior of his great department, and took his army by the river to the bottoms west of the Mississippi, with Vicksburg its sole and final objective, and a manner of attacking it which not only had no possibility of success, but in its several bayou and canal attempts was so destitute of military sense and of common sense as to be indignantly scoffed at by the intelligent volunteers.

Having no military sequence; having done nothing to end the war nor to gain a position or line for further operations; having opened a line of supplies for the Confederacy; having isolated GRANT's army while the real military operation was culminating, the military results of the Vicksburg campaign are reduced to a calculation of the comparative butchery and the comparative consumption of men and means. In this the excess of the consumption of the men and means of the nation was greater than our superiority to the Confederacy in these resources. The war never could have been brought to a successful termination by successes got at such cost as that at Vicksburg. And that diversion of the army from the interior, completely neutralizing it as to all true military operations, prepared the conditions of disaster to the

Army of the Cumberland as thoroughly as if it had been artfully planned. Instead of the drawn battle of Chickamauga being an occasion for blame, it is a cause for amazement that, with GRANT's army bottled up in the West, and the Army of the Potomac paralyzed in the East, and by the still more wonderful management from Washington, the army under Gen. BURNSIDE, in East Tennessee, separated and neutralized, the Confederacy was not able to seize such an opportunity to destroy that army; and that the invincible Army of the Cumberland, now bearing the brunt of all the war, was able to end the battle by a clear repulse of the enemy, and to gain its territorial objective.

CHAPTER LVI.

THE MATURED OPINIONS OF GENS. GRANT AND SHERMAN ON THE VICKSBURG CAMPAIGN—THE REVIEWER HUMBLY ACCEPTS THE JUDGMENT OF THESE GREAT GENERALS.

The military results of the Vicksburg campaign were so completed by the surrender of the place, that, as Gen. SHERMAN remarks in his memoirs: "GRANT's army had seemingly completed its share of the work of war," and it was now at rest where it had no influence on the great campaign now going forward in the interior of the Western zone, not even to the holding of any of the Confederate forces to the defensive against it in Mississippi, or detaining the troops recently under Gen. J. E. JOHNSTON from joining Gen. BRAGG in the concentration against Gen. ROSECRANS and the Army of the Cumberland." Says Gen. SHERMAN:

Our success at Vicksburg produced other results not so favorable to our cause—a general relaxation of effort, and desire to escape the hard drudgery of the camp; officers sought leave of absence to visit their homes, and soldiers obtained furloughs and discharges on the most slender pretexts; even the general government seemed to relax its efforts to replenish our ranks with new men, or to enforce the draft, and the politicians were pressing their schemes to reorganize or patch up some form of civil government, as fast as the armies gained partial possession of the States.

The "politicians" were simply acting upon the simple military idea of the time, that the capture of Vicksburg was a fatal blow to the Confederacy, and was at least equivalent to the occupation of the State of Mississippi, and this idea is set forth by BADEAU in his glorification of GRANT's achievement.

When a military operation has nothing further to do, and has left the army where it is neutralized as to the war, and its Commanding General departs on a hunt for another peripheral expedition, is a time for relaxation and furloughs, and for discharges of such as had become enfeebled by hardships in a malarious region, of whom there were thousands that had gone through the campaign, but were now too broken in health to be fit for another. But the war was yet to be fought, and now, while GRANT's army was lying idle out of the theater of the war, the Confederate chiefs were straining effort to gather a force under Gen. BRAGG to fall upon the army of Gen. ROSECRANS, now pushing into the heart of the Confederacy.

VAN HORNE's History of the Army of the Cumberland narrates that on the 30th of August, at the time when the Army of the Cumberland was crossing the Tennessee River, a loyal citizen, escaped from Chattanooga, brought Gen. ROSECRANS intelligence that 15,000 men were on the way from Mississippi to join Gen. BRAGG. Further along he states that BRAGG had been joined by two divisions from Mississippi. Also, in his general remarks on the battle of Chickamauga, he mentions as among the Confederate troops men paroled at Vicksburg.

The strategy of a campaign which thus ends by taking an army to a place where it has no influence on other operations, as if its part in the war were done, while the war is still increasing in magnitude and its greatest actions are yet to be, is a subject for the study of the military profession, and should have a prominent place in the text books at the military institute.

In going back from the immediate and finished results to make a brief review of the grand tactics of the campaign, the reviewer has the satisfaction of following the matured conclusions of the Commanding General as given by his supervised historian, and also of his greatest Captain, as given in his memoirs. Thus he has that confidence which the "layman" feels when he follows the judgment of men of the military profession, particularly of those who themselves, in their written memoirs, were the greatest part of the great events.

Says Gen. SHERMAN in his memoirs, after having recited the several failures in the bayou and canal cutting attempts:

I had always contended that the best way to take Vicksburg was to resume the movement which had been so well begun the previous November, viz.: For the main army to march by land down the country inland of the Mississippi River, while the gunboat fleet and a minor land force should threaten Vicksburg in its river front. I reasoned that with the large force then subject to Gen. Grant's orders—viz., four army corps—he could easily resume the movement from Memphis by way of Oxford and Grenada to Jackson, Miss., or down the ridge between the Yazoo and the Big Black.

Gen. SHERMAN also confirms the exhibit made by this history, that Gen. GRANT's attempt to go to join Gen. BANKS, by way of his Duckport canal, Willow Bayou, and Bayou Vidal, to New Carthage, was for the purpose of getting away from his hopeless situation at Vicksburg, without seeming to go back, which, as he says, was "for other than military reasons," meaning that it was to quiet the country by seeming to go forward, when, in truth, he was abandoning the expedition. For Gen. SHERMAN goes on:

But Gen. Grant would not, for reasons other than military, take any course which looked like taking a step backward, and he himself concluded on the river movement below Vicksburg, so as to appear like connecting with Gen. Banks, who at the same time was besieging Port Hudson from the direction of New Orleans.

Gen. SHERMAN narrates that his opinion of the interior line, as that by which the campaign would achieve great results, to which the fall of Vicksburg would be a consequence, was concurred in by Gen. GRANT after all was over. He says:

He has told me since the war that had we possessed in December, 1862, the experience of marching and maintaining armies without a regular base, which we afterward acquired, he would have gone on from Oxford, as first contemplated, and would not have turned back because of the destruction of his depot at Holly Springs by Van Dorn.

This is a candid statement by Gen. GRANT that he abandoned the true tactical line, because he had yet to learn how to move and subsist an army in a country of abundance, when his immediate depot of stores had been lost.

No lesson of the war was so strongly impressed on the public mind, and on the minds of the volunteer soldiers, as that the education at the military institute turned out officers knowing the whole art of war; and that on the other hand, without this passing through the institute, no degree of general education and no natural aptitude, genius, or experience, or achievement could make anything but a mere pretense of a soldier—a fiction, whose successes or failures were alike blunders. Upon this admirable rule were promotions and commands assigned and military operations judged. Yet the moving and subsisting of armies in the enemy's country is an elementary part of the art of war. But Gen. SHERMAN here states a simple confession by Gen. GRANT that after all the service he had seen in the war he abandoned a promising campaign and retreated ignominiously, and thereby finally abandoned the true tactical line, because he had not yet learned the rudimentary part of war, that an army may be subsisted in a country of abundant supplies for a few days, when by sheer neglect of another rudiment of war it has lost its immediate depot of supplies.

The younger part of this generation may get an idea of the way the war was made to last four years, and to cost seven thousand millions, and to call out more than a million of men, when our greatest General, now in command of a great department, and of 130,000 men, as good soldiers as the world ever saw, was yet serving an apprenticeship, and learning the very elementary parts of war, at the expense of sacrificing campaigns, and of flying from the tactical line to an impossible one. Gen. SHERMAN goes on:

The distance from Oxford to the rear of Vicksburg is little greater than by the circuitous route we afterward followed from Bruinsburg to Jackson and Vicksburg, during which we had neither depot nor train of supplies.

In other words, after all the cost of getting to Bruinsburg, the army was far worse situated for marching to Jackson then when, in November, six months before, it was at Oxford, and PEMBERTON had fallen back to the south of the Yallabusha. Upon this Gen. SHERMAN remarks—not as a criticism, but simply remarks:

I have never criticised Gen. Grant's strategy on this or any other occasion, but I thought then that he had lost an opportunity, which cost him and us six months of extra hard work; for we might have captured Vicksburg from the direction of Oxford in January, quite as easily as was afterward done in July, 1863.

These remarks by Gen. Sherman, which are not a criticism, relieve the reviewer from the disagreeable work of criticism. This, and Gen. Grant's concurrence therein, saves the lay reviewer from the presumption of differing from these great soldiers, and leaves to him the more pleasant work of agreeing entirely with their conclusion. The mutual admiration and confidence of these great Captains give great interest to their judgment of the radical blunder of the whole campaign. But Gen. Sherman, who states that it was for "other than military reasons" that Gen. Grant practiced the imposture on the country of pretending to go to Port Hudson because of his dead failure on Vicksburg, omits to state that it was also for other than military reasons that Gen. Grant left the interior line at Oxford, after he had arranged a co-operation with Sherman, and had sent him back to Memphis, and that it was the vision of Gen. McClernand, with Lincoln's commission in his pocket, coming to command a river expedition, that caused Gen. Grant to falter, to weakly inquire of Washington, "How far do you want me to go?" to halt, to leave the enemy, relieved from the pressure of his advance, free to operate in his rear, and then to make the loss of his communications a pretense for going back to head off McClernand, leaving Sherman to take his men to blind slaughter at Chickasaw Bluffs.

Gen. Sherman's statement of Gen. Grant's afterthought is further corroborated by Badeau, who, in narrating Grant's success in subsisting his army in the retreat from Oxford, after Van Dorn had destroyed his stores at Holly Springs, says:

Gen. Grant has told me, when discussing this campaign, that had he known then what he soon afterward learned—the possibility of subsisting an army of 30,000 men without supplies other than those drawn from the country—he could at that time have pushed on to the rear of Vicksburg, and probably have succeeded in capturing the place.

! This statement is the more interesting from being made upon Grant's discovery then, a Oxford, that an army in a campaign can draw supplies from the country, for, says Badeau:

For over a week he had no communication with the North, and for two weeks no supplies. But the country was found to be abundantly stocked. Everything for the subsistence of man or beast, for fifteen miles east and west of the railroad, from Coffeeville to La Grange, was appropriated to the use of the army. The families of the farmers suffered, but the soldiers were fed; and the lesson was taught which Grant afterward applied in the rear of Vicksburg, and which Sherman, having seen the application, practiced on a still larger scale in the marches through Georgia and the Carolinas—the lesson that an army may live, though its communications are destroyed.

Thus does Badeau, approved by Grant, corroborate Sherman's statement of Grant's admission, that if he had then known how to subsist an army for a short time in a country of abundance, as he afterward learned, he could then have gone on from Oxford to Jackson. And Badeau makes the admission more interesting by stating that it was after Grant had learned, on the Holly Springs and Oxford line, the simple lesson that he could subsist an army on the country, that he left that true tactical line and went to an imposable one, because his line of supply had been temporarily broken.

Badeau, revised by Grant, has to explain Grant's present disregard of the lesson which he had learned, and he does it shrewdly by this:

Although the soldiers found all that was necessary, Grant was anxious until he discovered the success of the experiment. It was one hitherto untried, and, while uncertain of its results, he moved his army back to La Grange, abandoning the campaign, which had been pressed to a distance of fifty or sixty miles.

Thus was the rudimentary educational acquirement by this costly lesson laid on the shelf, and Grant went to plant his army in the swamps west of the Mississippi, to learn further elementary lessons in the art of war. This gives an idea of what it cost to educate one General.

If Grant had gone on from Oxford to Jackson, and established himself strongly there, Vicksburg would be untenable to the Confederates, and would have fallen of itself. Gen. J. E. Johnston said that our possession of Jackson would eventuate in the loss of the State of Mississippi to the Confederacy. But reaching it by a raid from Grand Gulf, we could only raid it. By the interior line the army would have possessed and covered the country of the Department of the Tennessee, and the strategic places which had been the objective of a previous great campaign of an army of 100,000, but which were now abandoned to the enemy. Its progress down Northern Mississippi would have converted the resources of a rich country to the national use, which this strange abandonment left to supply the Confederate armies.

It would have given support and co-operation to the Army of the Cumberland, from which this strange departure isolated it as completely as if it had been taken out of the world. From the Department of the Cumberland to the Mississippi River, the Department of the Tennessee was laid open to the enemy, north to the Ohio River; and all that region, open to Confederate incursions, flanked ROSECRANS' army in the Stone River and Chattanooga campaigns. Happily the lay reviewer can avoid the presumption of drawing this conclusion on a purely military affair, and can escape the displeasure of differing with military men on their own achievements, when these great Captains concur in the judgment that the abandonment of the interior campaign was a blunder, and was because Gen. GRANT had yet to learn this elementary part of the art of war.

CHAPTER LVII.

GEN. GRANT AWARDED THE SOLE HONOR AND RESPONSIBILITY OF THE SEVERAL PLANS OF THE VICKSBURG CAMPAIGN—THE REASON WHY HE ABANDONED THE INTERIOR CAMPAIGN—HIS GREAT OPPORTUNITY.

Gen. GRANT's authorized historian affirms that all of the operations against Vicksburg were of GRANT's sole planning, and that not only did he unapproachably transcend all his Generals, but in the very turning point of the campaign, when it emerged from the swamp disasters and entered the triangular road to victory, he went contrary to the opinions of all his subordinate officers.

Gen. SHERMAN generously awards the same exclusive honor to GRANT. He says: "The campaign of Vicksburg, in its conception and execution, belonged exclusively to Gen. GRANT." He corroborates this by saying that when Gen. GRANT retreated from the interior campaign, "I thought then that he had lost an opportunity, which cost him and us six months' extra hard work; for we might have captured Vicksburg from the direction of Oxford in January quite as easily as was afterward done in July, 1863." No one has contested Gen. GRANT's sole credit for all the planning of the several operations which have been embraced in the general term as the Vicksburg Campaign, comprising a variety of campaigns and expeditions. And both SHERMAN and BADEAU quote GRANT as admitting that his retreat from the campaign by the line of the Mississippi Central Railroad was a mistake.

This admission of the military blunder of retreating from a promising campaign, on the true military line, where he had abundant force, great preparation of supplies, and had only to go forward to accept the success which was at hand, carries with it an admission of Gen. GRANT's sole responsibility for all the consequences of this error. The reviewer may avoid the sin of presumptuous criticism by accepting the matured judgment of the sole author and finisher of those operations, and of his great Captain, and he may plant himself impregnably on the base of their judgment in reviewing the direct consequences of this confessed blunder. And no operation in all the war had greater consequences, in the consuming of the volunteers and resources of the nation.

Both Gen. SHERMAN and ADAM BADEAU quote Gen. GRANT as excusing his abandonment of the Yallabusha campaign by his inexperience in war, in the elementary part of subsisting an army in the enemy's country; but this is an instance of modesty doing itself injustice. BADEAU's narrative of that retreat shows plainly that GRANT's object was to keep McCLERNAND from the command of the river expedition, and he narrates this as a sufficient reason. Gen. SHERMAN had just made an extraordinary march from Memphis, with three divisions, to join GRANT's army south of the Tallahatchie, and thus all was ready for a decisive advance, when GRANT heard that LINCOLN was favoring McCLERNAND's project of a river expedition.

He thought to head off McCLERNAND by hurrying SHERMAN back to Memphis to organize and embark a river expedition ahead of McClernand. By this, alone, did Grant sacrifice his campaign. He divided his army by a wide distance, where communication was impossible, and the force he had left was not sufficient for a bold offensive movement. That Grant intended any, after detaching Sherman, is incredible. To go forward was to expose his half of the army to destruction. The co-operation with Sherman in a concerted attack on Vicksburg, which was talked of, was, in the nature of things, impossible. Grant could not march to co-operate by attacking Vicksburg in the rear without having to cross the difficult Yallabusha, and expose his half of the army to Pemberton's concentrated forces.

According to all rational calculations this would have taken his army to destruction. He could not communicate with Sherman to arrange concert of action, if that had been possible. His talk of co-operation, as represented by Badeau, was vague as to leave a doubt of its sincerity. It was so vague that Badeau was enabled to cast on Gen. Sherman the sole responsibility for his slaughter of his troops at Chickasaw Bayou, by denying that he had reason to expect concert of action. He supports this by citing, as the "extent of Grant's promise of co-operation," the following: "I will hold the troops here in readiness to co-operate with you in such manner as the movements of the enemy may make necessary." In short, he had halted, while Sherman was to march back to Memphis, gather boats from all the rivers, and embark for Vicksburg, to beat McClernand, and there to sacrifice his troops by attempting the impossible.

When a General halts for an indefinite period, in an offensive campaign, he abandons it. Still more if when he has invaded the enemy's country, and stretched out his own communications, he sends back half his army out of sight, out of support and out of communications. But Badeau, in order to allow that Sherman, though in error, may have had some vague reason to expect co-operation, adds: "It was, however, understood in conversation that in case Pemberton retreated, Grant would follow him up, between the Yazoo and the Big Black rivers, to the Mississippi." Thus did Grant's subsequent movements now depend on Pemberton's retreating, and retreating between these rivers, all the way down to the Mississippi. Thus the plan was that when Grant sent back half his army, Pemberton was to return the compliment by retreating, and was to retreat in just the line that Grant desired. Otherwise Sherman was to be left without support. The lay reader has to admire that the lives of intelligent volunteers were placed at the mercy of such headless military plans as these.

These afterthoughts of Grant's historian do injustice to his military capacity, in the vain effort to cover the fact that he abandoned the campaign, to beat McClernand out of the command of the river expedition. He had abandoned it when he sent back half his army. To say that he meant to go forward after that is to charge him with the incredible incompetency of reducing his army one-half in the tide of an offensive campaign in a hostile country. To suppose that he thought that when Sherman got to Vicksburg, Pemberton would fall back to that place, and that then he would follow him and co-operate with Sherman, is to accuse him of military idiocy. No forward movement was possible after he had divided his army. His halting exposed the rest of his army to destruction, if an enterprising General had been against him. He got off cheaply from the consequences of his own conduct by the loss of his stores and some detachments captured. But after Sherman had gone, Grant heard from Halleck that Lincoln desired that McClernand's corps should form part of the river expedition, and that McClernand have "the immediate command under your direction."

Badeau's narrative shows clearly that Grant then determined to go back and take the direction of the river expedition by going with it, which would reduce McClernand to the command of his corps. To beat McClernand was the great military object for which Grant gave up that which, if pushed forward with energy, might reasonably have achieved greater results than were achieved by any campaign of the war. And in this he would let McClernand go and entangle his men in the West Mississippi swamps, till the malaria had eaten them up. A fleet from the lower river, a year previous, had found Vicksburg impregnable to naval attack, and inaccessible from the river, and had shown that the canal to turn the river was an impossibility. This was intelligence which a General should have had before he abandoned a great campaign to repeat this experiment. Gen. GRANT must have had it, but he seems to have thought that McCLERNAND might overcome these obstacles, and the great object of beating McCLERNAND obscured all other military objects.

The enemy's taking the offensive was the inevitable consequence of GRANT's slow, hesitating, and finally halting movement. The destruction of his immediate depot of supplies was not the cause, but the consequence of his desertion of the campaign. With SHERMAN, he had had a force twice as great as PEMBERTON could bring to oppose his advance. The season was favorable, the ground dry, the country rich in supplies. If he had marched to Jackson, PEMBERTON would have been compelled to try conclusions with him on that line. His defeat of PEMBERTON and occupation of Jackson would have made Vicksburg untenable to PEMBERTON. All that rich country of Northern Mississippi would have contributed supplies to our forces, instead of feeding the Confederate army to the end of the war.

Gen. J. E. JOHNSTON said that GRANT's possession of Jackson would bring the loss of Mississippi to the Confederacy. As a soldier he could not then believe that GRANT intended only a devastating raid on Jackson, and the destruction of a railroad center which military intelligence would convert to great power as a base for further operations. The firm occupation of Jackson would have threatened Meriden, another railroad center—the two commanding all the railroads of Mississippi. By the river to Vicksburg, and by the railroads to the North, GRANT would have lines of supplies for any further campaigns, and in no part of the South could these be more feasible, or more in the vitals of the Confederacy.

With such success as was within GRANT's easy reach, by faithfully keeping on in his campaign, the administration would have sent him all the forces he wanted, and he might then, by real and great achievements, have risen to that supreme dictatorial position over all the armies and over the administration which he gained after vast sacrifices, by comparatively small successes, which were magnified by the contrast of their broad setting in his own failures.

Even if he had rested at Jackson, the country which he would occupy, the disasters inflicted on the enemy, and the forces which the Confederacy would have to keep on the defensive against his commanding position, would greatly cripple the enemy, and would be direct co-operation with the campaigns of the Army of the Cumberland, from which this diversion isolated GRANT's army. All this sacrifice of his own great opportunity, and of his country's cause, and of the lives of the volunteers, was remorselessly made, to no other end than to beat Gen. McCLERNAND, whom he regarded as a personal rival, out of the command of the Mississippi River expedition, to which LINCOLN in his easy going mood had in an evil hour appointed him.

CHAPTER LVII.

A SUMMARY REVIEW OF THE OPERATIONS FROM THE TIME WHEN GRANT TOOK COMMAND OF THE RIVER EXPEDITIONS TO THE TAKING OF VICKSBURG.

By the time that Gen. GRANT had completed his success in beating Gen. McCLERNAND out of the command of the Mississippi River expedition by assuming it to himself, he realized that he had beaten himself by taking his great army and navy to a place where any rational military operation was impossible. At the very outset he was reduced to the strait of making projects and undertakings to keep up the pretense of a military operation, but from which nothing else was expected.

His Holly Springs disaster and retreat had disgusted the country, which now recalled all his failures, and looked upon this as cumulative proof of his incompetency. Erelong the utterly unmilitary character of his bayou, canal, and swamp undertakings, and the consuming of the volunteers in hardships in that malarious morass, caused a popular demand for his removal. Public opinion was only in part deceived by his bulletins to HALLECK, for the country had means of true intelligence. In the course of failures, this General, who had sacrificed a campaign to head off McCLERNAND, was put to a great strait to keep his own military head on.

The first plan ordered by Gen. GRANT, on taking formal command at Milliken's Bend, was a plan to abandon the Vicksburg expedition. Says BADEAU: "On the 30th of January, the day after he assumed command of the Vicksburg expedition, GRANT gave orders for cutting a way from the Mississippi to Lake Providence, and went himself to that place on the 4th of February." This was a project to get from the Mississippi, on the west side, about seventy miles above Vicksburg, through a swamp, into a small bayou, and from that into a chain of bayous, diverging forty or fifty miles from the river, and through a wonderfully crooked chain of supposed navigation of 400 to 600 miles, to fetch out in Red River.

Thus, after he had succeeded in putting himself in the place of McCLERNAND, at the cost of sacrificing a great campaign, his first plan was to run away—to take his army aimlessly somewhere, anywhere, so as to get off without seeming to retreat again. Fortunately, he could not make an entrance into this labyrinth, for it he had got his army and the gunboats and transports fairly in, it is not probable that they would ever have come out save as Confederate captures. The experience of the Steele's Bayou expedition, and of the Yazoo Pass expedition, proved that a few men with axes could shortly block this sort of navigation, and that the great guns of the navy were of no use against skirmishers. But while the country was made to believe that GRANT was evolving wonderful plans to capture Vicksburg, he was planning to retreat, and was consuming his army and risking its total destruction by sending it into labyrinth expeditions to keep the country deceived in order to save himself.

The plan to divert the Mississippi by a canal was also a plan to get away from Vicksburg. It is hard to believe that GRANT was so blind to the simplest physical forces as to suppose that this mighty river, running with vast volume a hundred feet below the surface of the earth, at the rate of five or six miles an hour, could be diverted by scratching the surface with a ditch. But BADEAU says that the idea took hold on LINCOLN's imagination. HALLECK told GRANT, for LINCOLN, to pay particular attention to the scheme to turn the Mississippi. GRANT was now in a predicament when he needed a pretense of a plan, and this pretense of diverting the river would divert LINCOLN and the public mind. As early as the 4th of February he wrote HAL-LECK that he had lost all faith in it. But still he kept up the pretense, and kept on abusing his troops by this depressing labor, at which their intelligence revolted. The after curtailing of this stupendous plan to the little one of making a canal through which shallow boats could pass, was alike impossible. The rise of the river at that point, by flood, is more than forty feet. Before the canal could be dug, the fall of the river would leave it in air. Yet GRANT kept the troops at this work for near two months after he had told HALLECK that it was impracticable, and that already the Confederates had erected batteries to command the outlet, and therefore it would be useless if made.

The Yazoo Pass plan was to cut the levee on the east side of the Mississippi, at a place which by direct line was 160 miles above Vicksbug, to open a passage for shallow boats through narrow and crooked bayous to the Tallahatchie, through that to the Yallabusha, and by that into the Yazoo. And then what? This detachment, whose long, narrow, and wonderfully tortuous communication a few axmen could obstruct by felling trees across, could not reach any ground from which it could attack Vicksburg by the rear, save where the Confederates could quickly concentrate a force to attack it, and where it would be impossible for GRANT to support it in any way. The further it got into this trap, the nearer it would get to destruction.

Fortunately for our troops, the Confederates had planted a battery at the junction of the Yallabusha and Yazoo, which, by an air line, is a hundred miles above Vicksburg, which our boats could not pass, and fortunately, the head of the expedition backed out before the Confederates had surrounded it. The Steele's Bayou expedition was partly undertaken as a diversion to relieve the entangled Yazoo Pass expedition. It took gunboats and SHERMAN's corps into a circuitous chain of narrow, crooked bayous, from which it was glad to make a very narrow escape. And if it had got further in, escape would have been less likely.

The wonderful fortune of the army was in its successive escapes from Gen. GRANT's plans. These various plans were carried along at the same time—the river diverting canal, the Lake Providence plan, the Yazoo Pass plan, the Steele's Bayou plan—severally aiming in opposite directions; and now came the most wonderful of all, the Duckport canal and bayou plan to get down to Gen. BANKS' Department, which may be called the Port Hudson plan. HALLECK and LINCOLN had come to the conclusion that all of GRANT's bayou undertakings were diversions, and that he could do nothing at Vicksburg, and they now urged him to get away and go and join BANKS. Thus the taking of Vicksburg had been eliminated from the campaign, and now the great objective was to get GRANT to move somewhere, and to seem to go forward, although really to retreat.

Under this peremptory urgency to move somewhere, GRANT formed the Port Hudson plan. The panic of a routed army, under a cavalry charge, could alone excuse such a plunging into the unknown as that which GRANT now ordered, under this pressure from the rear. The plan was to make a new canal, starting from Milliken's Bend, at Duckport, to a narrow bayou called Walnut, which fetches a great circuit to southeast and northeast, to Roundabout Bayou, then by great crooks to Bayou Vidal, which at a point in its circuit had a connection with the river by a crevasse at New Carthage. By this narrow and tortuous water route, whose navigation was in great part conjecture, which, if navigable at all, would cease to be as soon as the high flood fell, shallow barges were to supply the army, which was to march along the edge of these bayous to New Carthage, and from there by means of these flatboats to descend the river to Grand Gulf and carry that strongly fortified place by assault from these frail craft, in order to gain a point of departure to Port Hudson.

From Grand Gulf GRANT was to send 20,000 men to BANKS, while the rest abode at Grand Gulf, depending for supplies on this supposed navigable route of fifty miles in the enemy's country, through great woods, where a few choppers could quickly close it, until the corps of 20,000 had reached BANKS in some unknown way, and BANKS had taken Port Hudson, which might stand a siege as long as Vicksburg. Then BANKS, with his corps, was to come up to join GRANT, and then the combined army would begin anew some operation against Vicksburg. With moderation of speech it may be remarked that the escape of the army from this plan was a wonderful stroke of fortune.

The army was started on this retreating stratagem. The navigable route was never navigable. The falling river had left the canal in air at the very time when GRANT was reporting to HALLECK that it could be depended on to supply the army, and that "the navigation can be kept good, I think, by using our dredges constantly until there is twenty feet fall." The means for the supply of the army were found impossible after the army had begun its march. The impossibility was before evident to all but the willfully blind. The army was on the move into the unknown, with the line of supplies, on which the Commanding General's plan depended, dropped out; but it must move, although to destruction, or GRANT would be removed.

The advance corps of 20,000 men, having to build its own road along the edge of the bayous, just above the flood, strained the road's capacity for its own subsistence; and from the failure of the water route it had no boats to cross the Mississippi. The army was now saved from retreating from a retreat by the destructive resort of running boats past the Vicksburg guns. This was a desperate afterthought in a desperate situation. At first it cost the destruction of about half, but soon the Confederates strengthened their water batteries, and at the last venture only one out of three loaded transports got by, and so this desperate resort ended. But by this afterthought alone were boats got to cross the Mississippi. The plan to assault Grand Gulf by landing in front from towed flatboats was as pretty a plan for a colossal slaughter as the wit of man could devise. Fortune again saved the army from the Commanding General's plan.

The plan to divide the army at Grand Gulf by sending a part to Gen. BANKS, holding the rest at Grand Gulf passive, to abide the result of the Louisiana campaign, depending on a circuitous, narrow bayou route, its convolutions reaching far into the enemy's country, or on a road by the same route, now stretched seventy miles to Hard Times, was a complete plan, if the object had been to have both parts of the army made prisoners. The inability to make even a landing at Grand Gulf saved the troops from that premeditated slaughter. The accident of the finding of a landing at Bruinsburg, above the flood, and unguarded, with a road running to the high ground; the energy of the advance corps, which pushed on by a forced march to Port Gibson, and beat a Confederate detachment, and thereby made Grand Gulf untenable, gave to GRANT the chance to report not only a movement away from Vicksburg accomplished, but a victory, and his point of departure for Port Hudson gained. This was reasonable assurance that his head would stay on long enough for him to consider the situation, and he stopped to consider.

No reason can be found in BADEAU's history for GRANT's abandoning his Port Hudson plan, now that he had gained the place which was to be the point of departure. That which GRANT gave to BANKS as a reason was that he could not retrace his steps. BADEAU repeats this as if it were a reason. But although GRANT could give no reason for abandoning his great plan, reasons enough are apparent. The reasons were the impossibility of his plan; an impossibility as apparent when he conceived it as now. His navigable route of supply on which it was based never had an existence. Even if he could feed his army by that road, he could not protect it from the enemy. If he had halted, and had embarked part of his troops, the Confederates would have taken the offensive, and they could soon cut off his single road of supplies and besiege him at Grand Gulf. He had reasons enough, but to state them would be to confess the utter folly of his generalship.

And now, by his miraculous escape from his own devices, a great opportunity was present, and he had only to let his splendid troops go forward to achieve a victory which would have had the effect to wipe from the public memory all his blunders and failures. Although he had scattered his army by the necessity to protect the long line from Milliken's Bend, he yet had a movable force superior to PEMBERTON's, and soldiers confident in themselves and in their officers. The Confederate detachments had returned to Vicksburg. From GRANT's position at Hankinson's Ferry, a march of ten miles would reach Warrenton by the rear, and would make the Confederates evacuate that, as at Grand Gulf. This would restore the army to its base of supplies at Milliken's Bend, by a road of only two miles across the tongue of land, and would add to his offensive column the troops guarding the long road from Milliken's Bend to New Carthage.

From Warrenton a march of five miles would take his army upon the railroad communication of Vicksburg, and force PEMBERTON to an immediate issue, which our troops were eager for. Was there a soldier of that army, except GRANT, who feared the issue? The great opportunity was before his face. No military genius was required to seize it; no strategy; no tactics but of the simplest; nothing but to let his troops go forward, under their own officers, to victory. The only opportunity for the exercise of great military genius in this situation was the genius to avoid a great opportunity. This was the genius which GRANT exercised as conspicuously here as he had done in the Mississippi Central campaign.

The reason why GRANT shunned this opportunity, and the object for which he marched his army away from supplies and from Vicksburg, fifty miles into a hostile region, leaving PEMBERTON's army on his flank and rear, cannot be ascertained from any direct statement in BADEAU's history. Pretended reasons are alleged, which are contradictory to one another and are trivial in themselves and a reflection on GRANT's competency, and there is much of vagueness, from all of which the critical reader is left to find the reason, which plainly was that GRANT wished to avoid joining issue with PEMBERTON in a battle, and that his movement into the interior had for its original object nothing more than a raid, to keep up that policy of seeming to do, which he entered upon as soon as he took command of the river expedition, thinking to regain, by the rapid marches of an unencumbered army, a point on the Mississippi from which to call for re-enforcements to begin a campaign against Vicksburg.

No other objective than this can be sifted from BADEAU's narrative; nor, in his afterthought attempts to give reasons, is there any that does not border on military idiocy. The beginning of this raid was in a halting manner, as if GRANT had not made up his mind. BADEAU says the movements "were in the nature of developments." They were halting, shifting, and aimless until McPHERSON happened to stumble on a Confederate detachment at Raymond. Then all was shifted, and GRANT followed on to Jackson, where he applied his energies to destroy that which in a real campaign would have been important means for his own army. Then, upon a wild notion, he started all his army to race with JOHNSTON for the Mississippi River. This was a race to escape; for after he had avoided PEMBERTON alone at Vicksburg, it would be remarkably brilliant generalship to come to the issue with both PEMBERTON and JOHNSTON, having the stronghold of Vicksburg for their support.

His surprise by chance intelligence that PEMBERTON had crossed Big Black River, and was moving for his left and rear, turned him from that race, and now he was obliged to meet the enemy. And here, in spite of himself, the splendid quality of the volunteers, their indomitable marching, though with insufficient food, the energy and skill of a corps commander whom he was trying to defeat, the divided counsels of the Confederate army, PEMBERTON's mistaken advance, and the accidental advantage of coming upon him in the demoralization of retreat, offered GRANT an opportunity for an easy victory, which would have left no organized army to oppose his march into Vicksburg.

Remarkable military genius was requisite to bring an army near to repulse by a retreating enemy of half its force, but GRANT's was equal to the opportunity. He consumed the right of his army in assaults on a natural fortress, the only strong place in the enemy's line, which had a clear way round it to the enemy's road of retreat, because of his persistent idea that the enemy, who in fact was retreating by his right, was advancing upon his left rear. The heroic valor of the troops thus sent to needless slaughter won a victory in spite of the blunders of the Commanding General. Fortunately, he was remote from the battle of Black River Bridge, where the splendid volunteers, under their own officers, gave PEMBERTON's army a heavy disaster, with but little loss to themselves.

The time to storm Vicksburg was when SHERMAN's fresh corps reached it on the morning of the 18th, after the midnight when PEMBERTON's demoralized troops had entered it. To delay was to violate all military maxims. The defeated army must be of very bad material if its morale can not be restored in twenty-four or thirty-six hours behind intrenchments. The order to assault on the next day, the 19th, was to inevitable slaughter, and even then it was made in ignorance that the other two corps were not up to attack in concert, although this concert was in the alleged plan. The manner in which the assault of the 23d was ordered to be made was contrary to any manner of assaulting fortified places that was ever taught or practiced by military men. It was a terrible sacrifice of heroic volunteers by a Commanding General who seemed to have no feeling for the slaughter of his soldiers, and no idea of the art of war.

Such tactics as GRANT had in his aimless and shifting movements were intended to give to PEMBERTON the impregnable defenses of Vicksburg. He was as desirous to have PEMBERTON within the fortifications as PEMBERTON was to be there. His objective was not to meet and destroy PEMBERTON's army in the field, but to have it where he could lay siege to it. In real military operations, Generals in offensive campaigns seek to maneuver to come to issue with the enemy outside his fortified places; but GRANT's great military idea was to get the enemy into his fortifications. It was here, as afterward on a grander scale with LEE's army.

The labors at which GRANT kept his troops in the siege wore them out without hastening the end. The shooting of pickets, and the local games of killing, such as that of "the death hole," were not war, but butchery, which had no influence on the event. The deliberate reckoning that, in such affairs, we can afford to lose two men to kill one of the enemy, is simply a cold blooded calculation on the murder of one's own soldiers, which does not approach the dignity of even the wars of savages.

At length the starved garrison surrendered. So small had become the expectations of administration and country of military results from our great armies and enormous expenditure, so strained and protracted the discouragement by GRANT's operations, that this capture of a starved garrison by four times its number, after more than its whole number, sick and well, had been consumed in the various undertakings against Vicksburg, was hailed as a prodigious victory. And now the victory which the Commanding General's plans had so long shunned, and which had cost such vast consumption and sacrifice of intelligent volunteers, was glorified as an achievement of his genius, and it was stretched back to make his failure in the Mississippi Central campaign, and all his failures in his bayou and canal undertakings, and in his marching his army away from victory after he had reached solid ground, parts of intelligent strategy, all leading up to the crowning victory.

CHAPTER LVIII.

THE ART OF PROTRACTING THE WAR—THE DISJOINTED AND DIVERGING SYSTEM — SEESAW GENERALSHIP—TO PREVENT OTHERS FROM SUCCEEDING THE FIRST OBJECTIVE—THE PATRIOTIC VOLUNTEERS.

If the object had been to protract the war for the interest of an army faction, and therefor to consume the resources of a great nation and the most spirited and intelligent soldiers the world has ever seen, without decisive results, strategic genius could not contrive a more effective plan than by dividing the field of operations into different parallel departments, each under a separate commander, directed in his separate line from Washington.

Yet disjointed and bad as this system of separate and independent commands was, it had a theory that the several commanders of departments and of offensive campaigns would support and co-operate with each other. It supposed that these Generals would use their great discretion in loyalty to each other and to the country, and it had no thought that any one of them would have his mind divided between achieving success for his own advancement, and keeping a commander in a parallel department from succeeding; that any one placed in command of an army of citizens would care more for beating a rival than for beating the enemy.

If the object had been to so constitute departments and commanders, and so to order armies that one should give no support to another, or that the commander of one department should prevent the commander of the adjoining department from succeeding, strategy could not better contrive it than by Gen. GRANT'S withdrawing his great army—the principal army in the West—from the interior campaign, and from all the territory of his department, save a few ports on the Mississippi River, isolating his army, and laying open all that country to Confederate occupation, while the Army of the Cumberland was ordered on a campaign down the interior to Chattanooga.

The region which GRANT abandoned, to isolate his army in the Mississippi swamps included the strategic places which, in the previous season, had been the objective of a great campaign of an army of 100,000 men, and whose achievement had in its time been declared the breaking of the rebellion's backbone. West Tennessee and North Mississippi and Alabama were thus given up to supply the Confederate armies, and all these dearly gained strategic places were left to the enemy, on the right of Gen. ROSECRANS' army, while it had to go forward into the heart of the Confederacy, stretching out its line of supplies, with the enemy in full possession of the country on its flank.

The strategy was so perfected that even if GRANT had found the taking of Vicksburg practicable from the river, all the same it would have isolated his army so that it could give neither material nor moral support to the campaign of Gen. ROSECRANS, nor hold any Confederate troops from joining the army which was opposing him. If the object had been to destroy one army after another, by subjecting each in its turn, unsupported by the others, to the combined armies of the Confederacy, it is hard to conceive how it could be better planned than was done. And of all the segregating and isolating of our armies by separate and diverging operations, that of Vicksburg was the chief, for surpassing in the bottling up property even Gen. McCLELLAN'S taking his army from Northern Virginia and the interior to the peninsula.

Looking forward we behold the same wonderful management so ordering the Army of the Ohio in East Tennessee as to take it from co-operation with Gen. ROSECRANS, and to provide that all the Confederate forces between Virginia and the Mississippi should be concentrated against ROSECRANS, and even strengthened by LONGSTREET'S corps from Virginia, while our forces between the mountains and the Mississippi were divided into three isolated and non-co-operating parts. Further along in the war we shall find that Corinth, which was the great strategic objective of Gen. HALLECK'S campaign with 100,000 men, in the spring of 1862, was the base of supplies for HOOD'S army in his campaign against Gen. GEORGE H. THOMAS' army in December, 1864.

The declaration of Gens. GRANT and SHERMAN that the true line of operations was that down the Mississippi Central Railroad, which GRANT abandoned, and that all the results which came after wasting of the army and the season in the swamp operations, might have been gained in the fall of 1862, by simply keeping on in the line upon which he had started, admits much more than the wasting of that army by a palpable blunder, which ignored all principles of the art of war; admits the withdrawal of the support which this line and this territorial possession would have given to the Army of the Cumberland in its Chattanooga campaign.

Is it unreasonable to suppose that such support and co-operation in these departments might have changed materially the history of the war? Is it too much to say that good generalship, operating on these parallel lines, with such armies, might have swept all before them, and ended the war in the great central zone in 1863? All this is happily free from the temerity of a dispute of the judgment of professional army men by a mere layman; for this is only a direct conclusion from the after judgment expressed by these great Generals.

The severest military critic could not argue a greater military blunder than is thus confessed by the actors thereof; confessed with a plea of an alleged reason which confesses ignorance of the very elementary parts of the military profession. But in fact this abandonment of the interior campaign was done "for other than military reasons." Can we regard the long holding out of the Confederates in a war so conducted as proof of great generalship? On the other hand, can we set too high an estimate on the martial qualities of the Northern volunteers and their volunteer officers, whose invincible valor, heroic endurance of hardship, and hard fighting under all the disadvantage and discouragement of such leading generalship, fought the war through to the triumph of the nation?

Upon the surrender of Vicksburg, Gen. GRANT was promoted, and, upon his recommendation, SHERMAN and McPHERSON. According to BADEAU, this was the extent of his generosity to subordinates. The volunteers who had been consumed by his dreadful methods were considered as simply to have done the duty which every man owes his country. The volunteer officers, who, with the men of the ranks, had saved GRANT from his blunders, and had brought the succession of destructive operations out at last to victory, by sheer hard fighting, were regarded by GRANT and his approved historian as excessively honored by being permitted to serve as officers under a West Point commander, and to lead the volunteers into undertakings and sacrifices which their intelligence told them were ordered without military knowledge or good sense.

The more the war is studied the more does it inspire admiration for the soldierly qualities of the American volunteer, and the more does it raise pride in a country whose mass of citizens possess such martial superiority. The conscientious historian is obliged to say that the war did not evolve any Bonaparte to a leading command; but it did evolve a patriotic valor, and a military capacity in the mass of citizens above what any had believed. The citizen volunteers fought out the war to triumph in spite of blundering generalship in the highest commands. These splendid martial qualities and heroic patriotism in the universal citizen are immeasurably higher elements of national glory and pride than if all had been achieved by the genius of one or two Generals, with soldiers who were unthinking machines. The honor and glory of saving the nation belong not to any individual, but to the American patriotic volunteers.

From Vicksburg Gen. GRANT went to take command at Chattanooga. The Chattanooga campaign of the Army of the Cumberland under Gen. ROSECRANS, and the operations of Gen. GRANT on the river, were materially relative; not by co-operation, but by the departure of one from the line of co-operation, upon which a regard for military principles and a desire to end the war should have kept him. Because of this essential relation, and forasmuch as the battle of Chattanooga terminated Gen. GRANT's immediate command of the Western armies, a review of that battle will terminate this series of papers.

CHAPTER LIX.

THE BATTLES AROUND CHATTANOOGA AFTER GEN. GRANT TOOK COMMAND—RETROSPECTIVE GLANCE—THE DISJOINTED CONDUCT OF THE WAR—CAMPAIGN OF THE ARMY OF THE CUMBERLAND—LOSES ITS LINE OF SUPPLIES AT CHATTANOOGA—SHERMAN'S RELIEF EXPEDITION—STOPS TO REBUILD RAILROAS—LEISURELY MOVEMENT OF AN EXPEDITION OF URGENCY.

While Gen. GRANT's army was engaged in the Holly Springs campaign, the Army of the Cumberland, under Gen. ROSECRANS, on the 26th of December, 1862, began its movement which brought on the battle with the Confederate army under Gen. BRAGG at Murfeesboro, December 31.

The alternating, see-saw, desultory character of our disjointed department military operations has an apt illustration in the circumstance that while Gen. ROSECRANS was preparing to move on Gen. BRAGG's army in the Department of the Cumberland, Gen. GRANT, in the parallel Department of the Tennessee, had begun a forward movement down the Mississippi Central Railroad with a large army, which, if continued, would have been great co-operation with ROSECRANS, but as if it were devised that no co-operation should be with our several armies, Gen. GRANT had halted irresolutely at Oxford; had changed his mind, sent SHERMAN back to Memphis with three divisions, which he soon followed with the rest of the army. Thus he was retreating while ROSECRANS was advancing, and he was taking his army where no co-operation or mutual support could be possible in the future.

Gen. ROSECRANS, having refitted his army after the destructive battle of Murfreesboro, and awaited a season when military movements would be in a degree practicable in that region, started June 21, 1863, on his Tullahoma campaign against Gen. BRAGG's army, which was holding a strong and intrenched line north of Duck River, with Tullahoma as the chief depot of supplies, and Chattanooga as the base. The strategy of the plan, which, demonstrating to cover the design, avoided the enemy's strong front line, and marched the main force upon his line of communications, was completely successful, and showed good generalship; but heavy rains, floods, bottomless roads, and a mountainous country impeded the movement, and Gen. BRAGG, by a precipitate retreat, was able to save his army, which now fell back south of the Tennessee River, burning all bridges. The operation was completed by the 30th of June.

The march of the main body of the army in the Chattanooga campaign began August 16. The position of Chattanooga made it secure against direct attack, and was flanked by great mountains, making natural fortresses, whose few passes were easily defensible. A difficult river was to be crossed in the face of the enemy, and on any line of operations the defensive army might occupy positions almost impregnable, unless the strategy of the Commanding General could conceal his intentions and divert the enemy's forces from his route. In fact this, which was called the "Gateway to Georgia," and the most important military place in the South, was more difficult of attack than any place in the South.

But skillful generalship made Gen. BRAGG think the advance was to be made on the east, and thereby the crossing of the river on the west was made, and the mountain passes to the west and south of Chattanooga were occupied without resistance, and by the time that Gen. BRAGG comprehended the operation he realized that he must evacuate Chattanooga or be shut up there. He withdrew to the southeast, and one division of our army entered the place, and this primary objective of the campaign fell into our hands without a battle or any heavy skirmish. It was the solitary instance in the war in which a great advantage and objective were achieved by strategy.

Another illustration of the disjointed character of our military management is noted in the circumstance that the Army of the Ohio, under Gen. BURNSIDE, although it had now returned from Vicksburg and had moved into East Tennessee, was directed separately by Gen HALLECK's orders from Washington, and was not co-operating with Gen. ROSECRANS in this vital campaign. Thus, between the mountains and the Mississippi the army of the department on ROSECRANS' left was separate and independent, under direct orders from Washington, and the army of the department on ROSECRANS' right was also separate, independent, isolated, and idle at Vicksburg. If all had been planned by great generalship to waste our energies, it could not be more to the purpose.

The authorities at Washington, where Gen. HALLECK fancied that he was directing this campaign by telegraph, now accepted that BRAGG had fled, and they thought only of pursuit. In this grand delusion Gen. HALLECK, September 11, telegraphed ROSECRANS:

After holding the mountain passes on the west and Dalton or some other point on the railroad to prevent the return of Bragg's army, it will be decided whether your army shall move further south into Georgia and Alabama. It is reported here that a part of Bragg's army is re-enforcing Lee. It is important that the truth of this should be ascertained as early as possible.

If Gen. HALLECK had been directing by telegraph a campaign in the moon, he could not be more in ignorance of the situation. If our war were not so terribly tragical, a broad humorous side would be perceived which would make the strategy of Gen. Boum and of Corporal General Fritz seem real events. Gen. BRAGG had withdrawn to avoid being caught at a disadvantage, and now, re-enforced by LONGSTREET'S corps, he was aiming to attack ROSECRANS before he could gather up his separated corps from the several mountain passes.

At the time when ROSECRANS received this surprising telegraphic order to occupy Dalton and the passes to the west of it, preparatory to being ordered further south into Georgia and Alabama, he was straining every energy to get his army out of these passes to concentrate on the Lafayette & Chattanooga road, twenty miles north of Dalton, to cover Chatnooga and prevent BRAGG from falling on his forces in detail. But this review may pause to mention that Gen. HALLECK's resources were equal to the consequences, and that in his annual report he conveyed that Gen. ROSECRANS was going on a wild plan of advance into Georgia without warrant of prudence or authority, of which Chickamauga was the consequence. This is only another instance that in our war the longbow, in the hands of the truly great General, was more powerful than his sword.

That a campaign of invasion, of long distance and in a difficult country, is steadily diminishing its offensive force by the detachments required to guard its lengthening line of supplies, and that it needs steady re-enforcing to make up for these and to supply the waste of the campaign, is a circumstance known to all, but the authorities at Washington had in their wisdom resolved that Gen. ROSECRANS should begin and complete his campaign into the heart of the South, unsupported on either flank, with the number of troops which he had at the start, which before the Tullahoma movement began Gen. GARFIELD stated at 65,137, and which had in the battle of Chickamauga, according to the estimate of VAN HORNE's history, 56,160 men.

It appears to be in pursuance of this idea of ROSECRANS' advance further south into Georgia and Alabama that HALLECK on the 13th of September sent the following dispatch to GRANT at Vicksburg:

It is quite possible that Bragg and Johnston will move through Northern Alabama to the Tennessee River to turn Gen. Rosecrans' right and cut off his communication. All of Gen. Grant's available force should be sent to Memphis, thence to Corinth and Tuscumbia, to co-operate with Gen. Rosecrans.

This was to get GRANT's forces back into the interior of his own department. It marked some progress of HALLECK in learning the art of war, for it showed a perception that GRANT, in his department, would in a degree be co-operative with ROSECRANS, and that at Vicksburg he was withdrawn from all co-operation.

But Gen. BRAGG was now re-enforced by 15,000 men from Mississippi, and by LONGSTREET's corps from LEE's army, and his army now outnumbered that of ROSECRANS, and the battle for the possession of Chattanooga had yet to be fought. The result of that battle, although the enemy had expended all their power of attack, and had been repulsed, was that the army, on the 21st of September, after two days of battle, had to fall back to Chattanooga and to a state of siege, in which its communication to the north became so difficult and precarious that it was a question whether starvation would give the enemy a victory which they were not inclined to try to gain by an attack.

In the army there was no thought of defeat, or surrender, or retreat. It held the strategic objective. It knew that aid from the north was needed to open communication with supplies, but it knew that the government was able to send it on, and could not doubt its good faith and commensurate energy. Meanwhile the Commanding General was making the plan which eventually opened the communications, and the cavalry expeditions, in pursuit of the Confederate cavalry raids on the single road of supplies, were among the most heroic of all the war.

By a luck or something else which was characteristic of all the military conduct of the time, HALLECK's dispatch of the 13th to GRANT was delayed ten days after leaving Cairo. BADEAU says: "The messenger to whom it was intrusted failed to deliver it promptly." Singular coincidence! But on the 15th HALLECK was awakened from his dream of BRAGG's final retreat and of his sending part of his army to LEE, and of ordering ROSECRANS from Dalton further south into Georgia and Alabama, by intelligence that LONGSTREET's corps had joined BRAGG. He now began to see it all, and he telegraphed on the 15th to Gen. HURLBUT at Memphis:

> All the troops that can possibly be spared in West Tennessee and on the Mississippi River should be sent without delay to assist Gen. Rosecrans on the Tennessee River. Urge Gen. Sherman to act with all possible promptness. If you have boats, send them down to bring up his troops. Information just received indicates that a part of Lee's army has been sent to re-enforce Bragg.

This dispatch reached Vicksburg on the 22d, on which day GRANT had returned. That of the 13th was not yet delivered. GRANT issued orders on that day. SHERMAN took three of his four divisions, and says that the last reached Vicksburg on the 28th to embark.

Now comes one of the strange features of this military conduct. Gen. SHERMAN says in his memoirs:

> Gen. Halleck's dispatches dwelt upon the fact that Gen. Rosecrans' routes of supply were overtaxed, and that we should move from Memphis eastward, repairing railroads as we progressed as far as Athens, Ala., whence I was to report to Gen. Rosecrans at Chattanooga by letter.

The truth was that Gen. ROSECRANS' route of supply was cut off, both by railroad and river, by the enemy's possession of the valley of Lookout Creek, below Chattanooga.

To order this relieving expedition to repair and hold that railroad, running 140 miles along the enemy's front, as a line of supplies, was to give it permanent employment, and was the way not to relieve Gen. ROSECRANS. But HALLECK's dispatches, which are given in Gen. BOYNTON's review of SHERMAN's Memoirs [Historical Raid] sustain SHERMAN's statement that he was ordered to repair this railroad for a line of supplies for his troops. HALLECK's several dispatches were urgent that he should use all possible expedition, but they also required the repair and holding of the railroad, which forbade any expeditious movement.

Gen. HURLBUT, at Memphis, in answer to HALLECK's inquiries as to progress in re-enforcing ROSECRANS, dispatched to him September 21 that he had ordered a million rations and plenty of spare wagons to Corinth, and he had a cavalry corps to cover SHERMAN's movement; that the road was open to Corinth, and he had plenty of rolling stock to that place, and from thence to Chattanooga should not take more than eight days of hard marching. But HALLECK still insisted on the repair of the railroad east of Corinth. In a dispatch to HURLBUT October 4 he said: "Time is all important. The railroad must be kept up and guarded, in order to secure the supplies of your army. Should Gen. SHERMAN be assigned by Gen. GRANT to the command, you will furnish him with this and all other orders."

Time all important, and the repair of the railroad, which would consume the all important time. It is true that a dispatch of the 14th from HALLECK to SHERMAN, received on the 16th, had this modification of the railroad order: "When Eastport can be reached by boats, the railroad can be dispensed with; but until that time it must be guarded as far as used." SHERMAN narrates that at Iuka on the 20th he heard that two gunboats sent to his aid had arrived at Eastport, only ten miles off. Yet he kept on repairing the railroad, and was at Iuka on the 27th. The same dispatch concludes with the following moderate expectation from SHERMAN's expedition:

> Should the enemy be so strong as to prevent your going to Athens, or connecting with Gen. Rosecrans, you will, nevertheless, have assisted him greatly by drawing away a part of the enemy's forces.

This soars into the realms of grand strategy, but all this was the way not to assist the Army of the Cumberland. Such expedition as SHERMAN made with three divisions from Memphis to join GRANT at Oxford, and made again in his countermarch, would have brought him to Chattanooga in a fortnight from Memphis. But this was the way to relive ROSECRANS' army, and enable that to secure its victory.

At length, on the 27th of October, SHERMAN, still at Iuka, got intelligence that GRANT was appointed to supreme command from Virginia to the Mississippi, with power to remove ROSECRANS, and other plenary powers, including that of placing him (SHERMAN) in command of the Army of the Tennessee, in which it appears that HURLBUT was the ranking officer, but he was only a volunteer. With this exhilarating intelligence he received from GRANT an order to "drop all work on Memphis & Charleston Railroad, cross the Tennessee, and hurry eastward with all possible dispatch toward Bridgeport till you meet further orders from me."

No more delay of an urgent relieving expedition to rebuild a railroad which was not to be used, and was left in the enemy's hands! No longer was the railroad from the north overtaxed to supply ROSECRANS' army, for GRANT was now in the command. It was now thirty-three days since HALLECK'S urgent order of the 15th reached Vicksburg, and twenty-five days since SHERMAN'S first division reached Corinth, and in that twenty-five days his advance had reached Tuscumbia, about fifty miles from Corinth. That was the way GRANT'S army relieved ROSECRANS.

Gen. HALLECK's letter to Gen. GRANT, supplementing Secretary STANTON'S assignment of GRANT to the command of the three departments, gave his version of the operations toward East Tennessee, of the general failure of co-operation, and of ROSECRANS' operations in the Chattanooga campaign, sparing not the longbow in his own excuse. He also gave this piece of intelligence which rounds out, completes, and gilt edges the Vicksburg campaign:

It is now ascertained that the greater part of the prisoners paroled by you at Vicksburg, and by Gen. Banks at Port Hudson, were illegally and improperly declared exchanged and forced into the ranks to swell the rebel numbers at Chickamauga.

Gen. HALLECK said at the time that GRANT'S parole was not according to the cartel, and was not valid. But this is an exemplification of the nature of the co-operation which GRANT gave to other operations, and it considerably diminishes BADEAU's inventory of the results of the capture of Vicksburg.

Fortunately the relief ordered from the East was more expeditious than that from GRANT'S army, and its commanders were eager to help their brother soldiers in the West. Fortunately, by the aid of these the plan formed by Gen. ROSECRANS for opening the communication to Bridgeport, and left by him in the hands of Gen. GEORGE H. THOMAS, was ready to be put in operation before Gen. GRANT arrived, and was not opposed by him. Thereby the Army of the Cumberland was relieved by the reopening of its supplies without any assistance from GRANT and SHERMAN. Had it depended on them, it is safe to say that at the least the soldiers would have been reduced to very great straits. The operation which reopened the line of supplies was the first of the battles about Chattanooga, to which this preliminary chapter has now brought this review.

CHAPTER LX.

THE SOFT DELUSION AT WASHINGTON—THE AWAKENING—PROMPT MOVEMENT OF TROOPS FROM THE ARMY OF THE POTOMAC TO THE RESCUE—DESTRUCTION OF STORES AND TEAMS—ROSECRANS' PLAN TO REOPEN THE LINE OF SUPPLIES—ROSECRANS REMOVED—GRANT ARRIVES—ROSECRANS' PLAN EXECUTED UNDER GEN. THOMAS—BRILLIANT OPERATION AND BATTLE—THE LINE OF SUPPLIES OPENED AND THE ARMY TO RESUME THE OFFENSIVE.

At Washington the intelligence that LONGSTREET had joined BRAGG was a sudden awaking from the soft delusion that BRAGG had fled, and was dividing his army to send to LEE, and that the way for ROSECRANS was now open to Georgia and Alabama. Even as late as the 11th of September HALLECK thought that BRAGG was re-enforcing LEE, and on the 15th, in reply to a telegram from ROSECRANS, HALLECK telegraphed that no troops had gone from LEE to BRAGG.

Gen. ROSECRANS, in his testimony to the Committee on the Conduct of the War, stated that "LONGSTREET'S movement to support BRAGG was known to Gen. PECK as early as the 6th, and that Col. JACQUES, 73d Illinois, endeavored to communicate the fact that LONGSTREET'S corps was going to BRAGG, to the authorities at Washington, so long before the battle that he was able to wait in vain in Baltimore for a hearing, and then to reach us and take part in the battle of Chickamauga." Gen. HALLECK tries to show that he issued energetic orders for the aid of ROSECRANS; but a previous management which had deprived him of the support of the army on the Mississippi on his right, and of the army in East Tennessee on his left, and had conceived and clung to the strange delusion that BRAGG was scattering his army, could not retrieve all this after BRAGG had received his re-enforcements from east and west, and was advancing with intent to attack ROSECRANS before his widely divided columns could debouch from the mountain passes.

The authorities at Washington decided promptly to transfer 20,000 men from the Army of the Potomac, then inactive on the Rapidan, to re-enforce the Army of the Cumberland at Chattanooga, and through the energies of the Quartermaster General and Government Superintendent of Railroads, and the officers of the Baltimore & Ohio Railroad, 20,000 men, comprising the 11th Corps of Gen. HOWARD, and the 12th of Gen. SLOCUM, under the command of Gen. HOOKER, with their artillery, marching from the Rapidan to Washington to embark, were debarked at Nashville within eight days.

The officers of the Eastern army responded with loyal spirit to the need to relieve the beleaguered Western army. In the soldiers there was never any lack of this loyal spirit, either East or West. Thus it came about that troops from the army on the Rapidan were moved to the communications of ROSECRANS' army, co-operating with him, and eventually assisting the Army of the Cumberland to open the line of supplies, before any assistance had arrived from GRANT's army. Yet the remark must be made that this transfer of troops from the Army of the Potomac to relieve a situation caused by the transfer of Confederate troops from LEE's army and from the Mississippi, when concert of action in our Eastern and Mississippi armies would have given the Confederates enough to do on their several lines, was a most wasteful way of carrying on war, and that this and the concert of action now ordered in the Western armies was only an effort to retrieve a succession of blunders.

Gen. HOOKER's troops were moved without their transportation teams. The lack of these greatly restricted their co-operation with an army whose railroad line of supplies was cut off, and which had now lost a large part of its wagon equipment through the Confederate cavalry expeditions. WHEELER's cavalry had, on the 30th of September, captured and burned in the Sequatchie Valley a train of from 700 to 1,000 wagons laden with supplies, and then a train of wagons and of cars at McMinnville, in the heart of Tennessee, and had kept on to Murfreesboro, which being resolutely defended, he did not wait to attack, as he was pursued by Gen. CROOK with the cavalry of the Army of the Cumberland.

WHEELER moved upon other places on the railroad, burning bridges, stores, and trains, and although he was eventually driven from Tennessee with severe losses of men, and the destruction of his effective force for a time, he had inflicted heavy damage on the Army of the Cumberland by the destruction of its stores and transportation. HOOKER's arrival secured the railroad from Nashville to Bridgeport; but he had not the means of transporting supplies to join the army at Chattanooga, which was now on greatly reduced rations, and the geographical and military situation was such that the operation to open the line of supplies had to be made in the first instance from Chattanooga.

The Confederate historian, POLLARD, says of Chattanooga:

Chickamauga had conferred a brilliant glory upon our arms, but little else. Rosecrans still held the prize of Chattanooga, and with it the possession of East Tennessee. Two-thirds of our niter beds were in that region, and a large portion of the coal which supplied our foundries. It abounded in the necessaries of life. It was one of the strongest countries in the world, so full of lofty mountains that it had been called, not inaptly, the Switzerland of America. As the possession of Switzerland opened the door to the invasion of Italy, Germany, and France, so the possession of East Tennessee gave easy access to Virginia, North Carolina, Georgia, and Alabama.

Chattanooga is situated in a valley on the left bank of the Tennessee River, surrounded by lofty mountains and intervening valleys. These mountains, in a range from north to south, are cut by the Tennessee River in a serpentine southwest course till it strikes the north end of Lookout Mountain, about three miles below Chattanooga, when it turns shortly to the northwest, the loop making a tongue of land three miles long called Moccasin Point, from the fancied resemblance of its outline to a moccasin. The river keeping a northwest course for five miles, turns again abruptly to the south, making another narrow tongue of land, and then to southwest. Down the river twenty-six miles by railroad from Chattanooga is Bridgeport, and eleven miles further to the southwest is Stevenson, Ala., where the railroad from Chattanooga to Nashville turns to the north. This railroad, from Stevenson to Chattanooga crosses the Tennessee at Bridgeport and runs south of the river through a gap in Raccoon Mountains to Lookout Valley, through which valley it enters Chattanooga around the north base of Lookout Mountain.

This valley, together with Lookout Mountain, was held by Gen. Bragg's forces, whereby our army's line of supplies by both railroad and river was cut off. And now the only way in which supplies could reach the army at Chattanooga from Bridgeport was by a circuitous route up the Sequatchie Valley, and over the mountains north of the river, a distance of sixty miles, and by a road which the fall rains soon made a slough. The number of wagons had been greatly reduced by the cavalry expeditions; the quantity which the teams could haul was fast diminishing by the nature of the road and the lack of forage; the animals of the army had to be left unsupplied, and the rations for the men were getting very short.

The possession of Lookout Valley on the river would open to our army the navigation of the river up to the heel of Moccasin Point, and a road of less than a mile across this point would reach the river opposite Chattanooga, avoiding the guns of Lookout Mountain. Besides, a road from Brown's Ferry, at the heel of Moccasin Point, south and west through Lookout Valley, at the eastern base of Raccoon Mountains, to Kelly's Ferry, would open a practicable short road of supplies across a loop of the river to Kelly's Ferry, and thence by boat to Bridgeport. To get possession of Lookout Valley, between Lookout Mountain on the east, and Raccoon Mountains on the west, was, therefore, the object to which Gen. Rosecrans addressed himself as soon as he had made his position at Chattanooga secure by intrenchments so that he could safely detach a force for that object, in the face of Bragg's circumvallating army.

Gen. Halleck, in his letter to Gen. Grant giving his version of previous operations to excuse himself and accuse Rosecrans, wrote:

> If you reoccupy the passes in Lookout Mountain, which should never have been given up, you will be able to use the railroad and river from Bridgeport to Chattanooga. This seems to me a matter of vital importance, and should receive your early attention.

This has gone into history as a proper censure on Rosecrans for giving up these passes as unnecessary and a military blunder. Badeau's history, revised by Grant, repeats this censure. But generalship at Washington was much easier than in the field of operations, and was not limited by knowledge of the geographical situation.

Lookout Mountain, twenty-eight hundred feet above the sea, and fourteen hundred and sixty feet above the Tennessee River, is a hundred and fifty miles long. One of its passes is forty-two miles south of Chattanooga, the next nearest twenty-six miles, and the nearest at the northern end of the mountain. Did Halleck mean all these, or which of them? To hold Lookout Mountain, and to cover the line of supplies below Chattanooga, required the holding of a line across Chattanooga Creek Valley, three miles to Lookout Mountain, and then the holding of Lookout Valley, making a line of not less than ten miles, overlooked at Chattanooga by the natural fortress of Mission Ridge. This, to a badly hurt and retreating army, followed up by a victorious army, was equivalent to saying that it should restore the line of battle of Chickamauga, and that that "ought never to have been given up." In Lookout Valley the Confederates might concentrate any required force, to fall on that detached wing.

What was done was to intrench at Chattanooga, so that in the first instance our army could resist the expected immediate attack. Gen. Bragg gave as his plea for not following up his victory by an attack at Chattanooga, that he had lost two-fifths of his troops in the battle; and, second, that having cut off the line of supplies of the national army, he was confident that starvation would compel it to surrender. President Davis came to Lookout Mountain to anticipate the victory. This confidence resulted in BRAGG's ill fortune. Gen. ROSECRANS, having made his army secure by intrenchments which a part could hold, planned a movement for the other part to get possession of Lookout Valley.

ROSECRANS had previously ordered the construction of small steamboats and barges at Bridgeport, and two steamboats were now well advanced, and he was urging their completion. He directed Gen. HOOKER to concentrate his troops at Stevenson and Bridgeport, and advised him that as soon as enough of his train should arrive to subsist his troops, ten or twelve miles from his depot, he would be directed to move into Lookout Valley. He also ordered pontoons built at Chattanooga for a bridge at Brown's Ferry to connect with HOOKER's army, and preparations to build storehouses on Williams' Island, just beyond the narrowest part of Moccasin Point, with a view to making the island a cover for a steamboat landing. All of this meant that the army was at Chattanooga to stay.

The original plan was that the pontoons should be carried across Moccasin Point, and then floated to Brown's Ferry, where they were to form a bridge by which the expedition was to cross Lookout Valley, and there intrench until it was supported by HOOKER's troops, who were at the same time to move up from Bridgeport. The plan was far advanced in preparation when, October 19, Gen. ROSECRANS received an order to turn over the command to Gen. THOMAS. Gen. GRANT, on the same day, telegraphed Gen. THOMAS: "Hold Chattanooga at all hazards. I will be there as soon as possible. Please inform me how long your present supplies will last, and the prospect for keeping them up."

This was energetic, but as early as the 23d of September Gen. ROSECRANS' dispatches had shown that Chattanooga would be held against attack, and that its continued holding would be secured by prompt re-enforcements to open its line of supplies. Neither ROSECRANS, nor THOMAS, nor the soldiers had had any thought of giving it up. But now nearly a month had passed since GRANT had received orders of urgency to send aid to ROSECRANS, and none from that army had arrived, or was near enough to assure aid before starvation. Therefore this order did not render the decisive service to the holding of Chattanooga which BADEAU seems to ascribe to it.

Gen. THOMAS answered: "Two hundred and four thousand and sixty-two rations in storehouse; ninety-six thousand to arrive to-morrow, and all trains were loaded which had arrived at Bridgeport up to the 16th. We will hold the town till we starve." On the same day THOMAS directed HOOKER to hasten his concentration and his preparation to move as ROSECRANS had ordered.

Gen. GRANT reached Chattanooga in the evening of the 23d, and the plan for opening the line of supplies was laid before him. The next day, in company with Gen. THOMAS and Gen. W. F. SMITH, Chief of Engineers to ROSECRANS, he rode out to a view on the north side of the river, and approved the plan. Gen. SMITH was charged with the enterprise, which was now almost ready for action, and Gen. THOMAS immediately issued the necessary orders to Gen. HOOKER, who replied that he would move on the 27th. Gen. SMITH now decided that the risk would be less if he floated the pontoons down from Chattanooga, carrying part of the troops, and made a landing on the enemy's side, to cover the crossing of the rest.

The operation was a very delicate one. The boats had to float for seven miles along a line of Confederate pickets, and the landing to be made in the face of their fire. Fifteen hundred picked men, under Gen. HAZEN, embarked, while Gen. TURCHIN, with his brigade, the rest of HAZEN's, and three batteries of artillery under Major MENDENHALL, moved across and took position in the woods on the north bank, to cover the landing of the rest on the opposite bank, and to join them as soon as practicable.

The boats moved from Chattanooga at 3 a. m. on the 27th of October, directed by Col. T. R. STANLEY. A slight fog favored their concealment. They hugged the right shore, rounded Moccasin Point, and reached the place of landing unperceived. As the leading section of the boats landed, the pickets fired and fled. The other sections arrived in quick succession; the men leaped ashore and ascended a near hill to meet a small force which had hurried forward at the alarm of the pickets, which was driven back by a short engagement.

The boats were busy in bringing over the rest of the troops, while those before landed were busy in taking positions. HAZEN took position on a hill east of the railroad gap, and TURCHIN on one west of this gorge. Skirmishers were thrown forward, and then detachments with axes felled trees for barricades and abatis, and in two hours the defenses were such as to make the hold secure. Then the pontoon bridge was laid under the supervision of Capt. Fox, 1st Michigan Engineers. The enemy cannonaded from the foot of Lookout Mountain, but the loss of men in all this brilliant operation was but six killed, twenty-three wounded, and nine missing. The loss of the enemy was about the same.

While Gen. BRAGG was wasting ammunition cannonading the floating bridge, HOOKER was moving up from Bridgeport. He started early on the 27th, crossing on a pontoon bridge, turned through a gap in Raccoon Mountains into Lookout Valley, and at 3 p. m. the head of his column had reached Wauhatchie, three miles from the river. His road passed through hills, where resistance was expected, but no resolute opposition was made. As Gen. BRAGG's position on Lookout commanded a view of all the country, and as he must have perceived that a force coming down that valley to join the one which had crossed the river meant the opening of the line of supplies to the army he was expecting to starve, it was to be expected that he would make a strong attempt to oppose HOOKER's march, but he did not. There was a feeble resistance to the march beyond Wauhatchie, but after firing a volley the enemy withdrew, burning the bridge over Lookout Creek.

There was also on the march some loss of men from the batteries on top of Lookout Mountain. At 5 p. m. HOOKER's troops halted for the night about a mile from Brown's Ferry. Gen. GEARY's division of the 12th Corps remained at Wauhatchie to hold the road leading back to Kelly's Ferry. In the night the enemy attempted to take advantage of this separation of the troops. About midnight a regiment which had advanced toward Lookout got into a skirmish; soon after the sound of battle was heard from GEARY's division, which was attacked by part of LONGSTREET's corps.

HOOKER ordered HOWARD to send SCHURZ's division double quick to GEARY's aid. This division met resistance from the enemy on near hills. STEINWEHR's division came to the support, and an action was fought in the night, in which the enemy were successively driven from two strong positions, by charges with the bayonet. Through this the aid failed to reach GEARY, who had to fight it out with his own division. After a resistance to superior numbers for three hours, he took the offensive, broke LONGSTREET's line, and drove him from the field. In these actions the loss of HOOKER's army was 416.

This night attack showed that the Confederate General had at length realized the meaning of our lodgment in Lookout Valley, but his attempt to retrieve the loss was not made with sufficient force to overcome the splendid fighting of our troops. Two brigades were now moved, one from Chattanooga, to strengthen the hold on the valley, and the enemy's chance of recovering it was gone.

The relative situations of the national and Confederate armies were now changed. The question of supplies to our army was settled. The steamboat, which had now been repaired at Chattanooga, passed the batteries of Lookout on the night of the 28th, and one at Bridgeport was soon underway laden with rations. A road was made from Chattanooga to Brown's Ferry, thence to Kelly's, and work was begun to repair the railroad from Bridgeport to Chattanooga. And now, instead of Gen. BRAGG's question how long the national army could hold out against surrender from starvation, the question was how soon could it get ready to attack BRAGG's army.

This relief had been achieved through the plan formed by Gen. ROSECRANS, and the aid brought by Gen. HOOKER from the Eastern army, without any assistance from the two Western armies, one on the east and the other on the West, from which, in any rational military plan, co-operation was to be expected from the beginning, and from one of which, namely, that of Gen. GRANT, the first relief was rationaliy to be expected. This was the first of the battles about Chattanooga after Gen. GRANT took command. Although he had no part in the operation, the credit of the success redounded to his glory in BADEAU's history. And, considering the genius he had before exhibited, great credit is unquestionably due him for not preventing the execution of this well laid plan.

CHAPTER LXI.

THE MIGHTY PREPARATION—ARMIES AND ADMINISTRATION WORKING IN HARMONY FOR THE FIRST TIME—LONGSTREET DEPARTS TO ATTACK BURNSIDE—GRANT ORDERS AN IMPOSSIBILITY—SHERMAN AT LENGTH BEGINS TO MOVE WITH ENERGY—THE PLAN OF OPERATIONS AGAINST MISSION RIDGE—GRANT'S MISCONCEPTION OF THE SITUATION—THOMAS ORDERS TROOPS TO FEEL THE ENEMY—THEIR SPIRIT CONVERTS A DEMONSTRATION TO AN ADVANCE AND THE GAIN OF AN ADVANTAGE OF VITAL IMPORTANCE TO THE FINAL EVENT.

The firm hold on the left bank of the Tennessee River, in the valley between Lookout and Raccoon mountains, which had been made strong by the 27th of October, opened the way for supplies, which soon began to come by small steamboats, and thus the siege of Chattanooga was in effect broken, and now preparations began for driving the Confederate army from its positions.

In this preparation there was none of that dividing and diverting of resources which had given the chief of them to GRANT's army in Mississippi, while that of the Cumberland had to prepare for a greater campaign, nor of that stinting which had positively refused any additional force to Gen. ROSECRANS, when he was ordered on the most difficult campaign of the war; but now all the resources of the three departments which had been placed under GRANT's command were concentrated for the Chattanooga operation, with the aid of the two corps from the Army of the Potomac; and now the Washington authorities were bounteous in furnishing every sort of equipment and supply. At length three parallel departments and armies were placed under one commander, and the military administration at Washington was supporting. This was rare harmony in the great war.

Gen. SHERMAN was coming with the 15th Corps, comprising four divisions, to which, by an order issued from Iuka, he added a select force of 8,000 from the 17th (McPHERSON's) Corps, under command of Gen. DODGE. And now Gen. GRANT ordered forward another division from McPHERSON's corps. All the troops of both armies holding posts in the rear were ordered forward, so far as they could be spared, especially cavalry and artillery. Great energies and means were called out from the North to repair and equip the railroads, to increase the lines of supply. At Chattanooga Gen. BRANNAN, THOMAS' Chief of Artillery, was instructed to prepare the fortifications for heavier guns, and to make requisitions for these and for all ammunition that might be wanted. Two additional pontoon bridges were ordered to be laid to facilitate the movement of troops.

This sound of mighty preparation might have warned Gen. BRAGG that something more than the mere defense of Chattanooga was in the wind, but he supposed that his position on Mission Ridge and Lookout Mountain was impregnable, and now, in the face of this gathering power, he sent off LONGSTREET with 15,000 men to attack BURNSIDE in East Tennessee, having some grand project of ulterior operations after overwhelming BURNSIDE and recovering East Tennessee. Thus by a strange fortune, while forces from east, north, and west were gathering to GRANT, in his front BRAGG was dividing his army.

POLLARD, who has a severe mind toward President DAVIS, charges this dividing expedition to him, but it was resolved upon by a council of war after DAVIS had left, and after THOMAS' occupation of Lookout Valley had changed the situation. BRAGG and his Generals might reasonably reckon that his position was impregnable. If impregnable, so that part of his army could securely hold it, and hold GRANT's army in its front, he might reckon on recovering East Tennessee and threatening GRANT's rear by LONGSTREET's operation. It did throw the Washington authorities into panic, and if GRANT had given way to them he would have sent part of his army to help BURNSIDE, and thus the operations would have neutralized each other. But some military man has written that in real war the event depends on the question which side will commit the greatest blunders. There is a sort of satisfaction in the thought that blundering generalship was not all on the national side.

Gen. GRANT, having ascertained on the 7th of November that LONGSTREET was moving toward East Tennessee, became very anxious for BURNSIDE, but he saw no way of relieving him, save by attacking BRAGG on Mission Ridge. He sent another urgent message to SHERMAN, and on the same day ordered Gen. THOMAS to attack and carry the north end of Mission Ridge on the next morning. The order said:

The news * * is of such a nature that it becomes an imperative duty to draw the attention of the enemy from Burnside to your own front. I deem the best movement to attack the enemy to be an attack on the northern end of Mission Ridge with all the force you can bring to bear against it; and when this is carried, to threaten and even attack, if possible, the enemy's line of communication between Dalton and Cleveland. Rations should be ready to issue a sufficiency to last four days, the moment Mission Ridge is in our possession; rations to be carried in haversacks. * * * The movement should not be made a moment later than to-morrow morning.

To issue such an order is easy when the commander is utterly unconscious of physical possibilities. This was to attack at a point which subsequently Gen. SHERMAN, with six divisions, and more offered him, found impregnable. The operation which had seized Lookout Valley while the rations were at the shortest, had shown the indomitable spirit of Gen. THOMAS' soldiers. They had had no thought of surrender or retreat, and whatever faintness they suffered from hunger was quickly cured by a full meal. But in the strait for food men were preferred before the animals, and men recover more quickly from starvation.

Gen. THOMAS had neither horse nor mule to move artillery. Part of his army was in Lookout Valley as much as five miles from his left, separated by Lookout Mountain and Chattanooga Creek Valley. Four miles beyond the left of his line was the north end of Mission Ridge, which he was ordered to attack and carry. The order said also that HOWARD's cors of HOOKER's command could be withdrawn from Lookout Valley to be used in this attack. Thereby if the attack had failed, the loss of Lookout Valley might be expected. THOMAS, with his army stretched out more than twelve miles, and his center overlooked by the Confederate Army on Mission Ridge, was thus required to attack at one extreme a position which SHERMAN found impregnable to all the men he could use.

Further along it will be seen that the lack of animals to move a gun was a fortunate thing for the army, in saving it from an attempt to execute this order, which was given in absolute ignorance of the situation, and which reasonably might be expected to match the consumption of horses and mules by an equal number of soldiers slain and wounded in vain. GRANT announced to HALLECK and BURNSIDE this order, as if the operation were a certainty. But Gen. THOMAS and the Chief of Engineers, Gen. SMITH, after a thorough reconnaissance of the ground, and a consideration of the lack of draft animals and the inadequacy of the force for such an operation, agreed that the army was not in condition to make it. Gen. GRANT, therefore, revoked the order, and now applied himself to the forming of a plan of operation for the combined armies, to be carried out as soon as SHERMAN should arrive.

Gen. SHERMAN, upon receiving GRANT's order on the 27th, turned from the railroad at Tuscumbia, to cross to the north side of the Tennessee River. One division crossed, with very inadequate means of ferrying, and SHERMAN joined it at Florence, November 1. The other three divisions turned back eighteen miles to cross at Freeport by the aid of boats. From Florence he had to make a detour to northeast, up the Elk River to the Bridge at Fayetteville. At Fayetteville he received orders from GRANT to come to Bridgeport with the 15th Army Corps, and leave Gen. DODGE on the railroad which runs north from Decatur, Ala., to Nashville. He gave orders for the movement of the four divisions, and then went on to Bridgeport, arriving at night, November 13. From thence he was summoned to Chattanooga, which he reached on the 15th, as his official report says; his memoirs say the 14th.

Here Gen. GRANT informed him of his plan of operations, and he narrates that next day, to-wit, on the 15th (or 16th) they walked out to Fort Wood, a prominent salient of the defenses, to view the situation, and he thus narrates the impression made on him, and that expressed to him by Gen. GRANT:

From its parapet we had a magnificent view of the panorama. Lookout Mountain with its rebel flags and batteries stood out boldly, and an occasional shot fired toward Waubatchie or Moccasin Point gave life to the scene. These shots could barely reach Chattanooga, and I was told that one or more shot had struck the hospital inside the lines.

All along Mission Ridge were the tents of the rebel beleaguering force; the lines of trench from Lookout up toward Chickamauga Creek were plainly visible; and rebel sentinels in a continuous chain were walking their posts in plain view not a thousand yards off. "Why," said I. "Gen. Grant, you are besieged;" and he said, "It is too true." Up to that moment I had no idea that things were so bad. The rebel lines actually extended from the river below the town to the river above, and the Army of the Cumberland was closely held to the town and its immediate defenses.

Gen. Grant pointed out to me a house on Mission Ridge, where Gen. Bragg's headquarters were known to be. He also explained the situation of affairs generally; that the mules and horses of Thomas' army were so starved that they could not haul his guns; that forage, corn, and provisions were so scarce that the men in hunger stole the few grains of corn that were given to favorite horses; that the men of Thomas' army had been so demoralized by the battle of Chickamauga that he feared they could not be got out of the trenches to assume the offensive; that Bragg had detached Longstreet with a considerable force up into East Tennessee, to defeat and capture Burnside; that Burnside was in danger, and that he (Grant) was extremely anxious to attack Bragg in position, to defeat him, or at least him to force to recall Longstreet.

The Army of the Cumberland had been so long in the trenches that he wanted my troops to hurry up to take the offensive *first*, after which he had no doubt the Cumberland army would fight well.

The situation was, indeed, a revelation to Gen. SHERMAN, whose leading division in this rescuing expedition had been twenty-five days getting from Corinth to Tuscumbia, fifty miles, and whose troops now, when two months had elapsed since he received the word of urgency on the Mississippi, had only begun to arrive at Bridgeport on the 15th. But in order to get this view Gen. GRANT had to go backward a fortnight; for the soldiers had now enough to eat, and a part of this army, which Gen. GRANT said was so cowed by Chickamauga that it could not be got out of the trenches to fight until SHERMAN's men had shown how, had brilliantly carried out an expedition requiring the highest valor and intelligence; and this was in their greatest strait of rations.

Following events made even a more pointed commentary on Gen. GRANT's expressed opinion that the soldiers of THOMAS' army would not fight. SHERMAN's narrative now tells the plan which GRANT unfolded to him, and that next day they rode to the hills on the north side of the river opposite Chattanooga, to reconnoiter the ground from these heights. This plan makes necessary a general view of the ground.

The general course of the Tennessee River from Knoxville to Chattanooga is southwest. Striking the base of Lookout Mountain, three miles below Chattanooga, the river turns abruptly to northwest, and, after five miles, doubles on itself and then, after a loop, resumes its general southwest course.

Four miles north of Chattanooga South Chickamauga Creek, fetching a bend to northwest and southwest, enters the Tennessee. Mission Ridge starts from the south bank of this creek, nearly two miles east of the river, and about five miles north of Chattanooga, and runs a little east of south, and terminates at Rossville, in the valley of Chattanooga Creek, nearly east of the north end of Lookout Mountain, and about three miles south of Chattanooga. The bending of the river away from the ridge makes the distance from the river at Chattanooga to the ridge about three and one-half miles. In the valley between Lookout and the ridge, Chattanooga Creek runs in a general north course, and then turns to southwest to enter the river at the north end of Lookout. About two miles north of the South Chickamauga the North Chickamauga enters the river on the west side. The railroad from Dalton crosses the South Chickamauga, and runs through the north end of Mission Ridge by a tunnel, and thence southwest nearly four miles, to the town.

Chattanooga is in a rough valley on the east side of the river, which is a prolongation of the valley of Chattanooga Creek up along the river to the South Chickamauga. On the opposite side of the river the country is hilly. Gen. BRAGG's lines extended all the way from the South Chickamauga along the top of Mission Ridge to Rossville, a length of seven miles. The indented top of this ridge is from 400 to 600 feet above the valley. The Confederate army had also an intrenched line at the foot of the ridge, starting about two miles north of Chattanooga, and curving from the ridge south of the town to cross Chattanooga Creek Valley and connect with the head of Lookout Mountain.

About half way between the ridge and Chattanooga the Confederates had an intrenched position on and in front of a hill called Orchard Knob, with barricades of logs and stones for half a mile to the southwest of the knob, and a line of rifle pits for more than a mile to the north, following the curve of Citico Creek, which runs northwest to the river. Between this and the national line the ground is generally low, and was partly covered with trees and bushes. The Confederate picket line was as much as half way between

Orchard Knob and Chattanooga, reaching to the river above the town, and at the head of Lookout below.

The railroad which runs under the north end of Mission Ridge was BRAGG's line of supplies, and his depot was at Chickamauga Station, east of the north end of the ridge. Gen. GRANT conceived the idea that BRAGG had left this vital point unguarded. Says SHERMAN in his narrative: "GRANT explained to me that he had reconnoitered the rebel line from Lookout Mountain up to Chickamauga, and he believed that the northern portion of Mission Ridge was not fortified at all." His entire plan was formed upon this strange misconception, and its decisive part was to be the carrying of the head of Mission Ridge, which commanded BRAGG's line of supplies. This part was assigned to SHERMAN's army, to be assisted by one division from the Army of the Cumberland. SHERMAN, bringing his army from Bridgeport north through Lookout Valley, was to cross the Tennessee at Brown's Ferry, and then march by a long way over the hills west of the river, out of sight of the enemy, to the North Chickamauga.

Pontoons had been made at Chattanooga, and carried by this road to the North Chickamauga, to bridge the Tennessee for SHERMAN. Troops in these were to drop down the North Chickamauga, unperceived, to the Tennessee, make a landing on the east side, lay a bridge by which all of SHERMAN's troops were to cross, and carry the unguarded north end of the ridge by surprise before it could be fortified. THOMAS, meanwhile, was to hold the front, concentrating toward his left, and when SHERMAN came sweeping down the ridge, THOMAS was to join him and all were to sweep onward. HOOKER, with one of his corps and such of THOMAS' troops as had occupied Lookout Valley, was to hold that valley, and HOWARD with the other corps was to be held ready to act with either THOMAS or SHERMAN. But the General is not wise who risks his army in a general engagement on a plan based upon the supposition that his adversary is a fool.

The plan was an admirable plan, if BRAGG had been a General who would leave the vital point of his position unguarded; but because he did not so co-operate, but, on the contrary, had made strongest of all that part which SHERMAN was to take by surprise, the plan went all awry, and the success had to be achieved contrary to the plan in every particular.

Gen. GRANT communicated his plan on the 18th, and fixed the 21st as the day of battle, and Gen. THOMAS made his dispositions accordingly, one of which was to move HOWARD's corps from Lookout Valley to a position on the north side of the river, between Brown's Ferry and Chattanooga, calling up two of his own brigades from further down the river to fill the place left by HOWARD in the valley. His arrangements were completed by the 21st, but a rain delayed SHERMAN's movements, and the day of battle was changed to the 22d; but on that day GRANT notified THOMAS of further postponement, because two of SHERMAN's divisions had failed to cross at Brown's Ferry, the pontoon bridge having parted.

During all this time the authorities at Washington were very uneasy because of BURNSIDE, and HALLECK was telegraphing much worry and misinformation, and GRANT had not only his own anxiety to contend with, but had to quiet the Washington authorities with assurances which were not strictly according to the facts of the situation. And while thus waiting for SHERMAN he did not fail to cast the blame for delay on the immobility of THOMAS' army, all of which was eager to begin. THOMAS, at this juncture, suggested that, to avoid further delay, HOWARD's corps should take the place of those of SHERMAN's divisions, which were behind, and that these, in the place of HOWARD's, could join HOOKER's troops in Lookout Valley to attack the enemy on Lookout Mountain, or at least to divert his attention from SHERMAN's movement. But GRANT was desirous that SHERMAN's army should make the decisive movement, and he accepted THOMAS' suggestions only so far as to permit HOWARD's corps to be moved to Chattanooga.

Rumors now came that BRAGG was withdrawing his army, and Gen. GRANT on the 23d sent to Gen. THOMAS this:

> The truth or falsity of the deserter who came in last night, stating that Bragg had fallen back, should be ascertained at once. If he is really falling back, Sherman can commence at once laying his pontoon trains, and he can save a day.

To ascertain the truth or falsity of the deserter, Gen. THOMAS issued the following order to Gen. GRANGER:

The General commanding the department directs that you throw one division of the 4th Corps forward in the direction of Orchard Knob, and hold a second division in supporting distance, to discover the position of the enemy, if he still remains in the vicinity of his old camps. Howard's and Baird's commands will be ready to co-operate, if needed.

Granger issued the necessary order to Gen. Wood, to be supported by Gen. Sheridan. In an undulating valley, between Fort Wood, of the national line, and Orchard Knob, of the Confederate line, several divisions of the Army of the Cumberland now formed in line of battle, in plain sight from the enemy's commanding positions.

Both armies looked on with admiration at the movements of the well disciplined troops of the Army of the Cumberland. The Confederates thought it a parade, and made no preparations to oppose. Wood's division first deployed before Fort Wood. Then Sheridan's to the right and rear of Wood. Howard's corps was in mass in the rear of these divisions. Baird's division was to the right and rear of Sheridan in echelon. Johnston's division was in arms in the intrenchments. About 2 p. m. Wood's division moved rapidly forward, Hazen's brigade on the right, Willich's on the left, and Beatty's in reserve. As if on parade the compact lines marched, sweeping before them the enemy's pickets and their reserves, and then on to the enemy's line at Orchard Knob, carrying the whole line by a dash at the point of the bayonet, capturing the 8th Alabama Regiment. The short and sharp conflict cost 125 men killed and wounded in Wood's division.

As soon as Wood had driven the enemy from the position, Sheridan moved to Wood's right, occupying a series of small hills. The line now taken had nearly all the high ground between Fort Wood and Mission Ridge, making a base of operations against the enemy's main line almost a mile nearer to the ridge than the Confederate picket line had been on the morning of that day. The vital bearing of this on that which the failure of Sherman's attack made the decisive movement of the battle, will appear further along. And this was not in Gen. Grant's plan, but was achieved by a spontaneous movement, and by the dashing gallantry of those troops which Grant told Sherman could not be got out of the trenches to fight until Sherman's men had given them an example.

CHAPTER LXII.

GRANT'S WAITING FOR SHERMAN — THOMAS' ANXIETY THAT THE ACTION SHOULD BEGIN — THE OPERATION AGAINST LOOKOUT MOUNTAIN — ANOTHER VICTORY NOT IN GRANT'S PLAN, AND WHICH HELPED TO SAVE THE ARMY FROM HIS PLAN.

The brilliant demonstration of the 23d of November had made Orchard Knob the center of the battle front of Gen. Thomas' army, between which and the foot of Mission Ridge was easy ground of less than a mile. Another important consequence of the advance was that it caused Gen. Bragg to bring from Lookout Mountain Walker's division to strengthen his defense on Mission Ridge.

This had an important bearing on another operation which was not in Gen. Grant's plan — namely, Hooker's carrying Lookout Mountain. During the pageant of the 23d Sherman was struggling to get his divisions up to the North Chickamauga. Another division crossed at Brown's Ferry on that day, making three, but the bridge again parted, leaving Osterhaus' division on the left bank. Meanwhile it was improbable that this protracted movement could be concealed from the enemy, whose high positions looked out over all that region, and who had a chance to defeat the operation either by fortifying the north end of Mission Ridge, or resisting the crossing of the Tennessee, or by retreating.

Gen. Thomas, on the 22d, had urged Grant to take Howard's corps in place of the two divisions of Sherman's army, which were yet behind, letting these join Hooker in Lookout Valley in an attack on Lookout Mountain. But Grant had determined that Sherman's army should make the decisive attack, and so the operation was delayed. Fortunately, during this delay the unexpected seizure of the advanced line of Orchard Knob had greatly improved the situation, but still were fears that their aims would be defeated by Bragg's knowledge of them. As the proposition to make the attack with the aid of Howard's corps was rejected, Gen. Thomas, on the 22d, had moved it over the river to Chattanooga, thinking that this might deceive the enemy into the belief that all of Sherman's troops, whose crossing at Brown's Ferry was in full sight of the enemy, were simply re-enforcing Chattanooga.

On the 23d, as Sherman had now three divisions across Gen. GRANT decided to wait no longer for the fourth. Gen. J. C. DAVIS' division from THOMAS' army, which was to join SHERMAN, was already at the North Chickamauga ready for the operation. The chief energies of the Engineer Department of the Army of the Cumberland had been devoted to SHERMAN'S operation. The pontoons for a double bridge had been built and carried over the hills and placed in the North Chickamauga, with a brigade to man them, by the night of the 20th, ready for the operation which by GRANT'S first order was to be made on the 21st. A steamboat was sent up from Chattanooga to assist the crossing.

Gen. THOMAS now advised Gen. HOOKER that if SHERMAN'S remaining division should fail to cross to join SHERMAN, he should endeavor with it and his own command "to take the point of Lookout Mountain." Later he informed HOOKER that GRANT still hoped that OSTERHAUS' division could cross, but if he could not in time to join SHERMAN, the mountain should be taken if a demonstration should develop its practicability. BADEAU says that GRANT ordered OSTERHAUS that, unless he could get across by 8 o'clock of the morning of the 24th, he was to report to HOOKER. HOOKER sent a staff officer to the river to ascertain that the bridge could not be joined, and made his arrangements accordingly. The detention of this division turned out a lucky accident, leading to the taking of Lookout Mountain, which was not in GRANT'S plan, and which materially changed the situation, opening up Chattanooga Creek Valley around the southern point of Mission Ridge, and through that making BRAGG'S position untenable, even if all front attack had been found impracticable.

Gen. HOOKER was not the man to neglect an opportunity. At 4 a. m. of the 24th he reported that he was ready to advance against Lookout Mountain. His command now comprised GEARY'S division of the 12th Corps of the Army of the Potomac, OSTERHAUS' division of the Army of the Tennessee, and two brigades of CRUFT'S division of the Army of the Cumberland, under WHITTAKER and GROSE. He sent GEARY'S division and WHITTAKER'S brigade up the valley south to Wauhatchie, to cross Lookout Creek, and then to sweep down its right bank to cover the crossing of the rest of the forces. GROSE was to seize the wagon road bridge near the mouth of the creek, a little to the left of the head of Lookout Mountain, and repair it. The other bank of the creek was held by the Confederate pickets. The enemy's main force was encamped on the mountain side commanding the creek. OSTERHAUS' division was to move up from Brown's Ferry, under cover of the hills, to the point for crossing the creek, and was to support two batteries of artillery placed on hills to cover the crossing. HOOKER also sent a part of the 2d Kentucky Cavalry up the valley to Trenton, to give warning of danger from that direction.

The following description of the north end of Lookout is taken from VAN HORNE'S history of the Army of the Cumberland:

On the front of Lookout Mountain, intermediate between base and summit, there is a wide open space, cultivated as a farm, in vivid contrast with the natural surroundings of the wildest types. The farmhouse, known as Craven's, or "the white house," was situated upon the upper margin of the farm. From the house to the foundation of the perpendicular cliff or palisade, which crops out from the rockribbed frame of the mountain, the ascent is exceedingly steep, and thickly wooded.

Below the farm the surface is rough and craggy. The base of the mountain, next the river, has a perpendicular front of solid rock, rising grandly from the railroad track, which, though, in part, cut through the deep ledges, does not perceptibly mar nature's magnificent architecture. Over the top of this foundation front the narrow road passes, which in the western valley (Lookout Valley) throws off various branches leading west and south. East and west from Craven's farm the surface is broken by furrows and covered with shrubs, trees, and fragments of stone.

On the open space the enemy had constructed his defenses, consisting of intrenchments, pits, and redoubts, which, extending over the front of the mountain, bade defiance to a foe advancing from the river. At the extremities of the main intrenchments there were rifle pits, epaulments for batteries, barricades of stone and abatis, looking to resistance against aggression from Chattanooga or Lookout Valley. The road from Chattanooga to Summertown, an elegant village for summer resort, winding up the eastern side of the mountain, is the only one practicable for ordinary military movements within a range of many miles. So that, except by this road, there could be no transfer of troops from the summit to the northern slope, or to the valley, east or west, to meet the emergencies of battle, and this road was too long to allow provision from the top for sudden contingencies below.

To attack such a mountain seems to lift battle into the realm of romance; yet this description, and the plan of the attack, show that the heroic spirit of the soldiers was directed by military skill.

GEARY'S division crossed the creek at Wauhatchie at 8 a. m., captured the pickets, and then the column climbed the mountain side until its head reached the base of the palisaded top. Then with his right holding to the base of the palisades, the line, facing to the north, swept along the mountain side toward the north end. At the same time GROSE attacked and drove back the enemy at the bridge near the head of the mountain, and began to repair it.

This brought out the enemy in force, occupying intrenchments and rifle pits, and one part advanced to the railroad embankment, which formed a good cover from which to open fire upon troops advancing from the bridge. To avoid this fire in a direct advance HOOKER now directed OSTERHAUS to send WOODS' brigade to prepare a crossing half a mile further up the creek, under cover of woods. A part of GROSE'S brigade remained at the bridge, to hold the enemy's attention, and the rest followed WOODS. Meanwhile additional artillery was placed to enfilade the near positions of the enemy.

WOODS completed the bridge at 11 a. m., and soon after GEARY'S division and WHITTAKER'S brigade, in line reaching from the mountain base to the palisade, came abreast. The batteries now opened fire, and WOODS and GROSE, crossing the creek, placed their troops on GEARY'S left, extending it into the valley, and now the whole line swept forward, reaching from the creek up the mountain to the palisade, over crags, great detached rocks, bushes, trees, and all sorts of obstacles of a wild mountain side. The artillery at the northern bridge drove the enemy from their intrenchments at the foot of the mountain, and in their flight they fell into GEARY'S advancing line as it swept round to the head of the mountain.

At noon the victorious troops had reached a point where the orders required a halt to readjust the lines for a more cautious approach toward Summertown; but they kept on, driving the enemy's line out of its intrenchments, and making no halt until the middle of the open ground of CRAVEN'S farm was gained. Here the enemy met re-enforcements, and made a more determined stand, but the left of the national line closed up from below, and the enemy was driven from all the defenses on the open ground, and with broken ranks now retreated down the eastern side of the mountain. This skillful operation had struck the flank and rear of the Confederate defenses, turning them to naught. HOOKER'S report states the capture of between 2,000 and 3,000 prisoners, five colors, two guns, and upward of 5,000 muskets.

The heavy fighting ceased at 2 p. m. HOOKER'S troops had expended their ammunition, and now the fog which had enveloped the top of the mountain since morning settled far down its sides, completely covering the enemy. This prevented an effort to seize Summertown, and HOOKER now waited for ammunition and re-enforcements. At 5 p. m. CARLIN'S brigade from THOMAS' army came direct from Chattanooga, crossing Chattanooga Creek near its mouth, and ascended the mountain to HOOKER'S right, the troops carrying on their persons ammunition for HOOKER'S skirmishers. Skirmishing was kept up till midnight, the flash of the musketry seen from Chattanooga looking like a battle in the clouds.

This brilliant operation had neutralized the enemy's position on top of the mountain, even if not made it untenable. It had driven the enemy's picket line from the river, and opened to our troops the way across Chattanooga Creek Valley from Lookout to Chattanooga, connecting the national line, and opening a wide distance in the Confederate. And now there was a way open up Chattanooga Creek Valley and around the south end of Mission Ridge, whereby BRAGG'S position might be turned, and he forced to precipitate retreat without any direct attack on natural fortresses.

Gen. GRANT did not seem to appreciate the importance of HOOKER'S victory in its bearing on the main operation, and he expected nothing more from it than that next day HOOKER should complete the capture of the mountain. He said in his order of the 24th, for next day:

> If Hooker's present position on the mountain can be maintained with small force, and it is found impracticable to carry the top from where he is, it would be advisable for him to move up the valley with all the force he can spare, and ascend by the first practicable road.

This was to keep HOOKER, on the great day,

operating against the top of a mountain which he had before isolated and neutralized. But HOOKER believed that he had made the enemy's position untenable, and THOMAS, in his congratulatory order, gave this more pertinent direction to HOOKER:

Be in readiness to advance as early as possible in the morning into Chattanooga Valley, and seize and hold the Summertown road, and co-operate with the 14th Corps by supporting its right. Map sent by courier at 8 o'clock this evening,

This, instead of wasting HOOKER's forces in an operation around the top of Lookout, which now had no significance, would bring them into co-operation in the great attack on Mission Ridge. HOOKER had anticipated the enemy's abandonment of the top of Lookout, and at daylight next morning his enterprising soldiers found it so. He reported this to Gen. THOMAS, and received further orders to leave two regiments to hold Lookout, and with the rest of his forces to move on the Rossville road to Mission Ridge.

This may be numbered the third of the battles about Chattanooga since Gen. GRANT took command. Like the affair of Orchard Knob, it was not in GRANT's plan, and like that it gained advantages in the situation which were of great importance in the final event, in achieving a victory after it had been proved to be impossible upon the plan which Gen. GRANT had formed and had persisted in with characteristic firmness.

CHAPTER LXIII.

SHERMAN'S GRAND ATTACK ON BRAGG'S UNGUARDED RIGHT—FINDS IT THE STRONGEST PART OF BRAGG'S WHOLE LINE—SHERMAN'S ATTACK FAILS—GRANT'S PLAN AT A DEADLOCK—HOOKER ADVANCES TO SOUTH END OF THE RIDGE—THOMAS ORDERED FORWARD ON THE CENTER.

While Gen. HOOKER had been attacking Lookout Mountain, Gen. SHERMAN had been crossing the Tennessee, and making his first attack on the north end of Mission Ridge. At midnight of the 23d, 116 boats, carrying a brigade, floated down the North Chickamauga into the Tennessee, to the place of crossing, landing on the east bank of the river, both above and below the mouth of the South Chickamauga.

A steamboat aided the crossing of the troops. High water had now so widened the river that the boats intended for two would make no more than one bridge. By daylight two divisions were over, and the bridge construction was pushed with energy, and was ready at 11 a. m. At this time Gen. HOWARD, with a brigade and a cavalry escort, arrived, having come up the east bank of the river, which showed that the enemy had withdrawn their lines from the river and a great part of the valley. HOWARD left the brigade with SHERMAN, and returned with his escort.

At 1 p. m. Gen. SHERMAN moved forward with three divisions in echelon, covering the heads of columns with skirmishers. Meeting no serious resistance, they passed the foothills, and occupied the two most northern summits of Mission Ridge at 4 p. m. There had been no action, but he had not yet reached the right flank of the enemy. There intervened between him and the tunnel, which he was expected to carry on that day, a summit upon which BRAGG's right rested and which was fortified.

Mission Ridge is cut into distinct summits by deep depressions. The deepest of these separated that which SHERMAN had occupied from the next, which was the right of BRAGG's position, and was the strongest position for lateral defense within BRAGG's lines. CLEBURNE's division held this summit, which was broad enough for a strong force, and not too broad for solid lines. Heavy fortifications of logs and earth covered the troops on the first line, and higher ground to the south gave positions for supporting columns. Woods gave additional protection. An attacking force from any direction came under the guns of this position.

Gen. SHERMAN's report says:

The enemy was also seen in great force on a still higher hill beyond the tunnel, from which he had a fine plunging fire on the hill in dispute. The gorge between, through which several roads and the railroad tunnel pass, could not be seen from our position, but formed the natural place d'armes, where the enemy covered his masses to resist our contemplated movement of turning his right flank and endangering his communications with his depot at Chickamauga Station.

This place which Gen. SHERMAN had reached with so great labor and delay, and with such an expenditure of engineer energies and means; which Gen. GRANT expected to find unfortified, and to take by surprise; upon which delusion he had formed his plan so completely that it had no alternative, Gen. SHERMAN now found to be the strongest place, naturally and artificially, defensively and offensively, that could be found in BRAGG's line if he had freely searched for it. It was not only impregnable to his attack, but it had peculiar advantages for unexpected attack upon his attacking forces, as he found to his cost.

Gen. SHERMAN had come to a full stop. Yet all the same did Gen. GRANT telegraph to Washington:

The fight to-day progressed favorably. Sherman carried the end of Mission Ridge, and his right is now at the tunnel, and his left at Chickamauga Creek.

The rest told of HOOKER's success. In the hands of a truly great General, the telegraph is mightier than the sword. The relation of these events to GRANT's plan gives a touch of humor to HALLECK's reply: "I congratulate you on the success thus far of your plans." On that night GRANT issued the following order to Gen. THOMAS for the operations next day, in which may be noticed the valuable information communicated, and the vague alternative provided for THOMAS' army;

GENERAL: Gen. Sherman carried Mission Ridge as far as the tunnel with only slight skirmishing. His right now rests at the tunnel and on top of the hill; his left at Chickamauga Creek. I have instructed Gen. Sherman to advance as soon as it is light in the morning, and your attack, which will be simultaneous, will be in co-operation. Your command will either carry the rifle pits and ridge directly in front of them, or move to the left, as the presence of the enemy may require.

If Gen. GRANT thought that SHERMAN had carried the ridge as far as the tunnel, it shows again how a Commanding General, in a battle, who thinks he is the god of the machine, may be ignorant of the essential parts of the situation, and may issue orders unconscious of their impossibility and destructiveness. Gen. SHERMAN had not carried Mission Ridge to the tunnel, and was never to carry it, and the situation in which THOMAS was to co-operate, which was to be when SHERMAN's advance had made a junction with THOMAS, was never to arrive, and instead of attacking simultaneously, his forces were diverted to re-enforce SHERMAN.

Gen. SHERMAN opened the battle on the 25th soon after sunrise. CORSE's brigade moved down the southern slope of the second hill gained the night before, and ascended toward CLEBURNE's position under a heavy fire, gaining a place about eighty yards from the enemy's fortifications, from which he repeatedly advanced and was driven back, and in turn repulsed several attacks of the enemy, suffering slaughter without possibility of advantage. At the same time MORGAN L. SMITH's division advanced along the eastern base of the hill. LOOMIS' brigade, supporting CORSE on the left, was supported by two reserve brigades of JOHN E. SMITH's division.

Gen. M. L. SMITH pressed forward to the enemy's works, but gained no lodgment. Gen. GRANT, observing from Orchard Knob the nature of this fight, at 10 a. m. directed HOWARD's corps, which was in position on THOMAS' left, to go to SHERMAN's support. This corps was formed on the left of SHERMAN's line, its left reaching to South Chickamauga Creek. SHERMAN had now six divisions—three of his own, two of HOWARD's corps, and DAVIS' division of THOMAS' army.

Reducing his center, Gen. GRANT persisted in his original plan of turning BRAGG's right. Soon after HOWARD was in position SHERMAN made another effort to turn the enemy's right flank. CORSE's brigade, now under command of WALCUTT (CORSE being wounded), and BUSCHBECK's brigade again moved to the attack, and the brigades of JOHN E. SMITH advanced in support, the extreme right of the line reaching near to the depression in the rear of CLEBURNE's first line of works, through which the railroad runs to the tunnel. This gorge is that which SHERMAN describes as the place d'armes. It was now found so. From this gorge a heavy force, in complete concealment, came out upon SMITH's brigades, and drove them in disorder down the hill. But this was in turn taken in flank by WALCUTT's and LOOMIS' brigades, and the previous situation was resumed.

At Chattanooga the appearance was that SHERMAN was repulsed, but he denies it. Gen. GRANT, seeing this repulse, and clinging to his plan of making the attack on the north end of the ridge the decisive action, now ordered BAIRD's division, from the right of THOMAS' line, to move to SHERMAN's support. This order gave to SHERMAN seven of the thirteen divisions now before the enemy, leaving to Gen. THOMAS but eight brigades in line between Chattanooga and the ridge. HOOKER, with seven brigades, was as far removed on his right as SHERMAN on his left. And, according to GRANT's order of the night before, HOOKER was expected to have occupation at Lookout Mountain.

This sending of so great a preponderance of the forces to SHERMAN, precludes the afterthought which was cooked up, that the plan from the beginning designed SHERMAN's movement as only a demonstration, while the decisive attack was to be made by THOMAS against the breast of the ridge. To send away seven divisions for a demonstration, while the real battle was to be fought by eight brigades, would be strange battle tactics.

Gen. SHERMAN, who says in his memoirs that he has never criticised GRANT's strategy, but who does make remarks thereon, places italicized stress in his report on the fact that GRANT's order to him to attack at "dawn of day" gave him notice that Gen. THOMAS would attack in force early in the day. Relating the failure of his attack, he says of the situation at 3 p. m.: "I had watched for the attack of Gen. THOMAS 'early in the day.'" SHERMAN had reason to expect this, yet there was a vagueness in GRANT's order to THOMAS, in this: "Your command will either carry the rifle pits and ridge directly in front of them, or move to the left as the presence of the enemy may require."

Either carry the rifle pits and ridge in front, or move to the left, as the presence of the enemy may require! What could he make of that? Yet in the fore part of the order he gave this, which by itself is specific, but which was neutralized by the shifting alternative that followed: "I have instructed Gen. SHERMAN to advance as soon as it is light in the morning, and your attack, which will be simultaneous, will be in co-operation." Simultaneous with SHERMAN, at dawn, yet either to the front or to the left as the presence of the enemy might require. Besides, GRANT's post overlooked THOMAS' troops, and THOMAS was in his presence, yet he did not order him to attack, but on the contrary he diverted his troops to SHERMAN.

GRANT's original plan was still sticking in his mind, which was to hold THOMAS' army until SHERMAN had carried the north end of the ridge and thereby effected a junction with THOMAS, after which was this vague direction: "Further movements will depend on those of the enemy." In SHERMAN's reconstructed plan, after the event, he makes his attack the feint, and charges delinquency in that THOMAS did not attack simultaneously at dawn. In GRANT's reconstructed plan to fit the events, he makes his waiting to be for HOOKER to reach the south end of Mission Ridge, although in his original plan HOOKER was still to be in Lookout Valley, and in his order of the night before HOOKER was to occupy himself about the top of Lookout. The reality was that the operations were greatly encumbered by Gen. GRANT's plan, and that when success was gained in spite of it, the afterthought reconstuction of the plan to fit the successful events made a queer mixture.

Gen. BAIRD moved as ordered, following the road on the bank of the river until he had reached the rear of SHERMAN's right, when he was told by SHERMAN that he had all the force he could use. Thereupon BAIRD returned and now formed on THOMAS' left, to lessen the interval between him and SHERMAN. His report states that his division was again in line at half past 2 p. m. SHERMAN had found that the supposed undefended end of the ridge was impregnable, and that now the enemy's concentrative and offensive advantages made the attempt a vain slaughter, and he made no further effort.

That which GRANT's plan had made the decisive movement had failed, after drawing to it the bulk of the army, and now something else had to be done. Meanwhile Gen. HOOKER, following Gen. THOMAS' order, had moved up Chattanooga Creek Valley to the Confederate left flank at Rossville, driving the skirmishers before him. He had to rebuild the bridge over Chattanooga Creek. As soon as he could cross he pushed forward rapidly to Rossville, where he met considerable resistance. Forcing the enemy to retreat, he disposed of his three divisions to sweep north on the summit and on both sides of Mission Ridge.

While HOOKER was making these dispositions on the Confederate left flank, Gen. GRANT ordered a movement in the center, which was another radical departure from his original plan. Till now THOMAS' troops had been held to co-operate with SHERMAN, when he had carried the ridge to the tunnel, and, in the failure of this, had been detached to help SHERMAN; but now an independent movement was ordered from the center, after SHERMAN had spent his force, and had ceased his attempt. At last this strategic plan of a battle, whose main attack was to find the enemy's depot of supplies unfortified, had to resort to a direct attack by half the force, on a steep and rough ridge, from four to six hundred feet high, fortified at the base and on the top, which in any rational military calculation would be called impregnable, and which BRAGG said a skirmish line ought to hold against an assaulting column.

CHAPTER LXIV.

THE STORMING OF MISSION RIDGE—GRANT'S VAGUE ORDER—THE INTENT A DEMONSTRATION—THE TROOPS ASSAULT WITHOUT ORDERS—THE HEAVY LOSSES AND CAPTURES—HOOKER COMES IN AT THE SOUTH END OF THE RIDGE—THE ARMY RESTS ON THE RIDGE FOR THE NIGHT—SHERMAN INFORMED OF THE SUCCESS.

Gen. GRANT's order to Gen. THOMAS to advance to the ridge, like the rest of his orders to THOMAS in all this operation, was vague; but as it was verbal, it afforded facility for after reconstruction to fit the event. VAN HORNE's history, which may be accepted as that of Gen. THOMAS, says: "GRANT's order required that the enemy should be dislodged from the rifle pits and intrenchments at the base of Mission Ridge." He adds:

The statement is made in his official report that it was the design that the lines should be readjusted at the base for the assault on the summit; but no such instructions were given to the corps or division Generals. Neither does it appear from his report whether he meditated an independent assault of the summit from his center, or one co-operative with Sherman on the left, or Hooker on the right, as the original plan prescribed for the former, or as the issues of the day prescribed for the latter.

BADEAU says that GRANT seized the opportunity because BRAGG "was weakening his center and making a flank movement in the presence of an enemy," which BADEAU says is "the most difficult movement that can be executed in war." In military erudition BADEAU is great and precise. But a movement along the fortified crest of that ridge, with its intrenched base held, and "the enemy" nearly a mile away from the foot, could not be very hazardous save in a military maxim. And, in fact, BRAGG did not need to weaken his center in order to resist SHERMAN, and did not. It was still held by nearly four divisions, and the troops sent to strengthen HARDEE on the right had come from Lookout. But, on the contrary, GRANT had greatly weakened his own center by a "flank movement in the face of the enemy" to send aid to SHERMAN. BADEAU gives as another reason that GRANT was now satisfied that HOOKER must be on his way from Rossville, although not yet in sight, therefore he "determined to order the assault." But as late as the night before HOOKER's co-operation was no part of his plan, and, in fact, GRANT did not now "order the assault."

BADEAU, in order to show that GRANT was the god of the machine, says: "At first he simply directed THOMAS to order the advance; but seeing the corps commanders near him, GRANT repeated to them in person the command." This would be important. None of the corps commanders heard this instruction to carry the rifle pits and then halt and reform the lines "with a view to carrying the top of the ridge." Gen. GORDON GRANGER, whose corps consisted of WOOD's and SHERIDAN's divisions, says in his report:

Gen. Sherman was unable to make any progress in moving along the ridge during the day, as the enemy had massed in his front; therefore, in order to relieve him I was instructed to make a demonstration upon the works of the enemy directly in my front, at the base of Mission Ridge.

It is most likely that Gen. GRANT intended this movement as a demonstration to aid SHERMAN, still sticking to his original plan. Nor is it discreditable to his generalship that he hesitated to order an assault of that great fortress; for, although heroic soldiers might do it, it was hardly a thing for a General to order troops to do, still less to make the main part in a plan of battle. Even as BADEAU states it, the order is vague and indecisive, and if literally followed would have been almost certain to defeat the assault. If that high, steep, rough, and fortified ridge could be stormed at all, it must be by rapid movement and a surprise, following the Confederate troops from their intrenchments at the base, up the steeps, before they could reform and recover, just as it was done. To have halted in the intrenchments at the foot, under a storm of fire from the sides and crest, to reform the lines, "with a view to carrying the top of the ridge," would have given the enemy time to recover from panic, and reform their lines for defense, in that position which Gen. BRAGG said "ought to have been held by a line of skirmishers against an assaulting column."

The intelligence of the soldiers told them the foolishness of such generalship. The soldiers of THOMAS' army, which GRANT told SHERMAN were so demoralized by Chickamauga that they could not be got out of the trenches to fight, until SHERMAN'S troops had set them an example, had been chafing all day with impatience to attack. Says Gen. GRANGER:

For hours my command from behind their breastworks anxiously and impatiently watched this struggle of their brothers in arms away off to the left on the northern end of the ridge. * * * As the day wore on their impatience of restraint gathered force, and their desire to advance became almost uncontrollable.

This eagerness of the soldiers, let loose by the order to move forward, inspired by an enthusiasm which could not be stopped, threw the Confederate troops into complete panic, and carried that mountain, which by all rational military calculations was impregnable. It is evident that Gen. GRANT at this time had no clear idea of what he intended, and that he had not yet thrown off his original plan, by which the successful part was given to SHERMAN, and the demonstrating part to THOMAS. Fortunately the soldiers of the ranks and their immediate officers were far more intelligent than the commanding generalship.

This indecision and vagueness of the mind and orders of the Commanding General allow bold relief to the clear orders issued by Gen. THOMAS. That at 9:30 p. m. of the 24th, to HOOKER, concluded with this:

Be in readiness to advance as early as possible in the morning into Chattanooga Valley, and seize and hold the Summertown road and co-operate with the 14th Corps by supporting its right.

At 8 a. m. of the 25th he ordered by both signal and an aide:

Leave Carlin's brigade at Summertown road to rejoin Gen. Palmer. Move with the remainder of your force, except two regiments to hold Lookout, on the Rossville road toward Mission Ridge, looking well to your right flank.

At 10 a. m. he sent to HOOKER by signal the following:

I wish you and Gen. Palmer to move forward firmly and steadily upon the enemy's works in front, using Gen. Sheridan as a pivot.

Gen. THOMAS had now four divisions in front of Gen. BRAGG's center, which was held by three divisions and part of another, the other part having turned to help resist HOOKER's approach. WOOD's and SHERIDAN's divisions were in the center; JOHNSON's on the right of SHERIDAN, and BAIRD's on the left of WOOD. The brigades of these divisions were in the following order, from right to left: CARLIN's and STOUGHTON's, of JOHNSON's; SHERMAN'S, HOOKER's, and WAGNER's, of SHERIDAN's; HAZEN's, WILLICH's, and BEATTY's, of WOOD's; TURCHIN's, VANDERVEER's, and PHELPS', of BAIRD's. Two lines of skirmishers covered the battle front, and the several reserves were massed in the rear of their respective corps.

The Confederate forces and dispositions on Mission Ridge, on the morning of the 25th, are thus stated in VAN HORNE's history of the Army of the Cumberland:

Gen. Bragg now had his entire army on Mission Ridge. Cleburne's and Gist's divisions were on the extreme right opposed to Sherman; his left was held by Stewart's division; his center by Breckinridge's old division, and portions of the commands of Buckner and Hindman, under Gen. Anderson; and the divisions of Cheatham and Stevenson, fresh from defeat on Lookout Mountain, were in motion toward the right. The two parts of the army before Gens. Sherman and Thomas were commanded respectively by Gens. Hardee and Breckinridge.

Six successive guns on Orchard Knob gave to THOMAS' four divisions the signal to advance, between 3 and 4 p. m., and the lines moved forward in magnificent array. The batteries on the ridge opened upon them, and those of the national intrenchments answered, firing first at the intrenchments at the base of the ridge, and then, as our advancing troops quickly came in the way, at the top of the ridge. The advancing lines came first upon the enemy's pickets and their reserves, then his troops in the woods, and then, in their irresistible march, driving the line from the intrenchment at the bases in confusion up the hill. A thousand Confederates were here captured. All this operation was against the fire of as many as fifty guns along the crest, and against BRAGG's efforts to strengthen his lower line.

The troops had now done all that their orders required; but to halt under the fire of these guns on the crest was to halt for death, and to wait was to give the Confederate troops time to reform behind their strong intrenchments on the summit of the ridge. The completion of what GRANT had ordered had left them under a storm of fire from the crest and sides of the mountain, with no outcome. It had left the troops to their own intuitions under fire. It was a time when the intelligence of the ranks rose far above the generalship. With one spontaneous impulse the whole line, as much as two miles long, went on to climb the hill under a storm of fire of artillery and musketry. They advanced not in line, but in such parts as enabled them to avail of easier ascent or partial cover. They went up without firing, though receiving a destructive fire. The officers of all grades were inspired by the spirit of the men of the ranks, and so spontaneous was the spirit that the crest was reached and carried at six different points at the same time.

The Confederate troops were quickly driven from their intrenchments on the crest, and from all their guns. BAIRD's division, which had carried its whole front on the ridge, turned to the north in line across the crest, and advanced to meet CHEATHAM's division, which had been hurried forward by HARDEE to support ANDERSON's division, which was in confused retreat. A sharp contest followed, in which BAIRD drove this fresh division from several knolls, when night and the difficulties of the enemy's position closed the fight. Gen. WOOD's division, which VAN HORNE, from BRAGG's account, thinks was first to reach the summit, enfiladed the Confederates to right and left, and one of his brigades (WILLICH's) with SHERIDAN's division pursued the enemy down the eastern slope.

Gen. BRAGG's report relates that he had gone to his left to make disposition to secure that flank (from HOOKER's column), as by the road across the ridge at Rossville "a route was open to our rear." When the national troops advanced, he thought that the hot fire from the ridge had repulsed them, but "while riding along the crest, congratulating the troops, intelligence reached me that our line was broken on my right, and the enemy had crowned the ridge."

He dispatched to that point Gen. BATE, who had held the ground in his front, but he found the disaster too great for his force to repair. Then he learned that his extreme left had given way, and that his position was almost surrounded. He directed BATE to form a second line in the rear. BRAGG relates that Gen. HARDEE had moved from the north end of the ridge toward the left, when he heard the heavy firing; that he reached the right of ANDERSON's division just in time to find it had nearly all fallen back, commencing on its left where the enemy had first crossed the ridge; that he promptly threw a part of CHEATHAM's division across the ridge, and made a stand by which the further advance of the national troops toward the north end of the ridge was stayed.

But Gen. BRAGG says:

All to the left, except a portion of Bate's division, was entirely routed and in rapid flight, nearly all the artillery having been shamefully abandoned. ◊ * ◊ A panic, such as I had never before witnessed, seemed to have seized upon officers and men, and each seemed to be struggling for his personal safety regardless of his duty or his character. In this distressing and alarming state of affairs, Gen. Bate was ordered to hold his position. covering the road for the retreat of Breckinridge's command; and orders were immediately sent to Gens. Hardee and Breckinridge to retire their forces upon the depot at Chickamauga.

Fortunately it was now near nightfall, and the country and roads in our rear were fully known to us, but equally unknown to the enemy. The routed left made its way back in great disorder, effectually covered, however, by Bate's small command, which had a sharp conflict with the enemy's advance, driving it back. After night, all being quiet, all retired in good order, the enemy attempting no pursuit. Lieut. Gen. Hardee's command, under his judicious management, retired in good order and unmolested. As soon as all the troops had crossed, the bridges over the Chickamauga were destroyed to impede the enemy, though the stream was fordable at several places.

So disjointed had GRANT's operation become by the failure of Gen. SHERMAN in that which the plan designed for the decisive attack, that SHERMAN, during the battle of the ridge, was making no demonstration to prevent the withdrawing of a large force from the north end of the ridge, to resist the advance of THOMAS' troops along the summit. This eventually stopped their progress, and night ended the action, giving to BRAGG all night for retreat.

Gen. THOMAS' report, with characteristic modesty of language, has this account of the storming of the ridge, which was ordered as soon as Gen. BAIRD's division, returning from SHERMAN, had got into line on WOOD's left;

Orders were then given to move forward on Granger's left, and within supporting distance, against the enemy's riflepits on the slope and at the foot of Mission Ridge. The whole line then advanced against the breastworks, and soon became engaged with the enemy's skirmishers. These, giving way, retired upon their reserves, posted within their works, our troops advancing steadily in a continuous line. The enemy, seized with panic, abandoned the works at the foot of the hill and retreated precipitately to the crest, where they were closely followed by our troops, who, apparently inspired by the impulse of victory, carried the hill simultaneously at six different points, and so closely upon the heels of the enemy that many of them were taken prisoners in the trenches.

The report of Gen. GORDON GRANGER, whose corps was composed of WOOD's and SHERIDAN's divisions, has a more graphic and enthusiastic narration, in which is more distinctly set forth that the movement to the ridge was ordered as a demonstration, and that the ascent was without orders. It is likely that this report was unhealthy to Gen. GRANGER's subsequent fortunes, in the military necessity to show that all came about as Gen. GRANT had ordered. Says GRANGER:

Gen. Sherman was unable to make any progress in moving along the ridge during the day, as the enemy had massed in his front; therefore, in order to relieve him, I was ordered to make a demonstration upon the works of the enemy directly in my front, at the base of Mission Ridge. I accordingly directed Maj. Gen. Sheridan and Brig. Gen. Wood to advance their divisions at a given signal, moving directly forward simultaneously and briskly to attack the enemy, and, driving him from his riflepits, take possession of them.

At twenty minutes before 4 o'clock p. m. six guns, the signal agreed upon, were fired in rapid succession, and before the smoke had cleared away, these divisions, Sheridan on the right and Wood on the left, had cleared the breastworks that had sheltered them for two days, and were moving forward. * * * It pleases me to report that scarcely a straggler could be seen as this magnificent line, stretching one mile from end to end, swept through the valley up to the assault. At the moment of the advance of these troops Mission Ridge blazed with fire from the batteries which lined its summit. Not less than fifty guns opened at once, throwing a terrible shower of shot and shell.

The enemy now taking the alarm, commenced to move troops from both extremities of the ridge for the purpose of filling the ranks below and around these batteries. In the meantime the troops holding the woods were driven back to the works at the base of the ridge, their pursuers rapidly following. Here they halted and made a stout resistance, but our troops, by an impetuous assault, broke this line in several places; then scaling the breastworks at these points, opened a flank and reserve fire upon them, which, throwing them into confusion, caused their precipitate flight. * * *

My orders had now been fully and successfully carried out, but not enough had been done to satisfy the brave troops who had accomplished so much. Although the batteries on the ridge at short range, by direct and enfilading fire, were still pouring upon them a shower of iron, and the musketry from the hillsides were thinning their ranks, they dashed over the breastworks, through the riflepits, and started up the ridge. They started without orders. Along the whole line of both divisions, from right to left and from left to right, simultaneously and with one accord, animated with one spirit, and, with heroic courage, eagerly they rushed forward to a danger before which the bravest, marching under orders, might tremble.

Officers caught the enthusiasm of the men, and the men in turn cheered the officers. Each regiment tried to surpass the other in fighting its way up a hill that would try those of stout limb and strong lungs to climb, and each tried first to plant its flag on the summit. Above these men were an additional line of riflepits filled with troops. What was on the summit they knew not, and did not stop to inquire. The enemy was before them; to know that was to know sufficient.

At several points along the line my troops were ascending the hill and gaining positions less exposed to the enemy's artillery fire, though more exposed to the fire of the musketry. Seeing this, I sent my Adjutant General to inquire first of Gen. Wood and then of Gen. Sheridan, whether the troops had been ordered up the ridge by them, and to instruct them to take the ridge if possible. In reply to this, Gen. Wood told him that the men had started without orders, and that he could take it if he could be supported. In the meantime an aide-de-camp from Gen. Sheridan had reported to me that the General wished to know whether the orders that had been given to take the rifle pits "meant those at the base of the ridge or those on top."

My reply was that the order had been to take those at the base. Conceiving this to be an order to fall back to those rifle pits, and on his way so reporting it to Gen. Wagner, commanding 2d Brigade of Sheridan's division, this brigade was withdrawn from a position which it had gained on the side of the ridge to the rifle pits, which was being raked by the enemy's artillery, and from this point starting again under a terrible fire, made the ascent of the ridge. My Assistant Adjutant General, on his way to Gen. Sheridan, reported to me Gen. Wood's reply, but, by my instructions, went no further with the message I had given him, as I had already sent Capt. Avery, my Aide-de-Camp, directly to Maj. Gen. Sheridan, instructing him to go ahead and take the ridge if he could.

Gen. GRANGER says that the time from leaving Orchard Knob to reaching the crest was one hour; that SHERIDAN, with two brigades, passed over the ridge, pursuing the troops who fled down the southern slope toward Chickamauga Station, till in about a mile he came up with a large body, strongly posted, which, by a charge, he put to flight; that WOOD and BAIRD formed to meet a large force coming from the north end of the ridge, and a sharp contest lasted till dark. GRANGER claims the capture of thirty-one guns and 3,812 men, and says his command lost in the action 20.21 per cent. in killed and wounded. This brilliant action and unexpected success was not gained without heavy losses of brave men. GRANGER's corps lost 2.337 killed, wounded, and missing, of whom only two are classed as missing. JOHNSON's division lost 304 killed and wounded; BAIRD's division, 565, out of a total of 1,679, being over one-third. BAIRD claimed more than 300 prisoners; JOHNSON, 1,165 prisoners. The captures of men and guns belong, in justice, to all the troops alike, as well to those who pursued the enemy as to those who had time to gather up the abandoned guns and surrendered men.

All the evidence shows that not only did the troops storm the ridge without orders, but that a part of the line, in front of the strongest resistance, was disconcerted for a time, in the ascent, by a recall. The officers knew that the assault was unauthorized, and had good reason to fear the responsibility if it should fail. VAN HORNE says:

The division commanders did not arrest their troops, and for a time the corps Generals did not give official sanction to their advance. The impression, indeed, so far prevailed that the movement would not be authorized, that Turchin's brigade, on the right of Baird's division, was halted when far up the ascent; and Wagner's brigade, on the left of Sheridan's division, was recalled from its advanced position by a staff officer who was returning to Gen. Sheridan from Gen. Granger, with the information that Grant's order required only that the enemy's intrenched line at the base of the ridge should be carried. Soon, however, it was apparent to all that the eagerness of the troops had created a necessity superior to the limitations of orders, and this conviction gave unity and energy to the assault, whose transcendent issue justified its otherwise unauthorized execution.

Gen. HOOKER, coming from Lookout, had been detained three hours rebuilding the bridge over Chattanooga Creek. He then pushed forward to a gorge in the south end of Mission Ridge, which was strongly held, and here the enemy were trying to cover a train of wagons which was loading with stores at the Rossville House. Under HOOKER's threatening dispositions to carry the ridge on all sides, the enemy abandoned this gorge and the stores. HOOKER then swept up along the ridge on both sides and on top, meeting the enemy in a line of breastworks, but driving him by the impetuosity of his attack, and soon as they made successive stands where the ground favored them, until the greater part were scattered in flight, or killed or captured, and the remainder ran into JOHNSON's division, and were made prisoners. It was now night, and the troops rested on the ridge.

CHAPTER LXV.

THE PURSUIT FROM MISSION RIDGE—MOST DESTRUCTIVE TO THE PURSUERS—THE LOSSES IN THE BATTLE—THE RELATIVE FORCES—SHERMAN'S GREAT MARCH TOWARD KNOXVILLE—THE COUNTERMARCH—LONGSTREET STAYS IN EAST TENNESSEE.

Mission Ridge was carried too late in the day to admit of pursuit of such of the Confederate army as had fled down the eastern side, or to finish the fight against HARDEE's command, which still held the north end of the ridge opposite Gen. SHERMAN's army. A part of SHERIDAN's division and Gen WILLICH's brigade of WOOD's division had pursued down the eastern slope, and later on SHERIDAN had driven them from a strong position, but night put a stop to his pursuit and to further fighting on the north end of the ridge.

Gen. GRANT ordered Gen. THOMAS to recall WOOD's and SHERIDAN's divisions to join SHERMAN in an expedition to Knoxville to relieve BURNSIDE's army, which was threatened by both LONGSTREET and starvation, and to pursue Bragg with the rest. Accordingly Gen. Thomas ordered these to start for Knoxville, and Palmer and Hooker to make pursuit. Grant on the same night ordered Sherman to move to Knoxville, but toward the latter part of the order he doubted, like this:

> I take it for granted that Bragg's entire force has left. If not, of course the first thing is to dispose of him. If he has gone, the only thing necessary to do to-morrow will be to send out a reconnaissance to ascertain the whereabouts of the enemy.

But he changed his mind in a postscript as follows:

> P. S.—On reflection, I think we will push Bragg with all our strength to-morrow, and try if we can not cut off a good portion of his rear troops and trains. His men have manifested a strong disposition to desert for some time past, and we will now give them a chance. I will instruct Thomas accordingly. Move the advance force early on the most easterly route taken by the enemy.

Thus Granger's corps was withdrawn for Knoxville, and Sherman, the commander of the Knoxville expedition, went after Bragg. Hooker, however, was in the most advanced position, and he followed the enemy with great energy.

To follow this chase is not necessary to this review. One of Gen. Grant's principal military ideas was that the pursuit of a retreating army was the time for crowning achievements. He has made record of his complaints against Rosecrans and Thomas for lack of swiftness in such chase. He thought that from Washington he could order Thomas to pursue, after his victory of Nashville, better than Thomas could. He desired the administration to hold back any promotion of Thomas for that decisive battle until he had seen whether Thomas would pursue with swiftness. He complained that Rosecrans, after his victory at Corinth, did not chase the enemy.

But in this country, where the retreating enemy has to be followed in a stern chase by roads and defiles through woods and mountains, and by bridges, nothing can be made by pursuit of an army which has defiled into the roads and has got a good start. At the worst it can run as fast as the following troops can follow, and if it has an organized rear guard, it can obstruct the way by destroying bridges and felling trees, so as to make the chase not only vain, but destructive to the pursuers, who at each stand made by the retreating troops must deploy and attack against advantages of position.

Gen. Grant never made anything by such a chase, nor was anything made in all our war. Besides, a general battle is always preceded by hard marching, loss of sleep, and great nervous strain, and to order soldiers on forced marches after one or two days of battle is a hardness which assumes that they are nothing but machines. This pursuit was made with great energy for two days, Hooker's troops being in the lead, and, with a dashing valor which hesitated not for consequences; but it destroyed more of our victorious soldiers than of the enemy. And this forced march of Sherman's hardly used troops for two days, in a direction from which they had to return, seriously delayed his march to the relief of Burnside, while it accomplished nothing.

On the second day Hooker's troops had a long action with Cleburne's division at Taylor's Ridge, where it had taken position in a mountain gorge to cover the fording and withdrawal of the supply train. Artillery was brought up, dispositions made, and an attack, which, of course, was made with great gallantry; but when the train had passed, Cleburne defiled through the gorge in safety. Here the pursuit ended. It had been made without regard to the condition or the lives of the troops, and they had behaved with their wonted heroism, but it was, in fact, an abuse of the troops, and a sacrifice of brave veterans upon that dreadful calculation, which afterward had so vast an exercise in the Army of the Potomac, that we could afford to sacrifice three national soldiers to one Confederate.

Adam Badeau fails not to cast a reflection on Gen. Thomas for default in the pursuit, by this: "Grant was with the pursuing column, but on the night of the battle Thomas returned to Chattanooga, and did not rejoin his troops." Thomas had more important duties, as a General, than to follow in a hunt, and Hooker needed neither Thomas nor Grant. In the action at Taylor's Ridge Hooker lost 422 killed and wounded. Grant's idea that the great part of a battle was the after chase, had given to Cleburne the opportunity to wind up the affair by inflicting this check and loss of brave soldiers.

In this chase Gen. Davis' division of the

Army of the Cumberland, now with SHERMAN, crossed the South Chickamauga near the mouth, and moved in pursuit along the north side of that river. He came upon one column of the retreating enemy and had a sharp conflict, but the enemy made good his retreat, and DAVIS' line of march brought him into HOOKER'S rear. Gen. HOWARD crossed by the same way, and took a course further to the east, and detached a column to destroy the railroad between Dalton and Cleveland, with a view to sever connection between BRAGG and LONGSTREET. This done he returned. And now the expedition to relieve BURNSIDE was committed to SHERMAN, with HOWARD'S corps, GRANGER'S corps, and DAVIS' division from THOMAS' army, besides three divisions of his own army, This would seem to be an adequate force. HOOKER was ordered to remain at Ringgold to cover SHERMAN'S march from BRAGG, by keeping up a feint of pursuit, and Col. LONG was sent out with a cavalry expedition on SHERMAN'S flank to destroy communications and supplies.

Gen. SHERMAN'S report states his loss in the attack on the ridge as 1,949 killed, wounded, and missing, not including DAVIS' division. The attack by the troops under his command was made with great valor, but Gen. GRANT'S profound strategy in this battle had lighted upon the strongest place in BRAGG'S position for his main attack, just as his fortune had done at the battle of Champion's Hill. VAN HORNE states the aggregate losses of the armies of the Cumberland and Tennessee as 5,616, of whom 330 are set down as missing. He gives the loss of the enemy by capture as 6,142 men, 42 guns, and 7,000 small arms; their loss in killed and in such of the wounded as could get away, not known.

BADEAU says: "The enemy's losses were fewer in killed and wounded, owing to the fact that he was protected by intrenchments," but that "the rebel losses were reported at 367 killed, 2,180 wounded, and 4,146 missing." GRANT had added to the Army of the Cumberland four divisions from the Army of the Tennessee and four from the Army of the Potomac, while BRAGG, since Chickamauga, had reduced his force by sending off LONGSTREET with 15,000. That the victorious army lost more than twice as many as the defeated in killed and wounded is because the strategy of the battle had pitched upon BRAGG'S strongest positions for attack.

Gen. GRANT'S total force was probably double that of Gen. BRAGG, but was strangely separated and disposed by his plan of action, which had the singular fortune that the attack which gained the victory, after that which the plan meant for the decisive action had been repulsed, was made by four much reduced divisions, against nearly as large a force, on a natural fortress, while six divisions were inactive under SHERMAN. And this assault, which turned a defeated plan to a glorious victory, was made by those troops of the Army of the Cumberland, of whom GRANT told SHERMAN that they were so demoralized that they could not be gotten out of the trenches to fight until SHERMAN'S troops had set them an example. Although Gen. GRANT'S strategy had aimed to give the victory to Gen. SHERMAN'S army, holding Gen. THOMAS' army as demoralized, there was a fitness of things in its being carried in the main by the Army of the Cumberland, which had made the great campaign that gained the strategic objective of Chattanooga, and which had joined issue with BRAGG and LONGSTREET at Chickamauga.

Gen. SHERMAN'S march with more than seven divisions of infantry, and a strong cavalry force, might be expected to do something destructive to LONGSTREET in East Tennessee. but his objective was limited to the relieving of Knoxville, where BURNSIDE was now closely held, although not completely invested. LONGSTREET had made very active and resolute operations to recover East Tennessee, and wholly to cut off BURNSIDE, but had been repulsed and foiled in repeated engagements, while BURNSIDE fell back before his superior forces to Knoxville. LONGSTREET continued his intrenched approaches and tentative attacks at Knoxville from the 18th to the 29th, when he resolved to carry the place by assault. This was made in a most determined manner on a point of the works named Fort Sanders, and was repulsed, with a loss of 1,500 killed, wounded, and prisoners. [WOODBURY'S Burnside and the 9th Army Corps.] This was on the day that SHERMAN'S march from Chattanooga began. LONGSTREET now fell back; hearing of which SHERMAN halted before he got to Knoxville. He went there himself, and decided to return, leaving GRANGER'S corps.

Gen. SHERMAN began his return soon after the 7th of December. His report says: "By the 9th all our troops were in position, and we held the rich country between the Little Tennessee and the Hiawassee." This was a breadth of country east and west, about half way between Chattanooga and Knoxville. SHERMAN continues: "On the 14th of December all of my command in the field lay along the Hiawassee. Having communicated to Gen. GRANT the actual state of affairs, I received orders to leave on the line of the Hiawassee all the cavalry, and come to Chattanooga." LONGSTREET fell back but a little way, when finding that the relieving army was returning, he settled in East Tennessee for the winter.

CHAPTER LXVI.

REVIEW OF THE STRATEGY OF THE BATTLES—THE PLAN FOUNDED WHOLLY ON A FALSE CONCEPTION OF THE SITUATION—THE SPONTANEOUS ACTION OF THE SOLDIERS ACHIEVES VICTORY CONTRARY TO THE PLAN—GEN. THOMAS—THE AMERICAN VOLUNTEER—WAR TRADITIONS AND MILITARY GLORY.

The victory in the battle of Mission Ridge was achieved by attacking positions which, in a military sense, were impregnable—positions so strong that to plan a battle to depend on them would be a military crime, and, in case of repulse, these natural fortresses would stand as monuments of the monstrous generalship which ordered an army to certain butchery without a possibility of success.

The victory is distinguished as achieved by the soldiers of the ranks, when the Commanding General's plan had elaborately provided conditions which, upon all rational calculations, made defeat certain. According to the plan, the army's situation for the battle was to be as follows:

Part of the army, under Gen. HOOKER, was to be in Lookout Valley, separated from the center at Chattanooga by Lookout Mountain and a wide valley—both held by the enemy—and by two crossings of the river, making any support of either part by the other, in a battle, impossible, the Confederates possessing Lookout Mountain and having the opportunity to fall upon HOOKER's isolated force, and again cut off the army's supplies.

Another part of the army was to be in the Chattanooga fortifications, environed by the Confederate picket line, from the river below the town to the river above; this picket line and its reserves having the line of Pilot Knob for its base, and, across a plain from this, the intrenched base of Mission Ridge, beyond which the ridge, crowned with the Confederate army, seemed impregnable, and was so if resolutely defended by the troops who held it.

Four miles from the left of this central position SHERMAN, with another part of the army, was to make the attack, and the center was to await his success in carrying the head of the ridge. To give to SHERMAN this opportunity, his army was to be brought through Lookout Valley, past HOOKER, and then up the west side of the river past Chattanooga, his march concealed by the hills, and then was to cross by pontoons four miles above Chattanooga, and come upon BRAGG's flank and rear by surprise.

As thus divided and isolated by long distances and great barriers, each of the three parts of the army was confronted by a great natural fortress, which in a military sense was impregnable. But the plan was wholly based upon the strange delusion that Gen. BRAGG had left the head of Mission Ridge, on his right, commanding his depot of supplies at Chickamauga Station, unfortified. Upon this belief was made all this delay, this strategic march of SHERMAN, and all the great engineer preparations.

But prior to this plan and to SHERMAN's coming, Gen. GRANT, on the 7th of November, ordered Gen. THOMAS to "attack and carry the north end of Mission Ridge, and, when that is carried, to threaten and even attack, if possible, the enemy's lines of communication between Dalton and Cleveland." From the result of SHERMAN's attack on that point with six divisions, while THOMAS confronted the breast of the ridge, and HOOKER was advancing upon its south end, may be reckoned the probable consequences if THOMAS alone had tried to execute this extraordinary order. If THOMAS could do all that, he could have fought the battle and gone on into Georgia, and there was no need for SHERMAN to come. Fortunately, Gen. THOMAS' sound judgment saved his army from this ordered destruction.

When it was found that all this great preparation and effort had brought SHERMAN to the front of the strongest and most dangerous position in the Confederate line, and that not only was it impregnably fortified, but peculiar preparation had been made for counter attack, the plan was exhausted. It consisted so entirely in Bragg's being taken by surprise, unguarded, on the north end of the ridge, that when the mistake of this calculation was realized, the plan had no alternative.

But the affair was rescued from the plan of the Commanding General by the energy and sagacity of the subordinate commanders, and by the spirit of the soldiers, which went far ahead of the expectations of their officers. The length and hinderances of Sherman's movement, and meanwhile a mistaken report by a deserter that Bragg was retiring, caused Grant to order a reconnaissance by Gen. Thomas to ascertain the truth, which Thomas converted into an advance in force that carried the enemy's first intrenched line and gave to the army confronting the ridge a fortified base more than a mile nearer to Mission Ridge than its previous line. This had not been in the plan, and it may be seen how greatly it changed the situation with regard to the possibility of storming Mission Ridge.

The continued delays to Sherman's movement, and Gen. Thomas' solicitude lest the enemy's information should defeat it, caused Hooker's attack on Lookout Mountain, which wonderfully succeeded. This made a radical change in the situation. It was not in Grant's plan, nor would a General be justified in making plan of operations which depended on carrying such a mountain. This opened the way up the valley of Chattanooga Creek, around the south end of Mission Ridge, and up a valley on the east side of the ridge by which Bragg could be taken in rear.

Here was a fortunate deliverance from the plan, if there had been generalship to grasp the new situation. There was no longer any need to assault mountains. Completer results could be gained with less sacrifice. But Gen. Grant, with characteristic firmness, clung to his plan that Sherman should make the successful attack, and so Sherman hurled his brave troops against an impregnable position and slaughtered them. The center had been reduced to send aid to Sherman, but he found that to repeat the attack was only to repeat the slaughter in vain, and he rested; and now the plan was exhausted.

Gen. Thomas was ordered to make a demonstration in aid of Sherman, but Sherman did not respond. Grant's order of the demonstration was strange and undecided. To make a demonstration by storming the intrenchments at the base of the ridge, and then to stop, was to demonstrate in a way that might be expected to be slaughterous, and then to stop under a storm of fire from the sides and crest of the mountain.

Fortunately, the spirit of the soldiers of the ranks cast off this vague order, and went on to storm the great ridge. The spontaneous enthusiasm rescued the battle from the Commanding General's plan; rescued it by storming a position so strong that no General would have been justified in making its assault a part of his plan. The Commanding General's extremity was the opportunity for the volunteers of the ranks, and they gained a victory, whose glory all perched upon Gen. Grant's head.

To say that Gen. Grant, with an army twice as great as Gen. Bragg's, could find in all that region no way to operate against him, save by a front attack against Lookout Mountain and Mission Ridge, is to slander his military capacity. Justice to him demands that it be said that he did not plan such an operation, but that his plan depended wholly on Sherman's finding the north end of Mission Ridge unfortified, and thereby an open way to Bragg's depot of supplies, and that nothing fell out as Grant had planned.

Yet Adam Badeau admirably remarks:

Few battles have ever been won so strictly according to the plan laid down; certainly no battle during the war of the rebellion was carried out so completely according to the programme. Grant's instructions in advance would almost serve as a history of the contest.

He then reconstructs the plan to fit the event losing sight of the whole foundation—namely, that Sherman was to find the depot of supplies unguarded, and bringing in Hooker "to draw attention to the right," and converting Sherman's attack into a demonstration "to still further distract the enemy; and then, when re-enforcements and attention should be drawn to both the rebel flanks, the center was to be assaulted by the main body of Grant's force under Thomas."

But as it happened, two divisions were sent from our center to aid Sherman, giving him seven divisions to "distract" with, and leaving to THOMAS only three divisions for the real assault. And when one of these returned, still THOMAS' command at the center was far from being "the main body of GRANT's force." BADEAU winds up his effort with this: "Everything happened exactly as had been foreseen."

Gen. SHERMAN also disparages the brave fighting of his troops by the after assertion that it was only a feint at one end, while HOOKER was to feint at the other. He says in the memoirs:

The object of Gen. Hooker's and my attacks on the extreme flanks of Bragg's position was to disturb him to such an extent that he would naturally detach from his center as against us, so that Thomas' army could break through his center. The whole plan succeeded admirably.

Gen. SHERMAN forgot that only two pages previous to this he had narrated how GRANT told him that "he believed that the northern portion of Mission Ridge was not fortified at all," and how elaborately his plan of a concealed march was formed upon this belief.

In Flanders our army was remarkable for profanity; in the great secession war our greatest Generals were distinguished for veracity.

In fact, Gen. BRAGG did not strip his center, although SHERMAN "disturbed" his right with six divisions, and another in sight; his force in the center was enough, if the troops had fought with their usual valor; but the enthusiasm of our soldiers threw them into panic—a thing which could not be looked for, much less made a dependence in the plan of a great battle.

From the blind plan and indecisive orders of the Commanding General, the clear orders of Gen. THOMAS stand out admirably in relief. They show that he knew just what he wanted to do, and that his orders were all the time in advance of the mind of the Commanding General, comprehending the whole situation, and gaining successes in advance of orders, which were not in GRANT's plan, and which so changed the situation that the heroic spirit of the soldiers was able to snatch victory from the jaws of a planned failure. In all this he was brilliantly seconded by HOOKER's untiring energy and military skill. And this splendid achievement of the Army of the Cumberland was the fruit of a thorough training which began with Gen. BUELL and Gen. THOMAS, and had made it invincible.

The civil war extended the breadth of a continent; yet it was less than the solar system, which, vast as it is, allows but one sun, round which all the other planets must revolve, shining only by reflecting sunbeams. Even a continental army system can not be expected to be exempt from the conditions which govern the solar system. Glancing forward to Gen. GRANT's historian's third volume, the reader observes that Gen. GRANT was much dissatisfied with Gen. THOMAS' slowness at Chattanooga; that this was one of the alleged reasons for GRANT's order to remove THOMAS from command while the battle of Nashville was imminent—an order which, fortunately for the country, failed of connection; that after that completest victory of the war, which destroyed the offensive power of the Confederate army of the interior, Gen. GRANT determined to strip Gen. THOMAS of troops, and allow him no more a command in any active operations. All of this is more fully set down in GRANT's letters to SHERMAN, printed in his memoirs.

Another instance of the operation of the same solar law was seen in the Atlanta campaign of the following year, after Gen. MCPHERSON was killed, in that Gen. SHERMAN advanced to the command of the Army of the Tennessee, over Gen. HOOKER's head, Gen. HOWARD, HOOKER's subordinate, whose neglect of HOOKER's orders at Chancellorsville, and of all rational military precautions, upon his shallow conceit that LEE was retreating, subjected his corps to a surprise, and sacrificed the campaign.

The victory in the battles about Chattanooga was gained by the volunteers of the ranks. The more one studies the history of the great war, the more is he impressed with admiration for the qualities of the American citizen volunteer soldier, and with the fervent belief that they were the best soldiers in the world. The greatness of a whole people is a better cause for national pride than the eminence of an individual. These splendid martial qualities and this grand patriotism, in the volunteers of the ranks, are infinitely a higher national glory than the single genius of a Bonaparte, even if our war had developed a Bonaparte.

But war has a terrible sarcasm in its traditions, which heap all the glory of the patriotism, heroic valor, heroic death, and dear victories of the volunteers of the ranks, upon the head of a Commanding General who may even have been an incumbrance. The battles about Chattanooga raised Gen. GRANT's military fame to its zenith, and resulted in his call to the East to the command of all the national armies. His history affords an instructive lesson in the possibilities of commanding generalship and in the nature of military fame.

CHAPTER LXVII.

REVIEW OF THE EFFECT OF THE VICKSBURG CAMPAIGN ON THE ARMY OF THE OHIO AND BURNSIDE'S EAST TENNESSEE CAMPAIGN.

As soon as Knoxville had been relieved, Gen. BURNSIDE, who had asked to be relieved from the command because of ill health, as soon as he had gained East Tennessee, but had continued at LINCOLN's special request, now asked to be relieved, and he left on the 7th of December. Gen. FOSTER soon arrived to take command, the active command devolving on Gen. PARKE, BURNSIDE's Chief of Staff.

Gen. HALLECK had now rewarded Gen. BURNSIDE for the brilliant campaign which had seized the long coveted East Tennessee, and had held it by numerous engagements against superior numbers, by promoting him to the responsible office of scapegoat—a very essential office in all wars, and transcendently so in that romantic style of war whose remote campaigns are directed by dispatches from Washington, dictated by a General in Chief whose theory of war was so untrammeled by real conditions as Gen. HALLECK's telegraphic campaign orders.

The conduct of the Army of the Ohio after Gen. BURNSIDE took command had so important a relation to the Vicksburg campaign, the Chattanooga campaign of the Army of the Cumberland, and the subsequent operations under the command of Gen. GRANT, that a review of these would be incomplete which did not touch upon this part. When Gen. BURNSIDE was appointed to the command of the Department of the Ohio, in the last of March, 1863, he called for more force, and in April two divisions of the 9th Corps arrived in Kentucky. The Confederate expeditions into Kentucky were very active at this time, aiming at the communications of ROSECRANS' army.

On the 27th of April Gen. BURNSIDE organized the other troops in Kentucky into the 23d Army Corps. The intention was to move into East Tennessee, which from the beginning had been the cherished object of the government, and which was now to be undertaken by BURNSIDE with the two divisions of the 9th Corps and the hastily organized 23d Corps, under Gen. HARTSUFF. Says WOODBURY's history:

Gen. Burnside submitted to Gen. Rosecrans a plan for a co-operative movement upon East Tennessee. With the advice of Gen. Thomas it was accepted, and preparations were accordingly made by the two commanders. The troops were properly concentrated for the movement, and on the 2d of June Gen. Burnside left his headquarters at Cincinnati and proceeded to Lexington to take command. The time was ripe for the operation, and officers and men were eager for the service. The 9th Corps, strengthened by a division under Gen. Carter, was to march directly into East Tennessee by way of Monticello. Gen. Hartsuff was to follow in support. Gen. Rosecrans was to advance upon Chattanooga.

This plan gives a glimpse of real war—of war lifted out from raids and disjointed, centrifugal, seesaw campaigns, and placed upon a connected and mutually supporting plan. But it was not to be. Gen. GRANT's abandonment of the Mississippi Central movement, and his diffusive expedition 'to' isolate his great army at Vicksburg, had withdrawn the grand right wing of this operation, and now his situation was to withdraw the left wing just as the Army of the Cumberland in the center was about to start. If war is so near an art that rational calculations can be made upon positive conditions of forces and plans, is it too much to say that if these armies had been in the interior, co-operating, their march could not have been successfully opposed anywhere? Upon the same premises is it too much to say that when HALLECK withdrew the 9th Corps from BURNSIDE at this time to send to GRANT at Vicksburg, he dealt the campaign of ROSECRANS a fatal blow? This sacrifice was a part of the cost of the Vicksburg campaign. And upon the same premises is it presumptuous to say that if a great genius had been directing our armies with intent to thwart them, he could not have done it more effectually?

Gen. BURNSIDE, on the eve of starting for the field, received an ominous inquiry from Washington, if any troops could be spared from the Department of the Ohio to assist Gen. GRANT. Soon an order reached BURNSIDE, at Lexington, to send 8,000 men to GRANT. The 9th Corps, except one regiment, whose term of service was nearly out, was promptly dispatched upon this order of urgency. This enforced the suspension of the East Tennessee co-operation. And while the military authorities were stripping ROSECRANS of co-operation, and laying open his flanks west and east, and were devoting the great means of every sort to the supply and increase of GRANT's army, and were denying to ROSECRANS any further aid, they were peremptorily ordering him to advance, unsupported, more than a hundred miles further into the heart of the South, against the principal Confederate army, and upon the strongest Confederate position.

The 9th Corps went to Vicksburg. After the surrender, instead of being sent back to the East Tennessee operation, it was marched in SHERMAN's useless raid to Jackson. WOODBURY's description of the condition of the 9th Corps when it embarked to return from Vicksburg, in August, gives an idea of that terrible part of the cost of taking Vicksburg which is not set down by Gen. GRANT's historian, and is not given in the Commanding General's bulletins or reports. He says:

The campaign in Mississippi was especially severe in the effects upon the officers and men of the 9th Corps. The excessive heat, the malaria that settled like a pall of death around the camps upon the Yazoo River, the scarcity of water and its bad quality, the forced marches, and the crowded condition of the transports, told fearfully upon the troops.

All the accounts of the movement agree in their statements respecting the amount of disease and mortality which accompanied it. The hardships which all were obliged to endure were excessive. Water which the horses refused to drink the men were obliged to use in making their coffee. Fevers, congestive chills, diarrhea, and other diseases attacked the troops. Many sank down by the roadside and died from sunstroke and sheer exhaustion. The sickness that prevailed upon the transports upon the return voyage was terrible and almost universal. Nearly every night, as the boats lay up on account of low water and the consequent danger of navigation, the twinkling light of the lanterns on shore betokened the movements of the burial parties as they consigned the remains of some unfortunate comrade to the earth.

When the troops reached Cairo the men were scarcely able to march through the streets. They dropped in the ranks; and even at the market house, where the good citizens had provided an abundant and comfortable meal for the wornout soldiers, they fell beside the tables, and were carried away to the hospitals. More than half the command were rendered unfit for duty. There were not able men enough belonging to the batteries to water and groom the horses.

From the diseases contracted in that campaign, few ever recovered entirely. Yet these troops had not had the previous dreadful experience of four months in the hardships of the swamp operations, and of the first forced marches away to Jackson and back. This account of the condition of a corps which had come fresh from the North only two months before, gives some idea of the way in which the Vicksburg operation consumed a great army.

Gen. GRANT, as quoted by his historian, and Gen. SHERMAN in his memoirs, admit that they might have gone on from Oxford in the fall of 1862, and have taken Vicksburg from the interior. In this they confess that the Vicksburg operation by the river was in itself a blunder, and that this blunder caused the enormous expense of the river expedition, the consuming of the army in the swamp operations for four months, and the loss of at least six months of time. This confesses a blunder of great magnitude; but all this was but the lesser part. Vastly greater was the cost of the Vicksburg campaign in its sacrifice of other greater campaigns. In all this it was equivalent to a year's prolongation of the great war.

Meanwhile, in July, Gen. BURNSIDE had to direct the forces to pursue Gen. JOHN MORGAN's great raid into Kentucky, Indiana, and Ohio, which he did with great success, and his directions were supported by wonderful energy, and MORGAN's force was captured after a pursuit of nearly a month, which, for near twenty days, was in Indiana and Ohio. This raid again delayed preparations for East Tennessee. When the 9th Corps arrived the troops were unfit to join the expedition, and were sent to places in Kentucky for rest and recovery. The East Tennessee expedition was now organized of troops of the 23d Corps, some fresh levies in Kentucky, some from East Tennessee, and some from the North. The troops of the 9th Corps were to be disposed for following re-enforcements.

CHAPTER LXVIII.

GEN. BURNSIDE OCCUPIES EAST TENNESSEE—A BRILLIANT OPERATION—HALLECK'S DISTRACTING ORDERS—OPERA BOUFFE WAR—THE ACTIVE CAMPAIGN IN EAST TENNESSEE AFTER CHICKAMAUGA—THAT POSITION SAVED BY BURNSIDE IN SPITE OF HALLECK'S ORDERS—BURNSIDE PROMOTED TO THE PLACE OF SCAPEGOAT—LONGSTREET IN EAST TENNESSEE A STANDING MENACE.

The Confederate positions in East Tennessee were so strong, and could be so quickly re-enforced both from Virginia and from Bragg's army, that it was only by strategy that such a force as that of Burnside could expect to succeed. Burnside moved from Crab Orchard August 16, the infantry in two columns, the cavalry in another. Demonstrating toward Cumberland Gap, he moved to the mountains by more westerly gaps and more unfrequented roads, hitherto deemed impassable by a large army, his troops in light marching order, and after fourteen days of hard marching, the troops aiding the animals to haul the guns and wagons up the acclivities, they surmounted the summits, and Gen. Buckner was surprised by the appearance of an army approaching on differents roads, as if it had dropped from the clouds.

By this extraordinary march of 250 miles, over great mountains by difficult passes, Gen. Burnside gained East Tennessee, which, with due notice of his coming and line of march, might be called impregnable. His army consisted of about 18,000 men. On the 1st of September Col. Foster's cavalry entered Kingston, and on the 2d Burnside entered Knoxville. On the 9th Cumberland Gap was surrendered to Burnside, with 2,500 prisoners, eleven guns, small arms, and much ammunition. The recovery of East Tennessee was at last achieved, and it was done by an operation as bold, skillful, and brilliant as any in the war.

On the 10th Burnside received from Gen. Gordon Granger a dispatch stating his occupation of Chattanooga, and giving a highly colored view of the results, as if that operation were completed. Burnside was suffering from disease, and he now asked to be relieved; but Lincoln, with warm thanks for what he had done, besought him to stay. On the 11th he received this remarkable order from Halleck:

I congratulate you on your success. Hold the gaps of the North Carolina mountains, the line of the Holston River, or some point, if there be one, to prevent access from Virginia, and connect with Gen. Rosecrans, at least with your cavalry. Gen. Rosecrans will occupy Dalton, or some point on the railroad, to close all access from Atlanta, and also the mountain passes in the west. This being done, it will be determined whether the movable force shall advance into Georgia and Alabama or into the valley of Virginia and North Carolina.

The Grand Duchess of Gerolstein's council of war ceases to be burlesque in the contemplation of these and following orders issued by Gen. Halleck to Burnside. To hold the gaps of the North Carolina Mountains to prevent access from Virginia, to hold the line of the Holston, and connect with Rosecrans! Only an affair of 200 miles or so, besides the necessity of holding Cumberland Gap and other widely separated points in Tennessee. And meanwhile Rosecrans, instead of dreaming of Dalton and boundless marches into Georgia and Alabama, or into the valley of Virginia and North Carolina, was giving all his energies to getting his separated columns through the mountains west of Chattanooga, to concentrate them, before Bragg's re-enforced army could fall upon them in detail.

Burnside did what he could to make dispositions to carry out these diffusive orders, and had to do it against an active enemy, who had no intention of resigning East Tennessee. The utmost vigor and vigilance were required to repel the ever vigilant enemy, on a line now extended to 176 miles. On top of all this came to Burnside from Halleck the following distracting order dated September 13:

Move down your infantry as rapidly as possible toward Chattanooga to connect with Rosecrans. Bragg may hold the passes of the mountains to cover Atlanta, and move his main army through Northern Alabama to reach the Tennessee River, and turn Rosecrans' right and cut off his supplies. In this case Rosecrans will turn Chattanooga over to you and move to intercept Bragg.

To hold East Tennessee, the passes of the North Carolina Mountains, and move with his infantry to Chattanooga! Corporal General Fritz is without doubt an historical character. On the morning of the 17th Burnside started to overtake the troops whom he had sent up the valley on HALLECK'S first order, to march them back and down toward Chattanooga on his second order. Then came this from HALLECK on the 14th:

There are several reasons why you should re-enforce Rosecrans with all possible dispatch. It is believed that the enemy will concentrate to give him battle. You must be there to help him.

Gen. BURNSIDE got this order at Morristown, forty miles northeast of Knoxville, late on the 17th, and next day he ordered all troops in that quarter back to Knoxville and London. Thus was BURNSIDE from Washington ordered to hold the North Carolina Mountains against troops from Virginia, to hold the line of the Holston against Gen. JONES' army and re-enforcements from the south, and to join ROSECRANS with his main army, besides holding passes in the Cumberland Mountains on his own account. That which HALLECK'S orders required was like the traditional spread of the bird of freedom.

When ROSECRANS had fallen back to Chattanooga Gen. BURNSIDE submitted to HALLECK three different plans of movement to aid him, declaring his preference for the one to move on BRAGG's right and rear, and send the cavalry to destroy the machine works and powder mills at Rome. This would be a bold movement, but, if made immediately, who can say that it might not succeed? But HALLECK was still at cross purposes, and he disapproved, and gave this by way of censure for the past and direction for the future:

The purport of all your instructions has been that you should hold some point near the upper end of the valley, and with all your available force move to the assistance of Rosecrans.

And the purport and effect of all of HALLECK'S orders was to give up East Tennessee, if they had been followed.

A history would be required to give a full view of the absurd muddling of these and HALLECK'S other orders to BURNSIDE, which continued as long as BURNSIDE remained there. Of course a scapegoat was a military necessity, and the General who had made one of the most brilliant and important achievements of the war, and had done it with small means, and maintained it against great efforts of the enemy, was selected for this office. HALLECK still seemed unconscious of the ridiculous impossibilities of his orders, when he afterward cited them to show how vigorous he had been in ordering BURNSIDE to co-operate with ROSECRANS, and how delinquent BURNSIDE.

Then LONGSTREET was sent up in a determined campaign to recover East Tennessee. LONGSTREET could be re-enforced to any desired extent from Virginia. BURNSIDE, with his troops greatly extended, had to oppose this superior force, led by one of the most enterprising of the Confederate Generals. The peril of his army and of East Tennessee was very great, but BURNSIDE, though suffering from disease, was a sanguine and bold General, and he had brave troops. LONGSTREET planned his movements with good strategy to cut off and capture BURNSIDE, but he was met at each point, and was repulsed in all the important engagements of this very active campaign, as BURNSIDE retired skillfully upon Knoxville, where an assault and bloody repulse had expended LONGSTREET'S present resources, and had made his campaign a failure in its great objective, by the time that SHERMAN'S relieving march began.

The brilliancy of the operation by which East Tennessee was gained was surpassed by the energy, skill, and hard fighting by which it was held. Fortunately HALLECK'S orders of impossibilities were but little heeded, the Commanding General having constantly to hold against an active enemy. HALLECK'S fault finding was an attempt to cover his own blunders by disparaging one of the most important, spirited, and successful campaigns of the war. HALLECK would have sacrificed East Tennessee; BURNSIDE saved it in spite of his orders. Yet HALLECK pretended that BURNSIDE was weakly going to give up Tennessee. Although BURNSIDE's falling back before LONGSTREET to Knoxville was in accord with GRANT's views, who at that time thought it well to draw LONGSTREET further away, HALLECK took it as a purpose to give up East Tennessee, and on the 14th of November he sent to GRANT this mean and supremely ignorant telegram:

Advices from East Tennessee indicate that Burnside intends to abandon the defense of Little Tennessee River, and fall back before Longstreet toward Cumberland Gap and the upper valley. Longstreet is said to be near the Little Tennessee with from twenty to forty thousand men. Burnside has about thirty thousand in all, and can hold his position; he ought not to retreat. I fear further delay may result in Burnside's abandonment of East Tennessee.

Again HALLECK telegraphed GRANT on the 16th:

I fear he will not fight, although strongly urged to do so. Unless you can give him immediate assistance, he will surrender his position to the enemy.

This was from the hero of the fifteen miles of siege approaches of Corinth in thirty days, with a veteran army of a hundred thousand men; and it was concerning a General who had carried out one of the boldest campaigns of the war. Gen. BURNSIDE's reward was his promotion by HALLECK to the high office of scapegoat. He left Knoxville on the 7th of December.

Gen. PARKE moved a column from Knoxville after LONGSTREET on the 7th of December to Blain's Cross Roads, thirteen miles east of Knoxville. His cavalry was strung out sixteen miles beyond, where a force of WHEELER's cavalry fell upon a detachment far from support, and captured a wagon train laden with supplies. PARKE's advance then fell back to Blain's Cross Roads.

The winter was severe, and the troops in no condition for a campaign. ROSECRANS' army had crossed the Tennessee in light marching order for a campaign in warm weather. BURNSIDE's troops had crossed the mountains in light marching trim. HOWARD's corps had stripped at Bridgeport for Chattanooga. The movement of SHERMAN's army to Knoxville was one of great hardship from insufficient clothing and food and hard marching. BURNSIDE's troops were destitute, in rags, shoeless, and on semi-starvation rations. Not till spring were communications restored so that the troops at Knoxville could be properly supplied. During that winter the hardships of the troops in East Tennessee, on a much larger scale, surpassed the historical sufferings of WASHINGTON's troops at Valley Forge. Yet in the midst of their privations these hungry, ragged, and shoeless volunteers re-enlisted by regiments for three years. Yet our war traditions, following that hero worship which, in the evolution of tradition, creates the gods of mythology, hold that the National Union was saved by the military genius of an individual.

LONGSTREET abode all winter in East Tennessee. His attitude was a standing threat to our occupation, and even to GRANT's rear. GRANT's uneasiness was increased by reports that LONGSTREET was receiving more troops from Virginia, portending an offensive movement. BADEAU says that GRANT went to Knoxville about Christmas, to take steps to drive out LONGSTREET, but he found the troops so destitute, the weather so severe, and the difficulties of supplying the command so prodigious, that a campaign was impossible. He says:

The weather was extremely inclement, and many of the troops stood in line with only a blanket to cover their nakedness. The difficulties of supplying the demand were so prodigious that great suffering ensued. No railroad could be built under two months, at soonest; the fall in the rivers frequently interfered with the transportation of supplies; and now that the roads had become well nigh impassable by reason of snow and ice, to send re-enforcements would only be to put the men on more insufficient rations.

LONGSTREET's attitude was a standing menace. Re-enforcements could reach him from both Dalton and Virginia, and his plan of aggression might recover the mountain fortresses and passes of East Tennessee, and compromise GRANT's communications. Notwithstanding the destitution of the troops, a movement in force was made in January. Gen. WOOD's advance on the 15th drove the Confederate cavalry from Dandridge, twenty-eight miles directly east of Knoxville. LONGSTREET showed fight, and on the 17th and 18th there was skirmishing, and late on the 18th a brisk cavalry fight, which McCOOK, with three Ohio cavalry regiments, closed by a charge that cleared the field and covered the retreat, which a council of corps and division Generals had decided to be better than to risk a general engagement. They fell back to Strawberry Plains, and subsequently to Maysville, followed by LONGSTREET.

After this GRANGER's corps returned toward Chattanooga, and, BADEAU says, remained all winter stretched out between Cleveland and Knoxville. Not till some time in the spring were communications restored so that the army in East Tennessee could be fully supplied. But LONGSTREET seemed to GRANT to have the strategic advantage in East Tennessee, and, from his position, to be able to compel the course of the next campaign. He had heard also that LONGSTREET had received heavy re-enforcements. He therefore ordered Gen. FOSTER to prepare to take the offensive to drive out LONGSTREET, and Gen. THOMAS to prepare for an advance to Knoxville, with such forces as could be spared from the protection of Chattanooga and its communications, to assist Gen. FOSTER to drive LONGSTREET from East Tennessee. Gen. FOSTER wanted at least 10,000 men.

Gen. THOMAS' army was now greatly reduced by furloughs to regiments of re-enlisted veterans, and the waste of his artillery horses and train animals in the siege had not yet been supplied. He advised a postponement till the railroad could be put in running order to Loudon, thirty miles from Knoxville, where the bridge over the Tennessee was destroyed. Gen. SCHOFIELD had now arrived, and assumed command at Knoxville, Gen. FOSTER, on account of ill health, having been relieved. GRANT had a conversation with FOSTER, which, with SCHOFIELD's dispatches, led him to countermand the order. Again there was an alarm about LONGSTREET early in March, but it did not cause any large change of dispositions.

CHAPTER LXIX.

THE DIFFUSIVE DISPOSITIONS AFTER THE GREAT VICTORY—PERIPHERAL STRATEGY AGAIN—A RAID, WITH AN ALTERNATIVE—A SCAPEGOAT—MILITARY RAIDING GENIUS—GRANT'S FAME AND PRESTIGE AT THE ZENITH—GRANT LIEUTENANT GENERAL AND MILITARY AUTOCRAT—TAKES COMMAND OF THE ARMY OF THE POTOMAC—A GRAND ARMY READY TO BE CONSUMED—GRANT EMBRACES HIS OPPORTUNITY—THE END.

The victory of Mission Ridge was followed by a long period of diffusion, such as that which followed the operation on Corinth in the spring of 1862. From the beginning of the war much stress had been laid on the strategic importance of Chattanooga, but now no advance was made from it till in the following May. And that, after a vastly greater expenditure of troops, means, and time, was made abortive by its failure to disable the Confederate army, and by Gen. Hood's march north into Middle Tennessee, where he made his base at Corinth, which had been the great objective of HALLECK with an army of 100,000, in the spring of 1862. Thus the disjointed strategy in the West had the fortune that it was successively fighting back and forth over the same ground.

Great energies and means were applied to the rebuilding of bridges and roads, and to the gathering of munitions and supplies for the holding of Chattanooga, and for ulterior operations, whose nature was not yet decided upon. The region in the rear of the national advanced line was greatly infested by guerrilla parties, and raided by Confederate cavalry expeditions, against which were many national cavalry expeditions which were generally successful. Gen. JOSEPH E. JOHNSTON succeeded Gen. BRAGG, and made his base at Dalton, his dispositions covering all the country south of the national lines, and securing its supplies to the Confederate army.

Gen. GRANT, on the 7th of December, announced to Gen. HALLECK that "it may now safely be assured that the enemy are driven from the front, or, at least, that they n o longer threaten it in formidable numbers;" he therefore reverted to his former peripheral strategy, of an expedition from New Orleans against Mobile. He said the country south of Chattanooga was mountainous, affording little for the supply of an army, the roads bad at all times, and a winter campaign there impossible; therefore, he said: "I propose, with the concurrence of higher authority, to move by way of New Orleans and Pascagoula, or Mobile. I would hope to secure that place, or its investment, by the last of January."

The higher authority did not concur, and BADEAU says "GRANT himself ceased to urge it when he discovered that LONGSTREET was likely to winter in Tennessee." With LONGSTREET in East Tennessee and JOHNSTON's army still in front of Chattanooga, and the defensive attitude improved by the Confederate cavalry raids on his lines of supply, the sending of an army round the circumference to Mobile would be in the same order of diffusive strategy as that which retreated from Oxford to take the army to the Mississippi swamps, and would be likely to permit the Confederates to recover East Tennessee and to march into Kentucky.

Gen. GRANT on the 11th of December conceived a more ambitious expedition. He wrote to McPHERSON at Vicksburg: "I shall start a cavalry force through Mississippi in about two weeks, to clean out the State entirely of rebels." That would be an extensive cleaning out. Says BADEAU: "This was the germ of what has been known as the

Meridian raid." This contemplated raid grew in time and preparation to the force for a campaign. More than a month later, January 15, GRANT wrote to HALLECK:

> Sherman has gone down the Mississippi to collect at Vicksburg all the force that can be spared for a separate movement from the Mississippi. He will probably have by the 24th of this month a force of 20,000 men. I shall direct Sherman, therefore, to move out to Meridian with his spare force, the cavalry going from Corinth; destroy the roads and bridges south of there so effectually that the enemy will not attempt to rebuild them during the rebellion. He will then return, unless an opportunity of going to Mobile with the force he has appears perfectly plain.

Further along the letter has this sign of strategy: "I do not look upon any points, except Mobile in the South, and the Tennessee River in the North, as presenting practicable starting points from which to operate against Atlanta and Montgomery." It thus appears that the plan had the same alternative convenience as that of the movement from Hankinson's Ferry away from Vicksburg—namely, that it was to be a campaign if it succeeded in getting to Mobile, and a raid if it failed. Gen. SHERMAN says in his memoirs: "I never had the remotest idea of going to Mobile, but had purposely given out that idea to the people of the country, so as to deceive the enemy and divert their attention." That this stratagem would be likely to divert the attention from his movement is easy to be seen.

But Gen. GRANT wrote to Gen. THOMAS of this plan:

> He (Sherman) will proceed eastward as far as Meridian at least, and will thoroughly destroy the roads east and south of there, and, if possible, will throw troops as far east as Selma; or, if he finds Mobile unguarded so as to make his force sufficient for the enterprise, will go there. To co-operate with this movement you want to keep up an appearance of preparation of an advance from Chattanooga. It may be necessary to move a column even as far as Lafayette.

This was by the Commanding General who planned the expedition. BADEAU, whose strategic mind ranges as widely as the poet's frenzied rolling eye, has also this as one of the objects of the plan: "To relieve East Tennessee, as well as to secure the safety of the contemplated movement into Georgia during the ensuing spring." Gen. SHERMAN, February 3, moved from Vicksburg four divisions on this alternative. Gen. WILLIAM SOOY SMITH was to move with 7,000 cavalry from Memphis, at the same time, or thereabout, to join Gen. SHERMAN at Meridian, a route of over 250 miles, into the heart of the enemy's country.

It was about this time that Gen. GRANT ordered Gen. THOMAS to move to Knoxville—JOHNSTON then confronting Chattanooga. When he recalled that order, he issued another on the 19th to Gen. THOMAS, which was as remarkable—namely, to move in force toward Dalton, and if possible occupy that place and repair the railroad to it. This was to make a movement which SHERMAN required the three combined armies for in the following May. It was to attack JOHNSTON behind Rocky Face Ridge, which SHERMAN with the three armies found unassailable. GRANT'S object in this was to prevent JOHNSTON'S sending troops against SHERMAN. But the diverting movement would be a much greater thing than SHERMAN'S movement.

Two days after GRANT had issued this order he learned that JOHNSTON had at Dalton six divisions, and had sent away but one brigade; yet he did not recall his order, although he now knew that it was to attack superior numbers in an unassailable position. THOMAS moved on the 22d. On that evening Gen. PALMER advised GRANT that he had received intelligence that JOHNSTON had sent CHEATHAM'S and CLEBURNE'S divisions to re-enforce POLK, who was falling back before SHERMAN, and now all the available troops were moved up to attack JOHNSTON. The movements and dispositions were carried forward on the 23d and 24th, developing the enemy's positions, skirmishing, and driving him from the outer lines. Next day a resolute attack was made, which charged up the hill, and there met an overwhelming force.

Skirmishing and cannonading were continued till night, when our troops were withdrawn. Next morning Col. HARRISON was driven from a gap six miles south of Buzzard Roost, nearly opposite Dalton, by CLEBURNE'S division, one of the two which GRANT thought had been sent away. Gen. THOMAS had proved that not only had JOHNSTON an unassailable position, but more than his own force, and that to attempt to stay in front of JOHNSTON was to expose his army, besides the impracticability of supplying it. GRANT urged him to stay and threaten JOHNSTON and make him believe that he was making an advance into the South, until the result of SHERMAN'S campaign should be known. But THOMAS decided this to be impracticable, and gave orders to withdraw, his means of supply being inadequate. SHERMAN had before this started to return.

This operation cost more than 300 men. It effected nothing that GRANT had designed. But VAN HORNE's History states that upon the intelligence gained by this movement, THOMAS was impressed with the feasibility of a plan to turn JOHNSTON's position by a movement through Snake Creek Gap, and requested permission from GRANT to make preparation for it. But that THOMAS should do this was not in GRANT's ideas. In the following May this movement was made by Gen. SHERMAN, with the three armies combined, but made in such a manner as to leave the way open for JOHNSTON to retreat.

Gen. SHERMAN's march, bordered by Confederate cavalry, reached Meridian, 150 miles from Vicksburg, on the 14th of February. Here he set his infantry at work destroying the Mobile & Ohio Railroad south and north, and the Jackson & Selma Railroad east and west. The rolling stock of these roads had been removed. Meanwhile Admiral FARRAGUT, at SHERMAN's request, made a co-operative demonstration against the forts in Mobile harbor. Whatever indecision SHERMAN may have had hitherto, whether his movement was a raid, or a campaign to Mobile, was solved at Meridian, where he decided that it was a raid.

He issued a special order at Meridian on the 18th, beginning:

Having fulfilled, and well, all the objects of the expedition, the troops will return to the Mississippi to embark in another equally important movement.

This order gave directions for the return march, to begin on the 20th. It appears that after his return he began to doubt that his expedition had fulfilled all its objects, and he charged a default on Gen. SMITH for not moving at the appointed time, and for failing to join him at Meridian. But his communication to Gen. GRANT, including Gen. SMITH's report, expressed only a mild dissatisfaction, and closed with this satisfaction: "Nevertheless, on the whole, we accomplished all I undertook."

His dissatisfaction, however, grew with years, and in his memoirs he gave a stronger version of Gen. SMITH's conduct, and said:

Gen. Smith never regained my confidence as a soldier, though I still regard him as a most accomplished gentleman and a skillful engineer. Since the close of the war he has appealed to me to relieve him of that censure, but I could not do it, because it would falsify history.

Let the truth of history stand, though military heads fall! But Gen. BOYNTON's very accurate criticism of Gen. SHERMAN's memoirs, which he treats of as a raid upon history, reviews this affair from the records, and proves that SHERMAN's order to SMITH did not fix February 1, nor any exact time, for his start, but that he was to wait for a certain cavalry force, of which an entire brigade and a battery were to come from the North; that this brigade marched 250 miles, over a country covered with snow and ice, crossing difficult rivers, to reach Memphis on the 8th, after which SMITH gave them only three days to refit before he started.

Besides, Gen. SMITH's movement was opposed by FORREST's cavalry, estimated at 6,000, which was in no way diverted from him by SHERMAN's movement. To order a cavalry force of only 7,000 on an isolated march of 250 miles into the heart of a hostile country, opposed by a cavalry force so nearly equal, seems a wild operation. To go 140 miles of this way, and then return in safety, argues very good troops and a good General. SHERMAN says in the memoirs that SMITH suffered a defeat at West Point, but he simply found FORREST, with about an equal force, in a very strong position to resist his crossing of a river, and that was his turning point from the wild expedition. The damage which SMITH inflicted on the enemy seems about equal to SHERMAN's. He went further, and besides his great destruction of railroads, cotton, and corn, he brought in 3,000 horses and mules, and 1,500 negroes—these last in pursuance of orders.

Besides, from the unavoidable delay in starting, it was now impossible for him to join SHERMAN at Meridian on the day he had appointed to be there—namely, the 10th—even if it had ever been possible. SHERMAN did not get there till the 14th, and eight days after that he told his troops that they had done all they came to do. And SHERMAN was already going back when Gen. SMITH turned. Only in history did SHERMAN become implacable to SMITH; for when SHERMAN succeeded GRANT in the Western command he retained SMITH, who had been GRANT's Chief of Cavalry, as his own Chief of Staff, and intrusted him with the organization of the cavalry for the Atlanta campaign. Furthermore, Gen. SHERMAN assured Gen. SMITH that his own movements on Meridian and the contemplated operations there did not of necessity depend on a junction with the cavalry from Memphis. If it had been otherwise, and if movements from these remote points, on such long and widely separated routes into the unknown, had been planned by Gen. SHERMAN to depend on so exact a junction, it is hard to see how Gen. SMITH could ever have regained any confidence in SHERMAN as a soldier or as a man of sound mind.

If the expedition was only a raid to destroy railroads, what was the need of Gen. SMITH's joining SHERMAN at Meridian, when he was separately doing the same devastation? And if only a raid to Meridian, to destroy railroads, Gen. GRANT ordered a very costly co-operation when he ordered Gen. THOMAS to attack JOHNSTON at Rocky Face Ridge, to divert the enemy from SHERMAN, thereby to sacrifice his own veterans to help SHERMAN destroy railroads. This affair, like that of the previous spring in moving away from Vicksburg, showed the tendency of the minds of GRANT and SHERMAN to tentative raids, rather than connected and comprehensive campaigns. This had exercise on a still greater scale in the following autumn, when SHERMAN, with a great army, turned his back on the still unbroken Confederate army, and marched off to raid the undefended country, abandoning all the objectives of the enormously dear campaign, and leaving the real war to be sustained by Gen. THOMAS, with the lesser number of troops, widely divided in holding his lines of supply.

The winter thus wore away without apparently evolving any comprehensive plan of operations on either side. In anticipation of some campaign further into the South, Gen. THOMAS made active preparations to supply the army and to guard the lines of supply, by constructing block houses at the railroad bridges and depots. Early in March Gen. GRANT became apprehensive that JOHNSTON was to resume the offensive, but no important movement was made.

The victory in the battles about Chattanooga, like the Vicksburg campaign, was ascribed to Gen. GRANT's military genius. His fame was now raised to the zenith, and his prestige was irresistible to the executive administration and to the politicians of Congress. A bill was introduced into the House of Representatives by Hon. E. B. WASHBURNE —he whom BADEAU tells of as falling away from GRANT when the army was stuck in the Mississippi mud, and advising LINCOLN to remove him—to create the rank of Lieutenant General, "to command the armies of the United States." It became a law on the 26th of February. The President on the 1st of March nominated GRANT to this exalted rank, and he was immediately confirmed.

On the 3d of March GRANT was summoned to Washington, which he reached on the 8th. He returned to the West to close up his affairs, and on the 23d arrived in Washington to enter upon his great command. He was now military autocrat. The President and Secretary of War assured him of their intention to give him the absolute control of all military movements. Upon his requirement SHERMAN was placed in command of the military division of the Mississippi, over the head of Gen. THOMAS, his senior, and McPHERSON in command of the Army of the Tennessee, over the head of HURLBUT.

Gen. GRANT, in the East, found a great, thoroughly disciplined, high spirited, veteran army; seasoned by many battles, in which it had always shown fighting qualities of the highest order; officered by his seniors in service; ready to be taken in hand by him and consumed, and he did not come short of his great opportunity.

THE END.

ERROR.

On page 105, for LANDMAN read LANDRUM.

www.ingramcontent.com/pod-product-compliance
Lightning Source LLC
Chambersburg PA
CBHW032225230426
43666CB00033B/1532